Springer Series on Social Work

Albert R. Roberts, Ph.D., Series Editor
*Graduate School of Social Work, Rutgers
The State University of New Jersey*

Peter Lehmann, PhD, is Assistant Professor, School of Social Work, The University of Texas at Arlington. He has published in the areas of child witness to domestic violence, posttraumatic stress disorder, and crisis intervention. He teaches in the direct practice stream and currently trains child protective service workers in Texas on domestic violence issues.

Nick Coady, PhD, is Associate Professor, Faculty of Social Work, Wilfrid Laurier University, Waterloo, Ontario, Canada. He teaches direct practice and his practice background includes individual and family counseling with high-risk adolescents and group work with abusive men. Nick's publications have focused on various issues related to clinical social work practice, particularly on the importance of relationship factors to counseling outcome. His recent research has involved evaluations of innovative programs for high-risk populations.

Theoretical Perspectives for Direct Social Work Practice

A Generalist-Eclectic Approach

Peter Lehmann, PhD and
Nick Coady, PhD, Editors

 Springer Publishing Company

Springer Publishing Company, Inc.
536 Broadway
New York, NY 10012-3955

Acquisitions Editor: Bill Tucker
Production Editor: Janice Stangel
Cover design by Susan Hauley

00 01 02 03 04 / 5 4 3 2 1

Library of Congress Cataloging-in-Publication Data

Theoretical perspectives for direct social work : a generalist-eclectic approach / Peter Lehmann and Nick Coady, editors.
    p. cm.
    Includes bibliographical references and index.
    ISBN 0-8261-1369-9
    1. Social case work. I. Lehmann, Peter II. Coady, Nick.
HV43 .T42 2001
361.3'2—dc21

00-030744

Printed in the United States of America

To Delphine, Daley, and Rory; with thanks to Don Efron, MSW, who laid the groundwork in 1985.

Peter Lehmann

To my best friends: my partner Laurie, and my daughters, Devyn and Blaire (with honorable mention to current and former members of the longstanding Wednesday night poker club).

Nick Coady

Contents

About the Contributors

Dr. Ralph A. Brown is an Associate Professor in, and Director of, the School of Social Work at McMaster University, Hamilton, Ontario. Ralph is interested in social policy, practice, and program evaluation pertaining to families and children, with emphasis on "hard-to-serve" children and family violence. His current research includes an evaluation of wraparound services in seven Ontario communities.

Dr. Rudy Buckman is a therapist and trainer at the Salesmanship Club Youth & Family Centers, Inc. in Dallas. He was formerly an Assistant Professor of Psychology at the University of Texas at Tyler. Rudy has published on various aspects of family therapy, is a frequent presenter, and is known for his integration of yoga in therapy.

Dr. Scottye J. Cash is Assistant Professor, School of Social Work, Florida State University, Tallahassee, Florida. Scottye's research and teaching interests include child welfare, family preservation, and risk assessment.

Dr. Elaine P. Congress is Professor and Director of the Doctoral Program at Fordham University Graduate School of Social Service. Her most recent publications include *Multicultural Perspectives in Working with Families* (Springer, 1997) and *Social Work Values and Ethics: Identifying and Resolving Professional Dilemmas* (Nelson Hall, 1999). Elaine is the President of the New York City chapter of the NASW.

Dr. Jacqueline Corcoran is Assistant Professor, School of Social Work, Virginia Commonwealth University, Richmond, Virginia. She has published in the areas of family therapy, solution-focused therapy, and adolescent pregnancy. Her most recent book is entitled *Evidence-Based Social Work Practice with Families: A Lifespan Approach* (Springer, 2000).

Dr. Donald K. Granvold is Professor and Director of the Masters Program, School of Social Work, University of Texas at Arlington. He has published in the areas of cognitive-behavioral and constructivist treatment, including the edited volume, *Cognitive and Behavioral Treatment: Methods and Applica-*

tions. Don is an editorial board member with *Social Work* and *Crisis Intervention and Time-Limited Treatment.*

Dr. Delane Kinney is Director of Psychological Services, Salesmanship Club Youth & Family Centers, Dallas. Delane is an active presenter and trainer in narrative approaches to treatment and ethics. In addition, she serves in an advisory capacity to several nonprofit organizations and maintains a private practice with adults, couples, and survivors of child sexual abuse.

Dr. Karen Knox is Assistant Professor and Director of Field Practicum for the Department of Social Work at Southwest Texas State University. Her areas of specialization include survivors of violent crime and child abuse. Karen also works with Child Protective Services, the Austin Police Department Victim Services Division, and the Travis County Juvenile Court Adolescent Sex Offender Program.

Dr. Jim Lantz is director of The Midwest Existential Psychotherapy Institute, co-director of Lantz Counseling Associates, and a Professor at the Ohio State University College of Social Work.

Dr. James I. Martin is Associate Professor at the New York University Ehrenkranz School of Social Work. For several years Dr. Martin was Director of Social Work at a psychiatric hospital in Chicago, where he also maintained a private practice in clinical social work. His practice and research interests focus on the problems and needs of gay men and lesbians.

Dr. Christine Mello is a practicing school psychologist who has been trained by Dr. Kathleen Nader to screen and treat traumatized children. Her work has included treatment and on-going consultation following school disasters, and training mental health professionals in the use of PTSD screening instruments.

Dr. Kathleen Nader has worked nationally and internationally in the field of posttraumatic stress and related fields since 1974, and served for 10 years as the Director of Evaluations for the UCLA Trauma, Violence, and Sudden Bereavement Program. Her work and publications have focused on the provision of consultations, training, and specialized interventions for children, adults, and communities following catastrophic events.

Ann Reese, MSW, ACP, is a therapist and supervisor with Salesmanship Club Youth & Family Centers, Dallas. Ann works extensively with child survivors of physical and sexual abuse. She has coauthored "Beyond Family Systems—Toward Problem Systems: Some Clinical Implications" and "Therapeutic Loving: Opening Space for Children and Their Families" in the *Journal of Systemic Therapies.*

Dr. Cheryl Regehr is an Associate Professor of social work at the University of Toronto. Her practice background is in mental health, sexual assault recovery programs, sex offender treatment programs, and critical incident stress debriefing. Cheryl's program of research involves examining aspects of recovery from trauma in such diverse populations as victims of rape and firefighters who witness traumatic events.

Dr. Albert R. Roberts is a Professor at the School of Social Work, Rutgers University. He has authored, edited or coedited more than 20 books on the topics of crisis intervention, criminal justice, and domestic violence. Al is founding Editor-in-Chief of the journal *Crisis Intervention and Time-Limited Treatment.*

Dr. Michael Rothery is a Professor in the Faculty of Social Work at the University of Calgary. He holds an MSW degree from the University of British Columbia, and a PhD from the University of Toronto. His practice has been in the fields of child welfare and mental health, and his current research interests are in the family violence area.

Dr. Christine Flynn Saulnier is an Assistant Professor at Boston University School of Social Work. She is author of *Feminist Theories and Social Work* (Haworth, 1996). Christine has practiced in health, mental health, school, residential, and community settings. Her research and publications focus on women's alcohol and health concerns and group work practice.

Dr. Arthur Schwartz currently teaches at the School of Social Work at the University of Pennsylvania. His faculty appointments have included the Universities of Chicago, Maryland, Illinois, Hawaii, Rutgers and Widener University, where he was Scholar-in-Residence and Professor. His teaching and research interests have focused on comparative approaches to intervention and the brief treatments.

Dr. Carol A. Stalker is an Associate Professor in the Faculty of Social Work, Wilfrid Laurier University. She has twenty years practice experience in mental health settings. Her publications include an examination of attachment organization in women sexually abused as children. She is currently researching the associations between social support, insecure attachment patterns, and maintenance of treatment gains in traumatized adults.

Dr. Eleanor Reardon Tolson is an associate professor at Jane Addams College of Social Work, University of Illinois at Chicago, where she teaches practice, research, and human behavior. Her authored and edited books include *Generalist Practice: A Task-Centered Approach, The Metamodel and Clinical Social Work, Perspectives on Direct Practice Evaluation,* and *Models of Family Treatment.*

Dr. Leslie Tutty is a Professor in the Faculty of Social Work at the University of Calgary, where she has taught clinical and research courses since 1989. She received her PhD in Social Work from Wilfrid Laurier University. Her research has focused on abused women, sexual abuse prevention, and group treatment for women and children survivors of sexual abuse.

Preface

This book is intended to provide an overview of theories for clinical social work practice and strategies for integrating theory with practice. It is intended primarily for graduate-level social work students and practitioners. This book has similarities to other books that provide surveys of clinical theories; however, we think it has a number of distinctive and useful features. In brief, these features include (a) proposing a generalist social work framework as a necessary base for the eclectic use of theories in clinical practice; (b) documenting the trend toward and rationale for eclecticism in counseling, and reviewing strategies for eclecticism; (c) bringing order to and demystifying theories by differentiating among levels of theory, organizing clinical theories into like groupings, and providing an overview of the central characteristics of each grouping of theories; (d) including chapters on specialized service models for high-risk populations; and (e) giving credence to the artistic elements of practice and considering how a problem-solving model can provide a useful structure for integrating the artistic and theoretical/technical elements of practice (see Chapter 1 for a more detailed discussion of these features of the book).

This is the first time that either of us have edited a book and the first time that we have worked together. The process of writing and editing collaboratively has been challenging but very rewarding. One of the most challenging aspects has been managing the process collaboratively while separated from each other, and from many of the contributors whom we did not know personally, by vast geographical distance (this would have been much more difficult without e-mail). At the same time, collaboration has been one of the most rewarding aspects of this project in terms of getting to know each other, and many of the contributors, both professionally and personally.

We are enormously grateful to all the contributing authors for taking time from their busy schedules and lives to write original chapters contained herein. Their willingness to follow the structural guidelines for the chapters, the clarity of their writing, and their being amenable to editorial suggestions made our work that much easier. We feel privileged to have collaborated with a group of very gifted and personable academics and practitioners.

Special thanks go to Dr. Al Roberts, editor of the Springer series on Social Work and contributor to this book, for his commitment in "hanging in there" and for providing the advice, kind words, and constructive criticism that pushed us towards completion. His support of our ideas never wavered, which we believe is a credit to his considerable understanding of social work knowledge in direct practice. We are grateful to Bill Tucker, Managing Editor at Springer, for his generous advice, editorial suggestions, and patience with our need to "bend" the time lines on numerous occasions in completing this book. We would also like to thank the numerous colleagues, students, and support staff who provided helpful feedback and assistance with this project.

P. L.
Arlington, TX

N. C.
Waterloo, ON

PART 1

The Generalist-Eclectic Approach

An Overview of and Rationale for a Generalist-Eclectic Approach to Direct Social Work Practice

Nick Coady and Peter Lehmann

As the title suggests, the predominant focus of this book is on theoretical perspectives for direct (or clinical) social work practice. More specifically, the book focuses on theories for practice with individuals, although the relevance of these theories for practice with families and groups is also considered. The book is intended for graduate-level social work students and practitioners, whether they construe themselves as advanced generalists (Shatz, Jenkins, & Sheafor, 1990) or clinical specialists, who are seeking a more in-depth knowledge of the use of theory in direct practice. The majority of the chapters in this book present an overview of a theory that is used in direct social work practice. In this respect, it has similarities to other texts within social work (e.g., Dorfman, 1988, 1998; Payne, 1997; Turner, 1996) and psychology (e.g., Corsini & Wedding, 1995; Gilliland & James, 1998; Sapp, 1997) that provide a survey of various theories of counseling. This book shares many of the positive features of some of these other texts. For example, the chapters on the various theories have similar structure and headings to facilitate comparison, and case examples are provided to illustrate the use of theory in practice. At the same time, this book is different in a number ways that should make it appealing to social work educators, students, and practitioners.

Most obviously, this book is different from similar texts in psychology because it is written by and for social workers. Furthermore, it is different from the few similar social work texts, as well as from most similar texts in psychology, in the following ways.

We review the main elements of a generalist perspective for direct social work practice and present the argument that this perspective provides a necessary base for the eclectic use theories. This is important because most theories that clinical social workers use have been developed outside the profession. Although all theoretical perspectives can be potentially useful, they should always be adapted to the values and principles of our profession. For example, theories that place the worker in the role of expert need to be used in a more egalitarian, collaborative fashion, and theories that have a specific and narrow conception of human problems need to be broadened to include consideration of an expanded range of factors (i.e., biological, intrapsychic, interpersonal, environmental, and sociocultural factors).

An eclectic use of theory in practice is endorsed in this book. Although other texts endorse eclecticism in a general sense, in this book we review the theoretical arguments and empirical evidence that support eclecticism, and we document the general trend toward eclecticism in the broader field of counseling/psychotherapy. In addition, we review different approaches to eclecticism and delineate our own approach. Consideration of strategies for the eclectic use of theories and techniques is included in this discussion of eclecticism, as well as in the discussion of the problem-solving model in chapter 3.

The book includes chapters on, but differentiates between (1) metatheories (ecological systems and human development theories) (see Part 2) and (2) practice theories (see Part 3). We explain how the former provide general guidance for holistic assessment and the generation of ideas for intervention, whereas the latter provide more specific ideas and directions for assessment and intervention. A conceptual framework for making sense of the various levels of theory is also provided (see chapter 2).

In an effort to demystify theory, we present practice theories in like groupings (psychodynamic, cognitive-behavioral, humanistic and feminist, and postmodern). A brief overview of the distinguishing characteristics of each of these larger theoretical frameworks is provided (see chapter 2).

We devote a section of the book to specialized service models for high-risk populations. Chapters on family preservation services, wraparound services, and a model of treatment for traumatized children are presented in Part 4. We believe this is a valuable addition to the survey of more traditional clinical theories, because social workers frequently work with the most disadvantaged populations and these service models represent innovative ways of helping such clients.

Although the focus of the book is on the eclectic use of theory in practice, we present the argument that practice is as much art as science, and is based as much on intuition and inductive reasoning as on the deductive application of theoretical knowledge and technical skill. This is a contentious issue that is too frequently avoided or dismissed in texts that focus on the use of theory in practice. As part of our generalist-eclectic approach, we elaborate on how the problem-solving model provides a valuable and needed structure for an eclectic use of theories and techniques, as well as for an artistic, intuitive-inductive, theory-building, atheoretical, and commonsense approach to helping that is complementary to the more traditional deductive application of theory to practice (see chapters 2 and 3).

In the remainder of this chapter we (1) describe the central features of the generalist-eclectic approach to direct social work practice, (2) provide an overview of eclecticism and document the trend toward and rationale for the eclectic use of theory in practice, (3) discuss the various approaches to and models of eclecticism, and (4) delineate our approach to eclecticism.

THE GENERALIST-ECLECTIC APPROACH TO DIRECT SOCIAL WORK PRACTICE

There is very little difference between what we call a generalist-eclectic approach to direct social work practice and what is commonly referred to in a wide range of social work literature as a generalist approach, perspective, or framework for practice. The main difference is that the latter encompasses both direct and indirect (or macro) practice methods, whereas our book focuses only on direct practice (primarily on work with individuals). Our focus on direct practice is pragmatic in that our current overview of theories and models of clinical practice does not allow space to include consideration of macro practice (e.g., community work and policy development). Our predominant focus on work with individuals is based on the same pragmatic reasoning. Also, although we fully endorse a holistic conception of social work practice that includes openness to intervention on macro as well as micro levels, we do not think that this precludes specialization in one of these levels of practice. We believe, however, that a specialization in direct social work practice must be grounded in an understanding of and appreciation for generalist principles and values. Despite the fact that a generalist approach includes theoretical openness (see below), we have added the term *eclectic* to the title of our approach to emphasize this. After a brief summary of the major elements of generalist direct practice, we will elaborate on the issue of eclecticism.

The major elements of our generalist-eclectic approach to direct social work are adopted from a range of literature on generalist social work practice (Hepworth, Rooney, & Larsen, 1997; Johnson, 1995; Landon, 1999; Locke, Garrison, & Winship, 1998; McMahon, 1996; Miley, O'Melia, & DuBois, 1998; Shatz et al., 1990; Sheafor, Horejsi, & Horejsi, 1997; Sheafor & Landon, 1987). These elements are summarized in Table 1.1 and described, below.

TABLE 1.1 The Major Elements of Generalist-Eclectic Direct Social Work Practice

---

1. A person-in-environment perspective that is informed by ecological systems theory
2. An emphasis on the development of a good helping relationship that fosters empowerment
3. The flexible use of a problem-solving process to provide structure and guidance to work with clients
4. A holistic, multilevel assessment that includes a focus on issues of diversity and oppression and on strengths
5. The flexible/eclectic use of a wide range of theories and techniques that are selected on the basis of their relevance to each unique client situation

---

THE MAJOR ELEMENTS OF GENERALIST-ECLECTIC DIRECT SOCIAL WORK PRACTICE

A Person-in-Environment Perspective That Is Informed by Ecological Systems Theory

"The central focus of social work traditionally seems to have been on people in their life situation complex—a simultaneous dual focus on individuals and environment" (Gordon, cited in Compton & Galaway, 1994, p. 6). A generalist approach embraces this traditional person-in-environment perspective of social work practice. This perspective emphasizes the need to view the interdependence and mutual influence of people and their social and physical environments. Also, it recognizes the link between private troubles (i.e., individual problems) and public issues (i.e., social problems) (Mills, 1959). The person-in-environment perspective has been one of the primary factors that has distinguished social work from other helping/counseling professions (e.g., psychology, marriage and family therapy, and psychiatry).

Ecological systems theory (see chapter 4) is a conceptual framework for the person-in-environment perspective "that has achieved nearly universal acceptance in the profession" (Mattaini, Lowery, & Meyer, 1998, p. 12). This theory "recognizes an interrelatedness of human problems, life situations, and social conditions" (Shatz et al., 1990, p. 223). As explained in chapter 2, it is a metatheory that is particularly useful for helping workers to see the "big picture" in terms of the reciprocal influence of people and the various systems (e.g., family, work, and community) with which they interact. As such, it "provides an organizing theoretical framework for the generalist practice approach" (Miley et al., 1998, p. 23).

An Emphasis on the Development of a Good Helping Relationship That Fosters Empowerment

Historically, social work has led the helping professions in advocating the importance of a collaborative, warm, empathic, supportive worker-client relationship. Social workers have described this type of relationship as the "soul" (Biestek, 1957), "heart" (Perlman, 1979), and "major determinant" (Hollis, 1970) of the helping endeavor. Although clinical social work drifted away from such an emphasis over the last few decades in favor of attention to the theoretical/technical/scientific aspects of practice (Coady, 1993a; Perlman, 1979), the generalist perspective has reemphasized the importance of the helping relationship.

Along with a reaffirmation of the importance of a good helping relationship, the generalist perspective has promoted a focus on empowerment. A number of authors of generalist textbooks (Johnson, 1995; Landon, 1999; Locke et al., 1998) combine a consideration of empowerment and the strengths perspective (Saleebey, 1997). Miley and colleagues (1998) argue that "an orientation toward strengths and empowerment compels social workers to redefine their relationships to embrace the notion of collaboration and partnership" (p. 90). Gutiérrez (cited in Miley et al., 1998) notes that this involves "basing the helping relationship on collaboration, trust, and shared power; identifying and building on the client's strengths; actively involving the client in the change process; [and] experiencing a sense of personal power within the helping relationship" (p. 7).

The Flexible Use of a Problem-Solving Model to Provide Structure and Guidance to Work with Clients

Since Perlman's (1957) formulation of the problem-solving model for social casework, problem-solving has been an integral part of social work practice. Most generalist approaches to social work practice include some version of the problem-solving model. Although there are various conceptualizations of the stages or phases of problem-solving, all versions include guidelines for the entire helping process, from initial engagement to termination. It should be emphasized that, in a generalist approach, problem-solving is construed as a collaborative process between workers and clients that has the ultimate goal of empowering clients to solve their own problems (see chapter 3 for a more detailed discussion of problem-solving).

A Holistic, Multilevel Assessment That Includes a Focus on Issues of Diversity and Oppression and on Strengths

The person-in-environment perspective and ecological systems theory suggest the necessity of a holistic, multilevel assessment. The term *holistic* refers to a "totality in perspective, with sensitivity to all the parts or levels that constitute the whole and to their interdependence and relatedness" (McMahon, 1996, p. 2). This represents a focus on the whole person (i.e., the physical, emotional, and spiritual aspects) in the context of his or her surroundings. Multilevel assessment goes hand in hand with a holistic focus, because this means considering the entire range of factors, from micro to macro, that could be affecting a client. Thus, in conducting an assessment, the generalist direct practitioner should consider the potential influence of biophysical, intrapsychic, interpersonal/familial, environmental, and sociocultural factors. With regard to the latter class of factors, a generalist approach to direct practice assessment includes particular sensitivity to issues of diversity (e.g., gender, race, culture, class, sexual orientation, disability, age, and religion) and oppression (Shatz et al., 1990). A generalist approach also demands that the assessment process include a focus on clients' strengths, resources, and competencies.

The Flexible/Eclectic Use of a Wide Range of Theories and Techniques That Are Selected on the Basis of Their Relevance to Each Unique Client Situation

The commitment to a holistic, multilevel assessment precludes a rigid adherence to narrow theories of human problems. A generalist approach should be "unencumbered by any particular practice approach into which the client(s) might be expected to fit" (Sheafor & Landon, 1987, p. 666). Theories can be useful in the assessment process if they are considered tentatively as potential explanations for clients' problems; however, theories represent preconceived ideas about human problems and can blind one to alternative explanations.

Just as the assessment process must avoid rigid adherence to narrow theoretical perspectives, the "generalist perspective requires that the social worker be *eclectic* (i.e., draw ideas and techniques from many sources)" (Sheafor et al., 1997, p. 91) in the intervention process. Generalists are open to using theories and techniques that seem most relevant to the understanding of the unique client situation: "Single model practitioners do a disservice to themselves and their clients by attempting to fit all clients and problems into their chosen model" (Hepworth et al., 1997, p. 16). Guidelines for selecting theories and techniques for particular types of clients and problems are reviewed later in this chapter (see Approaches to Eclecticism, particularly Technical Eclecticism) as well as in chapter 3, but first it is important to provide an orientation to the issue of eclecticism.

AN OVERVIEW OF ECLECTICISM

As is evident from the discussion above, eclecticism is an inherent orientation in generalist practice and is endorsed by most authors of generalist social work practice texts (e.g., Hepworth et al., 1997; Locke et al., 1998; Sheafor et al., 1997). For example, Hepworth and colleagues (1997) argue that "because human beings present a broad array of problems of living, no single approach or practice model is sufficiently comprehensive to adequately address them all" (p. 16). One survey (Jensen, Bergin, & Greaves,

1990) found that the majority (68%) of social workers consider themselves eclectic, although this was the second lowest percentage among the four professional groups surveyed (corresponding figures for marriage and family therapists, psychologists, and psychiatrists were 72%, 70%, and 59%, respectively). Despite clear and logical arguments for eclecticism and its prevalence in practice, it is still a contentious issue in the helping professions, and we think this is particularly so in clinical social work (see below).

RESISTANCE TO ECLECTICISM

A historical perspective is necessary to understand the contentiousness of eclecticism. For most of the 20th century, the helping professions were marked by rigid adherence to narrow theories. Until the 1960s, psychodynamic theory remained relatively unchallenged as the dominant theory in the helping professions (Garfield & Bergin, 1994). As humanistic and behavioral theories gained increasing prominence in the 1960s, they began to challenge the dominance of psychodynamic theory. This initiated the era of the "competing schools of psychotherapy." For the most part, the next three decades were marked by rigid adherence to one or another of an increasing number of theoretical camps, rancorous debate about which theory was right, and extensive research focused on proving which therapeutic approach was the most effective. Although there were some efforts to bridge the differences among the numerous competing schools of therapy, eclecticism was clearly a "dirty word." As Norcross (1997) has commented: "You have all heard the classic refrains: eclectics are undisciplined subjectivists, jacks of all trades and masters of none, products of educational incompetency, muddle-headed, indiscriminate nihilists, fadmeisters, and people straddling the fence with both feet planted firmly in the air" (p. 87).

Unfortunately, such negative views of eclecticism are still prevalent within the field of counseling, particularly within clinical social work. Despite the endorsement of eclecticism by the generalist perspective, many social workers do not seem aware of or at least have not embraced the movement toward eclecticism that has been sweeping the larger field of psychotherapy (see a discussion of this trend, below). Also, despite the prevalence of eclecticism in practice, many social workers seem loath to admit this publicly because they know that eclecticism is still a "dirty word" in some circles. We have encountered many clinical social workers (academics and practitioners) who have disdain not only for eclecticism but also for a generalist perspective at the advanced/graduate level of training. Such social workers advocate instead for in-depth training in and adherence to one theoretical orientation.

It is not surprising that adherence to one theoretical orientation is most prevalent for those who were trained in an older, more traditional theory. The survey by Jensen and colleagues (1990) found that the most common exclusive theoretical orientation was psychodynamic. Furthermore, to bolster our contention about the conservative streak in clinical social work, this survey found that "of individuals endorsing an exclusively psychodynamic approach, 74% were either psychiatrists or social workers" (Jensen et al., 1990, p. 127) (25% of social workers and 36% of psychiatrists identified themselves as exclusively psychodynamic, whereas less than 10% of the other professional groups did so). It should also be pointed out, however, that this phenomenon of adherence to one theoretical perspective seems to be common for social workers who embrace the newer, "fashionable" therapeutic approaches (e.g., in the 1990s, solution-focused therapy [see Stalker, Levene, & Coady, 1999]; in the 1980s, family systems therapy [see Coady, 1993b]). One of the social work academics who we approached to write a chapter for this book declined to contribute because of our endorsement of both a generalist perspective and eclecticism. Unfortunately, such traditional negative views of eclecticism are difficult to change, and they quickly filter down to students. We have had students tell us that their field instructors counsel them to never admit to an eclectic orientation in a job interview because it would count against them. Thus, we felt that it was important to emphasize our endorsement of this perspective in the title of the book and to review the fact of and rationale for the trend toward eclecticism.

REASONS FOR THE TREND TOWARD ECLECTICISM

Although various writers have argued for eclecticism (e.g., Thorne, 1950) or have promoted the integration of various theories (e.g., Dollard & Miller, 1950) over the years, it is only in the last 20 years that a definite trend toward eclecticism has emerged in the broad field of psychotherapy. We should clarify briefly at this point that the term *integration* is often used together with or instead of the term *eclecticism*. "In common usage, these terms often have been employed interchangeably, with treatments labeled 'eclectic' in the 1960s and 1970s often having been more chicly relabeled as 'integrative' in the 1980s and 1990s" (Lebow, 1997, p. 5). Although there is a conceptual difference between these terms, which we will specify in our discussion of the types of eclecticism later in this chapter, until then we will use the term *eclecticism* to denote the general trend to use theoretical concepts and techniques from various theoretical schools.

The trend toward eclecticism has been fueled primarily by two interrelated factors. First, decades of psychotherapy research have failed to demonstrate the superiority of one type of psychotherapy over another. Summary reviews (e.g., Lambert & Bergin, 1994; Luborsky, Singer, & Luborsky, 1975) and meta-analyses (e.g., Smith & Glass, 1977; Wampold et al., 1997) of this vast body of research that was stimulated by the competing schools phenomenon have resulted in the "equal outcomes" or "Dodo bird effect" conclusion. That is, overall, studies indicate that the various types of therapy (psychodynamic, cognitive-behavioral, humanistic, etc.) have roughly equal effectiveness and therefore, in the words of the Dodo bird from Alice in Wonderland (Carroll, cited in Wampold et al., 1997), "Everybody has won, and all must have prizes" (p. 203). Although some authors (Lambert & Bergin, 1994) have pointed out tentative evidence that cognitive-behavioral approaches may yield superior outcomes for some specific, difficult problems (e.g., panic, phobic, and compulsive disorders) and others (Beutler, 1991) have surmised that in the future more sophisticated research designs may yield superior outcomes for specific therapy/client problem combinations, the equal outcomes conclusion generally has been accepted within the field of psychotherapy. The acceptance of this conclusion does not lead directly to an argument for eclecticism; however, it does promote acceptance of the validity of alternative approaches. This, along with the recognition that "no single school can provide all theoretical and practical answers for our psychological woes . . . [makes it seem sensible] to cross boundaries, to venture beyond one's borders in search of nuggets that may be deposited among the hills and dales of other camps" (Lazarus, 1996, p. 59).

Second, the cumulative results of psychotherapy research have stimulated interest in what has come to be known as "common (or nonspecific) factors." The findings of nonsignificant outcome differences among the variety of different therapies (the equal outcomes phenomenon) led many researchers to latch onto the ideas promoted earlier by Rosenzweig (1936) and Frank (1961) that factors specific to the various therapies (i.e., distinctive theory and techniques) had less impact on outcomes than factors that were common across therapies—particularly relationship factors. Early research on the client-centered core conditions of empathy, warmth, and genuineness and later research on the related concept of the therapeutic alliance established that relationship factors were the most powerful predictors of client outcome and that a good helping relationship was necessary for good outcome, regardless of the approach to therapy (Horvath & Symonds, 1991; Orlinsky, Grawe, & Parks, 1994). Some authors (e.g., Patterson, 1984) used the cumulative results of the research on relationship factors to resurface Rogers (1957) argument that such factors were "necessary and sufficient" for therapeutic change. Others (e.g., Lambert & Bergin, 1994) found empirical support for cognitive (e.g., reconceptualizing problems) and behavioral (e.g., mastery efforts) factors that seemed to be common across therapies. Research to date suggests that although factors unique to the various schools of therapy (i.e., specific techniques) may contribute something to therapeutic effectiveness, "factors common across treatments are accounting for a substantial amount of improvement . . . [and] common factors may even account for most of the gains that result from psychological intervention" (Lambert & Bergin, 1994, p. 163). Again, although the research on common factors does not lead directly to an argument for eclecticism with regard to theory and technique, it does promote openness to crossing therapeutic boundaries (see Approaches to Eclecticism, below, for further discussion of common factors).

Although there have been longstanding and persuasive arguments for eclecticism, the trend toward eclecticism has been fueled largely by research findings, both the equal outcomes phenomenon and the importance of relationship and other common factors. As Lambert and Bergin (1994) have noted, the trend toward eclecticism "appears to reflect a healthy response to empirical evidence" (p. 181). This has led practitioners to "increasingly acknowledge the inadequacies of any one school and the potential value of others" (Norcross, 1997, p. 86).

DOCUMENTING THE TREND TOWARD ECLECTICISM

More than a decade ago, with regard to the broad field of psychotherapy, Garfield and Bergin (1986) concluded:

> A decisive shift in opinion has quietly occurred; and it has created an irreversible change in professional attitudes about psychotherapy and behavior change. The new view is that the long-term dominance of the major theories is over and that an eclectic position has taken precedence. (p. 7)

The trend toward eclecticism is evidenced in a number of ways. First, the precedence of eclecticism has been demonstrated by surveys. The survey by Jensen and colleagues (1990) found that the majority of practitioners in each of the four groups of helping professionals were eclectic (68% overall). Although earlier surveys have yielded lower percentages for eclecticism, "the overall picture is relatively clear. Therapists identify themselves as eclectics more frequently than any other orientation" (Garfield & Bergin, 1994, p. 7). Second, two influential professional organizations have been formed to further the study of eclecticism (and the related concept of integration) in psychotherapy: (1) the Society for the Exploration of Psychotherapy Integration (SEPI) and (2) the International Academy of Eclectic Psychotherapists. Third, there has been a proliferation of literature, mostly outside social work, on eclecticism and integration. The two professional organizations named above each have established a journal: (1) *Journal of Psychotherapy Integration* and (2) *Journal of Eclectic and Integrative Psychotherapy*. The number of articles focused on eclecticism and integration that are published annually in these and other academic journals has continued to increase. This is also true for books on this topic. *Psychoanalysis and Behavior Therapy* (Wachtel, 1977), *Systems of Psychotherapy: A Transtheoretical Analysis* (Prochaska, 1979) and *Psychotherapy: An Eclectic Approach* (Garfield, 1980) were three of the first books that presented arguments for eclecticism and/or integration. Since then, the number of texts and handbooks on eclecticism and integration has continued to increase. Some of the more recent editions of such books include Beutler and Clarkin (1990), Dryden (1992), Garfield (1995), Gold (1996), Norcross and Goldfried (1992), and Prochaska and Norcross (1999).

Although the trend toward eclecticism and integration is clear in the broad field of psychotherapy and the profession of clinical psychology, as we have argued, it is less clear in direct social work practice. We think it is important for social workers to become familiar with the literature on eclecticism and integration in psychotherapy. Many of the ideas and principles in this literature (e.g., the valuing of multiple perspectives for understanding and intervening, the centrality of the helping relationship) are consistent with and can inform social work practice. We do, however, think that these ideas and principles need to be integrated within a generalist perspective for social work practice, and that is the general aim of this book.

APPROACHES TO ECLECTICISM

Three broad approaches to eclecticism are commonly identified in the literature: technical eclecticism, theoretical integration, and common factors (Alford, 1995; Arkowitz, 1989; Gold, 1996; Lazarus, 1996; Norcross & Grencavage, 1989; Safran & Messer, 1997). As noted earlier, although the term *integration* is commonly used in conjunction with or instead of eclecticism, there is an important distinction between these two terms.

> Eclectic therapies are relatively atheoretical, pragmatic, and empirical, made up of divergent techniques (Norcross & Grencavage, 1989). Integration-based therapies, on the other hand, are invested in a conceptual and theoretical creation beyond a technical blend of methods, so that higher order constructs are offered to account for change and to direct intervention. (Lambert, 1992, p. 95)

In simpler terms, "to take a culinary metaphor, the eclectic selects among several dishes to constitute a meal; the integrationist creates new dishes by combining different ingredients" (Prochaska & Norcross, 1999, p. 464). As alluded to earlier, the third approach to eclecticism, that of common factors, emphasizes the curative factors (e.g., a good helping relationship) that are generic to all counseling approaches.

We think there is evidence of and a need for a fourth classification of eclectic practice, which we call "theoretical eclecticism." This fourth classification is different from technical eclecticism in that it emphasizes the use of multiple theoretical perspectives, rather than focusing primarily on the techniques that derive from theories. It is different from theoretical integration because it does not attempt to synthesize theories.

Each of these four general approaches to eclecticism subsumes a number of more specific models of eclectic/integrative practice; however, not surprisingly, there is confusion in the literature with regard to classifying some models. Table 1.2 presents an overview of the characteristics of the four general approaches to eclecticism (or of the subtypes within the approaches). Although it is beyond the scope of this book to review specific

TABLE 1.2   Approaches to Eclecticism

Approaches	Approach subtypes and/or examples of eclectic therapies	General characteristics of approaches or subtypes
Technical eclecticism	(a) Theoretically Consistent Technical Eclecticism (e.g., Lazarus's [1989] Multimodal Therapy [MMT])	Adhering to one theoretical orientation while borrowing techniques from other theories on the basis of empirical evidence of efficacy and fit with client and problem
	(b) Cross-Theory Prescriptive Matching (e.g., Beutler & Clarkin's [1990] Systematic Treatment Planning [STP])	Using empirical evidence to select techniques from various theories that match with client variables (e.g., coping style)
Theoretical integration	(e.g., Wachtel's [1977] Integrative Psychodynamic Therapy)	Integrating/synthesizing the strengths of two or more theories to create a more comprehensive theory to explain and intervene with human problems
Common factors	(e.g., Weinberg's [1993] Relationship, Exposure, Mastery, and Attribution [REMA] Model)	Focusing on factors that are shared by all types of therapy and that are central to therapeutic effectiveness (e.g., a good helping relationship)
Theoretical eclecticism	(a) Uni-Theory Prescriptive Matching (e.g., Beck et al.'s [1979] Cognitive Therapy for Depression)	Choosing different pure type therapies for different kinds of client problems on the basis of empirical evidence of efficacy
	(b) Pluralistic Theoretical Eclecticism (e.g., General arguments advanced by Safran & Messer [1997])	Tentatively applying multiple theoretical perspectives to each client's situation to develop in-depth understanding and to choose interventive strategies that fit with such understanding

eclectic/integrative models in detail, the discussion of each of the four general approaches below gives examples of some of the specific models that fall under their domain. Following this, we elaborate on the type of eclecticism we endorse for our generalist-eclectic approach.

TECHNICAL ECLECTICISM

This is the most diverse and complex grouping of eclectic approaches. In general, technical eclecticism "refers to the relatively atheoretical selection of clinical treatments on the basis of predicted efficacy rather than theoretical considerations" (Alford, 1995, p. 147). Technical eclecticism is sometimes referred to as systematic eclecticism or prescriptive matching to emphasize that techniques are selected carefully and, where possible, on the basis of empirical evidence about effectiveness with certain types of problems or client characteristics. Lazarus (1996) differentiates this type of eclecticism from "the ragtag importation of techniques from anywhere or everywhere without a sound rationale" (p. 61). Technical eclectics are also leery of efforts to integrate theories because they believe that most theories have fundamental and irreconcilable philosophical differences.

Our reading of the literature suggests that there are two main subtypes of technical eclecticism. The first type involves adhering to one theoretical framework while incorporating empirically validated techniques from different theories that "fit" with the characteristics of the client and his or her problem. This type of eclecticism might be called *theoretically consistent technical eclecticism.* Lazarus's (1989) multimodal therapy (MMT) is the most prominent example of this approach. Lazarus (1996) is clear that he remains theoretically consistent with regard to his adherence to social and cognitive learning theory; however, he incorporates "effective techniques from any discipline without necessarily subscribing to the theories that begot them" (p. 61). Thus, in MMT, techniques from humanistic, psychodynamic, and family systems therapy are commonly used, but the practitioner continues to be guided by cognitive-behavioral theory.

The second type of technical eclecticism might be called *cross-theory prescriptive matching* and is best represented by Beutler and Clarkin's (1990) "systematic treatment planning" (STP). In this approach, there is an openness to using techniques from the entire range of therapies and an emphasis on selecting techniques on the basis of "empirical evidence of usefulness rather than by a theory of personality or of change" (Beutler & Harwood, 1995, p. 89). STP is one of the most ambitious models of eclecticism. In this model, a thorough assessment of client variables (e.g., demographic qualities, coping style, level of distress, level of resistance, expectations of therapy, social supports, and diagnosis) and a consideration of empirical evidence related to such variables lead to decisions about (1) treatment contexts (individual, group, marital, family therapy), (2) choice of therapist (e.g., based on interpersonal compatibility and demographic similarity),

(3) goal of therapy (i.e., focus on symptoms or underlying themes), (4) primary level of experience to be addressed (affect, cognition, or behavior), (5) style of therapist (e.g., degree of directiveness, support, or confrontation), and (6) therapeutic techniques. Also, reassessments of client variables that are most likely to change (e.g., level of distress, resistance, and symptoms) "are undertaken every few sessions in order to signal the clinician when to implement necessary treatment adjustments" (Beutler & Harwood, 1995, p. 96).

Another influential model that we think belongs in this second type of technical eclecticism is Prochaska and Norcross's (1999) "transtheoretical" model. Although this model has elements of integrative and common factors models (Gold, 1996), it has the same prescriptive matching nature of Beutler and Clarkin's (1990) STP model (Beutler & Harwood, 1995). In the transtheoretical model, the selection of interventions, or change processes, as they are called, is based on the assessment of two factors. First, consideration is given to the *stages of change* through which people progress. Thus, the worker needs to assess which of the five stages of change a client is in: (1) precontemplation (relatively unaware of problems with no intention to change), (2) contemplation (aware of a problem and considering but not committed to change), (3) preparation (intending and beginning to take initial steps toward change), (4) action (investment of considerable time and energy to successfully alter a problem behavior), or (5) maintenance (working to consolidate gains and prevent relapse). Second, the *level/depth of change* required needs to be assessed. Thus, the worker and client need to mutually determine which of five problem levels to focus on: (1) symptom/situational problems, (2) maladaptive cognitions, (3) current interpersonal conflicts, (4) family/systems conflicts, or (5) intrapersonal conflicts.

After an assessment of the client's stage of change and the level of change required, the transtheoretical model suggests that available empirical evidence of effectiveness be considered, as much as possible, to determine which interventions from different theoretical perspectives to use. In general, with regard to stages of change, techniques from cognitive, psychodynamic, and humanistic therapies are thought to be most useful in the precontemplation and contemplation stages, whereas "change processes traditionally associated with the existential and behavioral traditions . . . are most useful during the action and maintenance stages" (Prochaska & Norcross, 1999, p. 503). More specifically, when the level of change required is considered in the action stage, behavioral techniques would usually be chosen for the symptom/situational level, cognitive techniques would be employed at the level of maladaptive cognitions, and psychodynamic interventions would be used at the intrapersonal conflict level. The general principle in this model is to focus intervention initially at the symptom/situational level, then to proceed to deeper levels only if necessary.

THEORETICAL INTEGRATION

In this second category of approaches, "there is an emphasis on integrating the underlying theories of psychotherapy along with therapy techniques from each" (Prochaska & Norcross, 1999, p. 463). The goal is to produce a more comprehensive, overarching theoretical framework that synthesizes the strengths of individual theories. The ultimate form of theoretical integration would incorporate all of the various theories of therapy (i.e., those subsumed under psychodynamic, cognitive-behavioral, humanistic/feminist, and postmodern classifications, as well as biological and family systems approaches) into a synthesized/unified whole. Leaving aside the question of whether such a lofty goal is viable or not, to date "psychotherapy integration has not succeeded in that grand attempt, . . . the leading current approaches usually incorporate two, or at most three, of these perspectives" (Stricker, 1994, p. 6).

Wachtel's (1977) integration of psychodynamic and behavioral theories is the most commonly cited example of an integrative approach. Building on the earlier work of Dollard and Miller (1950), Wachtel integrated the strengths of the social-learning model of behavioral theory with his interpersonal type of psychodynamic theory to create integrative psychodynamic therapy (Wachtel & McKinney, 1992). The underlying theory of cyclical psychodynamics (Gold & Wachtel, 1993) posits that unconscious conflicts/anxieties and interpersonal interactions are mutually influencing and create vicious cycles (e.g., anxiety about dependency needs results in keeping people at arm's length, which heightens the anxiety, etc.). In this model, intervention involves integrating a psychodynamic focus on insight with a behavioral focus on action (e.g., skills training).

Safran and Segal (1990) have combined cognitive, interpersonal, and experiential theories into an integrative theoretical framework that has similarities to that of Wachtel. They use cognitive theory to elaborate on Wachtel's idea of cyclical psychodynamics. Thus, interpersonal schemas are generalized representations of interpersonal patterns. Cognitive and experiential interventions are used to interrupt and modify maladaptive patterns. It is interesting to note that, whereas early attempts at therapy integration usually involved psychodynamic and behavioral models, cognitive theory is the most common component of more recent integrative models (Norcross & Prochaska, 1999).

COMMON FACTORS

In this third category of approaches to eclecticism, there is an attempt to identify and utilize the "effective aspects of treatment shared by the diverse forms of psychotherapy" (Weinberger, 1993, p. 43). This approach has been influenced largely by the extensive work of Jerome Frank, particularly his classic book entitled *Persuasion and Healing* (1961, 1973, and coauthored with his daughter, Julia Frank, 1991). Building on the earlier ideas of Rosenzweig (1936), Frank developed the demoralization hypothesis, which proposes that most of the distress suffered by clients stems from being demoralized and that "features shared by all therapies that combat demoralization account for much of their effectiveness" (Frank, 1982, p. 32).

Frank (1982) identified four factors shared by all forms of psychotherapy, as well as religious and other secular types of healing, that represent means of directly or indirectly combating demoralization. First, and foremost, is an "emotionally supportive, confiding relationship with a helping person" (Frank, 1982, p. 19). If helpers can convince clients that they care and want to help, then this decreases their sense of alienation, increases expectations of improvement, and boosts morale. Second, is a "healing setting" that heightens the helper's prestige and increases the client's expectation of help. Third, is a theoretical rationale or myth that provides a believable explanation for the clients' difficulties. Frank uses the word *myth* to underscore the contention that the accuracy of the explanation is less important than its plausibility in the eyes of the client. Any explanation of their difficulties that clients can accept alleviates some distress and engenders hope for change. Fourth, is a set of therapeutic procedures or a "ritual" that involves the participation of helper and client in activities that both believe will help the client to overcome the presenting difficulties. On the basis of empirical studies of therapy, Frank contends that therapeutic procedures will be optimally effective if they (1) provide new learning experiences for the client (these enhance morale by helping clients to develop more positive views of themselves and their problems), (2) arouse clients' emotions (this helps clients to tolerate and accept their emotions and allows them to confront and cope more successfully with feared issues and situations, thus strengthening self-confidence, sense of mastery, and morale), and (3) provide opportunities for clients to practice what they have learned both within therapy and in their everyday lives (thus reinforcing therapeutic gains, a sense of mastery, and morale).

Weinberger (1993) has built on the work of Frank by reviewing the empirical evidence for the efficacy of common factors and developing a tentative model of common factors therapy. He calls this the REMA model, because it proposes that relationship, exposure, mastery, and attribution are the critical factors in all types of counseling.

> The relationship is ameliorative in its own right but insufficient in and of itself. Exposure to critical issues is only effective in the context of a therapeutic relationship and only works if it leads to mastery experiences, which together make up a corrective emotional experience. . . . Finally, change will last only if the patient attributes improvement to himself or herself. (Weinberger, 1993, p. 53)

Weinberger also notes that the therapeutic power of providing an explanation (or "myth") for the client's problem makes sense, but that no empirical work has focused on this hypothesis.

Another therapy model that has been classified as a common factors model is the "eclectic-integrative approach" of Garfield (1995). Garfield contends that despite the many apparent differences among the various therapeutic approaches and the fact that these schools of therapy tend to emphasize the importance of their specific techniques, factors that are common across therapies account for much of their success. Although Garfield does draw eclectically from many different theoretical approaches, he "places much more emphasis on the therapeutic relationship and on the common factors in psychotherapy" (p. 167). Echoing Frank, Garfield (1995) contends that "being given some explanation for one's problems by an interested expert in the role of healer, may be the important common aspect of these divergent therapies" (p. 34). Garfield (1995) rationalizes the theoretical openness of his approach:

> Although the absence of a unifying and guiding theory has its drawbacks, an awareness of one's limitations and of the gaps in our current knowledge is, in the long run, a positive thing even though it may make for uncertainties. It is better to see the situation for what it really is than to have what may be an incorrect or biased orientation. (p. 216)

Garfield's model, however, does provide some structure for practitioners by presenting general guidelines for the various phases of therapy (beginning, middle, later, and termination phases). This is very similar to the use of the problem-solving model in the generalist-eclectic approach (see below). Also, Garfield's approach has elements of technical eclecticism in that therapists are advised to choose techniques that "on the basis of empirical evidence seem to be most effective for the specific problems presented by the client" (p. 218).

THEORETICAL ECLECTICISM

We have created this fourth category of eclecticism for two other approaches that do not fit neatly into the three previous categories that are generally recognized in the literature. Some may argue that the first of these approaches is not a type of eclecticism at all; however, we think that a simple type of theoretical eclecticism is represented by what might be called *uni-theory prescriptive matching*. In this approach, different discrete therapies "are prescribed as optimal for different kinds of problems or clients, rather than combined in one client's treatment" (Safran & Messer, 1997, p. 142). Prominent examples of this type of eclecticism include interpersonal therapy for depression (Klerman, Weissman, Rounsaville, & Chevron, 1984; see chapter 7), cognitive therapy for depression (Beck, Rush, Shaw, & Emery,

1979; see chapter 9), and cognitive-behavior therapy for panic disorder (Barlow, Craske, Cerny, Jerome, & Klosko, 1989). Treatment manuals are commonly used in these approaches to guide the therapist and to ensure the model is followed. Beutler and Harwood (1995) differentiate this type of prescriptive matching from their own brand of cross-theory prescriptive matching and suggest that the unitheory approach "probably is still the most prominent model advocated among academics" (p. 91).

The second approach included in this category, which we call *pluralistic theoretical eclecticism*, values the potential relevance of all theories and promotes the use of multiple theories with individual clients. This perspective recognizes that "multiple, contradictory theories are necessary to capture different aspects of the underlying phenomenon, and that a given theory captures some of these aspects at the expense of others" (Safran & Messer, 1997, p. 149). This approach necessitates that practitioners "openly learn numerous psychotherapy *models* rather than simply applying various *techniques*" (Gaston, 1995, p. 84) and that they "be fluent in more than one therapy language and mode of practice" (Safran & Messer, 1997, p. 148). Rather than simply matching techniques to client characteristics or problems, as in most forms of technical eclecticism, theoretical eclecticism involves the tentative use of multiple theories to develop understanding of client problem situations before deciding on interventive techniques. The essence of theoretical eclecticism is to consider the relevance of multiple theoretical frameworks to each client's problem situation in order to develop a more complex, comprehensive understanding and to choose interventions that fit with this in-depth understanding.

OUR APPROACH TO ECLECTICISM

Given our commitment to the spirit of eclecticism, as well as the obvious overlap among many of the approaches to eclecticism, it should come as no surprise that our approach incorporates aspects of many of the approaches outlined above. In general, we endorse an approach that encourages both pluralistic theoretical eclecticism and technical eclecticism and that acknowledges the importance of common factors. Such an approach falls short of the lofty goal of theoretical integration (melding different theories into an overarching conceptual framework). We think it is useful to become familiar with the various integrative therapies that have been developed and to consider them, along with discrete theories, in a pluralistic approach to theoretical eclecticism. True, comprehensive integration, however, is a long-range goal at best, and it may be that "a continuing dialogue among multiple perspectives . . . [is more productive] than aspiring to one superordinate theory" (Safran & Messer, 1997, p. 147). Our approach also differs from those that remain theoretically narrow and simply adapt diverse techniques (i.e., theoretically consistent technical eclecticism, as in Lazarus's MMT) or that apply single models of treatment to different client problems (i.e., unitheory prescriptive matching, as in interpersonal therapy for depression). We find these approaches too theoretically narrow and restricting.

Given our generalist orientation, our approach is probably closest in spirit to pluralistic theoretical eclecticism and a common factors approach, but it also incorporates crosstheory prescriptive matching approaches (e.g., Beutler & Clarkin, 1990; Prochaska & Norcross, 1999). Thus, in line with the generalist perspective and theoretical eclecticism, we advocate for an open, holistic assessment that considers the entire range of theoretical perspectives in order to make sense of the client's problem-situation. In line with the generalist perspective and a common factors approach, we advocate for a collaborative, supportive, empathic helping relationship that is focused on instilling hope, boosting morale, and empowering the client. In line with the generalist perspective's openness to using a wide range of techniques on the basis of their relevance to each unique client situation, we also endorse the tentative use of cross-theory prescriptive matching of techniques to client variables (e.g., coping style, level of resistance, and stage of change). We stress "tentative" use of such matching efforts for two reasons. First, we agree with Stiles, Shapiro, and Barkham (1995), who contend that there is not enough empirical evidence to warrant firm decisions about matching. Second, because of this lack of empirical evidence, as well as the mechanistic flavor of some prescriptive matching models, we favor what has been called "responsive matching" (Stiles et al., 1995). "Responsive matching is often done intuitively, we suspect, as practitioners draw techniques from their repertoire to fit their momentary understanding of a client's needs" (Stiles et al., 1995, p. 265). This type of matching can draw on theory and empirical findings but is more tentative and open to modification based on sensitivity to the client's response: "[I]t is grounded in both theory and observation of the individual case" (Stiles et al., p. 265). In the same vein, Garfield (1995) has argued that

> [i]n the absence of research data, the therapist has to rely on his own clinical experience and evaluations, or on his best clinical judgment . . . and make whatever modifications seem to be necessary in order to facilitate positive movement in therapy. (p. 218)

Strategies for integrating these eclectic approaches with practice will be elaborated in chapter 3 in the discussion of the problem-solving phases, particularly the planning, contracting, and intervention phase.

A number of other specific issues should also be addressed with regard to our approach to eclecticism. First, although we endorse a common factors approach, we disagree to some extent with Frank's (1982) idea of myth, which posits that any explanation of the problem that the client can accept is good enough. This idea suggests that one theoretical framework may suffice as long as the worker can "persuade" the client to believe it. Although there may be some truth to this, we think that a holistic assessment

that considers multiple theoretical perspectives, and that is conducted collaboratively between the worker and the client, is preferable. The latter
approach is more likely to result in a comprehensive understanding that
fits with the client's experience. Also, this type of collaborative exploration
fosters the development of a strong therapeutic alliance and a sense of
empowerment for the client, both of which help to overcome demoralization.

Second, although we emphasize that pluralistic theoretical eclecticism is
important to developing comprehensive understanding of clients' problem-
situations and formulating plans for intervention, we don't think that good
practice is based solely on such a deductive application of theory. In chapter
2 we will discuss the limitations of using theory in practice and will elaborate
on how this needs to be augmented by creative, reflective, and intuitive-
inductive theory-building processes (Coady, 1995).

Third, and related to the previous point, we think that a general problem-
solving model (which is part of the generalist approach to social work
practice) provides useful guidance to an eclectic use of theory and technique, as well as to the artistic, intuitive-inductive part of practice. This
idea has similarities to Garfield's (1995) common factors approach, which
provides general guidelines for what he calls the stages of the therapeutic
process (beginning, middle, later, and termination stages). The various
formulations of the problem-solving model in literature on generalist social
work practice have similar (although usually more numerous) stages. In
chapter 3 we will review the problem-solving stages and elaborate on how
they provide useful guidelines for practice.

Fourth, it seems necessary to reiterate a point made earlier in this chapter.
Our approach to eclecticism necessitates that theoretical perspectives, most
of which have been developed by other professions, be examined critically
in light of the values and principles of our profession. For example, in
using various theories, it must be ensured that practice remains a collaborative venture between worker and client; that a person-in-environment/
ecological systems perspective is maintained; and that there is sensitivity to
issues of diversity, oppression, and empowerment. The fact that such values
and principles are integrated into most conceptions of problem-solving in
the generalist social work literature reinforces the importance of incorporating this framework in one's practice.

SUMMARY

This chapter has provided an overview of what we mean by a generalist-
eclectic approach to direct practice. It has included a description of the
major elements of generalist-eclectic practice, an overview of the rationale
for and trend toward eclecticism in direct practice, and a review of different
approaches to eclecticism. It was beyond the scope of this chapter to discuss
any of these topics in the depth that they deserve. The reader is referred

to the literature cited in our discussions for a more detailed review of these topics. In the next chapter, we extend our discussion of eclecticism by reviewing types, levels, and classification of theories for direct practice. In addition, we provide a critical examination of the use of theory in practice and a consideration of a complementary intuitive-inductive approach to practice.

REFERENCES

Alford, B. A. (1995). Introduction to the special issue: "Psychotherapy integration" and cognitive psychotherapy. *Journal of Cognitive Psychotherapy, 9*, 147–151.

Arkowitz, H. (1989). The role of theory in psychotherapy integration. *Journal of Integrative and Eclectic Psychotherapy, 8*, 8–16. *Can't find*

Barlow, D. H., Craske, M. G., Cerny, J. A., Jerome, A., & Klosko, J. S. (1989). Behavioral treatment of panic disorder. *Behavior Therapy, 20*, 261–282.

Beck, A. T., Rush, A. J., Shaw, B. F., & Emery, G. (1979). *Cognitive therapy of depression.* New York: Guilford Press.

Beutler, L. E. (1991). Have all won and must all have prizes? Revisiting Luborsky et al.'s verdict. *Journal of Consulting and Clinical Psychology, 59*, 226–232.

Beutler, L. E., & Clarkin, J. (1990). *Systematic treatment selection: Toward targeted therapeutic interventions.* New York: Brunner/Mazel.

Beutler, L. E., & Harwood, T. M. (1995). Prescriptive psychotherapies. *Applied and Preventive Psychology, 4*, 89–100.

Biestek, F. (1957). *The casework relationship.* Chicago: Loyola University Press.

Coady, N. F. (1993a). The worker-client relationship revisited. *Families in Society, 74*, 291–298.

Coady, N. F. (1993b). An argument for generalist social work practice with families versus family systems therapy. *Canadian Social Work Review, 10*, 27–42.

Coady, N. F. (1995). A reflective/inductive model of practice: Emphasizing theory building for unique cases versus applying theory to practice. In G. Rogers (Ed.), *Social work field education: Views and visions* (pp. 139–151). Dubuque, IA: Kendall/Hunt.

Compton, B. R., & Galaway, B. (1994). *Social work processes.* Pacific Grove, CA: Brooks/Cole.

Corsini, R. J., & Wedding, D. (Eds.). (1995). *Current psychotherapies* (5th ed.). Itasca, IL: F. E. Peacock.

Dollard, J., & Miller, N. E. (1950). *Personality and psychotherapy: An analysis in terms of learning, thinking, and culture.* New York: McGraw-Hill.

Dorfman, R. A. (Ed.). (1988). *Paradigms of clinical social work.* New York: Brunner/Mazel.

Dorfman, R. A. (Ed.). (1998). *Paradigms of clinical social work* (Vol. 2). New York: Brunner/Mazel.

Dryden, W. (Ed.). (1992). *Integrative and eclectic therapy: A handbook.* Buckingham, England: Open University Press.

Frank, J. D. (1961). *Persuasion and healing: A comparative study of psychotherapy.* Baltimore: Johns Hopkins University Press.

Frank, J. D. (1973). *Persuasion and healing: A comparative study of psychotherapy* (2nd ed.). Baltimore: John Hopkins University Press.

Frank, J. D. (1982). Therapeutic components shared by all psychotherapies. In J. H. Harvey & M. M. Parks (Eds.), *The master lecture series: Vol. 1. Psychotherapy research and behavior change* (pp. 9–37). Washington, DC: American Psychological Press.

Frank, J. D., & Frank, J. B. (1991). *Persuasion and healing: A comparative study of psychotherapy* (3rd ed.). Baltimore: Johns Hopkins University Press.

Garfield, S. L. (1980). *Psychotherapy: An eclectic approach.* New York: Wiley.

Garfield, S. L. (1995). *Psychotherapy: An eclectic-integrative approach* (2nd ed.). New York: Wiley.

Garfield, S. L., & Bergin, A. E. (1986). Introduction and historical overview. In S. L. Garfield & A. E. Bergin (Eds.), *Handbook of psychotherapy and behavior change* (3rd ed., pp. 3–22). New York: Wiley.

Garfield, S. L., & Bergin, A. E. (1994). Introduction and historical overview. In A. E. Bergin & S. L. Garfield (Eds.), *Handbook of psychotherapy and behavior change* (4th ed., pp. 3–18). New York: Wiley.

Gaston, L. (1995). Common factors exist in reality but not in our theories. *Clinical Psychology: Science and Practice, 2,* 83–86.

Gilliland, B. E., & James, R. K. (1998). *Theories and strategies in counseling and psychotherapy* (4th ed.). Boston: Allyn & Bacon.

Gold, J. R. (1996). *Key concepts in psychotherapy integration.* New York: Plenum Press.

Gold, J. R., & Wachtel, P. L. (1993). Cyclical psychodynamics. In G. Stricker & J. R. Gold (Eds.), *Comprehensive handbook of psychotherapy integration* (pp. 59–72). New York: Plenum Press.

Hepworth, D. H., Rooney, R. H., & Larsen, J. A. (1997). *Direct social work practice: Theory and skills* (5th ed.). Pacific Grove, CA: Brooks/Cole.

Hollis, F. (1969). Psychosocial approach to the practice of casework. In R. Roberts & R. Nee (Eds.), *Theories of social casework* (pp. 33–75). Chicago: University of Chicago Press.

Horvath, A. O., & Symonds, B. D. (1991). Relation between working alliance and outcome in psychotherapy. *Journal of Counseling Psychology, 38,* 139–149.

Jensen, J. P., Bergin, A. E., & Greaves, D. W. (1990). The meaning of eclecticism: New survey and analysis of components. *Professional Psychology: Research and Practice, 21,* 124–130.

Johnson, L. (1995). *Social work practice: A generalist approach* (5th ed.). Boston: Allyn & Bacon.

Klerman, G. L., Weissman, M. M., Rounsaville, B. J., & Chevron, E. S. (1984). *Interpersonal psychotherapy of depression.* New York: Basic Books.

Lambert, M. J. (1992). Psychotherapy outcome research: Implications for integrative and eclectic therapists. In J. C. Norcross & M. R. Goldfried (Eds.), *Handbook of psychotherapy integration* (pp. 94–129). New York: Basic Books.

Lambert, M. J., & Bergin, A. E. (1994). The effectiveness of psychotherapy. In A. E. Bergin & S. L. Garfield (Eds.), *Handbook of psychotherapy and behavior change* (4th ed., pp. 143–189). New York: Wiley.

Landon, P. (1999). *Generalist social work practice.* Dubuque, IA: Eddie Bowers.

Lazarus, A. A. (1989). *The practice of multimodal therapy.* Baltimore, MD: Johns Hopkins University Press.

Lazarus, A. A. (1996). The utility and futility of combining treatments in psychotherapy. *Clinical Psychology: Science and Practice, 3,* 59–68.

Lebow, J. (1997). The integrative revolution in couple and family therapy. *Family Process, 36,* 1–17.

Locke, B., Garrison, R., & Winship, J. (1998). *Generalist social work practice: Context, story, and partnerships.* Pacific Grove, CA: Brooks/Cole.

Luborsky, L., Singer, B., & Luborsky, L. (1975). Comparative studies of psychotherapies: Is it true that "everyone has won and all must have prizes"? *Archives of General Psychiatry, 32,* 995–1008.

Mattaini, M. A., Lowery, C. T., & Meyer, C. H. (Eds.). (1998). *The foundations of social work practice: A graduate text* (2nd ed.). Washington, DC: NASW Press.

McMahon, M. O. (1996). *The general method of social work practice: A problem-solving approach* (3rd ed.). Englewood Cliffs, NJ: Prentice Hall.

Miley, K. K., O'Melia, M., & DuBois, B. (1998). *Generalist social work practice: An empowering approach.* Boston: Allyn & Bacon.

Mills, C. W. (1959). *The sociological imagination.* New York: Oxford University Press.

Norcross, J. C. (1997). Emerging breakthroughs in psychotherapy integration: Three predictions and one fantasy. *Psychotherapy, 34,* 86–90.

Norcross, J. C., & Goldfried, M. R. (Eds.). (1992). *Handbook of psychotherapy integration.* New York: Basic Books.

Norcross, J. C., & Grencavage, L. M. (1989). Eclecticism and integration in psychotherapy: Major themes and obstacles. *British Journal of Guidance and Counseling, 17,* 227–247.

Orlinsky, D. E., Grawe, K., & Parks, B. K. (1994). Process and outcome in psychotherapy: Noch einmal. In A. E. Bergin & S. L. Garfield (Eds.), *Handbook of psychotherapy and behavior change* (4th ed., pp. 270–376). New York: Wiley.

Patterson, C. H. (1984). Empathy, warmth, and genuineness in psychotherapy: A review of reviews. *Psychotherapy, 21,* 431–438.

Payne, M. (1997). *Modern social work theory* (2nd ed.). Chicago: Lyceum.

Perlman, H. H. (1957). *Social casework: A problem-solving process.* Chicago: University of Chicago Press.

Perlman, H. H. (1979). *Relationship: The heart of helping people.* Chicago: University of Chicago Press.

Prochaska, J. O. (1979). *Systems of psychotherapy: A transtheoretical analysis.* Homewood, IL: Dorsey.

Prochaska, J. O., & Norcross, J. C. (1999). *Systems of psychotherapy: A transtheoretical analysis* (4th ed.). Pacific Grove, CA: Brooks/Cole.

Rogers, C. R. (1957). The necessary and sufficient conditions of therapeutic personality change. *Journal of Consulting Psychology, 21,* 95–103.

Rosenzweig, S. (1936). Some implicit common factors in diverse methods of psychotherapy. *American Journal of Orthopsychiatry, 6,* 412–415.

Safran, J. D., & Messer, S. B. (1997). Psychotherapy integration: A postmodern critique. *Clinical Psychology: Science and Practice, 4,* 140–152.

Safran, J. D., & Segal, Z. D. (1990). *Interpersonal processes in cognitive therapy.* New York: Basic Books.

Saleebey, D. (Ed.). (1997). *The strengths perspective in social work practice* (2nd ed.). New York: Longman.

Sapp, M. (1997). *Counseling and psychotherapy: Theories, associated research, and issues.* Lanham, MD: University Press of America.

Shatz, M. S., Jenkins, M. E., & Sheafor, B. W. (1990). Milford redefined: A model of initial and advanced generalist social work. *Journal of Social Work Education, 26,* 217–231.

Sheafor, B. W., Horejsi, C. R., & Horejsi, G. A. (1997). *Techniques and guidelines for social work practice* (4th ed.). Boston: Allyn & Bacon.

Sheafor, B. W., & Landon, P. S. (1987). Generalist perspective. In A. Minahan (Ed.), *Encyclopedia of social work* (pp. 660–669). Silver Spring, MD: National Association of Social Workers.

Smith, M. L., & Glass, G. V. (1977). Meta-analysis of psychotherapy outcome studies. *American Psychologist, 32,* 752–760.

Stalker, C. A., Levene, J. E., & Coady, N. F. (1999). Solution-focused brief therapy— one model fits all? *Families in Society, 80,* 468–477.

Stiles, W. B., Shapiro, D. A., & Barkham, M. (1995). Technical eclecticism. In J. C. Norcross (Ed.), *A roundtable on psychotherapy integration: Common factors, technical eclecticism, and psychotherapy research. Journal of Psychotherapy Practice and Research, 4,* 248–271.

Stricker, G. (1994). Reflections on psychotherapy integration. *Clinical Psychology: Science and Practice, 1,* 3–12.

Thorne, F. C. (1950). *Principles of personality counseling: An eclectic view.* Brandon, VT: Journal of Clinical Psychology.

Turner, F. J. (Ed.). (1996). *Social work treatment: Interlocking theoretical approaches* (4th ed.). New York: The Free Press.

Wachtel, P. L. (1977). *Psychoanalysis and behavior therapy: Toward an integration.* New York: Basic Books.

Wachtel, P. L., & McKinney, M. K. (1992). Cyclical psychodynamics and integrative psychodynamic therapy. In J. C. Norcross & M. R. Goldfried (Eds.), *Handbook of psychotherapy integration* (pp. 335–372). New York: Basic Books.

Wampold, B. E., Mondin, G. W., Moody, M., Stich, F., Benson, K., & Ahn, H. (1997). A meta-analysis of outcome studies comparing bona fide psychotherapies: Empirically, all must have prizes. *Psychological Bulletin, 122,* 203–215.

Weinberger, J. (1993). Common factors in psychotherapy. In G. Stricker & J. R. Gold (Eds.), *Comprehensive handbook of psychotherapy integration* (pp. 43–56). New York: Plenum Press.

An Overview of Theory for Direct Practice and an Artistic, Intuitive-Inductive Approach to Practice

Nick Coady

This chapter is divided into three parts. In the first part, an overview of the broad types and levels of theory for direct social work practice, as well as definitions of key terms, is provided. Second, we describe briefly the major classifications of direct practice theories (i.e., psychodynamic, cognitive-behavioral, humanistic and feminist, and postmodern). A critical examination of the use of theory in practice and a discussion of a complementary, artistic approach to practice (which we refer to as intuitive-inductive practice) are presented in the third part of the chapter.

BROAD TYPES AND LEVELS OF THEORY

Direct social work practice is informed by two broad types of theory: (1) theory for describing and explaining human behavior (i.e., explanatory theory) and (2) theory for facilitating changes in human behavior (i.e., interventive theory) (Fisher, 1978; Landon, 1999). Also, theories in each of these typologies exist at different levels of abstraction. Theories at higher levels of abstraction provide general ideas for understanding and/or intervening with a wide range of human behavior. Theories at lower levels of abstraction provide more specific ideas for understanding and/or intervening with more circumscribed types of human behavior. A simultaneous consideration of these general types and levels of theory provides a useful way of conceptualizing the multitude of theories that inform direct social work practice (see Figure 2.1).

The right-hand column of Figure 2.1 represents the artistic, intuitive-inductive side of practice, which will be discussed later in this chapter. For the present, we will concentrate on the rest of the figure, which conceptualizes how the theories that are reviewed in this book can be classified with regard to the broad types and levels of theory. One issue that becomes apparent in looking at the figure is the need to define some commonly used terms: *perspectives, theories, models,* and *therapies.* In most of this book, we use the term *theory* in a general sense to encompass all of these terms; however, more specific definitions are helpful. These terms are bandied about a great deal in the social work literature, and there are many different definitions for them. In presenting how we understand and use these terms, we acknowledge that there are alternate conceptualizations and that the boundaries around them are often fuzzy. In discussing these terms, we also elaborate on our understanding of the types and levels of theory.

Perspective denotes the highest level of generality among these terms and is referred to only at the highest level of abstraction in Figure 2.1. A perspective is a broad, general way of viewing human behavior and social work practice. Thus, as described in chapter 1, a generalist perspective provides a broad conceptual lens for viewing human behavior in that it reminds us to focus holistically on person-environment interactions, human strengths and resiliency, issues of diversity and oppression, and so on. It does not, however, provide explanations for human behavior. Similarly, a generalist perspective endorses the principles of theoretical and technical eclecticism, but provides no specific guidelines for employing these in practice. An example of another commonly referred to perspective for social work practice is the "strengths perspective" (Saleebey, 1997), which we have conceptualized as part of the broader generalist perspective. Although we include ecological systems "theory" and a problem-solving "model" as part of the generalist-eclectic approach to practice, these are depicted as separate from but linked to this perspective in Figure 2.1 to clarify distinctions among these terms.

The term *theory* is reserved for a conceptual framework that offers an explanation of human behavior. Additionally, some theories also provide guidelines for facilitating behavior change. For example, psychodynamic theory offers both an explanation of human problems and guidelines for helping people overcome problems. It should be noted, however, that the terms therapy and model are also commonly used for the part of a theory that provides guidelines for changing behavior. In Figure 2.1, theories are placed at either the high- or mid-level of abstraction. At the highest level of abstraction are ecological systems and human development theories (see Part 2 of the book). Although these theories provide a general way of understanding a broad range of human behavior, they provide few guidelines for intervention. Theories at the highest level of abstraction are com-

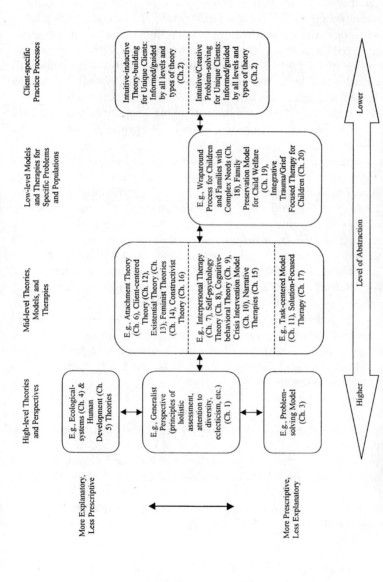

FIGURE 2.1 Types and levels of theory for direct social work practice.[1]

[1]The authors would like to thank Michael Rothery for allowing us to adapt a version of this figure that he had prepared for chapter 4 of this book.

monly referred to as *metatheories*. At the mid-level of abstraction are theories that provide more specific understanding of a broad range of human behavior, as well as guidelines for facilitating behavior change. These are typically what social workers think of when they think of *practice theories*, and most of this book (i.e., Part 3) is devoted to reviewing theories (as well as models and therapies) at this level. Although all theories at this level of abstraction offer both explanations for human behavior and guidelines for facilitating behavior change, some theories place more emphasis on one than the other. In Figure 2.1 the sub-groups of theories, models, and therapies in the mid-level box (divided by the dotted lines) reflect our assessment of the degree to which emphasis is placed on explanation or guidelines for change (e.g., attachment theory emphasizes explanation whereas solution-focused therapy emphasizes prescriptions for the change process).

Models and *therapies* are distinguished from theories by the fact that either they do not emphasize theoretical explanations of human behavior (e.g., the problem-solving model at the highest level of abstraction and solution-focused therapy at the mid-level of abstraction) or the explanation they offer is borrowed from one or more theories (e.g., with regard to the mid-level of abstraction, the crisis intervention model borrows from cognitive-behavioral and psychodynamic theories). Models and therapies are more focused on providing guidelines to facilitate change, and thus are placed in the lower half of Figure 2.1. There are many models and therapies at the lowest level of abstraction that have been developed for intervening with specific populations (e.g., the family preservation model for child welfare families at risk of child placement) or problems. The only distinction we make between these terms is that models can be at a high level of abstraction (e.g., the problem-solving model), whereas therapies are re-stricted to mid- and low levels.

Whether one accepts the definitions of the terms that we have provided or one prefers alternate conceptualizations, in order to avoid confusion it should be acknowledged that, in common usage (and often in the professional literature), many of these terms are used interchangeably. Thus, for example, one will find the therapeutic approach of Carl Rogers referred to variously as client-centered theory, client-centered therapy, or the client-centered model of practice. To us, terminology is much less important than understanding the different approaches to explaining and intervening with human problems.

MAJOR CLASSIFICATIONS OF DIRECT PRACTICE THEORIES

The direct practice theories, models, and therapies that are reviewed in Part 3 of this book are presented in like groupings. We have divided these theories into four major classifications: (1) psychodynamic theories, (2) cognitive-behavioral theories, (3) humanistic and feminist theories, and (4) postmodern theories. Below, we provide an overview of the common characteristics of the theories within the four classifications.

It should be noted that these four classifications of practice theories and the placement of the individual theories within these classifications are open to question. For example, some readers may question our grouping humanistic and feminist theories together. Others may question the classification of the task-centered and crisis intervention models under the cognitive-behavioral category. We attempt to rationalize these choices in the descriptions below; however, we acknowledge that, as with most classifications systems, the "fit" is not always perfect. The risks in such a classification system are overgeneralization and oversimplification. Thus, we encourage readers to pay attention to both the differences among the theories within each classification and the similarities across the classifications. The benefit of using classifications of theory, however, is to bring some order to the confusing multitude of theories that proliferate within the helping professions. The fact that there are well over 200 separate approaches to counseling (Herink, cited in Garfield & Bergin, 1994) makes it evident that efforts to classify approaches are necessary.

It was difficult to choose which theories, models, and therapies to include in the book as examples of the four major classifications of theory. Our choices were guided by one or more of the following factors: (1) the fit with the values and principles of generalist social work practice, (2) being widely recognized and used in current direct practice, and (3) being empirically validated. Although we cannot provide an exhaustive list of other theories that might be placed within each classification, in the discussion below we do provide examples of such.

PSYCHODYNAMIC THEORIES

We construe psychodynamic theories broadly to include all those that have evolved from Freud's theory of human psychological development. In general, psychodynamic approaches postulate that the root causes of most problems are painful, frightening, or unsupportive experiences in childhood. These theories hold that unconscious internal conflicts or developmental deficits underlie problematic behaviors, thoughts, and feelings. The goal of most psychodynamic therapies is to make the unconscious conscious. This is done primarily by using *interpretations* to help the client develop *insight* (cognitive and emotional understanding) into how the deprivations and frustrations suffered early in life have caused misperceptions and distortions of experience in the present (Gelso & Carter, 1985).

Although classical psychoanalysis, which is sometimes referred to as id (or drive) psychology (Strean, 1996), is no longer the most common type of psychodynamic therapy, many still consider it as the most thorough and powerful of these therapies (Gelso & Carter, 1985). Classical psychoanalytic theory holds that there are universal, biologically determined drives that are associated with psychosexual stages (oral, anal, phallic, oedipal, latency, and genital) through which personality develops. Problems represent unresolved conflicts that result in fixation at or regression to one or more of these stages. Classical psychoanalysis is a long-term (often lasting years), intensive (four to five sessions weekly) therapy. The client is encouraged to free associate (i.e., to talk about whatever comes to mind). The therapist is generally neutral and passive (acting like a blank screen), so that the client projects thoughts and feelings about early authority figures (especially parents) onto the therapist. This leads to the development of a transference neurosis, whereby the client confuses (on an unconscious level) the therapist with such early authority figures. The therapist then gradually interprets this transference to help the client develop insight into how his or her reactions to the therapist and other authority figures in the present are inappropriate and influenced by unresolved conflicts from childhood. Insight involves becoming aware of all aspects of the unresolved conflict: the childhood wish, fantasy, or memory; the anxiety or fear that was associated with this; and the defense mechanisms that were used to keep it from becoming conscious (Gold, 1996).

Many different types of psychodynamic therapies have evolved from classical psychoanalysis. Most therapies based on more recent psychodynamic theories are of shorter duration than classical psychoanalysis, and most have incorporated a greater recognition of the importance of social and interpersonal factors, as well as of the need for the practitioner to be more active, personal, and warm. Ego psychology was an important development within the psychodynamic school and was influential in placing more emphasis on social factors and the adaptive ability of the rational part of the mind (the ego). Erikson (1950) formulated the psychosocial (as opposed to psychosexual) stages of development across the life span (see chapter 5), and Hartmann (1951) elaborated on ego adaptation and mastery. Another important development involved a number of separate schools of psychodynamic thought that focused their attention on the importance of primary relationships on the developing individual. These theories, sometimes referred to collectively as the *relational structure model* (Greenberg & Mitchell, cited in Gold, 1996), include interpersonal psychoanalysis (Sullivan, 1953), object relations theories (e.g., Winnicott, 1971), self psychology (Kohut, 1977; see chapter 8), and attachment theory (Bowlby, 1980; see chapter 6). Each of these theories focuses in some way on how children internalize experiences of self, other, and relationships, and how these largely unconscious internalizations affect subsequent cognition, affect, and interpersonal behavior (Gold, 1996). These theories incorporated Alexander and French's (1946) idea of therapy as a "corrective emotional experience" to explain how a good relationship with a caring therapist could help clients to develop more positive internal images of self, other, and relationships, which in turn could lead to a healthier sense of self and more adaptive interpersonal functioning.

A more recent development has been the proliferation of psychodynamic approaches to brief therapy, which is defined generally as having an upper limit of 25 sessions (Koss & Shiang, 1994). Most of these approaches maintain some focus on the development of insight into the origins of one's problems; however, interpretations "focus on present circumstances, not on childhood experiences" (Koss & Shiang, 1994, p. 666). Some of the more prominent examples of brief psychodynamic therapies are interpersonal therapy (Klerman, Weissman, Rounsaville, & Chevron, 1984; see chapter 7), supportive-expressive therapy (Luborsky, 1984), and time-limited dynamic therapy (Strupp & Binder, 1984).

The goal of psychodynamic therapies is personality development and growth toward emotional maturity—resolution of specific symptoms and problems is expected to occur as the client "overcomes general difficulties such as internal conflicts, faulty assumptive systems, or emotional blocks" (Frank & Frank, 1991, p. 188). Thus, most psychodynamic therapies are relatively unstructured and nondirective, although the more recent, time-limited models focus on specific personal issues. The focus on insight suggests a primary focus on cognition in psychodynamic therapies; however, affect is also emphasized with regard to the need for emotional understanding and for working through issues from the past. In more traditional forms of psychodynamic therapy, the practitioner's role is that of a rather passive, neutral expert. More recent models (particularly the ones included in this book), however, place much more emphasis on collaboration, worker empathy, and the importance of a good therapeutic relationship.

The chapters in this book on psychodynamic approaches include (1) attachment theory (chapter 6), (2) interpersonal therapy (chapter 7), and (3) self psychology (chapter 8). These approaches are part of the relational structure model group of psychodynamic therapies and are among the psychodynamic approaches that have the most in common with generalist-eclectic social work principles and values.

COGNITIVE-BEHAVIORAL THEORIES

It used to be common for behavioral and cognitive theories to be classified separately. Early behavior therapies were based on classical (i.e., Pavlovian) and/or operant (i.e., Skinnerian) conditioning paradigms and focused on overt behavior only. Social learning theory (e.g., Bandura & Walters, 1963) broadened behavioral theory to include consideration of observational learning and modeling of social behavior. Cognitive theories (e.g., Beck, 1976) extended the application of learning theory principles to thoughts and beliefs, although some behaviorists were slow to accept this. Currently, although there is a continuum in terms of emphasis on behavior or cognition, it is common to group together, under a cognitive-behavioral classification, therapies that are based on a learning model of human functioning (Gelso & Carter, 1985). "To separate procedures that are truly behavioral from procedures that are purely cognitive is rather artificial. Most cognitive procedures have clear behavioral techniques in them, and, although less obvious, most behavioral procedures also contain cognitive elements" (Emmelkamp, 1994, p. 379).

As mentioned above, cognitive-behavioral approaches adhere to a learning model of human behavior. Thus, the basic premise of these theories is that maladaptive human behaviors and cognitions are learned. The corollary is that therapy involves the unlearning of problematic behaviors and thoughts and/or the learning of more adaptive ones. Furthermore, although it is acknowledged that such problematic behaviors and thoughts may have been learned in the past, cognitive-behavioral approaches focus on change in the present. Specific symptoms are the focus of the change effort, and specific procedures are used to help the client make changes, both within the counseling session and in daily life, between sessions. For instance, more behaviorally oriented therapies for depression often focus on social skills training to increase positive reinforcements for social interactions. More cognitively oriented therapies for depression focus on identifying and modifying covert self-statements and cognitive patterns (schemas) that support negative thinking (Emmelkamp, 1994).

There are a great number of cognitive-behavioral therapies. A primary reason for this is that so many of these therapies have been developed for very specific problems (e.g., panic attacks, agoraphobia, phobias, insomnia, and depression). These therapies can be placed at various points on a continuum of relative focus on behavior or cognition. On the behavioral end of the continuum, therapies can be divided into two main groups: counterconditioning (e.g., Wolpe's [1958] systematic desensitization therapy) and reinforcement (e.g., Paul & Lentz's [1977] token economy for clients with chronic mental health problems). Prominent therapies on the cognitive end of the continuum include Ellis's (1962) rational emotive therapy (RET) and Beck's (1976) cognitive therapy for depression. Other cognitive-behavioral therapies that can be placed somewhere in the middle of the continuum include Meichenbaum's (1977) cognitive-behavior modification (CBM), D'Zurilla and Goldfried's (1971) problem-solving training, and Barlow and Cerny's (1988) panic control treatment (PCT).

The goal of cognitive-behavioral therapies is to alleviate specific symptoms or solve specific problems—it is assumed that general improvement in personal functioning will follow from such changes (Frank & Frank, 1991). These therapies are much more focused and directive than psychodynamic therapies. Although early behavioral approaches did not emphasize the importance of the helping relationship, all cognitive-behavioral approaches now recognize the importance of collaboration and worker warmth as facilitating factors in therapeutic change. It is evident that the primary focus of such therapies is on behavior and cognitions; however, many approaches have integrated a focus on affect as well.

Due to the multiplicity of cognitive-behavioral theories, it was difficult to choose which ones to include in this book. After considerable deliberation, we decided to include one chapter (see chapter 9) that provided a more detailed overview of cognitive-behavioral theory than what we could provide in this thumbnail sketch. For the other two chapters, we chose models that are prominent within social work practice and, although not usually classified narrowly as cognitive-behavioral, that are largely consistent with this theory base. Thus, chapters 10 and 11 focus on the crisis intervention and task-centered models of practice, respectively. We recognize that the task-centered model is construed as an atheoretical structure for eclectic practice; however, it is most consistent with and has borrowed most frequently from cognitive-behavioral theory (Tolson, Reid, & Garvin, 1994). Similarly, although the crisis intervention model is an eclectic model that has roots in psychodynamic ego psychology, most of its principles (e.g., focus on the present, emphasis on structured/directive intervention, and use of contracts) have strong similarities to those of cognitive-behavioral theory, as well as to the task-centered model (Payne, 1991).

HUMANISTIC AND FEMINIST THEORIES

We know that some readers may have negative reactions to our having grouped humanistic and feminist theories together in the same section of the book. Although there are important differences between these two groups of theories, we believe there are many similarities. After providing separate overviews of humanistic and feminist theories, we will summarize the similarities and differences in these classes of theory.

Humanistic Theories

These theories have in common the following characteristics: (1) a focus on the "here and now"/present experience of the client from his or her perspective (i.e., a phenomenological focus); (2) a strong belief in the client's inherent capacity for growth or "self-actualization"; and (3) a belief in the central importance of an egalitarian, authentic worker-client relationship. Korchin (cited in Williams, 1997) has described the essence of humanistic approaches as follows: "Above all else, therapy involves an authentic encounter between two real individuals, free of sham and role-playing, rather than technical acts of an interpretive, advising, or conditioning sort" (p. 242).

The two humanistic theory chapters in this book are client-centered theory (chapter 12) and existential theory (chapter 13). Other examples of approaches that fall within this category are Gestalt therapy (Perls, 1969), existential-humanistic therapy (Bugental, 1986), and the experiential approaches of Gendlin (1981) and Mahrer (1983). In general, humanistic approaches hold that individuals' problems stem from losing touch with aspects of their experience. Thus, the key therapeutic task is to help clients to develop new awareness of and new meaning about their ongoing states of experience (Greenberg, Elliott, & Lietaer, 1994). In client-centered therapy, this involves overcoming "conditions of worth" that have been imposed by others and getting to know and accept oneself more completely and authentically. In existential therapy, this involves getting in touch with the painful realities of personal responsibility and free choice and developing new meaning in one's life.

Similar to psychodynamic therapies, humanistic therapies are concerned with total personality growth as opposed to specific problems or symptoms and are much less directive/prescriptive than cognitive-behavioral therapies. Compared to either psychodynamic or cognitive-behavioral therapies, humanistic therapies have a greater focus on affect and place more emphasis on the importance of an authentic, personal, and warm therapeutic relationship.

Feminist Theories

As stressed in chapter 14, there is a diverse group of feminist theories that differ from one another in a variety of respects. Thus, the reader should keep in mind that the broad characterization of feminist theories presented here does not do justice to the theoretical and practical diversity within this category. In general, feminist theories construe the root cause of individual and social problems as the institutionalized system of male privilege (i.e., the patriarchy) that relies on the domination and exploitation of people. Although most feminist theories focus primarily on the power and privilege of men over women, many feminist theories include a broader focus on the damage that patriarchal systems do to all groups of people (including men), as well as to the natural environment (Bricker-Jenkins & Hooyman, 1986).

Some of the common principles and goals of feminist practice include (1) to minimize the power differential between worker and client and to establish a partnership that is respectful of self-determination; (2) to raise consciousness about how the institutionalized system of male privilege results in the domination, exploitation, and abuse of women; (3) to explore the link between personal and political/social issues so that personal issues are contextualized and depathologized; (4) to validate the client's subjective experience and feelings and to highlight resiliency and strength; (5) to connect clients with each other and with community resources in order to facilitate empowerment, growth, and self-actualization; (6) to engage in social and political action to change conditions and beliefs that support the patriarchy; and (7) to value diversity and promote awareness of how all forms of oppression are linked and harmful to human well-being.

The range of feminist approaches to practice is immense. On one end of the continuum are feminist approaches that eschew a therapeutic focus because this is seen as a distraction from, or even an undermining of, social justice work. On the other end of the continuum are feminist approaches that focus primarily on individual healing and change. In the middle of the continuum are feminist approaches that see a therapeutic focus as a necessary prerequisite for effective social and political action. Also, feminist approaches that emphasize a therapeutic focus run the gamut with regard to theoretical orientation. There are feminist approaches that are predominantly psychodynamic (e.g., Luepnitz, 1988), cognitive-behavioral (e.g., Russell, 1984), experiential/humanistic (e.g., Laidlaw & Malmo, 1990), and postmodern (e.g., Van Den Bergh, 1995). The common thread that holds all feminist approaches together, however, is the focus on the damage done by a patriarchal system that uses power and privilege to oppress women and other marginalized groups.

Similarities and Differences Between Humanistic and Feminist Theories

There are obviously many differences between humanistic and feminist theories, and, at first glance, it may be difficult to detect many similarities. The obvious difference between these groups of theories is that humanistic theories do not incorporate the sociopolitical analysis and social change emphasis that is central to feminist theories. Also, even for feminist approaches that have a stronger therapeutic focus, the wide range of theoretical orientations that exist within feminist approaches (including the common eclectic orientation of many) would seem to preclude a particular affinity to humanistic theories. In our opinion, however, there are a number of important similarities between feminist and humanistic approaches to counseling. The primary similarity among these approaches is the emphasis that is placed on an egalitarian, collaborative, personal counseling relationship. Even feminist approaches that are psychodynamic or cognitive-behavioral in orientation construe counseling more as a dialogue between equals than do most approaches in these categories of therapies. Another similarity is the emphasis on depathologizing by avoiding labels, focusing on strengths, and assuming a movement toward self-actualization if blocks are removed. A third similarity is the importance placed on working on a feeling level and on the integration of mind and body by many humanistic (e.g., Perls, 1969) and feminist (e.g., Laidlaw & Malmo, 1990) approaches.

POSTMODERN THEORIES

Postmodern philosophy challenges the modernist viewpoint that truth can be discovered via objective scientific observation and measurement. As opposed to the modernist quest to discover universal principles and large-scale theories that underlie all human behavior, the postmodernist holds that there is no absolute truth, only points of view. Postmodern critiques have been applied to many fields (e.g., literature, political science, and education) to challenge the objective basis of accepted knowledge and to point out that such knowledge has been socially constructed (Nichols & Schwartz, 1998). A number of related postmodern philosophies have influenced the field of counseling. Two of the more dominant philosophies are constructivism and social constructionism. Constructivism holds that there is no objective reality and either that individuals construct mentally their own truths (radical constructivism) or that realities are created through the process of coevolution with others (Maturana & Varela, 1987). Social constructionism focuses on the power of social interaction and culturally shared assumptions for shaping knowledge and meaning. Of particular interest is the intersection among power, social discourse, and culture, which is seen as engendering meaning for people (Gergen, 1985).

A variety of postmodern approaches to counseling have emerged in the past decade. Although there are variations across postmodern therapies, in general these approaches are characterized by (1) a collaborative, egalitarian worker stance that recognizes clients as the experts on their experiences; (2) situating presumptions or theoretical ideas in order to concentrate on understanding clients' worlds from their perspective; and (3) a view of therapy as a mutual search for new, more empowering understanding of clients' stories.

Postmodern approaches to counseling view reality as psychologically and/or socially constructed and malleable. Thus, problems are believed to stem from the way people construe their experience and/or from the internalization of toxic cultural narratives. As a result, there is an optimism that people can overcome problems by developing more positive and empowering views of their lives. The goal of most postmodern therapies is to bring about overall improvement or general well-being—only solution-focused therapy focuses on solutions to specific problems. These therapies are typically unstructured and nondirective (except for solution-focused therapy, which is more prescriptive), and the worker's role is one of empathic listener and collaborator. The emphasis on the construction of meaning places the emphasis of these therapies more on cognition; however, affect is beginning to be attended to. Only the solution-focused model places much emphasis on behaviors.

The postmodern approaches to counseling reviewed in this book are (1) narrative therapies, including White and Epston's (1990) narrative deconstruction therapy and Anderson and Goolishian's (1988) collaborative language systems therapy (see chapter 15); (2) constructivist therapy (chapter 16); and (3) solution-focused therapy (chapter 17). These were chosen because they are among the most dominant postmodern approaches in social work practice. Other postmodern approaches can be found in the work of Andersen (1991), Cecchin, Lane, and Ray (1993), Hoffman (1988), and Tomm (1987).

INTUITIVE-INDUCTIVE PRACTICE[1]

As mentioned in chapter 1, because this book is largely a survey of theories for direct practice and our framework for practice stresses the eclectic use of theory in practice, we feel it is necessary to be explicit about the importance we attach to the artistic side of practice and how this is an integral part of our generalist-eclectic approach. There has been a longstanding debate within all of the helping professions about whether effective counseling consists primarily of (1) an objective, rational, scientific, deductive application of theoretical knowledge and technical skill or (2) a subjective, humanistic, artistic, intuitive-inductive process. Klein and Bloom (1995) have noted that, within social work, this debate continues to be confrontational and couched in either/or terms. We agree with Klein and Bloom's argument that good practice integrates "both of these two sources of knowledge rather than excluding one or the other" (p. 799). In this section of the chapter, we present an argument for the importance of the artistic elements of practice. In the next chapter, we discuss how the problem-solving model provides a useful structure for integrating intuitive-inductive practice with a deductive application of theory and technique.

HISTORICAL PREDOMINANCE OF A SCIENTIFIC VIEW OF PRACTICE

There is no doubt that the scientific view of practice held sway within the helping professions, as well as many other professions, for most of the 20th century (Schon, 1983). Schon argues that this view began to dominate professions as they gradually became ensconced in universities in the early part of the 20th century. He contends that universities have adhered, for the most part, to a positivistic, technical-rational view of knowledge that "fosters selective inattention to practical competence and professional artistry" (Schon, 1983, p. vii).

Goldstein (1986) noted that social casework began to move away from its idealistic, pragmatic, and humanistic roots in the 1920s, with the adoption of Freudian theory. In the 1930s and 1940s the Functional school of social work reasserted the importance of the humanistic and artistic elements of practice; however, this influence gradually faded out over the next couple of decades. In the 1970s, "the increasing demand for empirical testing and validation of our knowledge and practice" (Hartman, 1990a, p. 3), as well as the acceleration of the shift in power from the profession to the university (Hartman, 1990b), led to a heightened predominance of the technical-rational outlook. Prominent pronouncements such as "Science makes knowledge, practice uses it" (Rein & White, 1981, p. 36) and "If you cannot measure the client's problem, you cannot treat it" (Hudson, 1978, p. 65) reflected the positivistic position that the essence of good practice was the deductive application of empirically generated theory (Scott, 1990).

The predominance of the technical-rational outlook within social work has had a number of negative consequences. Hartman (1990b) noted that this has led to the academizing of schools of social work, whereby fewer instructors have "authentic knowledge about practice grounded not only in research and theory but in experience as well" (p. 48). This trend may be related to Gitterman's (1988) lament that professional social work education sometimes "formalizes our work and stiffens our approach" (p. 36) and can result in practitioners hiding "behind professional masks" (p. 37). This sort of professional stiffness is unfortunate but understandable given the fact that within a technical-rational outlook, "uncertainty is a threat; its admission is a sign of weakness" (Schon, 1983, p. 69). Mahoney (1986) commented on how the reliance on conceptual knowledge in training counselors has led to the unfortunate "unconscious search for a 'secret handbook' of practical 'how-to-do-it' knowledge and explicit techniques for achieving specified ends" (pp. 169–170). This point echoes Perlman's (1957) earlier observation that

> the more individualized and creative a process is, the more skill eludes being captured and held in the small snares of prefabricated kinds of behavior; and the paradox is that the less susceptible skill is to being caught and mastered by ready-made formulas, the more anxiously are formulas sought. (pp. 157–158)

THE RESURGENCE OF INTEREST IN INTUITIVE-INDUCTIVE PRACTICE

Fortunately, in the last two decades, numerous challenges to the predominance of the technical-rational outlook in the helping professions have resurfaced, and there has been a resurgence of interest in the artistic elements of practice. Schon's (1983) study of five professions (engineering, architecture, management, town planning, and psychotherapy) led to his challenging the idea that the essence of effective practice consists of the application of established theory and technique. He proposed that two complementary and largely intuitive processes were at the heart of much of professional practice. First, "knowing in action" represents the "spontaneous behavior of skilful practice which does not stem from a prior intellectual operation" (Schon, 1983, p. 51). Although he acknowledged that some knowing in action may be based on knowledge that has become internalized, Schon maintained that much of this develops naturally as "knowing how" and was never dependent on "knowing that." Second, and most important, "reflection in action" involves improvising or thinking on one's feet when faced with a unique or uncertain situation. Schon (1983) described this as reasoning inductively to "construct a new theory of the unique case" (p. 68). In a later publication, Schon (1987) argued persuasively that "professional education should be redesigned to combine the teaching of applied science with coaching in the artistry of reflection-in-action" (p. xii).

A number of social workers have linked Schon's ideas to earlier social work emphases on the art of practice and have called for social workers to reembrace this heritage. Papell and Skolnik (1992) identify Bertha Reynolds and Virginia Robinson, among other social workers of the Functional school, as social workers who emphasized the artistic and creative elements of practice. Referring to social work education, Reynolds (cited in Papell & Skolnik, 1992) stressed that "learning an art . . . cannot be carried on solely as an intellectual process" (p. 21). Similarly, Robinson (cited in Papell & Skolnik, 1992) contended that the goal of professional development should be "wisdom that goes beyond knowledge" (p. 21). Noting the modern-day emphasis on theory and technique, Papell and Skolnik (1992) argue for the "elevation of art, intuition, creativity, and practice wisdom to essential places in professional functioning" (p. 20). Goldstein (1990) has challenged the "insistent pursuit of a scientific image for social work" (p. 38) and has argued that "effective practice is less a technical enterprise than it is a creative, reflective, and, to a considerable extent, an artistic and dramatic event" (p. 38). As mentioned earlier, in a more moderate vein that approximates our own view, Klein and Bloom (1995) have argued for integrating a " 'subjective,' or intuitive-phenomenological, practice model" with the dominant " 'objective,' or empirical, practice model" (p. 799). We attempted to depict this integration in Figure 2.1 by including client-specific, intuitive-inductive processes along with the various levels of theory for practice.

It is ironic that a number of findings from research in the positivistic, technical-rational tradition have also fueled interest in the artistic elements of practice. First, cumulative research on individual psychotherapy has revealed "little evidence of clinically meaningful superiority of one form of psychotherapy over another" (Lambert & Bergin, 1994, p. 181). This calls into question the importance of "specific factors" such as theory and technique. Second, this questioning of the importance of theory and technique is reinforced by cumulative research evidence that "strongly suggests that under many if not most conditions, paraprofessionals or professionals with limited experience perform as well as or better than professionally trained psychotherapists" (Christensen & Jacobsen, 1994, p. 10). Third, cumulative research on the client-centered conditions of empathy, warmth, and genuineness, and on the therapeutic alliance, has led to the conclusion that relationship factors are the most powerful predictors for counseling outcome (Horvath & Symonds, 1991; Lambert & Bergin, 1994). Together, these findings suggest that counseling effectiveness has much to do with "relationship skills, facilitative attitudes, wisdom based on experience, and related nontechnical skills" (Lambert & Bergin, 1994, p. 181).

It should be noted that some theories have much in common with the intuitive-inductive approach to practice. Many humanistic (e.g., client-centered, chapter 12) and postmodern (e.g., the collaborative language systems type of narrative therapy, chapter 15) approaches have few preconceptions about the causes of problems and few specific guidelines for intervention. These approaches are more philosophical than prescriptive and promote general ways of looking at the world and of being with clients, which include the use of intuitive-inductive processes. The final chapter includes a more detailed consideration of the fit between the various practice theories reviewed in the book and aspects of the generalist-eclectic framework, including the intuitive-inductive element of practice.

SUMMARY

Comparing an approach to practice based on the deductive application of theory and technique to an approach based on intuitive-inductive processes is like comparing quantitative research to qualitative research. In quantitative research terms, the former approach applies established theory deductively to formulate hypotheses about the client's problem, which are then confirmed or disconfirmed by collecting and examining data. If the hypotheses are confirmed, the theory's empirically validated techniques for dealing with such problems are applied. In qualitative research terms, the latter approach "attempts to make sense of the situation without imposing preexisting expectations" (Patton, 1990, p. 44) and to build a theory that is grounded in the client's unique experience. Once a mutual, felt understanding of the client's unique situation is arrived at, together the worker and client use this understanding and their natural abilities for "reflection-in-action" to make desired changes. It is our view that these "scientific" and "artistic" approaches to practice are complementary, that effective practice represents an integration of these approaches, and that, as explained in the next chapter, the problem-solving model facilitates this integration.

NOTES

[1]The section of this chapter on intuitive-inductive practice has been adapted, in part, from an earlier chapter by Coady: Coady, N. F. (1993). A reflective/inductive model of practice: Emphasizing theory building for unique cases versus applying theory to practice. In G. Rogers (Ed.), *Social work field education: Views and visions* (pp. 139–151). Dubuque, IA: Kendall/Hunt.

REFERENCES

Alexander, F., & French, T. (1946). *Psychoanalytic therapy*. New York: Ronald Press.
Andersen, T. (1991). *The reflecting team*. New York: Norton.

Anderson, H., & Goolishian, H. A. (1988). Human systems as linguistic systems: Preliminary and evolving ideas about the implications for clinical theory. *Family Process, 27,* 371–393.

Bandura, A., & Walters, R. (1963). *Social learning and personality development.* New York: Holt, Rinehart & Winston.

Barlow, D. H., & Cerny, J. A. (1988). *Psychological treatment of panic.* New York: Guilford.

Beck, A. T. (1976). *Cognitive therapy and the emotional disorders.* New York: New American Library.

Bowlby, J. (1980). *Loss.* New York: Basic Books.

Bricker-Jenkins, M., & Hooyman, N. (Eds.). (1986). *Not for women only: Social work practice for a feminist future.* Silver Spring, MD: NASW Press.

Bugental, J. F. (1986). Existential-humanistic psychotherapy. In I. L. Kutash & A. Wolf (Eds.), *Psychotherapist's casebook* (pp. 222–236). San Francisco: Jossey-Bass.

Cecchin, G., Lane, G., & Ray, W. (1993). From strategizing to nonintervention: Toward irreverence in systemic practice. *Journal of Marital and Family Therapy, 19,* 125–136.

Christensen, A., & Jacobson, N. S. (1994). Who (or what) can do psychotherapy: The status and challenge of nonprofessional therapies. *Psychological Science, 5,* 8–14.

D'Zurilla, T. J., & Goldfried, M. R. (1971). Problem-solving and behavior modification. *Journal of Abnormal Psychology, 78,* 107–126.

Ellis, A. (1962). *Reason and emotion in psychotherapy.* New York: Lyle Stuart.

Emmelkamp, P. M. (1994). Behavior therapy with adults. In A. E. Bergin & S. L. Garfield (Eds.), *Handbook of psychotherapy and behavior change* (4th ed., pp. 379–427). New York: Wiley.

Erikson, E. (1950). *Childhood and society.* New York: Norton.

Fisher, J. (1978). *Effective casework practice: An eclectic approach.* New York: McGraw-Hill.

Frank, J. D., & Frank, J. B. (1991). *Persuasion and healing: A comparative study of psychotherapy* (3rd ed.). Baltimore: Johns Hopkins University Press.

Garfield, S. L., & Bergin, A. E. (1994). Introduction and historical overview. In A. E. Bergin & S. L. Garfield (Eds.), *Handbook of psychotherapy and behavior change* (4th ed., pp. 3–18). New York: Wiley.

Gelso, C., & Carter, J. (1985). The relationship in counseling and psychotherapy: Components, consequences, and theoretical antecedents. *The Counseling Psychologist, 13,* 155–243.

Gendlin, E. T. (1981). *Focusing* (2nd ed.). New York: Bantam.

Gergen, K. (1985). The social constructionist movement in modern psychology. *American Psychologist, 40,* 266–275.

Gitterman, A. (1988). Teaching students to connect theory and practice. *Social Work with Groups, 11,* 33–41.

Gold, J. R. (1996). *Key concepts in psychotherapy integration.* New York: Plenum Press.

Goldstein, H. (1986). Toward the integration of theory and practice: A humanistic approach. *Social Work, 31,* 352–357.

Goldstein, H. (1990). The knowledge base of social work practice: Theory, wisdom, analogue, or art? *Families in Society, 71,* 32–43.

Greenberg, L., Elliott, R., & Lietaer, G. (1994). Research on experiential psychotherapies. In A. E. Bergin & S. L. Garfield (Eds.), *Handbook of psychotherapy and behavior change* (4th ed., pp. 509–539). New York: Wiley.

Hartman, A. (1990a). Many ways of knowing. *Families in Society, 71,* 3–4.

Hartman, A. (1990b). Education for direct practice. *Families in Society, 71,* 44–50.

Hartmann, H. (1951). *Ego psychology and the problem of adaptation*. New York: International Universities Press.

Hoffman, L. (1988). A constructivist position for family therapy. *Irish Journal of Psychology, 9*, 110–129.

Horvath, A. O., & Symonds, B. D. (1991). Relation between working alliance and outcome in psychotherapy: A meta-analysis. *Journal of Counseling Psychology, 38*, 139–149.

Hudson, W. W. (1978). First axioms of treatment. *Social Work, 23*, 65–66.

Klein, W. C., & Bloom, M. (1995). Practice wisdom. *Social Work, 40*, 799–807.

Klerman, G. L., Weissman, M. M., Rounsaville, B. J., & Chevron, E. S. (1984). *Interpersonal psychotherapy of depression*. New York: Basic Books.

Kohut, H. (1977). *The restoration of the self*. New York: International Universities Press.

Koss, M. P., & Shiang, J. (1994). Research on brief psychotherapy. In A. E. Bergin & S. L. Garfield (Eds.), *Handbook of psychotherapy and behavior change* (4th ed., pp. 664–700). New York: Wiley.

Laidlaw, T., & Malmo, C. (1990). *Healing voices: Feminist approaches to therapy with women*. San Francisco: Jossey-Bass.

Lambert, M. J., & Bergin, A. E. (1994). The effectiveness of psychotherapy. In A. E. Bergin & S. L. Garfield (Eds.), *Handbook of psychotherapy and behavior change* (4th ed., pp. 143–189). New York: Wiley.

Landon, P. (1999). *Generalist social work practice*. Dubuque, IA: Eddie Bowers.

Luborsky, L. (1984). *Principles of psychoanalytic psychotherapy: A manual for supportive-expressive treatment*. New York: Basic Books.

Luepnitz, D. A. (1988). *The family interpreted: Psychoanalysis, feminism, and family therapy*. New York: Basic Books.

Mahoney, M. J. (1986). The tyranny of technique. *Counseling and Values, 30*, 169–174.

Mahrer, A. R. (1983). *Experiential psychotherapy: Basic practices*. New York: Brunner/Mazel.

Maturana, H., & Varela, F. J. (1987). *The tree of knowledge: The biological roots of human understanding*. Boston: New Science Library/Shambhala.

Meichenbaum, D. (1977). *Cognitive-behavior modification: An integrative approach*. New York: Plenum.

Nichols, M. P., & Schwartz, R. C. (1998). *Family therapy: Concepts and methods* (4th ed.). Boston: Allyn & Bacon.

Papell, C. P., & Skolnik, L. (1992). The reflective practitioner: A contemporary paradigm's relevance for social work education. *Journal of Social Work Education, 28*, 18–26.

Patton, M. Q. (1990). *Qualitative evaluation and research methods* (2nd ed.). Newbury Park, CA: Sage.

Paul, G. L., & Lentz, R. J. (1977). *Psychosocial treatment of chronic mental patients*. Cambridge, MA: Harvard University Press.

Payne, M. (1991). *Modern social work theory: A critical introduction*. London: Macmillan.

Perlman, H. H. (1957). *Social casework: A problem-solving process*. Chicago: University of Chicago Press.

Perls, F. (1969). *Gestalt therapy verbatim*. Lafayette, CA: Real People Press.

Rein, M., & White, S. (1981). Knowledge for practice. *Social Service Review, 55*, 1–41.

Russell, M. (1984). *Skills in counseling women—the feminist approach*. Springfield, IL: Charles C. Thomas.

Saleebey, D. (Ed.). (1997). *The strengths perspective in social work practice* (2nd ed.). New York: Longman.

Schon, D. A. (1983). *The reflective practitioner: How professionals think in action.* New York: Basic Books.

Schon, D. A. (1987). *Educating the reflective practitioner.* San Francisco: Jossey-Bass.

Scott, D. (1990). Practice wisdom: The neglected source of practice research. *Social Work, 35,* 564–568.

Strean, H. S. (1996). Psychoanalytic theory and social work treatment. In F. J. Turner (Ed.), *Social work treatment: Interlocking theoretical approaches* (4th ed., pp. 523–554). New York: The Free Press.

Strupp, H. H., & Binder, J. L. (1984). *Psychotherapy in a new key: A guide to time-limited dynamic psychotherapy.* New York: Basic Books.

Sullivan, H. S. (1953). *The interpersonal theory of psychiatry.* New York: Norton.

Tolson, E. T., Reid, W. J., & Garvin, C. D. (1994). *Generalist practice: A task-centered approach.* New York: Columbia University Press.

Tomm, K. (1987). Interventive interviewing: Part 2. Reflexive questioning as a means to enable self-healing. *Family Process, 25,* 167–184.

Van Den Bergh, N. (Ed.). (1995). *Feminist practice in the 21st century.* Washington, DC: NASW Press.

White, M., & Epston, D. (1990). *Narrative means to therapeutic ends.* New York: Norton.

Williams, M. H. (1997). Boundary violations: Do some contended standards of care fail to encompass commonplace procedures of humanistic, behavioral, and eclectic psychotherapies? *Psychotherapy, 34,* 238–249.

Winnicott, D. W. (1971). *The maturational processes and the facilitating environment.* New York: International Universities Press.

Wolpe, J. (1958). *Psychotherapy through reciprocal inhibition.* Stanford, CA: Stanford University Press.

The Problem-Solving Model: An Integrative Framework for the Deductive, Eclectic Use of Theory and Artistic, Intuitive-Inductive Practice

Nick Coady and Peter Lehmann

The problem-solving model is a critically important element in our generalist-eclectic approach because its general structure and guidelines for practice allow for both a deductive, eclectic use of theory and technique, and the use of creative, intuitive-inductive processes. In this chapter we (1) review the roots and founding principles of a problem-solving model for social work practice; (2) discuss how the problem-solving model is an integral part of generalist approaches to practice; (3) elaborate on how the problem-solving model allows for the integration of the scientific and artistic elements of social work practice; (4) provide an overview of the phases of the problem-solving model, with attention to how theoretical and intuitive-inductive processes interact; and (5) preview the contents and structure of the chapters in the last four sections of the book.

EARLY DEVELOPMENT: PERLMAN'S PROBLEM-SOLVING MODEL

The application of the problem-solving model to social work practice was first suggested by Perlman (1957) with the publication of *Social Casework: A Problem-Solving Process.* Perlman was influenced by John Dewey's (1933) description of learning as a problem-solving process. She believed that "the operations of casework are essentially those of the process of problem-solving" (p. v). Perlman's problem-solving model represented an attempt to integrate or at least bridge the differences between the two dominant schools of social casework of the time. Perlman had been trained in the scientific Freudian diagnostic school of social casework but was attracted to many of the ideas of the humanistic Functional or Rankian school of social casework. She blended the Diagnostic school's emphasis on applying psychodynamic theory through the scientific process of study, diagnosis, and treatment, with the Functional school's emphasis on starting where the client is in the present, partializing problems into manageable pieces, and developing a genuinely supportive relationship that serves to motivate clients and free their potential for growth (Perlman, 1986). Perlman (1986) has identified the problem-solving model as an eclectic construct, with theoretical roots in psychodynamic ego psychology and selected ideas from existential, learning, and ecological systems theories.

Perlman's model "stands firmly upon the recognition that life is an ongoing, problem-encountering, problem-solving process" (Perlman, 1970, p. 139). Perlman pointed out that effective problem-solving, whether in everyday life or in professional helping, consists of similar processes. In professional helping these processes include (1) identifying the problem, (2) identifying the person's subjective experience of the problem, (3) examining the causes and effects of the problem in the person's life, (4) considering the pros and cons of various courses of action, (5) choosing and enacting a course of action, and (6) assessing the effectiveness of the action (Perlman, 1970). Perlman (1970) stressed that the problem-solving process does not always take place as a linear, logical progression and that "in the spontaneity of action" (p. 158), the steps or phases can blend together, occur out of order, and repeat in a cyclical fashion. She pointed out that guiding people through a problem-solving process not only can help them cope more effectively with their presenting problems but also can help them cope more effectively with future difficulties. Most important, Perlman (1970) emphasized that problem-solving is not just a cognitive, rational process and that the development of a good relationship with clients is intertwined with the problem-solving process: "Relationship is the continuous context within which problem-solving takes place. It is, at the same time, the emerging product of mutual problem-solving efforts; and simultaneously it is the catalytic agent . . . " (p. 151).

THE PROBLEM-SOLVING MODEL AS A CENTRAL COMPONENT OF GENERALIST SOCIAL WORK PRACTICE

A problem-solving model, by one name or another, is a central part of most generalist models of social work practice. Compton and Galaway

(1994) identify problem-solving as one of six core components of social work practice, and McMahon (1996) refers to it as "the general method" of social work. Although Perlman's original adaptation of a problem-solving process to social work practice was confined to casework or individual practice, generalist models have extended the use of a problem-solving process to work with all levels of client systems (groups, families, organizations, and communities).

Perlman's central ideas about the problem-solving process are part of all current models; however, a couple of common changes in emphasis should be noted. First, most contemporary models of problem-solving place greater emphasis on collaboration and partnership between the worker and the client in all phases of the process—in Perlman's model, there was more of an emphasis on the worker's primary responsibility for assessment and treatment planning (Compton & Galaway, 1994). Second, most current models have delineated more clearly the stages in the problem-solving process and have been more specific in identifying the goals and activities in each stage. We think these changes in emphasis are positive, and they are reflected in our conception of the problem-solving process. One change that some models have instituted, which we do not agree with, is to move away from the term *problem-solving*. For example, Locke, Garrison, and Winship (1998) simply call their version of the helping process a "phase model." They express concern about construing social work practice as problem-solving because they think this reinforces a focus on deficiencies and pathology. We do not share this concern, and we agree with Compton and Galaway's (1994) argument:

> Describing a change process as a problem-solving model is quite different from characterizing it as a problem-focus model. . . . Social workers do start with a problem. . . . The process of working out a solution to that problem will involve the use of strengths brought by the client, the worker, and the environment. Thus the model might well be called problem-solving but strength-focused. . . . (p. 10)

We understand and support the trend toward depathologizing the concerns that clients typically bring to counseling—and it should be noted that Perlman was a pioneer in this regard. Rather than deny the existence of problems and the utility of a problem-solving process, however, we prefer to promote the understanding that problems are a normal part of life.

PROBLEM-SOLVING AS AN INTEGRATIVE FRAMEWORK FOR THE SCIENTIFIC AND ARTISTIC ELEMENTS OF PRACTICE

As discussed in chapter 2, the scientific aspect of social work practice is usually conceptualized as the deductive application of theory and technique to understanding and intervening with human problems. As identified in chapter 1, a generalist approach to practice requires the flexible and eclectic use of a wide range of theories and techniques. One of the primary dangers of eclecticism is that it can become haphazard and directionless. One of the primary values of a problem-solving process for practice is that it provides a general structure for the eclectic application of theories and techniques. The problem-solving approach contains no assumptions about the causes and solutions of client problems. The general guidelines that the problem-solving process provides for assessment allow for the tentative application of multiple theoretical perspectives to help develop understanding of each unique client situation. Similarly, problem-solving guidelines for intervention allow for the eclectic use of techniques from different theories to help clients overcome or cope more effectively with problems.

In the same fashion, the problem-solving process provides useful structure for the artistic, intuitive-inductive aspects of practice. Perlman (1957) contended that the problem-solving model meets the need

> for some dependable structure to provide the inner organization of the [case-work] process. . . . In no sense is such a structure a stamped out routine. It is rather an underlying guide, a pattern for action which gives general form to the caseworker's inventiveness or creativity. (p. vi)

As with eclectic practice, the main danger in an intuitive-inductive approach to practice is a lack of focus and direction. The guidelines for the various phases of the problem-solving process provide focus and direction for the worker while being general enough to allow for the use of intuition and creativity.

Beyond providing the general structure and guidelines to facilitate either an eclectic, deductive use of theory or an intuitive-inductive approach to practice, the problem-solving model allows for, and in fact encourages, the integration of these approaches. The essence of effective problem-solving of any kind might be construed as the judicious blending of knowledge and skill with imagination and creativity. At times, depending on the situation, one approach may predominate over and prove more effective than the other. At times, the two approaches may blend together or alternate over time. Of course, this is easier said than done. Our review of the stages in the problem-solving process will incorporate further discussion of combining the artistic and scientific elements of practice, and our final chapter will revisit this issue.

THE PHASES OF THE PROBLEM-SOLVING MODEL

Different conceptualizations of the phases in the problem-solving process proliferate in the social work literature. Although there are many differences with regard to the number of phases that are specified and in the language that is used to describe the phases, these differences represent only minor variations on the same themes. We have divided the problem-solving process into four phases for the purposes of our discussion. These phases are (1) engagement; (2) data collection and assessment; (3) planning, contracting, and intervention; and (4) evaluation and termination. Below, each phase is reviewed briefly with regard to general goals and strategies for achieving them.

ENGAGEMENT

We agree with Perlman's (1979) contention that the social work relationship is the heart of the helping process, and we believe that the engagement phase is crucial to creating the conditions from which a good helping relationship can grow. Even prior to the first contact with clients, workers will often have some information (e.g., via a referral letter or intake assessment) that allows them to do some preliminary "tuning in" (Shulman, 1992) to clients' situations and feelings. This should include a tentative ecological assessment of the particular problems and life circumstances of clients, and following from this, putting oneself in clients' positions and developing preparatory empathy. At the same time, it is important for workers to tune in to themselves, that is, to become more aware of how they are feeling with regard to what they know about the client (e.g., presenting problem, cultural background, and voluntary versus involuntary status). It is particularly important for workers to prepare themselves to work with clients who are involuntary and who may present as resistant or unwilling participants in the helping process. Understandably, workers are often leery of dealing directly with such issues; however, if these issues are not discussed openly and worked through, engagement can remain superficial. In tuning in to how one might engage with such clients, it is necessary to prepare for responding empathically versus defensively and to consider, in addition to any mandated goals, goals that might appeal to the client. The intent of the tuning-in process prior to initial contact with clients is for workers to establish a positive internal condition that can facilitate the engagement process.

The first session with clients is important for setting the tone, the focus, and the parameters for the helping process. Wherever the first meeting may take place, it is important for the worker to attend to basic issues such as privacy and comfort. If the meeting is in the worker's agency, it is appropriate for the worker to play host and attend to social amenities. For example, a handshake with the initial introduction is usually appropriate, as is some brief social chitchat (e.g., commenting on the weather or asking clients if they had any trouble finding the agency) to "break the ice." Following this, several basic issues need to be attended to. Clients need to be invited to clarify and elaborate briefly on why they have sought help and what help they hope to get. Workers also need to clarify their role and purpose (Shulman, 1992) and to discuss with clients how this fits with their expectations. Clients' situations need to be explored in more depth, and it is often helpful to establish some tentative goals. Then, a preliminary agreement (subject to change) about working together (e.g., general goals and time frame) needs to be achieved.

In attending to these engagement tasks, it is imperative that the worker's manner reflects warmth, empathy, and genuineness. Workers need to normalize clients' problems appropriately, communicate empathy and support for clients' struggles, highlight clients' strengths and coping abilities, credit them for reaching out for help, express a desire to work together, and promote a realistic hopefulness about the outcome of working together. Where appropriate, engagement can be deepened by the worker's sensitive exploration of how issues of diversity (e.g., race, culture, class, gender, sexual orientation, physical capacity, age, and religion/spirituality) may be related to the presenting problem or to concerns about engaging in counseling.

Not all of these tasks may be accomplished in a first session, and engagement should be construed as an ongoing process that blends together with initial data collection and assessment. In fact, aspects of later phases of problem-solving are also evident in the engagement phase. The provision of empathy and support is a type of intervention that can have an important effect even as early as the first session. Initial planning and contracting are evident in arriving at a tentative agreement to work together. Evaluation should be attended to with respect to eliciting client feedback about the first session, including how it fit with the client's expectations and whether there is anything he or she is unsure of or confused about. Also, it is important to address the issue of termination in the first session with respect to the anticipated time frame for working together.

DATA COLLECTION AND ASSESSMENT

As mentioned above, initial data collection often begins even before the first meeting with a client, and it is intertwined with the engagement process. In fact, as Perlman pointed out, relationship development and data collection are intertwined—ideally, each deepens the other. Data collection involves fact gathering with regard to issues that are most critical to the client's problem situation, and should include a focus on strengths and resources, as well as on vulnerabilities and stressors. Assessment is the culmination of data collection and involves distilling the facts that are most central to the client's concern and developing these into a succinct, coherent summary that reflects an overall understanding of the client's problem situation. Data collection and assessment are intertwined and in some sense continue to evolve throughout the problem-solving process. An assessment leads to an intervention plan but carrying out the intervention plan provides new data which may build on or alter the original assessment.

As mentioned in chapter 1, our generalist-eclectic approach to practice adheres to a person-in-environment (or ecological systems) view that emphasizes the need to consider the entire range of factors, from micro (e.g., biological and intrapsychic) to macro (e.g., environmental and sociocultural), that could impact positively or negatively on a client's problem situation. The eclectic nature of our approach also necessitates the consideration of multiple theoretical perspectives to help develop an understanding of the client's problem situation. In addition, in order to arrive at a comprehensive assessment, it is usually important to consider client history and factors that may have affected the development of the problem situation over time. The four "P"s—predisposing, precipitating, perpetuating, and protective factors (Weerasekera, 1993)—offer a useful framework for data collection and assessment that integrates the historical dimension, as well as a consideration of strengths (i.e., protective factors). The grid presented in Table 3.1 offers a conceptual framework that combines a consideration of (1) the broad person-in-environment perspective, (2) the range of theoretical perspectives covered in this book, and (3) predisposing, precipitating, perpetuating, and protective factors. Although a grid such as this could prove useful as a tool for organizing data collection, its primary utility is in providing a way of conceptualizing the range of data and perspectives that could be important to understanding any given client's problem situation.

The factors listed in Table 3.1 are only examples of the types of factors that could be considered in data collection and assessment. Obviously, the scope of information that could be relevant to any given client's problem situation is enormous. Although this may conjure the intimidating prospect of a long process of detailed, structured data collection and analysis, in practice most data collection usually flows naturally from allowing and encouraging clients to tell their stories. Aided by sensitive questions and probes that flow from the natural curiosity of the worker and his or her desire to more fully understand, clients' accounts often provide detailed information about the who, what, when, why, where, and how of their problem situations. As the worker and client collaboratively review and summarize their developing understanding of the issues, further questions usually emerge to clarify and deepen understanding.

The grid in Table 3.1 suggests how workers might use professional knowledge to guide data collection and assessment. First, in exploring the possible predisposing, precipitating, perpetuating, and protective factors related to clients' problem situations, workers should employ a person-in-environment perspective and be cognizant of the possible influence of micro (e.g., biological) and macro (e.g., environmental and sociocultural) factors. Second, workers should also use their knowledge of various theoretical perspectives to explore the possible impact of a wide variety of factors. This is not to say that workers should explicitly check with clients about every

TABLE 3.1 Holistic/Eclectic Grid for Data Collection and Assessment

	Factors related to general person-in-environment perspective					Factors related to theoretical perspectives					
	Biological	Environmental	Sociocultural	Ecological systems	Individual/family life cycle	Psychodynamic	Cognitive-behavioral	Humanistic	Feminist	Post-modern	Couple/family
Predisposing factors	Genetic vulnerability	Growing up poor	Member of oppressed group	Social isolation	Problems in earlier stages	Early attachment problems	Poor parental role modeling	Conditions of worth imposed by parent	Patriarchal society	Oppressive cultural story	Enmeshment in family of origin
Precipitating factors	Onset of illness	Loss of job	Experience of discrimination	Loss of social support network	Current developmental crisis	Relationship loss or problems	Classical conditioning leading to phobia	Conditions of worth imposed by adult partner	Battering incident	Problem-saturated story	Separation

TABLE 3.1 (*continued*)

	Factors related to general person-in-environment perspective					Factors related to theoretical perspectives					
	Biological	Environmental	Sociocultural	Ecological systems	Individual/family life cycle	Psychodynamic	Cognitive-behavioral	Humanistic	Feminist	Post-modern	Couple/family
Perpetuating factors	Chronic mental illness	Inadequate income	Institutional racism	Social isolation	Developmental crises of other family members	Maladaptive interpersonal patterns	Irrational beliefs	Low self-esteem	Internalizing blame	Oppressive internalized view of self	Poor communication
Protective factors	Good health	Adequate income	Connected to/proud of cultural heritage	Strong social support network	Earlier developmental successes	Corrective emotional experience	Positive reinforcement from career	Unconditional positive regard from parent	Relationship with positive female role model	Small victories, unique outcomes	Good couple relationship

Adapted from Weerasekera, P. (1993). Formulation: A multiperspective model. *Canadian Journal of Psychiatry, 38*, 351–358.
Note. The factors listed in this table are only examples of the types of factors that could be considered in data collection and assessment.

conceivable theoretical explanation for their difficulties. Workers need to use their developing understanding of a client's story in order to ascertain whether certain lines of inquiry seem relevant. For example, if it becomes apparent that there is a clearly identifiable, recent precipitating factor for a client's difficulties and that the client had a high level of social functioning prior to this, then it would make no sense to pursue an exploration of predisposing psychodynamic factors. Thus, workers need to exercise their judgment in order to keep the data collection process focused and pertinent.

The issue of worker judgment is related to the fact that data collection and assessment are also guided by intuitive-inductive processes. Workers often develop intuitive hunches about various aspects of clients' problem situations as they tell their stories. If these hunches or "gut instincts" are shared tentatively and checked out with clients, this can often lead to a deeper understanding. For example, if a client is talking about an intimate relationship in glowing terms, but a worker develops a sense that this is masking some underlying ambivalence about the relationship, this thought should be shared tentatively and empathically. Furthermore, as workers hear more and more of clients' stories, they often begin to "put pieces together" or "make links" in their minds. This type of inductive theory building should be checked with clients in a tentative fashion. For example, if a worker develops a sense that there may be an underlying theme of discomfort with intimacy to the various relationship difficulties that a client is recounting, this idea should be shared tentatively and empathically.

Deductive theory application and intuitive-inductive theory building in data collection and assessment should be construed as complementary processes. In the example cited above, if the worker's hunch about a pervasive, underlying discomfort with intimacy was confirmed by the client, the worker's knowledge of psychodynamic theory might be used to explore the potential connection with early experiences of intimate relationships as undependable or unsatisfactory. In turn, this theoretically informed exploration might lead to other hunches or theory building and so on.

Oftentimes the data collection and assessment process may involve more than client verbal reports and direct observation of the client. This might include, with client consent, the gathering of information and viewpoints from family members or other professionals who know the client, or referral for psychological (e.g., measures of anxiety or depression) or medical (e.g., neurological) testing. Decisions about how much information to collect from the variety of sources available should be based on the joint judgment of worker and client as to the potential benefits and costs.

Although data collection and assessment processes continue to some extent throughout the problem-solving process, this phase culminates in the development of an understanding shared by worker and client about the client's problem situation. The shared nature of this understanding is crucial and can only evolve from a truly collaborative exploration that is grounded in a relationship characterized by mutual trust, liking, and respect. This understanding needs to include an identification not only of the predisposing, precipitating, and perpetuating stressors (micro and macro), but also of the client's strengths and other protective factors. It is usually helpful, and usually required by agencies, that such understanding be summarized in an assessment report (see Sheafor, Horejsi, & Horejsi, 1997, and many other generalist texts for formats for such reports). The complexity of human life prevents any client assessment from being definitive and fully comprehensive. To a large degree, however, the effectiveness of the helping process depends on the quality of the assessment, because it leads directly to ideas for intervention.

PLANNING, CONTRACTING, AND INTERVENTION

Once the worker and client arrive at a shared understanding of the client's problem situation, they need to plan and contract with each other about a course of action or intervention, then implement the plan. Again, collaboration is key in these processes. The more clients are involved in and take ownership for the plan of action, the more likely it is that they will be motivated to implement the plan. Planning and contracting involve (1) clarifying and prioritizing the problems to be worked on, (2) identifying realistic goals, (3) considering the pros and cons of various strategies for achieving goals, (4) deciding on a course of action, and (5) specifying the roles and responsibilities of the worker and client and the anticipated time lines for working together. Intervention involves carrying out the plan.

Client need and preference, as opposed to worker theoretical orientation, should determine the goals and the action strategies, as well as the degree to which the plan and contract are specific and explicit. This is not to say that the worker is a silent and passive partner in such determinations. Workers have a right, and in fact a responsibility, to share their viewpoints on goals and action strategies. Ideally, decisions on these issues are consensual; however, where there are differences in opinion, workers should follow client preferences (unless, of course, these are illegal or involve threat of harm to self or others). As with assessment, planning and contracting should be construed as flexible and open to revision. If it becomes apparent that the intervention is not achieving the desired outcome, the plan and contract, as well as the assessment, should be revisited.

Planning, contracting, and intervention should be guided by the assessment. Sometimes the determination of problems, goals, and action strategies is relatively straightforward. For example, if it has been determined that a client's most pressing problem is having been evicted and having no money, then there is an obvious need to find shelter and financial assistance. Most times problems are not so easy to specify and prioritize, and solutions are not so clear. Still, the assessment provides a good place to start, and the specification of problems to work on and the exploration of courses of action should be guided by both deductive/eclectic theory application and intuitive-inductive processes.

The cross-theory prescriptive matching approaches of Beutler and Clarkin (1990) and Prochaska and Norcross (1999) that were reviewed briefly in chapter 1 offer examples of a deductive theory application approach to selecting theories to guide the process of intervention. Although empirical support has not been firmly established for any of the attempts to match client or problem characteristics with therapeutic approaches, there are a number of promising ideas with intuitive appeal in this regard. A client's natural coping style is one variable to consider in choosing a therapeutic approach. Thus, for example, Beutler and Harwood (1995) suggest that clients who tend to cope by externalizing blame and punishing others are best suited to cognitive-behavioral approaches, whereas clients who tend to cope by internalizing blame and punishing themselves are best suited to psychodynamic approaches. Weerasekera (1993) suggests that a more general assessment of clients' coping style might also be used to select a therapeutic approach. Thus, a client who is action-oriented and copes by "doing something" may do best with a behavioral approach, whereas a client who is motivated toward self-understanding and uses introspection to cope may be more amenable to a psychodynamic approach. Another variable to consider in choosing a theory to guide intervention is the level/depth of the client problem. Thus, it makes intuitive sense that problems at the symptom/situational level would be best suited to behavioral approaches, whereas problems at the intrapersonal conflict level would be best suited to psychodynamic approaches (Prochaska & Norcross, 1999).

It should be kept in mind that an eclectic use of theory might involve the sequential use and/or the simultaneous application of different theoretical perspectives. With regard to sequencing approaches, although a problem at the level of intrapersonal conflict might suggest a psychodynamic approach, a particular client may not be stable enough to tolerate painful introspection and revisiting difficult childhood issues. A cognitive-behavioral approach to building interpersonal skills and changing irrational beliefs might be a necessary step for preparing a client to do more emotional, insight-oriented work. With regard to simultaneous application of different theoretical perspectives, any combination of approaches may be appropriate to address different aspects of a client's problem situation. For example, as cognitive-behavioral techniques are used to help a client become aware of irrational thoughts, psychodynamic techniques may be used to help the client identify the origins of and work through the feelings associated with such thoughts. The holistic/eclectic grid presented in Table 3.1 could provide useful guidance to workers in choosing intervention approaches. This type of grid can function to remind workers of the range of theoretical perspectives to choose from, as well as of the possibilities for biological, environmental, and sociocultural intervention.

Inductive/intuitive processes should continue to interact with a deductive application of theory in planning, contracting, and intervention. The helping process is never a straightforward application of theory and technique. The complexity of human life precludes certainty in the helping process and necessitates that workers combine their intuition and inductive reasoning with an eclectic use of theory. Workers need to be reminded that a rigid or formula-like approach to using theory and technique in practice will take away from the humanity of the process and that the quality of the relationship with the client is the best predictor of outcome. Thus, throughout the intervention process, workers need to continue to listen, to provide empathy and support, to instill hope, and to use their intuition and commonsense reasoning to help clients achieve their goals.

EVALUATION AND TERMINATION

Evaluation is an ongoing process that should begin in the early phases of helping and continue as work progresses. It should address the process and outcome of helping. Workers need to constantly check with clients about their satisfaction with the helping process, and they should use client feedback to make adjustments (this is often referred to as formative evaluation). Evaluation of outcome relates to assessing the effectiveness of the interventions in relation to client goals (referred to as summative evaluation).

Evaluation of outcomes may be more or less formal and comprehensive, and, as with all aspects of the helping process, client need and preference should take precedence in such decisions. Outcome evaluation can be as simple as client verbal reports and worker judgment. On the other hand, it has become increasingly common to use more formal tools, including standardized scales (often within a single-subject design), task achievement scaling, goal attainment scaling, service plan outcome checklists, individualized rating scales, and client satisfaction questionnaires (Sheafor et al., 1997). In some situations, particularly where a client's presenting problems involve risk of harm to self or other, standardized scales and reports from others in the client's social milieu can add valuable information to client self-reports and worker judgment. Some clients, however, find the use of more formal measurement unnecessary and alienating.

As progress toward achieving client goals becomes evident, and/or as any prescribed time limitations on the helping process approach, the worker and client begin to discuss and negotiate the end of their work together. As mentioned previously, termination should be addressed at the beginning of the helping process with regard to contracting about the time period of work together. It should also be addressed regularly throughout the helping process by way of periodic discussions about progress toward goals and time limitations. Client reactions toward termination vary widely. Although some clients are more than happy to leave counseling, others have many regrets and fears. The intensity of the helping relationship and clients' previous experiences with endings may provide some indication of clients' probable reactions to termination, but these are often difficult to predict. To maximize the likelihood of a positive experience of termination, it is usually helpful to (1) discuss termination frequently and well in advance, (2) anticipate and explore feelings (the worker's as well as the client's feelings) about termination, (3) review the process and content of the work that was done together, (4) specify the gains that have been made and credit the client for his or her achievements, and (5) anticipate future difficulties and build in supports.

SUMMARY

It was beyond the scope of this chapter to provide more than an overview of the phases of the problem-solving model. The reader is referred to any of the generalist textbooks that were cited in chapter 1 for a more detailed review of the problem-solving phases. To reiterate Perlman's (1957) provisos, the reader should keep in mind that, in practice, the phases of the problem-solving process are not as distinct as they are presented here, and that the helping endeavor rarely proceeds in a linear, orderly fashion. We believe, however, that a flexible use of a problem-solving model provides valuable structure for, and facilitates the integration of, an eclectic, deductive use of theory and an intuitive-inductive approach to practice.

A PREVIEW OF THE REST OF THE BOOK

The first three chapters constitute Part 1 of this book, which has focused on explicating our generalist-eclectic approach to direct social work practice. The remainder of the book is divided into four additional parts. The next three review various theories, models, and therapies for direct practice, which are categorized according to level of abstraction (see Figure 2.1 in chapter 2).

In Part 2, high-level/metatheories for direct practice are presented. The two chapters in this part focus on (1) ecological systems theory and (2) individual and family development theory. These theories are differentiated from other theories that are reviewed in later sections of the book by their high level of abstraction. They provide a general way of looking at and understanding a broad range of human behavior and are particularly useful for holistic assessment. Although these theories may provide general ideas for intervention, they are much less prescriptive than practice theories and models.

Part 3 is the largest section and is devoted to theories, models, and therapies for direct practice that are at a mid-level of abstraction. This part is divided into four sections of three chapters each. These sections correspond to the major classifications of theory (psychodynamic, cognitive-behavioral, humanistic and feminist, and postmodern) that were reviewed in chapter 2. The chapters in this part of the book have similar, although not identical, structure. Contributors were provided with the same outline of structure for their chapters and were asked to follow this as much as possible to facilitate comparisons across chapters. Thus, with minor modifications, the chapters incorporate the following headings: (1) Introduction; (2) An Overview of the Theory, Model, or Therapy; (3) Historical Development; (4) Central Theoretical Constructs; (5) Phases of Helping; (6) Application to Family and Group Work; (7) Compatibility with the Generalist-Eclectic Approach; (8) Critique; (9) Case Example; and (10) Summary. The reader should note that the chapters in Parts 2 and 4, which represent theories that are at higher and lower levels of abstraction, respectively, are more diverse with regard to structure and headings.

Models and therapies at a low level of abstraction are presented in Part 4. The three chapters in this section focus on service models that have been developed for specific populations, particularly those who are disadvantaged and/or at high risk. These chapters address (1) wraparound services for children and families with complex needs, (2) a family preservation model for child welfare, and (3) integrative trauma/grief focused therapy for children.

Part 5 consists of a summary chapter. This chapter considers the similarities and differences between the theories, models, and therapies that are reviewed in the book and the principles and values that are integral to our generalist-eclectic approach. The issue of integrating the use of theory with intuitive-inductive practice via the problem-solving model is also revisited in this chapter.

REFERENCES

Beutler, L. E., & Clarkin, J. (1990). *Systematic treatment selection: Toward targeted therapeutic interventions.* New York: Brunner/Mazel.

Beutler, L. E., & Harwood, T. M. (1995). Prescriptive psychotherapies. *Applied and Preventive Psychology, 4,* 89–100.

Compton, B. R., & Galaway, B. (1994). *Social work processes.* Pacific Grove, CA: Brooks/Cole.

Dewey, J. (1933). *How we think* (rev. ed.). New York: D. C. Heath.

Locke, B., Garrison, R., & Winship, J. (1998). *Generalist social work practice: Context, story, and partnerships.* Pacific Grove, CA: Brooks/Cole.

McMahon, M. O. (1996). *The general method of social work practice: A problem-solving approach* (3rd ed.). Englewood Cliffs, NJ: Prentice Hall.

Perlman, H. H. (1957). *Social casework: A problem-solving process.* Chicago: University of Chicago Press.

Perlman, H. H. (1970). The problem-solving model in social case work. In R. W. Roberts & R. H. Nee (Eds.), *Theories of social casework* (pp. 131–179). Chicago: University of Chicago Press.

Perlman, H. H. (1979). *Relationship: The heart of helping people.* Chicago, IL: University of Chicago Press.

Perlman, H. H. (1986). The problem-solving model. In F. J. Turner (Ed.), *Social work treatment* (3rd ed., pp. 245–266). New York: Free Press.

Prochaska, J. O., & Norcross, J. C. (1999). *Systems of psychotherapy: A transtheoretical analysis* (4th ed.). Pacific Grove, CA: Brooks/Cole.

Sheafor, B. W., Horejsi, C. R., & Horejsi, G. A. (1997). *Techniques and guidelines for social work practice* (4th ed.). Boston: Allyn & Bacon.

Shulman, L. (1992). *The skills of helping: Individuals, families, and groups* (3rd ed.). Itasca, IL: Peacock.

Weerasekera, P. (1993). Formulation: A multiperspective model. *Canadian Journal of Psychiatry, 38,* 351–358.

PART 2

Metatheories for Direct Social Work Practice

4

Ecological Systems Theory

Michael Rothery

Ecological systems (or ecosystems) theory is a recent development in social work, representing a new way of conceptualizing our professional mandate and purpose. It is in the past three decades that most of the ongoing work on clarifying the language, refining the ideas, and coming to grips with the implications of this perspective has occurred (Compton & Galaway, 1994).

The profession's widespread interest in ecosystems thinking has not been applauded unanimously. Wakefield (1996a, 1996b), for example, considers our exploration of the perspective to be an unfortunate, misguided detour. At the same time, other researchers and scholars have worked to explore the advantages of an ecosystems analysis and support its usefulness as a framework capable of integrating (and extending) more traditional perspectives (e.g., Gilgun, 1996a, 1996b).

A basic concern advanced by Wakefield and others has been that the ecosystems perspective is so abstract or "metaphorical" that it cannot be operationalized reliably. Social work is an applied profession and needs concepts that inform its work at the concrete level of practice—"domain specific" knowledge about such areas as addictions, child welfare, or mental health. The search for a general theory that can inform all practice, it is argued, risks a serious loss of credibility respecting the delivery of concrete services. We are reduced to expounding general principles and philosophy, abandoning the real work of helping people to less lofty disciplines.

The author has shared such concerns to some extent, but remains persuaded that a general framework that can inform much of clinical social work practice most of the time is available through the development of ecosystems thinking. Furthermore, he believes such a model is useful for the profession, as a practical (if general) guide to assessment and planning across the range of domains in which we are employed.

This chapter represents an effort to present ecosystems thinking in a way that highlights its practical possibilities. The ideas it contains are not original, although their organization and integration are to a significant degree. The question of whether ecosystems thinking is useful in the real world can be addressed by conceptualizing it within a framework that incorporates social support ideas (Cameron & Vanderwoerd, 1997; Rothery & Cameron, 1985), the "stress and coping" models (Lazarus, 1993; Lazarus & Folkman, 1984), and elements of cognitive theory (Brower & Nurius, 1993).

First, however, it is worthwhile to indicate what ecosystems theory is and is not. Spokespersons for the perspective have been careful to stipulate limits to what we should expect from the model; it is an abstraction or "metaphor" that provides a basic orientation to clients and their problems, but it does not prescribe interventions (Germain & Gitterman, 1996; Meyer, 1988). It is offered as a conceptualization within which eclecticism with respect to models and methods can be organized. It provides a useful map and ideas about desirable destinations, but it is silent on the question of how, concretely, we and our clients can travel from points A to B.

It is commonly held that social work practice is based on theory of two types (Fischer, 1978), at different levels of abstraction: those that we use to describe and explain situations, and those that we use to understand and plan change. With respect to levels of abstraction, we rely on grand theory for our basic orientation to people and their problems. At other levels are less abstract theories and models that have been developed for use in defined practice domains and with particular common problems. At the lowest level of abstraction, the practitioner's more general beliefs and principles must be adapted creatively to the unique demands of each person or family and problems to be solved (see chapter 2 for further discussion of types and levels of theory).

We create difficulties when we confuse the functions of theory. Explaining or accurately describing situations is not the same as intervening to change them (although the relationship between the two functions is very close). Similarly with levels of abstraction: Responsible practitioners are not content to absorb grand theory without also learning the more concrete concepts and methods that make them useful to specific people with particular problems. From the other side, taking a particular technique that emerges in the creative encounter with a unique problem and attempting to elevate it to a general practice principle can have unhappy results. These may include an overly formulaic, scripted approach and a disrespectful effort to adapt clients to our techniques rather than the reverse—a point Pittman (1984) made convincingly.

With reference to the different levels and types of theory described in chapter 2, ecosystems theory can be seen as an example of grand theory with the primary function of helping to explain and describe situations. As such, it is potentially very useful, but it is not presented as sufficient, in and of itself, for shaping the thinking and actions of clinical social workers.

CASE EXAMPLE

Before exploring the ecosystems perspective and its contributions to our professional practice, there is a family to introduce. The Macdonnells have agreed to allow information about them to be used in this chapter, suitably altered to protect their anonymity.

Fifteen-year-old Colin Macdonnell attracted attention at his school as his grades dropped precipitously. When this was commented on in the staff coffee room, his English teacher added another concern: He had submitted an essay that was severely depressed in tone (well beyond normal adolescent angst), and in which he devoted considerable space to the question of suicide.

Colin was interviewed by the school social worker, who subsequently invited his parents to come with him for a family meeting. Colin's mother, Dawn, accepted the invitation, but his father, Eric, did not.

Both Colin and his mother were troubled and knew they had serious issues to address. Each was therefore motivated to talk, and because they were also quite articulate, the initial interviews provided considerable information. Dawn's assessment was that Colin had begun "losing it" when his older brother, Sean, was charged with selling drugs to other students in their high school. Two days later, Sean came to class inebriated, and was promptly suspended.

Sean was 2 years older than Colin, and they were students in the same school. Sean's troubles were, of course, highly public. For weeks, it seemed to Colin that the various student grapevines talked of nothing else. He felt humiliated and helpless, and withdrew from friends and his school activities, wishing he could somehow simply "disappear."

With very little prompting, Dawn also discussed deepening tensions in her marriage to Eric. In her view, Eric was an alcoholic, although he rejected the label, preferring to see himself as a hard living bon vivant, determined to live life to the full and contemptuous of other people's lives of banal moderation. Dawn considered that his drinking had cost the family dearly, both financially and emotionally, because he had often neglected and occasionally embarrassed them.

Another important tension concerned religious commitments. Dawn was devoutly Roman Catholic. Eric professed to be committed spiritually to the values of the church but was strongly anticlerical, for which reason he refused to participate in services or other church activities. Once, when he was very drunk, he accused her (in the presence of both sons) of having an affair with a young priest with whom she had been fund-raising for their parish.

Annoyed with his wife and son for talking about their family to a social worker, and wanting to correct any inaccuracies they might have put forth, Eric came to the third interview (and, sporadically, a number of sessions after that). He came across as a loquacious man with modest accomplishments and a romanticized view of himself. He was not overtly hostile toward the worker, but did communicate a degree of amused superiority respecting the helping enterprise, with frequent references to "psychobabble" and "wet shoulders for hire."

Eric worked as a journalist. Well into middle age, he was earning an adequate income and enjoyed a certain local reputation based on his willingness to put forth conventional opinions in a flamboyant style. When he talked of his work, one could easily imagine him running with the likes of Hemingway and Mailer, battling the perniciousness of the powerful, and struggling, against all odds, to expand the awareness of ordinary people. "Against human stupidity," he liked to recite, "the gods themselves contend in vain."

Eric was perplexed, he said, by his wife's unhappiness. He had no detailed analysis of what could explain it, but was attracted by the general idea that it implied a lack of understanding, or an unwillingness to be realistic on her part. Respecting his sons, he often declared that they were "wonderful" kids, dismissing Sean's difficulties as ordinary adolescent rebellion, perhaps even admirable in some ways. He thought Colin might be simply confronting some of his limitations, having done well in an educational system with low standards until he reached 10th grade and the sudden expectation that he should perform.

Eric acknowledged that his alcohol consumption was well above average. Harboring a certain fear of being "average," he was, at least at one level, proud of this. He could reference many accomplished people who didn't bother to contain similar appetites. Sir Winston Churchill was an example, as were many famous writers and heroic figures in the journalism trade. He stressed that he was not a "wino" but a person of discriminating taste—pointing out that he was an active member of the Opimian Society, a group that exists to celebrate the good life, especially as it is enhanced by fine wines and spirits. He also invoked the requirements of his profession, arguing that many important story ideas and leads were traded among his journalistic colleagues over drinks after work.

In an earlier time, a psychodynamically oriented social worker might focus very strongly on Eric's denial and narcissism, recognizing how frustrating such a father can be to his children. This alone helps explain the strength of Sean's acting out and the depth of Colin's hopeless despair. An ecosystems analysis does not prohibit such considerations (Meyer, 1988), although it does require that we not stop with them. There is a broader view available to us, with a more complex understanding of the sources of this family's pain and options for ameliorating it.

OVERVIEW OF ECOSYSTEMS THEORY

The ecosystems model evolved as a recent response to an old theoretical problem. Since its inception, social work has wrestled with the need for ways of thinking about clients' situations that included a respect for individuals' and families' capacities for effective coping, but also recognized the critical importance of environment—the physical and social contexts that support, constrain, and shape our efforts to live gratifying lives.

As one of the scholars identified with the initial development of this model, Meyer (1995) indicates: "Since the beginning . . . practice has focused on the person *and* the environment" (p. 16), but not without difficulties. For a host of reasons, a truly balanced view that gives proper weight to both sides of the person-in-environment equation has eluded us. More often than not, practitioners have indulged personal preferences for one focus over the other, and clients and their needs were imperfectly understood as a consequence: "For example, a child who refused to attend school might have been treated for depression, with no attention paid to the role of his school or his family . . . in his behavior" (Meyer, 1995, p. 16). Conversely, an unbalanced emphasis on environmental factors might have the equally undesirable effect of ignoring the personal reactions of the child and what these signify in terms of individual needs. The purpose in formulating the ecosystems perspective was to encourage social workers to view situations holistically, attending simultaneously to people, their families, and whatever other systems might be important to their needs. Furthermore, the desire was to create a theory that would encourage us to recognize, on an ongoing basis, that these different "levels" are always reciprocally influencing each other—ecological systems are inherently transactional in nature.

As its somewhat clumsy name suggests, the theory draws on two related schools of thought originating in the life sciences: general systems theory and ecological theory (Meyer, 1995). Introduced to social work in the 1950s (Hern, 1958), general systems theory has been enormously important in highlighting how interconnected we are as people embedded in various social systems. Colin Macdonnell's problems are not simply adolescent depression. Rather, his experience is better understood as the consequence of a much larger set of interacting factors: his family situation, his relationships to peers, the impact of the school, the school's treatment of his older brother (and the vicarious effect of that on him), and so on. How such elements interact, reciprocally influencing each other, is the purview of systems theory.

Ecological theory was wedded to systems theory in the 1970s, in order to enhance it in important ways. "Ecology," according to Meyer (1995), "is the science that is concerned with the adaptive fit of organisms and their environments. . . . [E]cological ideas denote the transactional processes that exist in nature and thus serve as a metaphor for human relatedness through mutual adaptation" (p. 19). When systems concepts are used to understand better how people like Colin achieve (or fail to achieve) a goodness of fit with the various aspects of their environment, ecosystems thinking is the result. We are not simply interested in Colin's symptoms, nor in how they might be explained in terms of the actions of complex systems of which he is a part. We also attend to the critical question of how well Colin and those systems are adapting to each other, and the implications of that adaptation for his ability to get his needs (including his developmental needs) met.

CENTRAL THEORETICAL CONSTRUCTS

Ecosystems theory incorporates concepts from a number of different theoretical perspectives. In addition to general systems and ecological theory, concepts are drawn from social support and stress and coping perspectives, as well as from cognitive-behavioral theory.

CRITICAL CONCEPTS FROM GENERAL SYSTEMS THEORY

Key ideas from general systems theory that inform the ecosystems perspective include the following:

1. All people or groups of people in a system share a reciprocal influence on one another. "When a gnat blinks," says Nissen-Weber (1923), "the universe adjusts itself" (p. 244), which is the extreme statement of the systems theory recognition that everything in a system is constantly influencing everything else (however intangibly).
2. In systems, causes are considered to be circular rather than linear. Colin Macdonnell's depression and withdrawal are a consequence of a complex set of interactions between different people in the systems of which he is a part. When his brother comes to school drunk, he initiates events that lead to Colin's withdrawing. If Colin's friends feel abandoned and become angry, they may in turn distance themselves from him. This distancing confirms Colin's belief that he is an outcast, and he withdraws further, becoming more acutely unhappy. When systems theorist talk about circular causality, they have such reciprocal transactions in mind, as opposed to simpler arguments—attributing Colin's depression to a neurotransmitter deficiency (and nothing else) would be an example of a nonsystemic, linear causal model.
3. Systems possess structure, consisting of predictable patterns of behavior and boundaries. Boundaries are always somewhat arbitrary, but not entirely so. Given the impossibility of relating effectively to Nissen-Weber's universe, we arbitrarily "draw" boundaries around a more manageable unit for analysis and intervention. We might decide, for example, to focus on the Macdonnell nuclear family, or more broadly on the family plus its proximal community, including the school,

the church, and Sean's friends. This illustrates the idea of boundaries in the arbitrary sense. It is also the case that the school, the church, and the Macdonnell nuclear family possess boundaries in a nonarbitrary sense, which is that there is a flow of information within a given system that is different (quantitatively and qualitatively) from the information exchanged with people or groups outside itself. The Macdonnell family members know things about each other that others do not know, for example, and this represents a boundary. Dawn and Eric, as parents (or, more ponderously, a *parental subsystem*), share information with each other that their children (the *sibling subsystem*) know nothing of, and vice versa. Thus, there are boundaries within the family defining its parts, just as there are boundaries that separate it from other elements of its environment.

4. Boundaries are qualitatively different, in that the type and amount of information they restrict vary. Systems that exchange information relatively freely are considered open, whereas systems that rigidly restrict the flow of information are relatively closed. Social systems like families are never completely impervious to influence from outside, so they are always open to some extent and can only be relatively closed. Completely open boundaries lead to a loss of identity and other risks, whereas boundaries that are completely closed result in deprivation, starvation, and eventual death. A balance is what is desirable, with systems like families being open enough to access the resources they need to thrive, but closed enough that undesirable influences can be screened out and identity maintained. Some authors use the term *permeability* to describe ideal boundaries that are well defined but sufficiently open (Nichols & Schwartz, 1995).

5. Along with a degree of structure, which lends them predictability, the complexity of systems lends them the opposite quality. Because everything affects everything else in a circular, reciprocal fashion, it can be observed that different interventions can have similar effects. Colin might experience relief if his father and mother reduce the conflict in their relationship, or if Sean is provided effective treatment for his substance abuse, or if the teachers in his school find a way to rally to his support. A corollary is that very similar interventions can have rather different outcomes, depending on how the system responds to them. A prescription of antidepressant medications could help Colin feel better, decreasing his social withdrawal, and signaling his father that the situation is serious and revisions to their relationship are in order. On the other hand, if such an intervention results in scapegoating—dismissal as an emotional weakling, for example—then Colin's symptoms may be made worse. This unpredictability is referred to by the terms *equifinality* (to indicate similar outcomes evolving from different beginnings) and *multifinality* (to indicate that similar beginnings can lead to multiple consequences).

CRITICAL CONCEPTS FROM ECOLOGICAL THEORY

As a complement to general systems thinking, ecological theory adds an important new dimension to the foregoing concepts. As noted earlier, this is the emphasis on "goodness of fit," or the adequacy of the many relationships that link clients to their social (and physical) environments (Brower & Nurius, 1993; Germain & Gitterman, 1996; Meyer, 1988; Rothery, 1999).

The idea of goodness of fit can be understood largely (though not entirely) in terms of two general types of factors: demand factors and resource factors. Part of our environment is always the demands it places on us—it constantly presents us with realities requiring an adaptive response. These are often called stresses, or needs, or problems, but the term *demands* has the advantage of neutrality. Although the terms *stress* and *problems* may connote something harmful, demands are not seen negatively—they may be challenging and enlivening or onerous, depending on other variables, resource factors being an important example.

In addition to demanding adaptive responses, our environment provides us with access to resources. Hunger is a demand, and if we are lucky our refrigerator has the resources we need to adapt to it. When the supports we can access are plentiful enough, we usually can cope effectively with whatever demands life throws our way, and our goodness of fit with our environment is satisfactory. However, when our supports are deficient, we cope less well and are more likely to become distressed in some way.

The equation is not so straightforward as I have just implied, because the balance of demands with supports is mediated by differences among individuals and their families. Given the same set of demands and supports, differences in how we perceive our situations, our beliefs about ourselves and our world, and our competencies will all affect how well we meet our needs.

Figure 4.1 (adapted from Rothery, 1999) illustrates and expands upon the goodness of fit idea: The balance of demands and resources is emphasized, but the figure also emphasizes context. Context could include any aspect of the physical, social, and cultural environment, and what is most important will vary with individuals, time, and geography. The impact of a particular stress or the importance of a specific resource is not the same for women and men, for children and adults, or for people from different cultures. If Colin Macdonnell were 6 rather than 16, or female, or from an Asiatic family, the meaning of his brother's acting out (or his father's drinking) would be considerably different as a result.

Having all the circles overlap is an effort to recognize how much the critical factors are interdependent. Although it is useful to separate them conceptually for analysis, we do not *experience* them as separate, because each influences the other in myriad ways. Also, as has already been emphasized, the ecosystems model is thoroughly transactional, and a commitment

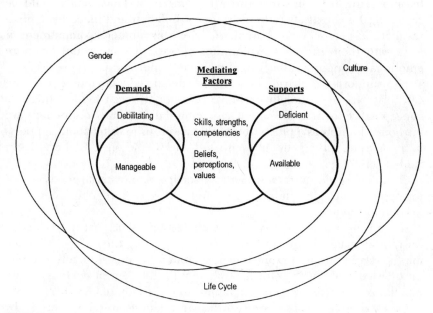

FIGURE 4.1   An ecological perspective: People in context.

to a transactional viewpoint alerts us to the fact that it is seldom either possible or necessary to declare a demand or resource to be located in the person as opposed to the environment. For example, a domestic assault victim suffers from damage originating in her environment—in her immediate family. However, having been treated in such a damaging way results in emotional and psychological needs that are personal to her. Part of the cause of Colin Macdonnell's distress is in his environment: his brother's misbehavior and his social network's reaction to those, along with his father's inability to be helpful. However, his humiliation and alienation are also part of his person—his private experience.

Figure 4.1, therefore, is useful but imperfect. Its limitations should be borne in mind, because it is a tool (like most) that can be misleading at the same time as it helps us understand better.

CRITICAL CONCEPTS FROM THE SOCIAL SUPPORT AND STRESS AND COPING PERSPECTIVES

Although ecosystems theory is not intended to prescribe interventions, the framework's emphasis on the balance of supports and demands does have general implications regarding possible goals. Often, improving the goodness of fit a client experiences by finding ways to shore up resources can be important. If Colin's relations with some important friends could be repaired, this might alleviate his sense of isolation and make his embarrassment less consequential. Similarly, given his mother's commitment, if work with them included exploration of ways that she could be more emotionally supportive, that might make an important difference for him.

The supports we all rely on can be categorized into four types. The categories are not mutually exclusive, and not all social support theorists conceptualize them in this way. These admittedly arbitrary distinctions are introduced simply as a practical tool that allows us to think about supports in a concrete, sufficiently differentiated way (Cameron & Rothery, 1985; Rothery, 1999).

First, *concrete, instrumental supports* are services and material goods we use to cope with life's demands. If we are hungry, we require food; when cold, we require shelter.

Second, *information supports* are knowledge and skills that help us cope with the demands in our lives. Education regarding the cycle of violence may be very important to someone in an abusive relationship, for example, or knowledge about the effects of alcohol on the central nervous system may improve a depressed person's ability to make helpful lifestyle changes.

Third, *emotional supports* are provided in relationships characterized by *understanding* and *safety*. When we can discuss our affective experience, receive an understanding response, and know we are safe in doing so, we are receiving emotional support. An adult survivor of childhood abuse may well benefit from the opportunity to discuss the feelings of vulnerability, fear, and helplessness that often remain with people who have been hurt in this way—again, assuming this is met with empathy and credible assurances of safety.

Fourth, *affiliational supports* come to us when we have access to meaningful social roles and when we are validated as competent. Roles that we value provide both meaning and a sense of belonging. Recognition by others of our competence to perform our roles also enhances belonging and contributes to our sense of efficacy. A young single parent, new to the complex demands of caring for a child, will benefit greatly from experiences that validate her in her new role and recognize her growing ability to manage it capably.

Each of us copes best in life when the demands placed on us are manageable, and this is likely to be true when we have adequate supports of each of the four types described above. Also, it is a good thing if the sources from which we draw supports are relatively diverse, comprising a mix of formal and informal service providers—friends, social workers, educators, family, neighbors, doctors, churches, competent mechanics, and so on. The loss of one source of support will not have the same damaging effect for someone with a rich diversity of sources of support as it would for someone who has been overly reliant on that one source and has not developed alternatives.

When he was feeling his worst, Colin Macdonnell, for example, had virtually no sources of emotional support. He had isolated himself to the extent that he had nobody to talk to about his troubles, and this inevitably made them worse. When he finally signaled his distress, he was lucky; the school social worker and his mother both were able to mobilize effectively and reach out to him. Had those resources not been available, his story may well have ended less happily.

In addition to strengthening resources, goodness of fit can be improved through reduction of stressful demands. If Eric were to stop abusing alcohol, for example, this would reduce the demands that his drinking places on his marriage and his family. This stress reduction might well free family members to explore more creative solutions to the problems they face, with the parents finding ways to relate more positively and address Sean's problems more effectively.

MEDIATING FACTORS: CRITICAL CONCEPTS FROM COGNITIVE-BEHAVIORAL THEORY

Like many depressed people, Colin Macdonnell has come to certain powerful conclusions about himself and his possibilities. He thinks his situation is hopeless, for example. His acute discomfort in his school setting is fueled by a belief that he is the object of derision and is not really wanted there in any positive sense.

Such beliefs are influenced by circumstances, but this influence is reciprocal. Steps to decrease his social isolation may help him regain his sense of belonging, but his beliefs that his situation is hopeless and that he is widely regarded with disdain by his peers are going to be an impediment to such changes. However potentially useful the supports available to him are, it will be difficult for him to utilize them effectively as long as he is convinced that he is hopeless and alone.

Thus, goodness of fit is not a simple matter of being in an environment where there are sufficient resources to balance the demands with which a person is coping. This balance is very sensitive to the person's beliefs; it is not our circumstances alone that determine our well-being, but also how we interpret the situations we are in. It is in this sense that beliefs (which include perceptions, interpretations, and values) are considered to be mediating factors.

Another category of mediating factors is competencies. Competencies are not separate from beliefs, but include action as a second dimension. Accurate perceptions and an ability to understand situations obviously contribute to our ability to cope adequately, but this is only true to the extent that we can translate our understanding into effective action. Competencies are a combination of cognitive abilities and a repertoire of behavioral skills working together to achieve an effective adaptation to the demands we face.

Much direct social work is intended to affect pernicious beliefs and to support or facilitate development of competencies. In her work with Colin, the social worker would very likely spend time identifying his painful beliefs about himself and his situation, indicating how they are contributing to his depression and making it difficult to find creative responses to his problems. She may also, at some point, look for ways to challenge Eric Macdonnell's unwillingness to look squarely at his drinking and its consequences. With respect to competencies, Colin's intelligence and insight, as well as his mother's, are very important, and supporting him in his ability to analyze his situation and options would be an obvious thing to do. If Colin were to decide to rekindle some of his old friendships, helping him rediscover the social skills and areas of interest that characterized those relationships may well be a focus for work with him.

Again, we should not lose sight of the transactional nature of people and their environments in our work with them. Reviving his social abilities and using them to repair formerly supportive friendships may involve very concrete behaviors and plans on Colin's part. He may be helped to develop a schedule of phone calls and contacts with particular people at specific times and so on. Planned and implemented with sufficient care, these relatively simple actions can have deep effects—they may help him access important supports, but they may also ameliorate his beliefs about himself not being worth much to other people. Obtaining resources can be beneficial in its own right, but the benefits are more profound and longer-lasting if new supports bring with them a positive cognitive change and a renewed sense of efficacy.

THE ECOMAP: A TOOL FOR ANALYSIS

Not surprisingly, ecosystems theorists have experimented with various ways of diagraming the complex person-in-environment systems that they see as being the focus for social work practice. Genograms (see chapter 5) are a popular tool for helping us understand nuclear and extended families, looking for the patterns that have affected the people with whom we work. From sociology and anthropology, approaches to diagramming social networks (in addition to kinship systems) have also been adapted.

The ecomap (Hartman, 1978, 1994) is a flexible tool that has been widely used, and is employed here to expand our understanding of Colin Macdonnell and his difficulties. It should be noted that there is not a standard approach to drawing ecomaps; rather, different authors suggest different formulas. Some approaches are very simple (Meyer, 1995), whereas others attempt to capture the full complexity of clients' contexts (Lachiusa, 1996).

The degree of complexity to be observed in constructing an ecomap is a practical matter. Such diagrams cannot be complete; indeed, they are useful *because* they are somewhat reductionistic. The more we include, the more complicated and difficult to understand the diagram will become; however, we need to include enough information that we and our clients achieve a practical awareness of important contextual aspects of their problems and opportunities. A middle-of-the road approach, similar to Johnson's (1998), will be used here.

To begin, a simple genogram of the Macdonnell nuclear family is drawn and enclosed in a circle, representing a boundary (see Figure 4.2). Then, more circles are used to represent systems outside the family that are important (or potentially important) influences, impinging on the Macdonnells.

Note that this is not (indeed, as we have noted, cannot be) complete. The systems represented are those that have been identified in discussion with family members. Partly, they are a function of the priorities the family introduces, and partly they reflect the social worker's theoretical biases, training, and experience.

One immediate advantage to this exercise in visualization is that it can direct our attention to systems that may have been neglected in the preliminary discussions. For example, where are Eric and Dawn's extended families in the above picture?

When this is inquired into, further information is acquired. Dawn's father is dead, and her mother is a rather depressed person, distant geographically

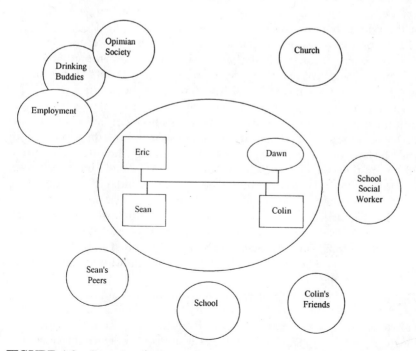

FIGURE 4.2 Step 1 ecomap.

and emotionally. Although they keep in touch, Dawn believes that her mother and her siblings have had a steadily waning influence on her since she left home as a young adult.

Eric's extended family is another matter. Dawn is ambivalent toward them, mixing admiration with misgivings. Eric likes to talk about them and, not surprisingly, describes his father and brothers (he has no sisters) as larger than life and as models for his relentless pursuit of good times. None live nearby, but there are annual stereotypically male reunions at his parents' mountain cabin, described by Eric as a convivial (if exhausting) few days of skiing, drinking, telling stories, and "smoking our brains out." Eric's mother is presented as a genteel person, who does not participate in such events and who, as Eric describes her, does not possess the color or presence of the men in the family.

Once the major systems have been identified, the next step is to diagram relationships between them. There are no standard formulas for doing this—Figure 4.3 incorporates suggestions by Hartman (1978, 1994) and Johnson (1998), somewhat modified. Different social workers and agencies evolve similar adaptations of the basic idea, in the service of their priorities and focuses.

The completed ecomap (Figure 4.3) is a rich stimulus for thinking about Colin and his family. Once the legend becomes familiar, the visual representation of their situation suggests numerous avenues for further exploration. In most cases, it is desirable to include the client(s) in such discussions, because a picture such as the above can be both illuminating and affecting for the people featured in it.

Ecomaps are snapshots, frozen in time. Thus, they represent a piece of a client's reality at one point—they are necessarily incomplete and only temporarily valid. In fact, they are often redrawn at selected intervals as an aid in identifying and emphasizing changes as they occur.

When the map in Figure 4.3 was drawn, Colin's isolation was made painfully clear: The only positive relationships he identified were with his mother and the school social worker. Relations with his father and brother (and the school) were mixed at best, and although he attended church with his mother, he was uncertain about its importance to him as a support. He had been actively avoiding his friends for weeks and did not know what, if any, relationships still existed (or could be retrieved).

As the diagram highlights Colin's plight, it also identifies opportunities for change—positive relationships that can be used and valued, tenuous relationships that could be strengthened, and resources (his friends, for example) that have been unavailable to him but with which reconnections could be attempted.

Consider Colin's older brother Sean. With Sean's relations to his parents mixed and connection to the school highly acrimonious, the only clearly positive relationship he has is with his friends. This makes these relationships very powerful in his life, and, because his friends are implicated in his substance abuse problems, that aspect of the ecomap is ominous.

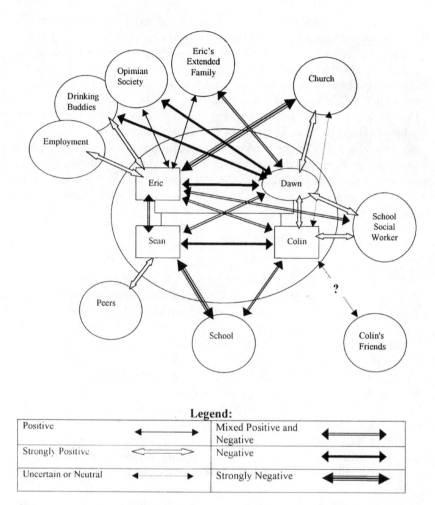

FIGURE 4.3   Developed ecomap.

Similarly, Eric's inducements to continue abusing alcohol are very power-ful. His family is not as comfortable a place for him as one might wish, and his positive relationships to work and his drinking friends (which overlap), along with the Opimian Society and his extended family, all encourage his overuse of alcohol. Like his son Sean, if he were to give up abusing, he would risk losing very important sources of social support.

The fact that Dawn's only positive extrafamilial involvement is with the church makes it extremely important to her. Eric's very negative relation-ship to the clergy, therefore, also represents a distancing factor in their marriage, for which there is no existing antidote. A more general feature of the ecomap is the extent to which these marital partners are being pulled in different directions. Because their own relationship has become hostile, the fact that they have no shared positive relations elsewhere suggests that the marriage will not last, unless corrective measures are undertaken.

Interestingly, it was through the drawing of the ecomap that Eric finally began to recognize how serious his marital difficulties were and to acknowledge that his alcohol use was a contributing factor.

A final aspect is the position of the social worker in this picture. The reader who tries to imagine being in the social worker's place will immediately sense the difficulty the worker has in maintaining balance when trying to engage helpfully with different people who are at odds with one another. The opportunities to become unhelpfully triangulated in this situation are many, and the worker will need to exercise considerable sensitivity and skill to sidestep such risks.

SUMMARY

The promise and concerns associated with the ecosystems perspective have attracted considerable attention in recent years. The elaboration of the theory presented in this chapter has recognized the very real advantages of "thinking ecosystemically" without discounting legitimate concerns.

One concern identified earlier has to do with the abstract nature of this theory, which can often distance us from the real world of clients and social agencies. A major goal in writing this chapter was to indicate how, despite its abstract nature, the perspective can nevertheless provide a useful orientation, with practical consequences for our work.

Another difficulty with the ecosystems model derives from its emphasis on adaptation and coping. The danger, of course, is that it does not automatically encourage a social critique—there is no evaluation of the social arrangements to which we and our clients are adapting. In the ecomap in the preceding section, for example, there is no healthy pressure to consider how sexism may be affecting Dawn and her freedom to confront her husband's behavior, or whether Sean's options and opportunities are unnecessarily constrained.

In the discussion of the ecosystems model centering on Figure 4.1, the problem of the inherently conservative nature of the ecosystems perspective was addressed by including a focus on context, but this is seen as a partial solution to the problem. The more complete solution is for social workers to continue to insist that whatever models and perspectives are embraced, they must be informed by an ongoing respect for our professional values, including a mandate to recognize and speak against oppressive contexts. Ecological systems are, as has been emphasized, transactional. Adaptation, therefore, can mean change by environments in response to clients as easily as it means clients' accommodating to circumstances; this is obviously important to remember when we are confronted by situations where a "goodness of fit" implies accepting social arrangements that should not go unchallenged.

REFERENCES

Brower, A., & Nurius, P. (1993). *Social cognition and individual change: Current theory and counseling guidelines.* Newbury Park, CA: Sage.

Cameron, G., & Rothery, M. (1985). *An exploratory study of the nature and effectiveness of family support measures in child welfare.* Toronto: Ontario Ministry of Community and Social Services.

Cameron, G., & Vanderwoerd, J. (1997). *Protecting children and supporting families: Promising programs and organizational realities.* New York: Aldine de Gruyter.

Compton, B., & Galaway, B. (1994). *Social work processes* (5th ed.). Pacific Grove, CA: Brooks/Cole.

Fischer, J. (1978). *Effective casework practice: An eclectic approach.* New York: McGraw-Hill.

Germain, C., & Gitterman, A. (1996). *The life model of social work practice: Advances in theory and practice* (2nd ed.). New York: Columbia University Press.

Gilgun, J. F. (1996a). Human development and adversity in ecological perspective, Part 1: A conceptual framework. *Families in Society, 77,* 395–402.

Gilgun, J. F. (1996b). Human development and adversity in ecological perspective: Part 2. Three patterns. *Families in Society, 77,* 459–476.

Hartman, A. (1978). Diagrammatic assessment of family relationships. *Social Casework, 59,* 465–476.

Hartman, A. (1994). Diagrammatic assessment of family relationships. In B. Compton & B. Galaway (Eds.), *Social work processes* (5th ed., pp. 154–165). Pacific Grove, CA: Brooks/Cole.

Hern, G. (1958). *Theory building in social work.* Toronto: University of Toronto Press.

Johnson, L. (1998). *Social work practice: A generalist approach* (6th ed.). Boston: Allyn & Bacon.

Lachiusa, T. A. (1996). Development of the graphic social network measure. *Journal of Social Service Research, 21*(4), 1–35.

Lazarus, R. (1993). Coping theory and research: Past, present and future. *Psychosomatic Medicine, 55,* 234–247.

Lazarus, R., & Folkman, S. (1984). *Stress, appraisal, and coping.* New York: Springer.

Meyer, C. (1988). The eco-systems perspective. In R. Dorfman (Ed.), *Paradigms of clinical social work* (pp. 275–295). New York: Brunner/Mazel.

Meyer, C. (1995). The eco-systems perspective: Implications for practice. In C. Meyer & M. Mattaini (Eds.), *The foundations of social work practice* (pp. 16–27). Washington, DC: NASW Press.

Nichols, M. P., & Schwartz, R. C. (1995). *Family therapy: Concepts and methods* (3rd ed.). Needham Heights, MA: Simon & Schuster.

Nissen-Weber, C. (1923). *Essays and aphorisms* (Wolfgang Streicher, Trans.). Berlin: Steinalter Koenig-Kohl Press.

Pittman, F. (1984). Wet cocker spaniel therapy: An essay on technique in family therapy. *Family Process, 23,* 1–9.

Rothery, M. (1999). The resources of intervention. In F. Turner (Ed.), *Social work practice: A Canadian perspective* (pp. 34–47). Scarborough, ON: Prentice Hall Allyn & Bacon Canada.

Rothery, M., & Cameron, G. (1985). *Understanding family support in child welfare: A summary report.* Toronto: Ontario Ministry of Community and Social Services.

Wakefield, J. C. (1996a). Does social work need the eco-systems perspective? Part 1. Is the perspective clinically useful? *Social Service Review, 70,* 2–32.

Wakefield, J. C. (1996b). Does social work need the eco-systems perspective? Part 2. Does the perspective save social work from incoherence? *Social Service Review, 70,* 184–213.

Individual and Family Development Theory

Elaine P. Congress

Theories of individual and family development provide an important knowledge base for direct social work practice. These theories are particularly helpful in the data collection and assessment phases of helping because they direct the practitioner to explore the potential significance of issues that individuals and families commonly face at different stages of development. Although individual and family development theories are primarily explanatory, they often provide general ideas for intervention.

Individual and family development theories need to be studied together, as families are made up of individuals and 75% of individuals live within families (U.S. Bureau of the Census, 1993). This chapter will focus specifically on the individual development theory of Erikson (1959, 1982) and the family life-cycle theory of Carter and McGoldrick (1980, 1989) within a changed and continually changing social context. Because the United States is becoming increasingly culturally diverse, these developmental theories will be viewed through a cultural lens. Family assessment tools, including the ecomap (Hartman & Laird, 1983), genogram (McGoldrick & Gerson, 1985), and culturagram (Congress, 1994), that can help clinicians apply development theories to their work with individuals and families will be presented.

INDIVIDUAL DEVELOPMENT THEORY

The developmental theory of Erikson fits well with the biopsychosocial orientation of social work. Departing from Freud's psychoanalytic approach, Erikson acknowledged the importance of social factors, including the family, community, and culture, in shaping the individual (Greene & Ephross, 1991). His theory is an optimistic one, as he believed individuals had the capacity to master their environment. This theme is echoed in the strengths perspective, in which clients are seen as having inherent capabilities for succeeding in life's activities (Saleebey, 1997). Unlike Freud, whose development stages stopped at adolescence, Erikson formulated eight life stages, starting with the infant at birth and ending with old age and death (Greene & Ephross, 1991). Each life stage is viewed as an opportunity to learn new skills to help the individual move on to the next stage. Based on the strengths perspective, each individual is viewed as having the capacity to master successfully the developmental challenges presented by that stage. Each stage is characterized by two contradictory extremes, which produce a psychosocial crisis. Crisis has been defined as something that upsets the usual psychological equilibrium of the individual. Although providing a challenge, each crisis produces an opportunity for the individual to grow and develop (Roberts, 1990). These crises are normative, universal experiences, and the expectation is that individuals will be able to integrate often conflicting themes and move on to the next developmental stage. The eight stages of individual development (Erikson, 1959) are described below. Following this, a recently added ninth stage and a feminist critique of the theory are discussed.

TRUST VERSUS MISTRUST (0–2 YEARS)

Occurring between birth and 2 years of age, the first stage parallels Freud's oral phase. The main issues for the infant relate to conflicts about trust and mistrust. Ideally, the infant learns about trust—the mother will be there to meet the dependent baby's needs. Early infancy provides a learning environment about trust and mistrust. If this stage is mastered successfully, the end result is hope; that is, the individual emerges with the belief that he or she can attain his or her goal. This early developmental stage is universal throughout cultures. External social factors, however, including poverty, social dislocation, and physical and emotional neglect, can affect the development of trust. If not mastered successfully, emotional and social detachment will result. An adult manifestation might be the individual who has difficulty making a commitment to any close, interpersonal relationship. Although it is important to achieve this goal in order to move successfully onto the next stage of development, failure to achieve it is not irreversible. Erikson believed that teachers, clergy members, therapists, and other supportive people might help individuals revisit and resolve this psychosocial crisis in a positive way (Greene & Ephross, 1991).

AUTONOMY VERSUS SHAME (2–4 YEARS)

Erikson's second stage, which corresponds to Freud's anal stage, is described as early childhood. Between the ages of 2 and 4, the struggle is between autonomy and shame. During this stage, children first learn to act independently without a loss of self-esteem. They struggle with overcoming a sense of shame and doubt. The positive outcome is will—that is, the promotion of autonomous behavior. A failure during this stage can lead to compulsion and guilt-ridden behavior in adults.

INITIATIVE VERSUS GUILT (4–6 YEARS)

This third stage corresponds to Freud's genital phase. In contrast to Freud, however, Erikson focuses primarily on the social interaction rather than individual psychosexual development. Described as the play stage, children face the crisis of initiative versus guilt. Ideally, children learn to initiate and take pride in their activities; they also develop a sense of what is right and wrong. The goal for this stage is the development of purpose, in which the child has "the courage to imagine and pursue valued goals" (Newman & Newman, 1987, p. 46). One sees manifestations of failure to pass successfully through this stage in the adult who procrastinates, avoids, and is fearful of initiating any new project.

INDUSTRY VERSUS INFERIORITY (6–12 YEARS)

Erikson (1959) describes this period of a child's life as characterized by industry versus inferiority. At this time, the child first goes to school and develops knowledge and skills in a structured way. Children are interested in learning in the classroom, in the community, and from peers. However, because of external or internal factors, a child may have difficulty moving successfully through this period. There may be factors in the external environment of the community or school that detrimentally affect mastery at this level. For example, the child may live in a dangerous neighborhood, and going to school may be a threatening experience. The school itself may not be a receptive environment, with a deteriorating building, lack of supplies, and an overburdened, unresponsive teacher. The family may not provide support, which is essential in mastering this stage. The mother may be overwhelmed by socioeconomic problems to the point that she is neglectful and abusive. Children may also have learning difficulties, such as hyperactivity, developmental disabilities, and health problems that impede the development of competence during the latency years.

Although the latency years mark a school-related separation from family for all children, these years may be especially traumatic for an immigrant child. Attending school marks the entrance into an environment that is very different from the home environment. The child may be uncomfortable with English as the primary language or with the policies of American schools. In a previous article (Congress & Lynn, 1994), the author presented the case example of an 8-year-old immigrant child who was extremely upset after assignment to a classroom apart from his 7-year-old sibling. His unhappiness prevented him from learning and achieving mastery within the school environment.

IDENTITY VERSUS IDENTITY CONFUSION (12–22 YEARS)

The period of adolescence, between the ages of 12 and 22, is characterized by the psychosocial crisis of identity versus identity confusion (Erikson, 1959). The adolescent becomes more independent of the parents and may look more to the peer group for support and guidance. This period is often rife with struggle and conflict, both intrapsychic and interpersonal, within the family. Much attention has been given to the adolescent's attempts at separation—wanting his or her own private space, extended curfew, and dress and behaviors that differ markedly from the family. This period, however, is best characterized by ambivalence. The teenager who fought so hard for an extended curfew may call home several times to see how everything is. There is a need for parents to provide structure in order to promote the establishment of identity. It should be noted that adolescence may begin before 12 years of age, as children often develop physically and socially at an earlier age than at the time that Erikson first developed his theory. Also, for some youth, adolescence may end in the late teens, as they form families of their own. For others, this adolescent phase may extend well into their 20s, as they pursue graduate and postgraduate education.

Many immigrants may come from backgrounds in which the adolescence stage did not exist or was extremely curtailed. For families in which children married young and/or left school in early adolescence to begin working, identity formation occurs at a much younger age. There may be much conflict within families in which the parents' adolescence was limited, whereas their adolescent children seek the lengthy American adolescent experience of their peers.

INTIMACY VERSUS ISOLATION (22–34 YEARS)

Erikson (1959) characterized the young adult era by the psychosocial crisis of intimacy versus isolation. Successful achievement during this period is measured by finding a love object, as well as satisfying work. The age parameters for this stage should be viewed as very flexible. Many young adults are so involved in developing this stage that the development of an intimate relationship does not occur. For others, developing an intimate relationship may have occurred at a younger age. Also, in a society in which the divorce rate approaches 50%, developing a permanent love relationship in the early 20s is not a desirable goal for some people. Although Erikson did not address the gay and lesbian population, it should be noted that the love object can be a person of the same sex. Finally, some adults choose never to find an individual person for a love relationship.

GENERATIVITY VERSUS STAGNATION (34–60 YEARS)

The seventh stage occurs between 34 and 60 years and involves the psychosocial crisis of generativity versus stagnation. This period involves learning to care for others and may include having a family and/or pursuing a career. Initially it was thought that the midlife period presented a time of crisis for men, with the realization of failure to achieve previous goals, whereas, for women, the crisis involved children leaving the home. More recently, the mid-life crisis period has been considered a myth, as both men and women tend to make positive career changes during the midlife years (Hunter & Sundel, 1989). Also, because most women now work outside the home, the end of their role of child caretaker has declined in importance. Furthermore, one can question if this stage in truth ends at 60, as many continue to work much longer.

INTEGRITY VERSUS DESPAIR (AGE 60–DEATH)

Erikson (1959) described the final stage of old age as characterized by the psychosocial crisis of integrity versus despair. The psychologically healthy older person is seen as one who has come to terms with past successes and failures, who has few regrets, and who has accepted death. Those who do not resolve this crisis experience despair at impending death and lost opportunities. Erikson's eighth stage did not include the recent phenomenon of many older adults who now assume caretaking roles for their grandchildren. It could be argued that these grandparents may experience the generativity of an earlier stage of development.

A NINTH STAGE (80 YEARS AND BEYOND)

Since Erikson's theory was first published in 1959, life expectancy has increased to 71.8 years for men and 78.8 years for women (Wright, 1993). The number of older people in our society is rapidly increasing, and the fastest-growing group of older people are the "old old," who are defined as 85 and older (U.S. Senate, 1988). To address this phenomenon, Erikson formulated a ninth stage of development for those who live into their 80s and 90s (see J. Erikson, 1997). This stage is characterized ideally by gerotranscendence. An older person achieves this stage by mastering each previous stage, as well as by transcending the physical and social losses associated with old age.

FEMINIST CRITIQUE OF TRADITIONAL THEORIES OF INDIVIDUAL HUMAN DEVELOPMENT

Traditional theories of individual development, such as Erikson's, have been recognized as being based largely on a male, middle-class, White, western European model. The discussion of Erikson's theory in this chapter attempted to include considerations of various types of diversity (e.g., culture, class, and sexual orientation). It is important to consider the feminist critique of traditional theories of individual development. The main point of feminist critiques of such theories has been that they have ignored women's experience of development. Gilligan (1982) argued that traditional theories of development represent the male experience of self-development through separation and ignore the female experience of progression toward interdependence through relationships and attachments. Similarly, Miller (1991) has pointed out that women's sense of self develops through emotional connections with and caring for others and that such experiences are ignored and undervalued by traditional theories, thus undermining the development of self-esteem for women. Surrey (1991) has explicated the self-in-relation theory of women's development, with the dual goals of "response-ability" to others and the ability to care for oneself. Feminist critiques have argued convincingly that theories of development that undervalue the importance of emotional connections are detrimental to both men and women. These critiques have made an important contribution to broadening theories of individual development so that attachment, affiliation, and relationship are valued as much as separation and self-development.

FAMILY DEVELOPMENT THEORY

Families are made up of individuals of different ages and at different stages of development. Although early family literature focused primarily on the nuclear family in which members ranged in age from infancy to adulthood, many families now are intergenerational and may have members of all ages. In order to work effectively with individuals and families, the clinician must have an awareness of the development stage of each family member, as well as the stage of the family life cycle. Carter and McGoldrick (1980, 1989) have developed a family life cycle model that delineates predictable stages in family development. Similar to Erikson's model of individual development, families experience a crisis when they pass from one life cycle stage to another. If not resolved, a family developmental crisis can lead to family conflict and breakup (Congress, 1996). The six stages of the traditional middle-class family life cycle delineated by Carter and McGoldrick (1980, 1989) are (1) Between Families—the Unattached Young Adult, (2) The Joining of Families through Marriage—the Newly Married Couple, (3) The Family with Young Children, (4) The Family with Adolescents, (5) Launching Children and Moving On, and (6) The Family in Later Life.

New roles for women, social and economic trends, an increasing divorce rate, and class differences have all contributed to diverse forms of the family life cycle (Carter & McGoldrick, 1989). Approximately one out of every two marriages in the United States ends in divorce (U.S. Bureau of the Census, 1993). Also, most of the divorced remarry within a few years (Congress, 1996). To address these phenomena, Carter and McGoldrick (1989) have identified family life cycle stages for divorced and remarried families. Also, approximately 22% of people choose never to marry, which represents a dramatic increase over the last two decades (U.S. Bureau of the Census, 1993). Some of the unmarried are lesbian and gay couples involved in long-term intimate relationships. Although the literature has focused primarily on the family life cycle as heterosexual, the family life cycle for lesbians and gay men has also been discussed (Appleby & Anastas, 1998; McFadden, 1997). In addition, it is important to note that approximately 50% of couples choose to remain childless (U.S. Bureau of the Census, 1993); therefore, alternate conceptions of stages 3, 4, and 5 in Carter and McGoldrick's family life cycle are needed for this population. Unfortunately, it is beyond the scope of this chapter to consider the many population-specific variations of the family life cycle—the reader is referred elsewhere for this important information. The following discussion pertains to Carter and McGoldrick's (1980, 1989) formulation of the traditional middle-class family life cycle. Attempts are made to acknowledge how issues of diversity limit the generalization of these stages and to relate these stages to those in individual development theory.

STAGE 1: BETWEEN FAMILIES—THE UNATTACHED YOUNG ADULT

This first stage of family development usually occurs in late adolescence and early adulthood. Developmental tasks for this period traditionally have included emotional and physical separation from the family of origin, developing peer relationships, and establishing oneself in work (Carter & McGoldrick, 1980). This period may span the late part of Erikson's adolescence stage and the early part of the adult stage. Both the young adult and the parents must participate in this separation process. Ambivalence about separating may produce a family crisis. Separation involves more than physical disconnection. Often young adults who do not successfully complete this process of emotional separation may have difficulties establishing their own independent family.

The age at which individuals marry for the first time is increasing; there-fore, the stage of the young, unattached adult may be extended. Economic factors may contribute to young adults remaining physically and financially dependent on their parents for housing and financial support. Parents may also apply adolescent rules to young adults still living in their house, which can precipitate family crises and conflict.

A lengthy stage of young unattached adulthood may be very much an Anglo middle-class phenomenon. The United States has become increas-ingly culturally diverse, and it is estimated that by the mid 21st century the majority of people will be from backgrounds other than western European (Congress, 1994). Many cultures continue to have an expectation that young adults remain at home until married, thus keeping offspring emo-tionally connected and dependent on their families. Furthermore, as adoles-cent single parenthood increases (Ashcroft & Strauss, 1993), this stage leading to marriage may not exist. Young unattached adolescents/adults may not choose to establish their own home, but rather continue to live in an intergenerational family. Although mothers and grandmothers in-volved in raising adolescents'/adults' children may provide needed emo-tional and concrete support, family conflict often occurs with regard to parental roles and power.

Serious romantic involvements during this stage pave the way for young adults to leave home and form their own families. Again, there may be family conflict when parents and adult children disagree about a future marriage partner. An increasing number of young adults choose to live together before marriage (U.S. Bureau of the Census, 1993).

STAGE 2: THE JOINING OF FAMILIES THROUGH MARRIAGE—THE NEWLY MARRIED COUPLE

The second family life cycle stage identified by Carter and McGoldrick (1980), that of the newly married couple, is often challenging for young people. Each partner must learn that the other may have differing expecta-tions, choices, and goals (Congress, 1996), and together the couple must learn to make compromise decisions. Although one might assume that this stage would be less challenging for couples who have lived together before marriage, relating to in-laws as a married couple is still apt to produce conflict (Carter & McGoldrick, 1989). The increasing rate of divorce among couples, especially in the first few years of marriage, is often the outcome of family crisis and conflict during this stage.

Marriages occur not only among young adults, but at different ages along the individual life cycle. Whereas marriage in adolescence is decreasing, an increasing number marry and remarry in their 30s, 40s, and 50s. Marriage also occurs among people in Erikson's eighth stage, that of old age. Al-though the developmental tasks involved in establishing an intimate rela-tionship may be similar, other psychosocial tasks related to work issues may impact differently on newly married couples. For example, when young adults marry, they may be struggling to establish careers. Also, when middle-aged adults with existing careers marry, they may be faced with the demands of finding time for their new marriage partners or relocating for one partner's career. Older adults who marry or remarry may face conflict around retirement and shrinking financial resources.

STAGE 3: THE FAMILY WITH YOUNG CHILDREN

The third family life cycle stage has been described as the "pressure cooker" phase, in that the majority of divorces occur within this period (Carter & McGoldrick, 1989). The major developmental task is faced when the couple must move to thinking of themselves as a triad rather than a dyad. An infant is extremely demanding of time and attention. While the family is in this developmental phase, the child is in the first stage of individual development during which trust is so important. There are many occasions for conflict to arise during this period.

Current social trends may contribute to the stress of this period. Women are usually older and working while children are young, which produces additional stress. Also, the increase of the single-parent household often means role overload for the primary caretaker. Furthermore, remarriages and blended families may result in the need to negotiate complicated relationships with stepparents and stepchildren (Carter & McGoldrick, 1989).

Having children of one's own often reenacts and reawakens old unresolved issues in individual members. For example, a spouse who has not been able to resolve the developmental psychosocial crisis of establishing trust may be especially threatened by the birth of a baby, who now receives special attention.

Another complicating factor is that, in most families, children are often at different stages of individual development. For example, a multichild family may be challenged by having a new infant, who is very demanding of time and attention, and also a latency-age child, who needs help to develop peer relationships. Families may experience a crisis in handling sibling conflict, especially for siblings of different ages with different psychosocial needs.

STAGE 4: THE FAMILY WITH ADOLESCENTS

This fourth phase has been identified as a major family crisis point (Carter & McGoldrick, 1989). While adolescents are struggling with identity and separation issues, their parents may be coping with their own issues around employment and health. Parents often have difficulty in granting adolescents any independence and may wish for a return to the latency years, when their children were more connected with the family. Although adolescents seem to want more independence, there continues to be a need for structure, and parents may alternate between being too restrictive and too lenient. Intrafamilial differences also affect culturally diverse families during this period, as adolescents often want to associate only with their American peers, whereas parents prefer the family relationship patterns they have learned in their country of origin.

STAGE 5: LAUNCHING CHILDREN AND MOVING ON

Although previously referred to as the "empty nest" phase, this term may not reflect what actually occurs in families. First, because of economic factors, many young adults do not leave home until they are much older, and even then they frequently return to the parental home. Second, two factors mitigate the impact of the empty nest syndrome. The majority of women with children work outside the home, and many women in midlife actively pursue new careers and higher education. This family life cycle stage may be linked to individual development issues. The parents may be struggling with midlife concerns around career changes, while their offspring are only beginning to pursue their work objectives. Difficulties may arise when parents try to enforce their unrealized career wishes on their children, as, for example, when a middle-aged father who worked in a clerical social service position insisted that his son attend law school after graduating from college.

During this phase the family changes from being a small group with one or more offspring to a dyad again. For couples who have spent most of their married years raising a family, relating as a dyad may be challenging. Many couples, however, look forward to this phase and welcome the opportunity to be relieved of demanding child care responsibilities. Time can be spent on advancing careers, pursuing education, and traveling.

STAGE 6: THE FAMILY IN LATER LIFE

The final stage of the family life cycle, the family in later life, occurs when children have left home. With increasing life expectancies, this phase may span over 30 years. Although the number of older people in our population is rapidly increasing, especially as the "baby boomers" hit 60, the increase of the old (85 or older) is especially striking (Gutheil, 1994). The transitions and tasks in later life include issues of retirement, grandparenthood, illness and dependency, and loss and death. One common challenge for individuals and couples in this period, especially for those with failing health, is the experience of role reversal with their children.

As life expectancies increase and women continue to live longer than men, the number of widowed women will continue to increase (U.S. House of Representatives, 1988). The majority of older people live alone in the community, not in institutional care or with their families (American Association of Retired Persons, 1992). Although elders living with families has been the pattern for many American cultural minorities, there is some evidence that this is changing (Congress & Johns, 1994). Regardless of where they live, many culturally diverse grandmothers do not "retire" from the family in old age, but rather are called upon to serve as parents to grandchildren whose parents have died or are unable to care for their children.

Does the family cease when there is one remaining member, often an elderly woman whose husband has died and whose children have developed their own families? The interest in reminiscence groups, both in nursing homes and in senior centers, attests to the continuing importance of family throughout the life cycle.

Loss may be an especially difficult issue for lesbian and gay families during the later years. The loss of a partner may be more traumatic for the remaining person, because he or she may not be comfortable sharing with others about the loss in what is yet largely a homophobic society (Humphries & Quam, 1998).

IMPLICATIONS AND TOOLS FOR PRACTICE

The social worker needs to remain cognizant of developmental theory in work with individuals and families. Making an assessment about what is the stage of development for each individual, as well as the total family, is particularly helpful, as there are certain needs and tasks of individuals and families at different stages. For example, a young newly married couple in their 20s is very different from a recently divorced single-parent family with two adolescent children. In the former, each member must work on establishing a commitment to each other and the marriage; they must be able to work out issues of appropriate emotional separation from their family of origin, yet realign relationships with extended families and friends to include the spouse. In the latter situation, the family must work out financial and familial relationships with the departing spouse. Unless contraindicated by issues of safety, contact with the absent spouse must be maintained and a visitation plan developed. Also, according to individual development theory, adolescents are in the process of establishing their own identity apart from their parents and families. They often turn to their peers for support and guidance during this phase rather than their parents, which may cause increased conflict within a family that has already endured the crisis of separation and divorce.

Even when couples seem to be in the same family life cycle stage, there may be important differences based on their individual ages. A young couple in their 20s who are engaged may be struggling with issues of separation from their family of origin, whereas a middle-age couple engaged to be married may have to work out issues of separation and connection with previous spouses and children.

There are a number of family assessment tools that can help the practitioner identify and understand individual and family development issues. Below, a brief overview is provided of three such tools: the ecomap, the genogram, and the culturagram.

ECOMAP

The ecomap (Hartman & Laird, 1983) is built on an ecological approach to practice and outlines the relationship of the family as a whole, and its members, with the outside world. It provides a snapshot of the family at a certain point in time. By looking at the ecomap, the clinician can assess to what extent the developmental needs of the family and its individual members are being met. For example, the previously discussed newly divorced family with two adolescents should show some connection with the absent parent. If this link is missing or conflictual, family problems can be addressed in treatment. Also, the ecomap demonstrates connection with different resources in the community. It would be of concern if the ecomap illustrated that an adolescent had no connection with peers for recreational activities. The reader is referred to chapter 4 for a more detailed discussion and an example of an ecomap.

GENOGRAM

The genogram (McGoldrick & Gerson, 1982) is a second family assessment tool that examines the intergenerational relationships within a family. The genogram maps out family constellations, relationships, and events over three generations. This tool allows the social worker to become aware of the current and past connections in the immediate family, as well as connections with extended family. The clinician is able to assess the individual and family development stages when therapeutic work begins. Also, the clinician can gain an understanding of historical issues in individual and family development.

Figure 5.1 is a genogram of the recently divorced family with two adolescent children that has been referred to previously. The genogram allows the clinician to examine the connection of parents and children with extended family, as well as the absent parent. Also, it is possible to look at what was happening at key points in the family history; for example, at the time of the divorce, at the time of the children's birth, and at the time of the parents' marriages. Key events such as births, separations, divorces,

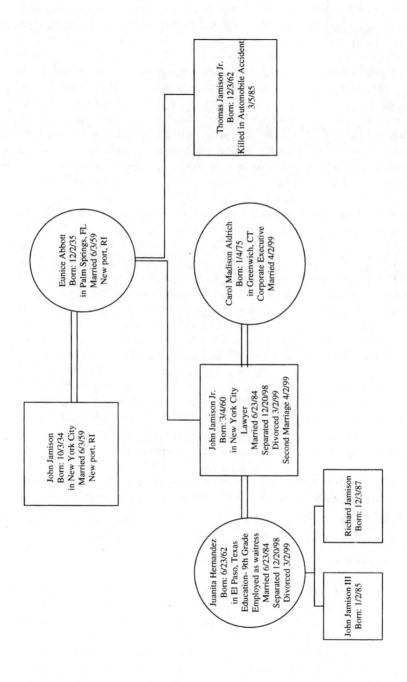

FIGURE 5.1 Sample genogram.

death, serious health problems, employment reversals, relocations, and other crisis events all affect individual and family development. The genogram can help to clarify when these events occurred and their impact on family development. For example, an examination of Figure 5.1 indicates that the Jamison/Hernandez family have experienced many crises. John Jamison, Jr. and Juanita Hernandez were divorced in 1999, and shortly afterwards John remarried. Also, we are aware that John's new wife is 15 years younger than he and only 10 to 12 years older than her stepsons. The two boys live with their mother, and there is indication that both have experienced academic and behavioral problems around the time of the divorce. Although Juanita has continued as the custodial parent, the social worker would want to explore what arrangements have been made for the adolescent sons to visit their father.

In terms of important historic facts, we note that John Jamison III was born only 6 months after his parents were married, which may suggest that the couple had little time to adjust to living together before they were married. Also, there is the possibility that John Jamison, Jr. and Juanita "had" to get married and that John III was not planned. The Jamison family experienced a major crisis when John III was an infant when John, Jr.'s brother was in a fatal accident. There may be pressure on the oldest male child John, Jr., and now John III to carry on the family tradition. Also we note ethnic, geographic, and class differences between the Jamison and the Hernandez side of the family. The Jamisons and the new wife, Carol Madison Aldrich, are from the Northeast, whereas Juanita was born in Texas. The Jamisons appear to be from a White, Anglo-Saxon, Protestant background, whereas Juanita is Mexican American. John, Jr. has a postgraduate education, whereas Juanita did not graduate from high school. Both sons are in the adolescent phase of development, during which children strive to become more independent of their parents. Yet parental roles and values are very important in shaping adolescent and adult identity. Because both parents come from such different backgrounds, the social worker would want to explore the impact this has had on the family in the past as well as in the present.

CULTURAGRAM

The ecomap and genogram are useful tools in assessing the development of the family, as well as the developmental stages of its members. These tools, however, neglect the important role of culture in assessing and understanding the family. To increase understanding of the impact of culture on the family, the culturagram (Congress, 1994, 1997) has been developed and applied to work with people of color (Lum, 1996), battered women (Brownell & Congress, 1998), children (Webb, 1996), and older people (Brownell, 1997). The culturagram grew out of the recognition that families in the United States are becoming increasingly culturally diverse. Although earlier immigrants were primarily men, recent waves of immigration have been mostly women and children. The presence of families from 125 nations in one zip code attests to the increasing diversity of the nation ("All the World," 1998).

Generally, practitioners are not well prepared to work with individuals and families from different cultures. U.S. schools, agencies, and governmental organizations are all rooted in western Europe. Individual and family development theories originally were based on an understanding of and work with traditional White middle-class families. Cultural differences do affect individual and family development. For example, individuals and families from other cultures are often more familial and communal than their White American counterparts. Class also may be an important factor. Middle-class families from other cultures may be more assimilated and follow Carter and McGoldrick's family development patterns more closely than do poor families. The social worker must guard against judging individuals or families as pathological because they do not follow traditional individual and family development patterns. The adolescent who chooses not to separate from his parents to attend a distant college despite a full scholarship, for example, is not pathological, but perhaps heeds a cultural norm that continuing familial connection is more powerful than individual achievement. The culturally diverse family in the launching stage in which adult children choose not to move out and live independent of their parents may believe that ongoing connection with family provides essential lifetime support.

Many culturally diverse families exhibit much strength in handling the crisis of each developmental stage. Some examples of this include the single adolescent mother who struggles with achieving her general education diploma while working full time to support her child; the working-class family in which father, as a janitor, and mother, as a housekeeper, manage to provide for and raise a large family; and the grandmother who, despite serious health problems, cares for her grandchildren.

When attempting to understand culturally diverse families in terms of individual and family development theory, it is important to assess the family within a cultural context. Some researchers have written about the unique characteristics of different cultures (Ho, 1987; McGoldrick, Pearce, & Giordano, 1996). Considering a family only in terms of a specific culture, however, may lead to overgeneralization and stereotyping (Congress, 1994). For example, a Puerto Rican family who has lived in New York City for 40 years is very different from a Mexican family that emigrated last month, although both families are Hispanic. Also, one cannot assume even within a particular cultural group that all families are similar.

The culturagram (see Figure 5.2) is a family assessment tool that represents an attempt to individualize culturally diverse families (Congress, 1994). Completing a culturagram with a family can help a practitioner develop a better understanding of the family in terms of individual and family development theory.

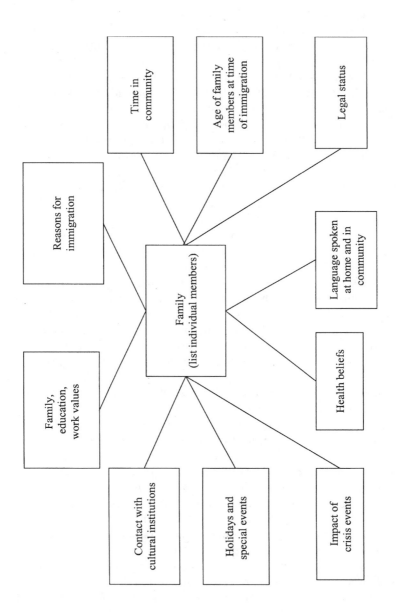

FIGURE 5.2 The culturagram.

As is apparent in Figure 5.2, the culturagram consists of 10 major areas that are important to consider in order to understand culturally diverse families. They are (1) reasons for immigration; (2) length of time in the community; (3) age of family members at time of immigration; (4) legal status; (5) language spoken at home and in the community; (6) health beliefs; (7) impact of crisis events; (8) holidays and special events; (9) contact with cultural institutions; and (10) values about family, education, and work.

Reasons for Immigration

Reasons for immigration vary among families. Many families come to the United States because of economic opportunities, whereas others relocate because of political and religious discrimination in their country of origin. For some, it is possible to return home again, and they often travel back and forth for holidays and special occasions. Others know that they can never go home again. Economic and social differences between the country of origin and the United States can affect immigrant families. For example, in the United States, latency-age children often attend large schools far from their communities and begin to develop peer relationships apart from their families. For culturally diverse families that come from backgrounds in which education is not highly valued, and in which even young children are supposed to work and care for younger siblings, the American school system, with its focus on individual academic achievement and peer relationships, may seem strange. Furthermore, immigrant children who bring a history of individual or family oppression may feel very isolated and lonely in their new environments. Individual development theory for latency-age children, as well as family development theory for families with young children, needs to be understood in the context of immigration issues involving loss, change, and assimilation.

Length of Time in the Community and Age of Family Members at Time of Immigration

These two areas of a culturagram assessment are interrelated and provide important context for understanding culturally diverse families. Usually the family members who have arrived earlier are more assimilated than other members. Also, because they attend American schools and develop peer relationships, children are often more quickly assimilated than their parents. This may lead to conflictual role reversals in which children assume a leadership position. A current phenomenon involves mothers first immigrating to the United States, then sending for their children. These circumstances can certainly affect individual and family development. An infant left in the care of relatives in the homeland may have difficulties in developing trust because of the lack of continuity in parenting during this crucial development period. Also, the family with young children that is disrupted when the mother emigrates may face challenges in reuniting as a family after a lengthy hiatus.

Legal Status

The legal status of a family may have an effect on both individual and family development. If a family is undocumented and fears deportation, individual members, as well as the family as a whole, may become secretive and socially isolated. Latency-age children and adolescents will be discouraged from developing peer relationships because of the fear of others knowing their immigration status.

Language

Language is the mechanism by which families communicate with each other. Often families use their native language at home, but may begin to use English in contacts with the outside community. Sometimes children prefer English as they learn that knowledge of English is needed for survival in their newly adopted country. This may lead to conflict in families. A literal communication problem may develop when parents speak no English and children speak only minimally their native tongue.

Health Beliefs

Families from different cultures have different beliefs about health, disease, and treatment (Congress & Lyons, 1992). Often health issues affect individual and family development, as, for example, when the primary wage earner with a serious illness is no longer able to work, a family member has HIV/AIDS, or a child has a chronic health condition such as asthma or diabetes. Also, mental health problems can impact negatively on individual and family development. Families from different cultures may encounter barriers in accessing medical treatment, or may prefer alternative resources for diagnosing and treating physical and mental health conditions (Devore & Schlesinger, 1998). Many immigrants use health care methods other than traditional western European medical care involving diagnosis, pharmacology, X rays, and surgery (Congress & Lyons, 1992). The social worker who wishes to understand families must study their unique health care beliefs.

Crisis Events

Families can encounter developmental crises, as well as "bolts from the blue" crises (Congress, 1996). As discussed earlier, developmental crises can occur when a family moves from one life cycle stage to another. Life cycle stages for culturally diverse families may be quite different from those for traditional middle-class families. For example, for many culturally diverse families, the "launching children" stage may not occur at all, as single and even married children continue to live in close proximity to the parents. If separation is forced, this developmental crisis might be especially traumatic.

Families also deal with "bolts from the blue" crises in different ways. A family's reactions to crisis events are often related to their cultural values. For example, a father's accident and subsequent inability to work may be especially traumatic for an immigrant family, in which the father's providing for the family is an important family value. While rape is certainly traumatic for any family, the rape of a teenage girl may be especially traumatic for a family who values virginity before marriage.

Holidays and Special Events

Each family has particular holidays and special events. Some events mark transitions from one developmental stage to another, for example, christenings, bar mitzvahs, weddings, and funerals. It is important for the social worker to learn the cultural significance of important holidays for the family, as they are indicative of what families see as major transition points in their family development.

Contact with Cultural Institutions

Contact with cultural institutions often provides support to an immigrant family. Family members may use cultural institutions differently. For example, a father may belong to a social club, the mother may attend a church where her native language is spoken, and adolescent children may refuse to participate in either because they wish to become more Americanized.

Values about Family, Education, and Work

All families have different values about work, education, and family, and culture is an important influence on such values. The social worker must explore what these values are in order to understand the family. For example, employment in a status position may be very important to the male breadwinner. It may be especially traumatic for the immigrant family when the father cannot find work or only work of a menial nature. Sometimes there may be a conflict in values. This occurred when an adolescent son was accepted with a full scholarship to a prestigious university 1,000 miles away from home. Although the family had always believed in the importance of education, the parents believed that the family needed to stay together and did not want to have their only child leave home even to pursue an education.

SUMMARY

Social workers need to integrate knowledge of individual and family development theory in their work. Such knowledge can help workers identify and normalize individual and family problems. The stages of individual and family development, however, should not be applied rigidly. There is a risk of characterizing individuals or families as pathological if they do not follow the expected guidelines for the stage. Any attempt to describe "normal" development runs the risk of pathologizing those who do not fit the theoretical descriptions. It is important to recognize that theories of individual and family development have been based largely on a White, male, middle-class model. These theories must continue to be expanded to take into account various types of diversity and changing social trends.

With regard to individual development, more recognition must be afforded to women's experience, and affiliation and connection need to be valued as much as separation and self-development. With regard to family development theory, the need for flexibility and multiple conceptions of normal development are necessitated by phenomena such as single-parent, blended, gay and lesbian, and culturally diverse families. Even when changing social trends and diversity are given due recognition, individual and family development theories provide only broad guidelines in work with clients. Social workers must apply these theories in the context of the specific, unique individuals and families with whom they are working.

REFERENCES

All the world comes to Queens. (1998, September). *National Geographic.*

American Association of Retired People. (1992). *Profile of retired persons.* Washington, DC: Author.

Appleby, G., & Anastas, J. (Eds.). (1998). *Not just a passing phase: Social work with gay, lesbian, and bisexual people.* New York: Columbia University Press.

Ashcroft, J., & Strauss, A. (1993). *Families first: Report of the National Commission on American's Urban Families.* Washington, DC: U.S. Government Printing Office.

Brownell, P. (1997). The application of the culturagram in cross-cultural practice with elder abuse victims. *Journal of Elder Abuse and Neglect, 9*(2), 19–33.

Brownell, P., & Congress, E. (1998). Application of the culturagram to assess and empower culturally and ethnically diverse battered women. In A. Roberts (Ed.), *Battered women and their families: Intervention and treatment strategies* (pp. 387–404). New York: Springer.

Carter, B., & McGoldrick, M. (1980). *The family life cycle: A framework for family therapy.* New York: Gardner Press.

Carter, B., & McGoldrick, M. (1989). *The changing family life cycle: A framework for family therapy* (2nd ed.). New York: Gardner Press.

Congress, E. (1994). The use of culturagrams to assess and empower culturally diverse families. *Families in Society, 75,* 531–540.

Congress, E. (1996). Family crisis—life cycle and bolts from the blue: Assessment and treatment. In A. Roberts (Ed.), *Crisis intervention and brief treatment: Theory, techniques, and applications* (pp. 142–159). Chicago: Nelson Hall.

Congress, E. (1997). Using the culturagram to assess and empower culturally diverse families. In E. Congress (Ed.), *Multicultural perspectives in working with families* (pp. 3–16). New York: Springer.

Congress, E., & Johns, M. (1994). Cultural diversity and practice with older people. In I. Gutheil (Ed.), *Work with older people: Challenges and opportunities* (pp. 65–84). New York: Fordham University Press.

Congress, E., & Lynn, M. (1994). Group work programs in public schools: Ethical dilemmas and cultural diversity. *Social Work in Education, 16*(2), 107–114.

Congress, E., & Lyons, B. (1992). Ethnic differences in health beliefs: Implications for social workers in health care settings. *Social Work in Health Care, 17*(3), 81–96.

Devore, W., & Schlesinger, E. (1998). *Ethnic-sensitive social work practice.* Boston: Allyn & Bacon.

Erikson, E. (1959). *Identity and the life cycle.* New York: Norton.

Erikson, E. (1982). *The life cycle completed.* New York: Norton.

Erikson, J. (1997). *The life cycle completed—Erik H. Erikson: Extended version with new chapters on the ninth stage of development.* New York: Norton.

Gilligan, C. (1982). *In a different voice: Psychological theory and women's development.* Cambridge, MA: Harvard University Press.

Greene, R., & Ephross, P. (1991). *Human behavior theory and social work practice.* New York: Aldine De Gruyter.

Gutheil, I. (Ed.). (1994). *Work with older people: Challenges and opportunities.* New York: Fordham University Press.

Hartman, A., & Laird, J. (1983). *Family oriented treatment.* New York: The Free Press.

Ho, M. K. (1987). *Family therapy with ethnic minorities.* Newbury Park, CA: Sage.

Humphries, N., & Quam, J. (1998). Middle-aged and old gay, lesbian, and bisexual adults. In G. Appleby & J. Anastas (Eds.), *Not just a passing phase: Social work with gay, lesbian, and bisexual people* (pp. 245–267). New York: Columbia University Press.

Hunter, S., & Sundel, M. (1989). *Midlife myths.* Newbury Park, CA: Sage.

Lum, D. (1996). *Social work practice and people of color: A process-stage approach* (2nd ed.). Pacific Grove, CA: Brooks Cole.

McFadden, S. (1997). Redefining the family: The concept of family for lesbians and gay men. In E. Congress (Ed.), *Multicultural perspectives in working with families* (pp. 167–180). New York: Springer.

McGoldrick, M., & Gerson, R. (1985). *Genograms in family assessment.* New York: Norton.

McGoldrick, M., Pearce, J., & Giordano, J. (1996). *Ethnicity and family therapy* (2nd ed.). New York: Guilford.

Miller, J. B. (1991). The development of women's sense of self. In J. V. Jordan, A. G. Kaplan, J. B. Miller, I. P. Stiver, & J. L. Surrey (Eds.), *Women's growth in connection: Writings from the Stone Center* (pp. 11–26). New York: Guilford.

Newman, B., & Newman, P. (1987). *Development through life: A psychosocial approach.* Chicago: Dorsey Press.

Roberts, A. (Ed.). (1990). *Crisis intervention handbook: Assessment, treatment, and research.* Belmont, CA: Wadsworth.

Saleebey, D. (1997). *The strengths perspective in social work practice.* New York: Longman.

Surrey, J. L. (1991). The self-in-relation: A theory of women's development. In J. V. Jordan, A. G. Kaplan, J. B. Miller, I. P. Stiver, & J. L. Surrey (Eds.), *Women's growth in connection: Writings from the Stone Center* (pp. 51–66). New York: Guilford.

U.S. Bureau of the Census. (1993). *Statistical analysis of the United States, 1993.* Austin, TX: Reference Press.

U.S. House of Representatives. (1988). *Exploding the myth: Caretaking in America* (Select Committee on Aging Publication No. 100–665). Washington, DC: U.S. Government Printing Office.

U.S. Senate. (1988). *Developments in aging: 1987* (Vol. 1). Washington, DC: U.S. Government Printing Office.

Webb, N. B. (1996). *Social work practice with children.* New York: Guilford Press.

Wright, J. (1993). *Universal almanac.* Kansas City, MO: Andrews & McMeel.

PART 3

Mid-level Theories for Direct Social Work Practice

SECTION A

Psychodynamic Theories

6

Attachment Theory

Carol A. Stalker

Attachment theory developed out of the research and writing of John Bowlby, a British child psychiatrist and psychoanalyst. During the 1930s and 1940s, Bowlby studied the effects on children of lengthy institutional care and frequent changes in the primary caregiver. One of his early papers, entitled "Forty-four Juvenile Thieves: Their Character and Home Life" (Bowlby, cited in Holmes, 1993a), reported that the histories of these young offenders were marked by "prolonged separation from their mothers in their infancy and early childhood" (p. 431). In 1951, Bowlby published a report, commissioned by the World Health Organization, that reviewed the considerable evidence supporting the idea that children's mental health was severely compromised by early separation from their mothers. As a result, hospitals throughout the world, reversing earlier policies, began to permit parents to visit their sick children, and the prevalence of large institutional orphanages with multiple, rotating caregivers declined dramatically (Rutter, 1995).

Attachment theory is a variant of the object relations school of psychodynamic theory (Bowlby, 1988). Primarily a theory of human development, which initially focused on the development of affectional ties between infants and caregivers, it has evolved into an explanation of the role of attachment across the life span and the transmission of attachment patterns across generations. The theory has attracted much interest, primarily because of the considerable empirical research that supports it, and in the last decade, numerous papers and books describing the implications of attachment theory for clinical practice have appeared (e.g., Holmes, 1993a, 1994; Rutter, 1995; West & Sheldon-Keller, 1994).

AN OVERVIEW OF THE THEORY

UNDERSTANDING OF HUMAN PROBLEMS

Contrary to traditional psychoanalytic theories, attachment theory holds that psychological problems derive not from internal conflict about sexual and aggressive drives, but from deficits in relationships and from deficits or distortions in internal representations of self, others, and relationships. Whereas traditional psychodynamic theories are prone to overvaluing independence and stigmatizing dependency needs, attachment theory stresses that the need to be close to another person, even as an adult, is not pathological. Indeed, it is held that the frustration of this need often leads to depression and anxiety. According to attachment theory, humans cannot be self-reliant until they experience a relationship in which an attachment figure can be relied upon to respond to their normal and natural attachment needs. Attachment theory, therefore, is an interpersonal, rather than an intrapersonal, theory (Holmes, 1994).

CONCEPTION OF THERAPEUTIC INTERVENTION

Bowlby put relatively little emphasis on a theory of psychotherapy (West & Sheldon-Keller, 1994), but he did address the clinical implications of attachment theory on a few occasions (Bowlby, 1977, 1988). In his most complete statement, Bowlby (1988) indicated that the role of the therapist is to provide "the conditions in which his patient can explore his representational models of himself and his attachment figures with a view to reappraising and restructuring them in the light of the new understanding he acquires and the new experiences he has in the therapeutic relationship" (p. 138).

Contrary to some psychodynamic theories, in attachment theory the central change agent is not insight provided by the correct interpretation of the transference. Insight is deemed to be important in terms of understanding the nature of one's internal working models of self, others, and relationships; however, insight is not seen as sufficient to produce lasting change. Attachment theory posits that effective psychotherapy must also provide a "corrective attachment experience" (Lieberman, cited in Erickson, Korfmacher, & Egeland, 1992, p. 501) or "a new kind of relationship that is therapeutic in itself" (Sable, 1992, p. 277). The provision of this kind of a relationship is deemed necessary in order to challenge existing maladaptive internal working models and permit their revision.

HISTORICAL DEVELOPMENT

Bowlby trained in Britain as a psychoanalyst when there was much turmoil in psychoanalytic circles. Freud and his daughter, Anna, had arrived in

London in 1938, and this exacerbated the rift that had developed between the followers of Freud and the followers of Melanie Klein (Holmes, 1994). Bowlby, embracing neither the Kleinian theory of object relations nor the classical Freudian theory, was critical of psychoanalysis' isolation from contemporary science and doubtful of theories of development that derived from clinical work with adults rather than observations of normal children (Holmes, 1994). He also rejected the minimization of the role of the environment in psychoanalytic theory at that time. As a result of his work with children, Bowlby became convinced that the environment, particularly the responsiveness of the primary caregiver, was central to psychological development.

Bowlby also rejected the centrality of sexual impulses in infant development, and with it, the significance of the oedipal complex. The idea that development is organized around drives and that children develop bonds with their mothers because they feed them was replaced by the idea that development depends on relationships, and that infants are preprogrammed to seek proximity to their attachment figures out of the evolutionary need for protection. Psychological development was seen as organized around interactions with the primary caregivers, which become internalized as representations of self, of other, and of relationships, and which strongly influence the quality of later relationships (Osofsky, 1995).

Although initially rejected by psychoanalysts, Bowlby's theory was embraced by developmental psychologists, apparently because of its inclusion of concepts from biology, ethology, and cognitive psychology. An "explosion in mother-infant research" (Holmes, 1994, p. 65) over the past two decades has been led by such Bowlby followers as Mary Ainsworth (1989) and Mary Main (1996) (some of this research is reviewed below). As a result of the empirical support for attachment theory that this research has provided, all fields of study concerned with human development have been forced to take notice.

CENTRAL THEORETICAL CONSTRUCTS

SECURE BASE

The central premise of attachment theory is that responsive caregivers provide a secure base from which infants can explore both the material and the interpersonal world, and from which they can freely apply their abilities and maximize their inherent potential. Bowlby also believed that individuals who do not experience responsive parenting, and consequently develop insecure internal working models of attachment, can be helped to modify these internal models in the direction of security through later relationships that provide the experience of a secure base. Examples of such relationships include a positive marital relationship and a trusting relationship with a therapist.

INTERNAL WORKING MODELS

Another key construct that Bowlby introduced was related to the common observation that patterns of attachment, once formed, tend to endure (Ainsworth, 1989; Bowlby, 1980; Sable, 1992). Bowlby postulated that, based on real experiences with their parents or caregivers, children develop inner representational models of themselves and others that include both cognitive and affective aspects. These models then guide feelings about self and others, expectations of self and others, and behavior in relationships with others. These inner models become unconscious and consequently do not change easily, but can be revised and updated in response to experiences that do not support the current working model.

ATTACHMENT BEHAVIOR

Attachment behavior is defined as "any form of behavior that results in a person attaining or maintaining proximity to some other clearly identified individual who is conceived as better able to cope with the world" (Bowlby, 1988, p. 27). It is most apparent during childhood, but it can be observed throughout the life cycle, especially when the individual, whether young or old, is frightened, fatigued, or ill. The biological function of attachment behavior is protection, and when it is adequately responded to, the individual's subjective experience is one of security. Attachment behavior includes clinging to caregivers when frightened, protesting caregivers' departure, following caregivers when able, and greeting caregivers' return. Thus, any behaviors that increase the probability of caregivers' availability are deemed attachment behaviors. When children's attachment behaviors are adequately responded to, they move freely away from caregivers and explore the environment, suggesting that the attachment behavior system operates in balance with the exploratory behavior system (Bowlby, 1988).

During the first year of life, attachment behaviors become directed toward a specific person or a small number of persons called attachment figures. The behavior is seen as the observable aspect of a behavioral system that responds to subtle changes in the environment and is governed by "felt security." The word *attachment* properly refers to the "focusing (preferential activation) of this system with respect to a small hierarchy of familiar figures and its resistance to 'reprogramming' " (Bretherton, 1985, p. 7). Children are hypothesized to construct increasingly complex "internal working models" that guide their behavior in new situations so that attachment figures' availability and responsiveness do not need to be reprocessed repeatedly.

Attachment theory views attachment behavior as an essential and biologically rooted behavior that serves a survival function. Attachment behavior continues throughout life, although it is more easily observed in young children. Adults, especially when ill, fatigued, or overwhelmed by life events, also seek proximity to an attachment figure, who is often a sexual partner as well. West and Sheldon-Keller (1994) suggest that adult attachment relationships are characterized by five criteria: "proximity seeking, secure base effect, separation protest, anticipated permanence of the relationship, and reciprocity" (p. 101).

PATTERNS OF ATTACHMENT

Bowlby's Patterns of Insecure Attachment in Adults

Bowlby identified three patterns of insecure attachment that are seen in clinical practice with adults, and which he believed were manifestations of parenting that was unresponsive to attachment behavior. These patterns included anxious attachment, compulsive self-reliance, and compulsive caregiving. The individual who is anxiously attached clings to the attachment figure and constantly seeks proximity. Bowlby postulated that such individuals have experienced interruptions of care by the primary attachment figure, substitute care that failed to provide one primary caregiver, or threats of abandonment. From these experiences, the child learns that no caregiver response to attachment behavior is reliable. The consequence is that the individual learns that "activation of attachment behavior must always include watchfulness and uncertainty" (West & Sheldon-Keller, 1994, p. 76).

Persons who are compulsively self-reliant act as though they do not need others for affection or assistance, and insist on appearing self-sufficient. The parenting that Bowlby saw as leading to such a pattern is one of repeated rejection, which teaches the child that attachment behaviors lead to rejection and are therefore dangerous. He hypothesized that for these individuals, the attachment system is, in effect, deactivated because the perception of anything that might activate attachment behavior is defensively excluded (Bowlby, 1980).

Persons who are compulsively caregiving are those who always place themselves in the nurturing role and do not allow themselves to be on the receiving end of help or care. Bowlby hypothesized that such individuals typically had a parent who was depressed or ill and was unable to care for the child, but welcomed being cared for and perhaps expected help in caring for siblings. This attachment pattern is seen as a solution to the child's dilemma of learning that her or his attachment behavior elicits distress in the parent. Caregiving for the parent allows for proximity to the parent, even though it requires suppression of the child's attachment behavior (West & Sheldon-Keller, 1994).

In the years since Bowlby delineated these patterns of insecure attachment in adults, empirical research with children and adults has suggested a slightly different classification of attachment patterns. But, as the reader will see, the patterns that have emerged from this research are similar.

Patterns of Attachment Behavior in Children

Mary Ainsworth, a Canadian-born psychologist who worked with Bowlby, developed the Strange Situation Protocol, which has been referred to as the "Rosetta stone" of infancy research (Karen, 1990). It is a laboratory procedure designed originally to assess the effect of maternal absence on 12-month-old infant exploration, but the focus of attention has shifted to the infant's behavior when the mother returns from a brief absence. Employing close study of videotapes of the child's behavior in the Strange Situation, Ainsworth and her colleagues identified four patterns of attachment relationship—secure, insecure-avoidant, insecure-ambivalent, and disorganized (Ainsworth, Blehar, Waters, & Wall, 1978; Main & Solomon, 1990).

The babies who are labeled "securely attached" typically explore the unfamiliar playroom and toys of the Strange Situation but frequently return to their mother, apparently for reassurance. They protest or cry when the mother leaves the room and greet her with pleasure on her return, often wanting to be picked up and molding to the mother's body when held. If they are crying when the mother returns, they are likely to be easily comforted.

Those children who explore the new environment without checking to be certain of their mother's presence, and who appear not to be affected when their mother leaves the room, are called "avoidant." Upon the return of the mother, these babies often avoid looking at her or coming close to her.

The third group, called "ambivalently attached," are those babies who cling to their mother and seem to be afraid to explore the room. When the mother leaves the room, they typically become extremely agitated and cry relentlessly, and when she returns they seek contact, but often arch away from her and seem angry. They resist all efforts to be soothed.

A fourth group displays disorganized/disoriented behavior and was identified following the study of a group of children who were originally considered "unclassifiable" in the original three-pattern classification. Main (1996) notes that most of these infants "exhibited a diverse array of anomalous or conflicted behaviors in the parent's presence, as evidenced, for example, in rocking on hands and knees with face averted after an abortive approach; freezing all movement, arms in the air, with a trance-like expression; moving away from the parent to lean on the wall when frightened; and rising to meet the parent, then falling prone" (p. 239).

These patterns of attachment behavior have been found in many studies to be associated with observations of the parent's sensitivity to the child in various contexts (Ainsworth et al., 1978; Ainsworth & Eichberg, 1991; Grossmann, Grossmann, Spangler, Suess, & Unzner, 1985). The pattern of attachment also tends to be stable, with secure children at 12 months tending to be secure when assessed years later, and insecure children tending to remain insecure. The attachment pattern is also associated with other indicators of mental health: Children classified as secure in the Strange Situation have been found several years later to be more socially competent, more empathic, and happier than children rated in one of the insecure categories (Main & Weston, 1981).

Adults' Internal Working Models of Attachment that Correspond to Attachment Patterns in Children

Taking this research further, Mary Main, a student of Ainsworth, and her colleagues, developed the Adult Attachment Interview (AAI) (George, Kaplan, & Main, 1996). The AAI assesses an adult's "state of mind in respect to attachment," a concept that is postulated to be reflective of the adult's internal working models of attachment. The AAI is an audiotaped, semi-structured interview that asks the adult to describe childhood relationships with parents and to provide specific biographical episodes that support more general descriptions. The interviewer asks directly about experiences of rejection; being upset, ill, and hurt; and experiences of loss, abuse, and separation. Transcripts of the interview are studied carefully and rated on a number of variables, of which the coherence of the narrative is the most significant.

Main and others (see van Ijzendoorn, 1995) have found that parents of securely attached children tend to value attachment relationships and are able to discuss their experiences in a coherent way. Even when their childhood experiences were painful and abusive, these parents demonstrate that they have been able to think about what happened, make some sense or meaning of their experiences, and talk about it coherently. The AAI classification system labels such adults as "autonomous" (free to evaluate attachment relationships).

Parents of children judged "insecure-avoidant" in the Strange Situation tend to have difficulty recalling the events of childhood, and/or they dismiss or devalue childhood events in terms of their current impact on their personalities. The narratives produced by these parents usually reflect a claim to strength, normalcy, and independence, and lack coherence because biographical details do not support or actually contradict these claims. They are classified as "dismissing" of attachment.

Parents of "insecure-ambivalent" children tend to produce long, confusing narratives that reflect mental entanglement or unresolved anger with their own parents and/or difficulty in coherently describing attachment-related experiences. These adults are classified as "preoccupied" with or by early attachments.

Finally, the AAIs of parents of children judged "disorganized" in the Strange Situation are significantly more likely than other parents to be classified as "unresolved" with respect to loss or trauma because of "lapses in the monitoring of reasoning or discourse, or reports of extreme reactions during discussion of these events" (Main, 1994, personal communication).

INTERGENERATIONAL TRANSMISSION OF ATTACHMENT PATTERNS

Studies using the Strange Situation and the Adult Attachment Interview have provided support for the intergenerational transmission of attachment patterns. These studies have also supported Bowlby's concept of internal working models of self, other, and attachment relationships as the means by which attachment experiences are internalized and come to guide behavior in significant relationships, including parenting behavior. One study (Fonagy, Steele, & Steele, 1991) has shown that the attachment pattern of a child at 12 months can be predicted from the assessment of the mother's attachment pattern prior to the child's birth.

Early research based on attachment theory focused primarily on nonclinical samples, but more recently, samples are increasingly drawn from clinical populations. This broader focus has led to more attention to the disorganized infant category, which has been shown to have the highest risk for later mental disorder (Main, 1996). Similarly, in research using the AAI with clinical populations, the "unresolved" (in terms of loss or trauma) category is much more highly represented than in nonclinical samples. Some studies have also suggested that a subgroup of the "preoccupied" category is associated with the diagnosis of borderline personality disorder (Fonagy et al., 1996; Patrick, Hobson, Castle, Howard, & Maugn, 1994).

DEVELOPMENTAL PATHWAYS

Another principal part of Bowlby's theory, and one that does not always receive a lot of attention, is his concept of developmental pathways. Bowlby did not agree with Margaret Mahler (Mahler, Pine, & Bergman, 1975), who theorized that infants for whom caregiving was inadequate during the symbiotic phase of development (2–4 months) would fail to completely move beyond this phase and instead continuously experience themselves as psychologically undifferentiated from significant others. In attachment theory, infants are seen as having a variety of possible ways of developing, depending on the interactions between them and their caregivers and other aspects of the environment. The implication is that there are many pathways that lead to mental health and adaptive functioning, as well as many routes to pathology and maladaptive outcomes. Even when the child begins early in life on a pathway that could lead to a negative outcome, changes in the caregiving environment can lead to a more promising pathway. Alternatively, a child who begins life with responsive parenting can move to a less favorable pathway if later life events are adverse. Bowlby believed that the potential for change continues throughout the life cycle. Although he recognized that this potential may diminish with age, he held a very optimistic view about the human capacity to respond to the experience of a secure base and the possibility of altering internal working models that have inhibited adaptive behavior (Bowlby, 1988).

PHASES OF HELPING

Bowlby's description of the therapist's role provides a framework for treatment, but it does not provide specific techniques or directives regarding phases of helping. Although McMillen (1992) notes that the tasks required of the therapist using attachment theory share much with current social work practice, there is a lack of specific guidelines in the literature for therapists who wish to use attachment theory in practice. The following discussion attempts to tailor Bowlby's (1988) general description of the therapist's role to some of the traditional phases of helping.

ENGAGEMENT

In general, the task for therapists in the engagement phase is to establish themselves as a secure base from which clients can explore unhappy and painful aspects of their life in the past and in the present. The therapist needs to act as a "trusted companion" who provides support, encouragement, and sympathy. Bowlby insisted that, although some clients bring past experiences to therapy, which make it very difficult for them to trust the therapist or have realistic expectations of therapy, it is crucial that therapists be aware of their own contribution to the relationship and not be too quick to attribute problems to the client. He noted that if the therapist is not able to provide the client with some sense of security, therapy cannot even begin. Because the client, when seeking help, is usually in a state of anxiety or distress, the therapist "is in a natural position to become an attachment figure for the client" (Kobak & Shaver, cited in Farber, Lippert, & Nevas, 1995, p. 205).

DATA COLLECTION/ASSESSMENT AND INTERVENTION

Although some models of therapy tend to differentiate between data collection/assessment and intervention, these phases tend to blend together in therapy based on attachment theory. The central task for therapists in this phase of helping is to encourage clients to examine the ways in which they relate to significant people in their present life, what their expectations of themselves and others are, and how unconscious biases may affect their selection of individuals with whom to make a close relationship. The assumption is that individuals often (because of the internal working models of self and other) unconsciously act in ways that contribute to later distress.

Therapists also should encourage clients to examine the therapist-client relationship, and thereby learn how they have transferred perceptions and expectations to the current attachment figure (the therapist) from working models based on experiences with early caregivers. Bowlby emphasized that the focus during therapy should be on the interactions between the client and therapist in the here and now, and that discussions of past events and relationships are necessary only in order to better understand the present way of feeling and coping.

Therapists help clients to consider how their current expectations, perceptions, and feelings are influenced by early experiences with parents or by what significant others told them. Therapists should expect that it will be a painful process as clients consider ideas and feelings about parents and other important people that previously were "unthinkable." Attachment theory does not attribute emotional problems to fantasy, but rather to understandable human responses to what clients actually experienced or were told about reality. Furthermore, therapists need to avoid making judgments about the caregivers, and instead encourage clients to think about what may have motivated their caregivers to behave as they did. Attachment theory does not simplistically encourage "parent bashing," but supports increased understanding and working through of the complexity of one's experiences, thoughts, and feelings.

The goal for therapists is to help clients to recognize where their internal models (cognitive and affective) are not appropriate to the present or the future. Then, clients need to be encouraged to let go of the old and formerly unconscious perceptions and expectations, and to think, feel, and act in new ways based on models compatible with their current life. The importance of a strong, trusting relationship between the therapist and the client is central to making positive changes to the client's internal models of self, other, and relationships.

TERMINATION

The literature on attachment theory does not provide specific guidelines for the process of termination, but the theory's focus on the damaging effects of unresolved losses and separations implies that a therapist should encourage the client to express the complete range of thoughts and feelings about the ending of the relationship with the therapist, and use the feelings and thoughts evoked by this ending to increase understanding of the client's reactions to earlier losses and separations.

With regard to length of treatment, attachment theory would alert therapists to be skeptical of models that advocate brief interventions with clients
who present with pervasive and longstanding difficulties in interpersonal
relationships. Attachment theorists believe that brief interventions can be
helpful for individuals who have experienced secure attachment relationships and who are dealing with situational and life transitional issues. But,
with clients who have experienced significant losses in early life, rejection
of attachment behaviors by primary caretakers, and experiences of abuse
and neglect and other traumatic experiences that preclude the construction
of secure working models of relationships, attachment theory would predict
that longer term therapy, or at least the availability of a therapist or an
agency over an extended period, would almost always be required. Therapists basing their practice on this theory accept that many clients need to
use them as a temporary attachment figure and as a secure base; they also
recognize that clients need to work at their own pace, and that maladaptive
internal working models often do not change quickly and easily.

APPLICATION TO FAMILY AND GROUP WORK

FAMILY WORK

Byng-Hall (1991) notes that Bowlby wrote one of the first papers on family
therapy when he described conjoint sessions with a client and her parents
in order to resolve an impasse that had developed in individual therapy
(Bowlby, 1949). He also attests, from his experience of working with Bowlby
at the Tavistock clinic, that Bowlby was a supporter of family therapy
throughout his life (Byng-Hall, 1991).

Byng-Hall (1995) believes that attachment theory provides a framework
that can integrate a number of ways of working with families, but he sees
no need to develop a new school of family therapy based on attachment
concepts. He argues that attachment theory suggests the concept of a secure
family base, which can be seen as an overall aim or superordinate goal of
family therapy. Once achieved, this would allow the family to explore new
solutions to family problems both during and after therapy. An attachment
framework allows for a variety of techniques to be used in the pursuit of
more specific goals, but the family therapist is required to model and
reinforce behavior and attitudes that increase the sense of security in the
family for all family members. Byng-Hall argues that knowledge of insecure
attachment dynamics can help family therapists to reframe behavior that
on the surface appears to be hostile or controlling. He also believes that
attachment theory supports the hypothesis, commonly expressed in family
therapy models, that children's problematic behavior is part of a regulatory
system that allows parents to maintain distance when their working models

of attachment require it. In other words, he suggests that acting out or symptomatic behavior on the part of a child serves a function in terms of the insecure attachment patterns of the parents.

GROUP WORK

An excellent example of group work based on attachment theory is provided by Egeland and Erickson (1993) and Erickson and colleagues (1992). These authors discuss and evaluate a group in which young, high-risk mothers were brought together for biweekly group sessions from the time their babies were born until the child was 1 year old. This group work approach assumed that therapy can affect internal working models in two ways: (1) through insight, in which the parent becomes conscious of thoughts and attitudes that were previously unconscious; and (2) through the therapeutic relationship itself, in which the "therapist maintains a healthy, supportive alliance with the parent, proving to the parent that such relationships are possible" (Erickson et al., 1992, p. 501).

In this group, structured exercises were used to encourage the examination of the mothers' memories of their own childhoods, and their understanding of how their own early experiences were influencing their interactions with their baby. For example, mothers were encouraged to identify messages that they heard from their parents when they were growing up and to talk about how it felt to hear those messages. Later, they were asked to discuss the messages they wished they had received from their parents, as well as the messages they wanted to pass on to their own child.

An evaluation of this intervention found that the mothers who had received the treatment demonstrated better understanding of their babies' needs, had lower depression and anxiety scores, and provided a more stimulating and organized home environment than mothers in the control group (Egeland & Erickson, 1993).

COMPATIBILITY WITH THE GENERALIST-ECLECTIC APPROACH

The reader will recognize that attachment theory is very compatible with the generalist-eclectic framework for direct social work practice. Holmes (1993b) argues that attachment theory should not be seen as simply another form of psychotherapy, but rather as having "defining *features that are relevant to therapy generally*—individual, group, family . . . " (p. 151) (emphasis added). He suggests that attachment theory is similar to Jerome Frank's theory of common factors. With its conceptualization of the therapist as a "trusted companion" (Bowlby, 1988) who provides a secure base from which to explore problems, attachment theory shares with Frank and the generalist-eclectic framework a strong emphasis on the development and maintenance of the worker-client relationship. Also, attachment theorists recognize that there are many ways to provide a secure base, most of which require empathic skills, intuition, and creativity. Bowlby explicitly stated that the therapeutic stance he advocated was "You know, you tell me" rather than "I know, I'll tell you" (Bowlby, 1988, p. 151). This defines his approach as collaborative rather than expert-oriented. The concept of potentially innumerable developmental pathways also supports a view of individuals that recognizes the uniqueness, potential resilience, and strengths of each.

Attachment theory can also be seen to embrace a systemic perspective and a holistic, multilevel assessment. It was Bowlby's criticism of previous theories' rigidity, and lack of attention to environmental factors, that spurred the development of the theory. Sable (1995a) has been a strong advocate of the usefulness of attachment theory in social work practice and its compatibility with the biopsychosocial perspective of systems thinking. Similarly, Egeland (1998), whose longitudinal studies of high-risk families have supported the tenets of attachment theory, argues for the use of a comprehensive ecological model that recognizes that poverty and other social stressors have a significant impact on parents' ability to provide a secure base for their children. Egeland points out that attachment theory implies that wise societies invest considerable resources into prevention programs, and programs that support parents and families, rather than rely on psychotherapy to repair the results of insecure attachment at a later date. He argues that attachment theory has much to offer the design of prevention programs and that high-risk populations (e.g., those subjected to childhood abuse or neglect, poverty, and discrimination or oppression) must be the targets of such programs.

With regard to eclecticism, for some time clinicians have recognized that attachment theory can be integrated with concepts from other models of therapy. McMillen (1992) demonstrated that attachment theory "can easily be integrated into several approaches to clinical (social work) practice" (p. 211), and he identified these as psychosocial therapy, self psychology, cognitive therapy, and family therapy. Many writers (Holmes, 1993a; McMillen, 1992; Rutter, 1995) have commented on the compatibility of attachment theory with cognitive-behavioral techniques in view of the similarities in the concepts of internal working models, basic assumptions, and cognitive schemata. McMillen (1992), however, points out that, although both cognitive therapy and attachment therapy aim to change cognitive processes, attachment theory suggests a "relationship-based approach to change" (p. 214) that cognitive therapies, at least initially, did not emphasize. He notes that Safran and Segal (cited in McMillen, 1992) have proposed a "relationship-based cognitive therapy with principles similar to Bowlby's recommendations for clinical practice" (p. 215).

Some writers (Fish, 1996; Holmes, 1993b) have also recognized that attachment and narrative theories can be productively integrated. Holmes

(1993b) argues that attachment theory supports the concept of psychotherapy as a process in which the therapist and client work together on a "tentative and disjointed" story brought by the client until a more "coherent and satisfying narrative emerges" (p. 158). "Out of narrative comes meaning—the 'broken line' of insecure attachment is replaced by a sense of continuity, an inner story which enables new experience to be explored, with the confidence that it can be coped with and assimilated" (Holmes, 1993b, p. 158).

CRITIQUE

STRENGTHS

The greatest strength of attachment theory is the growing empirical support for its tenets (McMillen, 1992; Paterson & Moran, 1988). The idea that the ability to be an adequate parent, and the ability to relate to others in satisfying ways, is transmitted from one generation to another through experiences beginning in early life is no longer just a hypothesis; it has reached the status of a well-supported proposition. Furthermore, we have a much clearer understanding of the mechanism for this transmission, and therefore more specific ideas about how to intervene with high-risk families.

A second, related strength is that attachment theory has made clearer the relationship between certain kinds of early experiences with caregivers and attachment strategies commonly seen in adult clients. This knowledge can also help therapists to understand and respond empathically to difficult clients whose behaviors are often confusing, upsetting, and distancing.

A third strength is the accessibility of attachment theory. "Ideas are expressed simply and directly, in everyday language and without traditional jargon" (Sable, 1995a, p. 34). Attachment theory retains many of the strengths of other object relations theories (e.g., viewing relationship as the crucial factor and recognizing the power of the unconscious and internalized ideas) without the difficult and confusing terminology. Such accessibility in language reflects the "experience-near" quality of the concepts of attachment theory, which likely contributes to workers' comfort with the theory and their ability to be responsive to the client (Sable, 1992). Other strengths of this theory referred to earlier include a focus on normalcy versus pathology and a recognition of the prime importance of the worker-client relationship.

WEAKNESSES

One might argue that a weakness of attachment theory is the lack of specific guidelines and techniques for therapy (Holmes, 1993a). Certainly, new workers will need more direction than that solely provided by the literature on attachment theory to become competent therapists. However, its lack of structured techniques is also its strength—like a responsive parent, it provides a firm enough framework to help therapists feel secure in the basic assumptions and approach to clients, but permits autonomy and flexibility in the specific implementation of therapy with different clients.

POPULATIONS MOST SUITED TO ATTACHMENT THEORY

Attachment theory, in view of its focus on human development, offers a perspective that shows promise for working with a range of problems (Sable, 1995a). In principle, it has something to contribute to the understanding of all clients. The most obvious populations to which attachment theory can be applied are those of all ages dealing with bereavement and loss, and children who, for whatever reason, have been separated from parents or have experienced maltreatment. McMillen (1992) has listed papers written by social workers applying attachment concepts to child welfare issues and to populations dealing with bereavement and loss. Pearce and Pezzot-Pearce (1994) have produced an excellent description of the implications of attachment theory for clinical work with maltreated children. Sable has described the application of attachment theory to a variety of specific problems with which adult clients present, including borderline personality disorder (Sable, 1997), posttraumatic stress disorder (Sable, 1995b), and anxiety and agoraphobia (Sable, 1991).

CASE EXAMPLE

The following case example illustrates how attachment theory helps the therapist to challenge the tendency of many clients to label as weakness or pathology their human need to have supportive and nurturing relationships. It is also an example of how the therapist allows the client to use him or her as a secure base so that the client can explore his or her feelings, thoughts, and attitudes, both present and past, and modify those ways of thinking and perceiving that are interfering with positive feelings about self and others.

Virginia was a 25-year-old married woman with no children who sought therapy because of a history of periodic depressive episodes for which she had received short-term cognitive-behavioral treatment on three previous occasions. When depressed, she had suicidal thoughts, had difficulty getting up in the morning, had difficulty concentrating, had little appetite, and felt worthless. When not depressed, she had lots of energy, worked very hard, and had aspirations to have a successful career in a demanding field. She had always been a good student and had completed a university degree.

Virginia was the second of three children. Her father had worked hard from difficult beginnings to become a successful executive. He was very critical of co-workers and acquaintances, who never seemed to meet his high expectations. He was also very disparaging of his wife's "weakness." The client's mother had suffered a number of illnesses during Virginia's childhood, and Virginia felt that her mother had been frustrated by her own inability to pursue a career. She described a good relationship between herself and her father, whom she felt was less demanding with her than with her brothers. She also felt she had a positive relationship with her mother, which she described as one in which they took turns looking after one another.

Virginia acknowledged in the first session that it was hard for her to seek help because she wanted to be independent, and she felt she had failed when she couldn't pull herself out of the depression. She indicated that her husband was very supportive and understanding. In fact, they had met at a time when she was quite depressed, and he had been very sympathetic and helpful to her whenever she had been "down." Virginia knew that, especially when she was depressed, she was very self-critical and that her negative self-statements were irrational. Still, she had not been able to change them.

The therapist pointed out the strength and determination that Virginia was showing by coming for help and by continuing to look for ways to overcome her depression. She also acknowledged how hard it is to get up and go to work when one is depressed, and praised Virginia for her efforts to do the things that were likely to help herself, such as seeing her family doctor about antidepressant medication, forcing herself to eat, and getting some exercise. She contracted to see Virginia initially for 10 weekly sessions, with the plan to reevaluate at that point the need to continue. She indicated that Virginia could call her between sessions if she felt overwhelmed and needed additional support. She explained that her approach was to work with her clients to understand better what past and current experiences had led to thoughts and feelings that were hindering optimal functioning in the present.

The client was encouraged by the therapist to talk more about her expectations of herself and how she had come to be so critical of herself when she felt her performance was less than stellar. The client recognized that she had, as a child, decided that she would not be like her mother, and that she would be more like her father—a strong, independent, and successful person. She also identified her mixed feelings about being like her father. She felt sorry for her mother when she thought about her father's attitude toward her, and thought that he had not been fair to her.

Over time, as the therapy conversation went back and forth between current feelings and behavior and past feelings and experiences, Virginia became aware of anger toward both of her parents for what she came to recognize as unrealistic and inappropriate expectations. She recalled that at age 7, when she complained of being picked on at school by older children, her parents asked Virginia to consider how she had contributed to the problem, and told her that she could solve the problem herself. She recognized that she interpreted this as meaning that she was the cause of the problem, and there was something wrong with her if she couldn't solve it. This insight elicited memory of feelings of great despair in the face of what she now recognized was cruel bullying by bigger and stronger children.

Virginia came to recognize that she only felt acceptable when she perceived herself as solving her own problems and needing no one. This idea had come from many experiences but certainly from both parents, who, with positive intentions, had been trying to encourage self-sufficient behavior in their daughter. The therapist reminded Virginia that all humans need support and care from others, and that this was not a sign of weakness or "dependence." Virginia began to postulate that some part of her rebelled at the internal pressure to constantly be strong and self-sufficient, and the depression might be an unconscious attempt to receive care and nurture from others without consciously acknowledging her need for support. Over time she began to perceive that in her current life, she actually received very little support when she was not depressed, as her husband's behavior seemed to change to a more critical stance when she was feeling good and being more assertive in her work and home life.

After 3 months of therapy, Virginia was no longer depressed; however, she chose to continue therapy in order to better understand how ways of coping that were adaptive in the past were interfering with healthy and satisfying choices in the present. The therapist saw Virginia on a weekly basis for 10 months, and once monthly for 3 more months. The therapist felt that the support and safety afforded by the therapeutic relationship allowed Virginia to modify internal models of self, other, and relationships so that she could better accept her needs for nurturing and achieve greater intimacy in a reciprocal and respectful relationship with her husband.

SUMMARY

Attachment theory is a theory of human development that has served as the theoretical framework for perhaps more empirical research than any other theory of human development. This research continues to both support and amplify the basic tenets of the theory and to grow at phenomenal rates. The theory provides a way of understanding human relationships that is very compatible with the best of traditional social work practice. Attachment theory has the flexibility to incorporate concepts and techniques from a variety of therapeutic models, and it is applicable to individual, family, and group interventions. It also has much to offer interventions that aim to prevent mental health problems in future generations.

REFERENCES

Ainsworth, M. D. S. (1989). Attachments beyond infancy. *American Psychologist, 44*, 709–716.

Ainsworth, M. D. S., Blehar, M. C., Waters, E., & Wall, S. (1978). *Patterns of attachment: A psychological study of the strange situation.* Hillsdale, NJ: Erlbaum.

Ainsworth, M. D. S., & Eichberg, C. G. (1991). Effects on infant-mother attachment of mother's unresolved loss of an attachment figure or other traumatic experience. In P. Marris, J. C. Stevenson-Hinde, & C. Parkes (Eds.), *Attachment across the life cycle* (pp. 160–183). New York: Routledge.

Bowlby, J. (1949). The study and reduction of group tensions in the family. *Human Relations, 2*, 123–128.

Bowlby, J. (1977). The making and breaking of affectional bonds. *British Journal of Psychiatry, 130*, 201–210.

Bowlby, J. (1980). *Attachment and loss: Vol. 3. Loss: Sadness and depression.* New York: Basic Books.

Bowlby, J. (1988). *A secure base.* New York: Basic Books.

Bretherton, I. (1985). Attachment theory: Retrospect and prospect. In I. Bretherton & E. Waters (Eds.), *Growing points of attachment theory and research* (Monographs of the Society of Research in Child Development, Serial No. 209, Vol. 50, Nos. 1–2, pp. 3–35). Chicago: University of Chicago Press.

Byng-Hall, J. (1991). An appreciation of John Bowlby: His significance for family therapy. *Journal of Family Therapy, 13*, 5–16.

Byng-Hall, J. (1995). Creating a secure family base: Some implications of attachment theory for family therapy. *Family Process, 34*, 45–58.

Egeland, B. R. (1998, October). *The longitudinal study of attachment and psychopathology.* Paper presented at the Second International Conference on Attachment and Psychopathology, Toronto, Canada.

Egeland, B. R., & Erickson, M. F. (1993). Attachment theory and findings: Implications for prevention and intervention. In S. Kramer & H. Parens (Eds.), *Prevention in mental health: Now, tomorrow, ever?* (pp. 21–50). Northvale, NJ: Jason Aronson.

Erickson, M. F., Korfmacher, J., & Egeland, B. R. (1992). Attachments past and present: Implications for therapeutic intervention with mother-infant dyads. *Development and Psychopathology, 4*, 495–507.

Farber, B. A., Lippert, R. A., & Nevas, D. R. (1995). The therapist as attachment figure. *Psychotherapy, 32*, 204–212.

Fish, B. (1996). Clinical implications of attachment narratives. *Clinical Social Work Journal, 24*, 239–253.

Fonagy, P., Leigh, T., Steel, M., Steele, H., Kennedy, R., Mattoon, G., Target, M., & Gerber, A. (1996). The relation of attachment status, psychiatric classification and response to psychotherapy. *Journal of Consulting and Clinical Psychology, 64*, 22–31.

Fonagy, P., Steele, M., & Steele, H. (1991). Maternal representations of attachment during pregnancy predict the organization of infant-mother attachment at one year of age. *Child Development, 62*, 880–893.

George, C., Kaplan, N., & Main, M. (1996). *Adult Attachment Interview* (3rd ed.). Unpublished manuscript. Department of Psychology, University of California, Berkeley.

Grossmann, K., Grossmann, K. E., Spangler, G., Suess, G., & Unzar, L. (1985). Maternal sensitivity and newborn's orientation response as related to quality of attachment in Northern Germany. In I. Bretherton & E. Waters (Eds.), *Growing points of attachment theory and research* (Monographs of the Society of Research in Child Development, Serial No. 209, Vol. 50, Nos. 1–2, pp. 233–256). Chicago: University of Chicago Press.

Holmes, J. (1993a). Attachment theory: A biological basis for psychotherapy? *British Journal of Psychiatry, 163,* 430–438.

Holmes, J. (1993b). *John Bowlby and attachment theory.* London: Routledge.

Holmes, J. (1994). The clinical implications of attachment theory. *British Journal of Psychotherapy, 11,* 62–76.

Karen, R. (1990, February). Becoming attached. *The Atlantic Monthly,* pp. 35–70.

Mahler, M. S., Pine, F., & Bergman, A. (1975). *The psychological birth of the human infant.* New York: Basic Books.

Main, M. (1996). Introduction to the special section on attachment and psychopathology: 2. Overview of the field of attachment. *Journal of Consulting and Clinical Psychology, 64,* 237–243.

Main, M., & Solomon, J. (1990). Procedures for identifying infants as disorganized/disoriented during the Ainsworth Strange Situation. In M. T. Greenberg, D. C. Cicchetti, & E. M. Cummings (Eds.), *Attachment in the preschool years* (pp. 121–160). Chicago: University of Chicago Press.

Main, M., & Weston, D. R. (1981). The quality of the toddler's relationship to mother and to father: Related to conflict behavior and the readiness to establish new relationships. *Child Development, 52,* 932–940.

McMillen, J. C. (1992). Attachment theory and clinical social work. *Clinical Social Work Journal, 20,* 205–218.

Osofsky, J. D. (1995). Perspectives on attachment and psychoanalysis. *Psychoanalytic Psychology, 12,* 347–362.

Paterson, R. J., & Moran, G. (1988). Attachment theory, personality development and psychotherapy. *Clinical Psychology Review, 8,* 611–636.

Patrick, M., Hobson, P., Castle, P., Howard, R., & Maughn, B. (1994). Personality disorder and the mental representation of early social experience. *Development and Psychopathology, 94,* 375–388.

Pearce, J. W., & Pezzot-Pearce, T. D. (1994). Attachment theory and its implication for psychotherapy with maltreated children. *Child Abuse and Neglect, 18,* 425–438.

Rutter, M. (1995). Clinical implications of attachment concepts: Retrospect and prospect. *Journal of Child Psychology and Psychiatry, 4,* 549–571.

Sable, P. (1991). Attachment, anxiety, and agoraphobia. *Women and Therapy, 11,* 55–69.

Sable, P. (1992). Attachment theory: Application to clinical practice with adults. *Clinical Social Work Journal, 20,* 271–283.

Sable, P. (1995a). Attachment theory and social work education. *Journal of Teaching in Social Work, 12,* 19–38.

Sable, P. (1995b). Attachment theory and post-traumatic stress disorder. *Journal of Analytic Social Work, 2,* 89–109.

Sable, P. (1997). Attachment, detachment and borderline personality disorder. *Psychotherapy, 43,* 171–181.

van IJzendoorn, M. V. I. (1995). Adult attachment representation, parental responsiveness, and infant attachment: A meta-analysis on the predictive validity of the Adult Attachment Interview. *Psychological Bulletin, 117,* 387–403.

West, M. L., & Sheldon-Keller, A. E. (1994). *Patterns of relating: An adult attachment perspective.* New York: Guilford.

7

Interpersonal Therapy[1]

Arthur Schwartz

Interpersonal therapy (IPT) was developed initially by Klerman, Weissman, Rounsaville, and Chevron (1984) for the treatment of depression. IPT evolved from the psychodynamic tradition, particularly from the interpersonal relations school of psychiatry (Sullivan, 1953). IPT shares with other psychodynamic approaches a concern with the entire life span and an acknowledgment of the importance of childhood experiences and personality patterns. However, unlike traditional psychodynamic approaches that focus on intrapsychic issues rooted in the past, IPT focuses on interpersonal relationships in the here and now (Klerman et al., 1984). Thus, IPT is a psychodynamic approach only in the broadest sense of the word.

AN OVERVIEW OF THE THEORY

UNDERSTANDING OF HUMAN PROBLEMS

IPT emphasizes that psychological problems, including depression, result from a person's relationships with other people in his or her environment. It is hypothesized that there is a link between interpersonal difficulties and the development and continuance of psychological problems; that these problematic interpersonal interactions lead to mood disturbances, and a vicious cycle is often set into effect. Although the theory focuses on interpersonal relationships, the theory also recognizes the role of genetic, biochemical, developmental, and personality factors in causation of and vulnerability to depression and other disorders (Klerman et al., 1984).

THERAPEUTIC INTERVENTION IN IPT

The primary focus of treatment is to effect change by altering interpersonal relations. The purpose of intervention is to interrupt the vicious cycle of interpersonal and mood disturbances. The focus is on both understanding and changing the linkages between interpersonal and psychological problems. The proponents of the approach specifically state that the goal of therapy is not "personality reconstruction," but the easing of psychological problems through better understanding of interpersonal difficulties and the adoption of more adaptive coping mechanisms, along with accompanying attitude and cognitive changes.

IPT is time-limited, usually consisting of 12 to 20 sessions, with the client being seen once a week. IPT practitioners are assisted by manuals that specify in considerable detail the concepts, techniques, and methods of the approach, including the roles of therapist and client (Klerman & Weissman 1993; Klerman et al., 1984). A manual for clients has also been developed. It was designed to facilitate client participation and includes exercises, homework assignments, and other procedures (Weissman, 1998).

HISTORICAL DEVELOPMENT OF IPT

PRECURSORS

IPT follows in the tradition of Dr. Adolph Meyer, of Johns Hopkins University Hospital, in Baltimore. Dr. Meyer was one of the first psychiatrists to focus on the influence of social and interpersonal (i.e., environmental) matters, as well as biological factors in mental disorders. He believed that psychiatric symptoms reflected clients' efforts to adapt to stresses in their environments, and that adaptive capacities, although formed in early family relations, are influenced in the present by one's relationships with individuals and with different social groups (Schwartz & Schwartz, 1993).

The originators of IPT were also heavily influenced by G. H. Mead of the Chicago school of sociology and his writings on the "self" (Mead, 1934). Mead viewed the "self" as arising from people's interactions with others, originating in the initial interactions of children with parents, and continuing with a positive or a negative impact throughout an individual's life.

IPT evolved from the general framework of psychodynamic theory and therapy, particularly from the tradition of the interpersonal relations school of psychiatry of Harry Stack Sullivan (1953). Sullivan thought that much "psychiatric illness" is associated with, if not caused by, faulty interpersonal relationships. The interpersonal relations school of psychiatry incorporated many concepts from the social sciences, particularly the importance of primary groups, such as the family, and relationships with immediate "significant others." It stressed the importance of the different roles people play, the different statuses they occupy, and the rewards or consequences of successful or unsuccessful fulfillment of these role requirements. "Role adaptation" includes the significance of assuming what Parsons (cited in Markowitz, 1998) called the "sick role."

The work of Bowlby (1969) was another influence on the development of IPT. Bowlby rejected earlier psychodynamic theory that linked depression to excess dependency in childhood and resultant repressed hostility. Instead, he emphasized the link between depression and disruptions in attachment and bonding.

DEVELOPMENT OF IPT

IPT was developed at Yale University, and in Boston, as a short-term, time-limited, focused therapy for depressed clients. Attention was also given to the use and integration of antidepressant medications in this treatment, a topic that is still being examined carefully and continuously reconsidered as newer developments in medications occur.

Dr. Klerman and his associates began their work in the late 1960s, continuing with experimentation and improvements throughout the 1970s. They published their primary, and still very useful, handbook in 1984. The original clinical work was carefully evaluated and the theory and procedures modified according to the data collected. It should be noted that the founders of IPT were an interdisciplinary team, grounded not only in psychiatry but also in medicine, psychopharmacology, social work, epidemiology, sociology, psychology, and other related disciplines.

LATER DEVELOPMENTS AND CURRENT STATUS

A form of IPT (IPT-A) has been developed and tested for use with depressed adolescents (Mufson & Moreau, 1998; Mufson, Moreau, Weissman, & Klerman, 1993). Another adaptation, for use with geriatric clients, both acutely depressed and for those with recurrent depression, has been called IPT—Late Life Maintenance (IPT-LLM). A manual was developed for use with these older clients (Reynolds, Frank, Houck, & Mazumdar, 1997).

Similarly, IPT has been adapted, and manuals developed, for treating other forms of depression and depression-related conditions, such as dysthymia, bipolar disorder, bereavement, antepartum and postpartum depressions, social phobia, panic disorder, body dysmorphic disorder, chronic somatization, borderline personality disorder, insomnia, breast cancer, myocardial infarction, and a number of other medical and psychiatric conditions (for an overview, see Weissman & Markowitz, 1998). Particularly promising is the work being done, primarily in England, with clients with bulimia nervosa (Fairburn, 1998), as well as work with clients with HIV (Swartz & Markowitz, 1998). Opportunities for training in IPT have been rapidly expanding, and the manuals and studies have been translated into a number of foreign languages (Weissman & Markowitz, 1998).

In an attempt to make counseling available to those who would not seek treatment from a mental health professional, or for those whose symptomatology does not fulfil a DSM-IV diagnosis, a form of IPT called interpersonal counseling (IPC) has been developed for use primarily by those without formal psychiatric training, chiefly nurse practitioners. IPC usually lasts six sessions, and, although initial sessions can be as long as 30 minutes, following sessions are usually shorter (Weissman & Markowitz, 1998). IPC is also currently being tested as treatment, via the telephone, for cancer patients (Weissman & Markowitz, 1998).

PAST AND CURRENT CONNECTIONS TO SOCIAL WORK

The emphasis on interpersonal relations, on social roles, on expectations of self and others—in short, the incorporation of concepts from the social sciences—makes IPT highly compatible with the orientation and the value assumptions of social work. Myrna Weissman, the colleague and widow of one of the primary developers of IPT (Klerman), was trained as a social worker before she became a distinguished professor of epidemiology at Columbia University. The interdisciplinary team that developed IPT included many other social workers.

CENTRAL THEORETICAL CONSTRUCTS

THREE COMPONENT PROCESSES IN DISORDERS

IPT conceptualizes disorders as consisting of three processes. The first is *symptom formation*, which refers to the development of signs and symptoms, and which may have biological and/or psychological bases. The second process is *social and interpersonal relations*, which involves interaction with others in social roles, and which reflects past learning, social reinforcement, and/or current coping efforts. The third process is *personality and character problems*, which refers to personality traits, deficits in communication, and lack of self-esteem. These are personality patterns that are thought to predispose individuals to depression (Klerman et al., 1984). According to its founders, the briefness of IPT therapy tends to rule out changes or lasting effects on personality structure. They do emphasize, however, that "personality function is assessed" (Klerman et al., 1984).

Intervention in IPT is focused on the first two processes mentioned above. In intervention with symptom formation and social and interpersonal relations, emphasis is placed on helping the client to develop new and more effective ways (strategies) of handling the current interpersonal problems that are linked with the beginning of symptomatology. In such work, "reliance is upon well-established techniques such as reassurance, clarification of emotional states, improvement of interpersonal communication, and testing of perceptions and performance through interpersonal contact" (Klerman et al., 1984, p. 7).

FOUR PROBLEM AREAS IN DEPRESSION

Although IPT may be similar to other therapies in techniques and orientation, it differs on the "level of strategies," emphasizing specific strategies oriented to particular and specific problem areas. With regard to depression, the main problem areas are conceptualized as (1) abnormal grief, (2) role transitions, (3) interpersonal deficits, and (4) interpersonal role disputes. A brief description of each of these problem areas is provided below. The treatment goals and strategies for each of these four problem areas are summarized under "Phases of Helping."

Abnormal Grief

It is sometimes difficult to tell the difference between abnormal grief and "normal mourning"; however, it is generally felt that "normal" grief lessens and diminishes within 2 to 4 months, a gradual return to everyday activities occurs, and there is a lessening preoccupation with the memories of the person who has died (Klerman et al., 1984). One of the assumptions of IPT, regarding abnormal grief, is that "inadequate grieving" leads to delayed or distorted grief reactions. In delayed grief, the person does not show grief immediately after the death but may react strongly later, often in response to another event: the death of a pet, the loss of a favorite possession, and so on. In distorted grief reactions, which may come immediately or may be postponed, the grief is not expressed in the usual manner, but it surfaces in physical symptoms and/or other problems.

Role Transitions

We all experience changes in our lives—some positive, some negative, some planned, and some unplanned. These changes may lead to alterations in one or more of our "roles." Our various roles both determine and are determined by our interactions with others. They are closely linked to how we view ourselves—our self-esteem. Role transitions are sometimes associated with troubling emotions: feelings of rage, fright, fear, failure, and more. This is especially true if a new role is seen as too demanding. New roles may require social skills and behaviors that are not in a person's repertoire; they may result in such drastic changes in an individual's patterns of behavior (including the way he or she copes with these changes) that they may produce both depression and an accompanying drop in self-esteem (Klerman et al., 1984). An individual may feel reluctant to give up old roles. New behaviors cause anxiety; old roles and statuses may have at least provided security, and deprivation of this security may be experienced as a loss. Inability to function in new roles may worsen a depressive reaction. This depressive reaction may be related to the individual's lack of awareness of what is involved in the new roles—often a focus in IPT treatment.

Interpersonal Deficits

Clients may appear with a history of severe loneliness due to a lack of social (interpersonal) relations, which frequently dates back to childhood, even early childhood. These clients often seem to lack social skills and show inadequacies in relating to other people. There may also be temporary or chronic deficits in social skills. For example, if the person is alone or does not work, there may not be much opportunity for intimate relationships. This lack of contact with others may be a crucial factor in depression and may become a focus of treatment.

Interpersonal Disputes

Interpersonal role disputes involve circumstances in which two people have differing definitions or "expectations" of their relationship. For some people, these differences are central to the formation and the continuance of depression. If the disputes continue, and there seems little chance of resolution in the future, these people often feel the disputes are all their fault and evidence of their own worthlessness (Klerman et al., 1984). In IPT, a role dispute is assessed as being at one of three stages: (1) renegotiation, where the client and the other person know that there are disagreements and they may even be attempting to resolve the differences; (2) impasse, where there is no dialogue between the two, although the emotions may persist; and (3) dissolution, where the client feels the relationship cannot be healed or reestablished (Klerman et al., 1984).

PHASES OF HELPING

In IPT, the process of helping is viewed as occurring in three stages: an initial phase, an intermediate phase, and a termination phase. Because IPT was originally designed for use with depressed clients, the focus in this section will be on the treatment of the depressions.

INITIAL PHASE (ENGAGEMENT AND ASSESSMENT)

The initial phase usually lasts for one to three sessions. The major task in this phase is a review of symptoms, signs, and complaints, leading to assessment and diagnosis. In depression, and in some other disorders, there is also an assessment of the possible need for medication.

In the initial phase, and throughout the helping process, there is an emphasis on being open and direct with the client. The therapist-client relationship is viewed as a "model" for relationships outside of the therapeutic work. As early as the first interview, the therapist gives his or her perception of the problem, and there is a discussion of the treatment goals and work toward agreement on the goals (a "contract"). The mechanics of the therapy are also discussed, such as frequency of visits, length of therapy, fees, and other policy matters (Klerman et al., 1984; Weissman & Markowitz, 1998). The client is encouraged to report both positive and negative feelings to the therapist. IPT practitioners emphasize that it is important to discuss the client's feelings and behaviors toward the therapist in order to maximize client involvement and commitment.

Even though IPT was created by therapists highly social in their orientation, clients are told that the depression they are suffering is a "medical illness." IPT therapists believe that this is justified by the reassurance many depressed individuals feel when they are given a label for what they have been experiencing, and that this offers hope that the client can be helped.

As part of a psychiatric history, an "interpersonal inventory" is administered, which reviews the client's current social functioning and interpersonal relations (Weissman & Markowitz, 1998). The major problem areas are then specified, and these problem areas are related to the current disorder. In other words, the problems the client is experiencing are interpreted to the client as being related to difficulties, in the present and in the past, that the individual has in interactions with "significant others," and whatever expectations they have of each other (Klerman et al., 1984). Pinpointing which relationships or factors in a relationship are connected to the disorder leads to a consideration of possible changes that can be made in these relationships.

INTERMEDIATE PHASE (INTERVENTION)

The intermediate phase focuses on the problem areas mutually defined by the client and the therapist. The emphasis of IPT is on relieving symptoms by focusing on communication and other problems with "significant others" in any one or more of the selected current problem areas.

Special "strategies" have been developed to deal with specific problems and problem areas. These "strategies" have been described closely in manuals for IPT therapists and have been supplemented by a manual, and "scoring sheets," specifically designed for clients (Weissman, 1998). Structured tasks are commonly used, including homework assignments that direct the client to try out, in actual life situations, the skills and self-confidence he or she has been acquiring in the therapy sessions. Discussion of the client's experiences in practicing these new skills provides the opportunity for feedback from the therapist. It is important for the therapist to reinforce each accomplishment of the client by praising attempts at new ways of coping, buttressing the hope that change is possible and achievable. The IPT goals and strategies for treatment of the four problem areas are summarized below.

Abnormal Grief

The goals for this problem area are to help the client to mourn and, through mourning, to reestablish relationships and interests to compensate for the loss. The strategies for treating grief involve (1) examining the symptoms of depression and relating these to the death of the significant other, (2) discussing the client's relationship with the deceased, (3) reviewing the sequences and consequences of the events leading up to and following the death, (4) exploring negative and positive feelings about these events, and (5) considering ways of establishing relationships with others (Klerman et al., 1984).

Role Transitions

The goals in working on the problem area of role transitions are to help the client (1) mourn and accept the loss of the old role, (2) see the new role more positively, and (3) develop mastery of the new role and restore self-esteem (Klerman et al., 1984). The strategies for dealing with such problems include (1) examining the symptoms of depression and relating these to problems in coping with a recent life change, (2) identifying the positive and negative aspects of the old and new roles, (3) helping the client express feelings about the losses and changes, (4) identifying potential in the new roles, (5) evaluating what has been lost and encouraging the expression of affect, and (6) helping the client develop a social support system and requisite skills for the new role (Klerman et al., 1984).

Interpersonal Deficits

The treatment goals for clients with interpersonal deficits are lessening their social isolation and learning how to form new relationships. This may well include helping the client to learn new social skills. The strategies for dealing with interpersonal deficits involve (1) identifying depressive symptoms and relating these to social isolation or unsatisfying social relationships, (2) reviewing the positives and the negatives in past significant relationships, (3) recognizing repetitive patterns in relationships, and (4) detecting parallels between the positive and negative feelings about the therapeutic relationship and feelings about other relationships (Klerman et al., 1984).

Interpersonal Disputes

The goals of the intermediate phase of treatment are (1) to identify the disputes, (2) to spell out their nature within interpersonal terms, and (3) to help the client decide on a course of action to resolve the disputes. It is important to identify and differentiate among the three stages of interpersonal disputes, for each stage necessitates a different strategy. If the stage is "renegotiation," part of the therapist's task may be to restrain both individuals so that they can talk with each other. In an "impasse" situation, one possible strategy is to increase the conflict temporarily in order to start a dialogue. With "dissolution," similar to grief, the therapist works with the client to understand what happened in the relationship, helping him or her to realize the relationship is dead, and facilitating mourning so the client is able to move on to form new relationships (Klerman et al., 1984).

The strategies for dealing with interpersonal disputes include (1) reviewing symptoms of depression and relating these to the onset of a current dispute with a significant other, (2) establishing the stage of the dispute (i.e., renegotiation, impasse, or dissolution), (3) examining how nonreciprocal role expectations contribute to the dispute (identify issues, differences, options, alternatives, and available resources), (4) illustrating the function of the client's behavior and parallels to other relationships, and (5) identifying how the dispute is perpetuated (Klerman et al., 1984). A case illustration of IPT treatment of interpersonal disputes is presented later in the chapter.

TERMINATION PHASE

Clients must form a relationship with the therapist, examine their problems, work on them, acquire skills to deal with future stresses, then relinquish the relationship, all within a comparatively short period of time. This is often difficult for clients, who may perceive termination as rejection by the therapist and may respond with additional symptoms, particularly hopelessness.

The IPT manual calls for the therapist and client to begin talking of termination from two to four sessions before the end of treatment. They should review the client's progress and should expressly discuss the termination of treatment and the naturalness of a feeling of loss, and possibly of mourning, which revives past deprivations and losses. There also should be an acknowledgment by the client of his or her new skills and new competencies (Klerman et al., 1984).

Included in the termination process are discussions of possible future difficulties. It is deemed important to alert the client that symptoms may reoccur under some conditions. The client should be informed that the therapist (and the agency or clinic) will be available if the need should arise in the future.

APPLICATION TO FAMILY AND GROUP WORK

Since its very beginning, the founders of IPT have highlighted the role of family factors in the etiology of depression (Klerman et al., 1984). The theoretical core of IPT, with its focus on interpersonal factors, emphasizes the role of the family in the causation and maintenance of psychiatric disorders. There is often a strong association between strained marital and family relationships and depression, and one form of IPT has been developed specifically for conjoint marital therapy (IPT-CM; Weissman & Markowitz, 1998). There is also a manual for IPT-CM. More positive results have been shown in reduction of depressive symptoms, and improvement in marital and sexual relations, when IPT-CM is used with couples, than in those couples treated only with IPT (Foley, cited in Weissman & Markowitz, 1998).

Regarding group work, a 10-session group format has been developed and tested, showing positive results in treating social phobics and bulimic clients (Weissman & Markowitz, 1998). This author believes that the development of group forms of intervention is one of the most outstanding aspects of the current advancements in IPT.

COMPATIBILITY WITH THE GENERALIST-ECLECTIC APPROACH

Although IPT is a specific type of psychodynamic therapy, it is compatible with the elements of a generalist-eclectic framework for social work practice. As much as is possible in a brief and time-limited treatment, the practitioners of IPT attempt a holistic assessment that is sensitive to the possible effects of biological, social, and historical factors. In relation to depression (still the main focus of IPT), the therapist pays particular attention to the effect of changes in the life cycle, especially those involving role and status changes. On issues such as diversity, oppression, and empowerment, IPT most certainly is oriented toward problems associated with gender bias and discrimination, particularly around the social roles of women that foster depression and eating disorders. IPT practitioners who work with HIV-positive men and women have recognized how such groups are "disenfranchised" (Swartz & Markowitz, 1998). Although this author believes that the practical, here-and-now emphasis of IPT lends itself to work with oppressed populations, it should be acknowledged that larger societal issues may tend to be overlooked in any time-limited approach that focuses on problems of immediate concern.

Similar to the generalist-eclectic framework, IPT promotes a therapeutic climate that emphasizes a collegial relationship. IPT is most certainly collaborative in that it encourages and requires the client to participate actively in the entire treatment process. Since its origins, the developers of IPT have stressed the positive qualities of their clients. Although critics might focus on the use of the "expert role" to "label" the client's depression as a medical illness, this is usually positively received by clients. It provides relief to those who either feel they are malingering or have been accused of malingering by significant others. For example, in client groups where there is an extremely strong work ethic, the retarded behavior of depression is often seen as malingering (Schwartz & Schwartz, 1993).

IPT's use of a variety of strategies and techniques to improve interpersonal relations can be viewed as a kind of "pragmatic eclecticism" (Goldfried & Padawer, 1982). Although we have pointed out that IPT has its genesis within the general psychodynamic orientation, it has similarities to behavioral and cognitive approaches. In IPT, the close, detailed examination of the interpersonal relationships of the client, along with the relating of these factors to mood and other changes, resembles the "contingency analysis" of the operant, or applied behavior, therapist (Schwartz, 1982). For instance, similar to IPT, much of Arieti and Bemporad's (1978) cognitive-behavioral focus on "dominant others" involves relating depression to disturbed interpersonal relations and unrealistic, unfulfilled expectations. There has, in fact, been some effort—deemed promising and successful—to combine IPT with cognitive-behavioral therapy (Jensen, 1990, 1994). Klerman and colleagues (1984) acknowledge that, ideally, a comprehensive approach to treatment would incorporate many different theoretical orientations (psychodynamic, cognitive-behavioral, biological, etc.). The IPT group sees such a comprehensive approach as a longer-term goal: "[G]iven the current state of science and health care, we believe it is valuable to focus on one approach and to explore its validity and utility" (Klerman et al., 1984, p. 18).

A CRITIQUE OF IPT

STRENGTHS

Since its inception, the practitioners of IPT have subjected their methods to careful investigation, and the evidence supporting IPT as a therapy for depression is extensive. Perhaps the most famous "test" of IPT was in the National Institute of Mental Health (NIMH) Treatment of Depression Collaborative Research Program. Two hundred and fifty depressed clients were assigned, at random, to cognitive-behavioral therapy (CBT), to IPT, to an antidepressant drug (Imipramine), and to a placebo and clinical management combination. Clients treated with IPT had the lowest dropout rate of any of the groups (23%) as compared to 32% for CBT and 32% for the entire sample (Elkin et al., 1989). For those clients who were the most depressed and impaired, IPT seemed more effective than CBT, but less effective than Imipramine plus clinical management. Among the "less severely depressed," the differences among the four conditions were "not significant" (Elkin et al., 1989). One follow-up study reported that IPT was superior to CBT for more seriously depressed clients (Klein & Ross, cited in Weissman & Markowitz, 1998).

IPT has proved to be useful as a maintenance approach for a longer period of time, even years, for depression-prone individuals. Periodic "booster" sessions have been shown to be effective by lessening the reappearance and seriousness of depressive symptoms (Markowitz & Weissman, 1995). IPT is the only treatment for depression that has been tested as a maintenance intervention for recurrent major depression (Spanier & Frank, 1998).

IPT has focused increasingly on different populations and problems. In the treatment of depression, IPT has been used with adolescents and seniors (Markowitz, 1998). As mentioned previously, IPT has proven valuable with HIV-infected clients who are depressed (Swartz & Markowitz, 1998) and with clients who suffer from bulimia nervosa (Fairburn, 1998).

Much of the ongoing research on IPT is aimed at specifying exactly which aspects of the IPT process are responsible for effecting change. Not surprising for a therapy oriented toward interpersonal relations, it was found that the severity of the client's presenting problem was less relevant to positive outcome than the client's ability to become involved in a "productive" relationship with the therapist (Foley, O'Malley, Rounsaville, Prusoff, & Weissman, 1987). This same study found that clients with negative expectations of therapy proved to be more difficult to treat; consequently, therapists were less successful with these clients (Foley et al., 1987). This research seems to buttress the importance of the therapeutic relationship and positive expectations of outcome in IPT for depression.

Another attribute of IPT is the growing evidence that experienced therapists, especially those with psychodynamic training, can use IPT manuals to become competent in the approach after a short training period. The fact that IPT is outlined and described in a usable treatment manual also heightens its ability to be examined methodologically, including making comparisons from therapist to therapist and from client to client (Mufson & Moreau, 1998).

LIMITATIONS

The literature on IPT suggests that it may not be applicable to the most
seriously depressed, especially those requiring institutionalization. For similar reasons, this author feels that IPT probably would not be useful with
psychotic or mentally handicapped clients. Attempts to apply IPT to substance abusers have proven to be unsuccessful (Weissman & Markowitz,
1998), although Mufson and Moreau (1998) have not ruled out using IPT-
A with substance-abusing adolescents. They recommend, however, that
these adolescents be referred for treatment of drug abuse before using
IPT-A, if they are not "clean." Currently, there does not seem to be any
form of IPT for use with children. This author thinks that IPT and IPT-A
could be adapted for preadolescent children of school age.

CASE EXAMPLE

IDENTIFYING AND BACKGROUND INFORMATION

Mary McCarthy (a pseudonym), 23 years old, had been tearful, sleepless,
experiencing "dark thoughts," and seeing the future as hopeless. She was
referred to the clinic by a neighbor who had been treated successfully for
depression. Mary, who was employed as a data processor and computer
technician at an insurance company, was very bright and successful in her
work. She had started to take night courses at a local college. She liked
these courses and the people she met, but discontinued night school when
her boyfriend, David, complained that he wanted more of her company.
Mary had been dating David for more than 4 years. She had known him
since they were both in grade school. She had always been eager to marry
David, but recently she had been feeling increasingly uncomfortable in
the relationship.

INITIAL PHASE (SESSIONS 1 AND 2)

In the first interview, Mary stated that she could no longer talk to David.
Communication between the two had dwindled and now, more often than
not, consisted of arguments or extended silences. They went out infre-
quently, either to a local movie or to the neighborhood pub, where they
drank, often to excess, with David's friends. The sexual relationship between
the two, which Mary initially found pleasurable, had become perfunctory
and unsatisfying.

Recently their arguing had become quite ugly, with verbal (but no physical) abuse from David. Arguing centered on Mary's wishing to return to

school, which David vehemently opposed. After these arguments, she would feel that "life has no meaning." She felt "like a worm," slept a lot, and was tired and listless at work. In the evenings, when she wasn't seeing David, she watched a lot of television. She had thought of suicide. She felt that the future was bleak, and she did not know what she was going to do. She kept avoiding pressure from David to "set a date."

Mary responded positively to the therapist's diagnosis of depression. She quickly grasped the connection between the depressed moods and the unresolved relationship with David. Part of the depression was related to the decreasing ability to communicate with David, and Mary's growing—but not consciously acknowledged—doubts about marrying him. Mary also quickly understood the relationship among the arguments, David's assaults, the feelings of depression, and the subsequent lowering of her self-esteem.

Both the therapist and Mary felt that medication was not indicated at this time because of the primarily reactive nature of the symptomatology. In setting the "contract" for the therapy, Mary and the therapist agreed that in the initial phase they would examine the current and past relationship between the couple. They would assess the positives and negatives, as well as the behaviors (and attitudes) on both their parts that might be feeding into the currently poor relationship, ultimately to determine Mary's true feelings for David prior to making a decision about marriage. They also would assess the realistic possibilities of changing the relationship, in particular, whether it could be improved by either of them.

Mary determined her "options" in the situation, which seemed to be staying with David and working on the relationship, temporarily interrupting the relationship (not seeing David), or ending the relationship. She rejected the last two options. David had refused to attend the sessions, calling the therapy "nonsense" and stating that all Mary had to do "to get better" was to "snap out of it" and marry him.

A portion of the discussion was to focus on Mary's occupational status and her desire for more education—on what this meant to Mary and what it implied for the relationship. Also to be examined were her friendships and relationships aside from David, an assessment of her "social networks" and what could be done to improve them. Central to these discussions was an examination of the relationship of the depressive reactions to these interpersonal disputes.

MIDDLE PHASE (SESSIONS 3 TO 11)

Mary and the therapist agreed that the discussions about marriage seemed to be at the "impasse" stage of resolution. Because David chose not to be involved in the therapy, Mary and the therapist explored Mary's perception of the agreements and disagreements in the couple's hopes for the relationship. Central to the dispute, and to her increasing resistance to the marriage, was Mary's thwarted desire for more education. She received high praise for her work as a computer technician but had risen as far as she could within the company where she worked without further technical training or, preferably, a college degree. In the course of the sessions, Mary came to realize how badly she wanted this advanced training and how unwilling she was to "settle" for the "traditional" role of a wife. David had stated his expectation that *his* wife would not have a career; she would stay at home, take care of their house, and raise their children.

Mary attempted to convey these feelings to David, who responded either with verbal abuse or with silence, often not calling Mary for several days and not returning her phone calls. When Mary told David how hurt she was by his behavior and by his lack of even trying to understand how she felt, he responded, "Then let's break up."

Mary and the therapist examined the alternatives. Although Mary tried to draw the therapist into making decisions for her, the therapist steadfastly avoided this. They discussed the future of the relationship and the possibility of working out some alternative that would allow Mary both the relationship and the future job training. Mary, herself, decided against marriage in the near future.

With the therapist's encouragement, Mary explored her options for education. She found that her company would pay for her college courses if she earned certain minimum grades and would make a commitment to remain with the firm for a specified time period. The company would even allow her a few hours of paid time off each week so that she could attend classes. With this information, she enrolled in school. Upon being presented with another ultimatum by David, she ended the relationship.

Termination Phase (Sessions 12 and 13)

In the termination phase, Mary discussed her now-ended relationship with David, her previous denial of her own needs and wants, and her lack of assertive behavior with David. Initially devastated by the breakup, Mary nonetheless responded enthusiastically to school. As she began to verbalize her hostility to David and her long-suppressed discontent with the relationship, her depressive moods lifted. She also began to shop for new clothing, in preparation for expanding her social life.

An avid reader, Mary began to read "self-help" books on depression and on male-female relationships, recommended by the therapist. She increasingly was able to draw connections between her "down feelings" and her interactions with others, particularly men, in her environment. She was symptom-free for the last three sessions and, upon follow-up, was busily attending school and dating several "eligible" young men.

Discussion

The above vignette has been edited to illustrate the main areas of IPT focus. In practice, most cases are not so clear-cut. Although the "strategy" of IPT calls for a focus on one problem area, sometimes two, it is conceivable that problem areas might be handled serially (e.g., grief, then role transition). It is also not uncommon that progress in one area has a "ripple" effect on another.

SUMMARY

IPT as a focused, short-term therapy appears to show promise for being an economical, effective, and useful approach not only for depression but also for a number of other problems. In the opinion of this author, the emphasis in IPT on the interpersonal aspects of clients' disorders is its main contribution. This represents a reawakening to the positive contribution of Sullivan and others, and may even serve a function to social workers as a clarion call to remember, and to reemphasize, the social in social work. Elements of this approach most likely will become part of even more effective models in the future.

NOTES

[1]Much of the content of this chapter, and the case example, are drawn from *Depression: Theories and Treatments,* by Arthur Schwartz and Ruth M. Schwartz © 1993 Columbia University Press. This content is used here with the permission of the publisher.

REFERENCES

Arieti, S., & Bemporad, J. (1978). *Severe and mild depression: The psychotherapeutic approach.* New York: Basic Books.

Bowlby, J. (1969). *Attachment.* New York: Basic Books.

Elkin, I., Shea, T., Watkins, J. T., Imber, S. D., Sotsky, S. M., Collins, J. F., Glass, D. R., Pilkonis, P. A., Leber, W. R., Docherty, J. F., Fiester, S. J., & Parloff, M. B. (1989). National Institute of Mental Health Treatment of Depression Collaborative Research Program: General effectiveness of treatments. *Archives of General Psychiatry, 46,* 971–982.

Fairburn, C. G. (1998). Interpersonal psychotherapy for bulimia nervosa. In J. C. Markowitz (Ed.), *Interpersonal psychotherapy* (pp. 99–128). Washington, DC: American Psychiatric Press.

Foley, S. H., O'Malley, S., Rounsaville, B., Prusoff, B. A., & Weissman, M. M. (1987). The relationship of patient difficulty to therapist performance in interpersonal psychotherapy of depression. *Journal of Affective Disorders, 12,* 207–217.

Goldfried, M. R., & Padawer, W. (1982). Current status and future directions in psychotherapy. In M. Goldfried (Ed.), *Converging themes in psychotherapy: Trends in psychodynamic, humanistic and behavioral practice* (p. 11). New York: Springer.

Jensen, C. C. (1990). *A new treatment modality for social work practice: Integrating cognitive behavioral theory and interpersonal theory in the treatment of major depression.* Unpublished doctoral dissertation, University of Denver, Colorado.

Jensen, C. C. (1994). Psychosocial treatment of depression in women: Nine single-subject evaluations. *Research on Social Welfare Practice, 4,* 267–282.

Klerman, G. L., & Weissman, M. M. (Eds.). (1993). *New applications of interpersonal psychotherapy.* Washington, DC: American Psychiatric Press.

Klerman, G. L., Weissman, M. M., Rounsaville, B. J., & Chevron, E. S. (1984). *Interpersonal psychotherapy of depression.* New York: Basic Books.

Markowitz, J. C. (Vol. Ed.). (1998). *Interpersonal psychotherapy: Vol. 17. Review of Psychotherapy Series.* Washington, DC: American Psychiatric Press.

Markowitz, J. C., & Weissman, M. M. (1995). Interpersonal psychotherapy. In E. E. Beckham & W. R. Leber (Eds.), *Handbook of depression* (2nd ed., pp. 376–390). New York: The Guilford Press.

Mead, G. H. (1934). *Mind, self and society.* Chicago: University of Chicago Press.

Mufson, L., & Moreau, D. (1998). Interpersonal psychotherapy for adolescent depression. In J. C. Markowitz (Vol. Ed.), *Interpersonal psychotherapy: Vol. 17. Review of psychotherapy series* (pp. 35–66). Washington, DC: American Psychiatric Press.

Mufson, L., Moreau, D., Weissman, M. M., & Klerman, G. L. (1993). *Interpersonal psychotherapy for depressed adolescents.* New York: The Guilford Press.

Reynolds, C. F., Frank, E., Houck, P. R., & Mazumdar, S. (1997). Which elderly patients with remitted depression remain well with continued interpersonal psychotherapy after discontinuation of antidepressant medication? *American Journal of Psychiatry, 154,* 958–962.

Schwartz, A. (1982). *The behavior therapies: Theories and applications.* New York: The Free Press.

Schwartz, A., & Schwartz, R. M. (1993). The interpersonal psychotherapy (IPT) approach. In A. Schwartz & R. M. Schwartz, *Depression: Theories and treatments: Psychological, biological, and social perspectives* (pp. 187–209). New York: Columbia University Press.

Spanier, C., & Frank, E. (1998). Maintenance interpersonal psychotherapy: A preventive treatment for depression. In J. C. Markowitz (Vol. Ed.), *Interpersonal psychotherapy: Vol. 17. Review of psychotherapy series* (pp. 67–97). Washington, DC: American Psychiatric Press.

Sullivan, H. S. (1953). *The interpersonal theory of psychiatry.* New York: Norton.

Swartz, H. A., & Markowitz, J. C. (1998). Interpersonal psychotherapy for the treatment of depression in HIV-positive men and women. In J. C. Markowitz (Vol. Ed.), *Interpersonal psychotherapy: Vol. 17. Review of psychotherapy series* (pp. 129–155). Washington, DC: American Psychiatric Press.

Weissman, M. M. (1998, April). The many uses of interpersonal therapy. *Harvard Mental Health Letter, 14*(10), 4–5.

Weissman, M. M., & Markowitz, J. C. (1998). An overview of interpersonal psychotherapy. In J. C. Markowitz (Vol. Ed.), *Interpersonal psychotherapy: Vol. 17. Review of psychotherapy series* (pp. 1–33). Washington, DC: American Psychiatric Press.

8

Self Psychology Theory

James I. Martin

Self psychology is a psychodynamic theory that originated in the United States only in the last 30 years. Although it was first conceived as a theory of psychoanalysis, self psychology is applicable to a wide variety of practice contexts and client populations. It is primarily used in clinical work with individuals.

According to this theory, people require an empathically responsive interpersonal environment to fuel their development and sustain their adaptive functioning. Many problems experienced by people today derive from an insufficiently responsive interpersonal environment. Practitioners using self psychology restore clients' adaptive functioning by meeting their needs for empathic understanding. To enhance adaptive functioning, practitioners help clients to influence their interpersonal environment more effectively so that it is more responsive to their psychological needs. Clients whose developmental process stalled because of a chronic lack of responsiveness in their interpersonal environment may need long-term intervention in order to build missing psychic structure.

HISTORICAL DEVELOPMENT

Self psychology originated with Heinz Kohut, who, as a young psychoanalyst, escaped the Nazi Holocaust and settled in the United States in 1942. Kohut eventually became president of the American Psychoanalytic Association. As a result of his clinical experience in postwar America, Kohut began to amend traditional psychoanalytic theory. Increasingly, Kohut found that the theory he had learned as a student of psychoanalysis did not fit the "narcissistic" problems of the clients he treated (Cushman, 1995). He gradually developed a new theory that attempted to explain and treat these problems, as they became more common in the growing "Culture of Narcissism" (Lasch, 1979). Kohut died in 1981, after which the development of self psychology continued on several different paths.

According to Bacal and Newman (1990), self psychology had its roots in both British object relations and ego psychology theories. Unlike classical psychoanalytic theory, which maintained that personality development resulted from the resolution of intrapsychic conflicts associated with biological drives, object relations theory claimed that development resulted from experiences in interpersonal relationships. Similarly, ego psychology theory minimized the importance of both the drives and intrapsychic conflict, instead stressing the development of "conflict-free" adaptive abilities. All three theories focused on early childhood as the boilerplate for adult psychopathology, for which the recommended treatment was psychoanalysis. Preceding Kohut, ego psychology theorist Hartmann (1939) and object relations theorist Winnicott (1965) expressed interest both in the self as the core of the personality and in the important role of an average expectable environment for normal development.

Since Kohut's death, self psychology's influence has gone far beyond the domain of psychoanalysis. Writers in several fields have continued to develop the theory in a variety of ways. Some theorists continue to examine the theory within the context of psychoanalysis and long-term psychoanalytic psychotherapy, although among them there are different perspectives on important clinical and theoretical issues (Fosshage, 1998; Stolorow, Brandchaft, & Atwood, 1987; Wolf, 1988). New developments are continuing in the application of self psychology theory to interventions with couples (O'Connor, 1993), families (Pinsof, 1995), and groups (Harwood, 1992), and to short-term interventions with individuals (Gardner, 1991; Martin, 1993). The theory is used increasingly to understand and treat people's problems across the life span (Goldmeier & Fandetti, 1992; Miller, 1996; Shreve & Kunkel, 1991). In an even greater departure from its psychoanalytic origins, some writers are examining the theory's relevance to practice in child welfare settings (Goldmeier & Fandetti, 1991), in supervision of clinical trainees (Gardner, 1995), and for understanding health risk behaviors in large populations (Martin & Knox, 1995, 1997).

Social workers have been exposed to self psychology theory since its early development. In 1970, the University of Chicago Student Mental Health Clinic's chief psychiatric social worker, Miriam Elson, invited Kohut to lead a year-long multidisciplinary seminar on the treatment of young adults. Case vignettes were presented for discussion and analysis, resulting in two published volumes of Kohut's work (Elson, 1986, 1987). Since Kohut's death, numerous social workers have continued to interpret and expand the theory and its application to direct practice (Chenot, 1998; Elson, 1986; Goldstein, 1997; Martin, 1993; Mishne, 1993; Paradis, 1993; Young, 1994).

CENTRAL THEORETICAL CONSTRUCTS

SELF-COHESIVENESS AND SELF-FRAGMENTATION

Self psychology concerns itself with the relative cohesiveness of the human *self*, the enduring central core of the personality. The self may be evaluated on a continuum from *cohesive* to *fragmented*, as both a long-term characteristic and a short-term state. Thus, even a person with a relatively cohesive self may experience states of *self-fragmentation*. An individual's abilities to regulate self-esteem, monitor and regulate stress, and pursue realistic goals indicate *self-cohesiveness*. In states of self-cohesiveness, people may feel energized, self-efficacious, focused, and whole. They may function relatively well in their social and occupational roles. Conversely, unstable self-esteem, inability to self-soothe, and problems with goal attainment are indicators of self-fragmentation. In states of self-fragmentation, people may feel weakened, hopeless, confused, and scattered. They may experience difficulties in role performance. Addictive behaviors, depression, insomnia, suicide, panic, somatic preoccupations, social withdrawal, and nonorganic cognitive impairments may indicate a state of self-fragmentation.

BASIC STRUCTURE OF THE SELF

Most contemporary theorists consider the self to be a tripolar structure. The three poles—called the *pole of ambitions*, the *pole of ideals*, and the *pole of twinship*—are actually major themes of self-related experience that develop over a lifetime. The pole of ambitions consists of experiences of uniqueness, vigor, and greatness. The pole of ideals consists of experiences of calm, support, and uplift. The pole of twinship consists of experiences of essential belonging and likeness to others. Kohut (1977) theorized that people are born with a primitive *virtual self* that contains the seeds from which the three poles of self-structure grow. These poles consist of needs for admiration, praise, and confirmation (*mirroring needs*); for calming, supportive, and uplifting responses from others (*idealizing needs*); and for acceptance and kinship responses (*twinship needs*). Self-structure develops in the three poles as a result of interactions between the virtual self (and later, the developing self) and the interpersonal environment. To the extent that any of these needs are understood and met with appropriate responses from significant others over time, self-structure is built in each of the poles. However, to the extent that any of these needs are repeatedly misunderstood or disregarded, self-structure fails to develop.

SELFOBJECT NEEDS AND FUNCTIONS

Self psychology calls the needs for mirroring, idealizing, and twinship *selfobject needs*, appropriate responses to them *selfobject functions*, and the sources of those responses *selfobjects*. Selfobjects are one's subjective experiences of people as they respond in ways that enhance one's self-cohesiveness. Selfobjects that respond empathically to mirroring needs are mirroring selfobjects, and selfobjects that respond to idealizing or twinship needs are, respectively, idealizing and twinship selfobjects. When parents provide what they believe to be reassurance and calming responses to their child's distress, they themselves are not idealizing selfobjects. In this case, the selfobjects are simply those dimensions of the parents that the child experiences as providing reassurance and calm. In addition, although a parent might provide reassurance and calm, it might not be quite the response that the child needs at that moment. In other words, a person's subjective experience of having his or her selfobject needs met is far more important than any outsider's objective view of the interaction. Therefore, the only way to know whether an interpersonal response provided a selfobject function for a person is to examine whether that response resulted in enhancement of the person's self-cohesion.

Self psychology views the development of the adult self as the result of innumerable experiences of empathic responsiveness to an individual's selfobject needs. Gradually, selfobject functions provided externally become internalized as self-functions through a process called *transmuting internalization*. Self psychology theorists have debated the process by which transmuting internalization results in the building of self-structure. Kohut (1977) proposed that development of self-structure requires some frustration of selfobject needs (*optimal frustration*). According to this formulation, children whose selfobject needs are understood and met perfectly have no reason to internalize the selfobject functions, so they will remain dependent on external sources. However, occasional lapses in empathic responsiveness by external sources provides motivation for children to take over a bit of the mirroring, idealizing, or twinship functions for themselves. As long as the lapses are not too frequent or severe, they will result in the gradual building of self-structure. Later theorists (Bacal, 1985; Stolorow, 1983) argued that the inevitable lapses in empathic responsiveness during development are incidental to the development of self-structure. Rather, self-structure develops as a result of the gradual accumulation of experiences of empathic responsiveness (*optimal responsiveness*).

Although self psychology considers the process of development as one in which individuals gradually increase their ability to meet their own selfobject needs, it also asserts that people never become completely independent of selfobjects (Elson, 1986). Especially during periods of severe stress, disappointment, loss, or illness, adults who have cohesive self-structures can still experience heightened needs for externally provided selfobject functions in order to restore or maintain their self-cohesiveness. Kohut and Wolf (1978) called such episodes *secondary disorders of the self*, or temporary self-fragmentation states that occur in a person with a cohesive self-structure. They called problems associated with deficits in self-structure *primary disorders of the self*. These disorders exist because of chronic lapses in empathic responsiveness to selfobject needs associated with at least two of the three poles during the course of development. Although people usually can compensate for deficits in one pole of self-structure with strengths in another pole, they cannot overcome deficits in two or more poles in this way (Kohut, 1977). People with primary disorders of the self are highly vulnerable to experiencing self-fragmentation states. They may experience emotional distress and cognitive or behavioral symptoms in reaction to a much wider variety of stressors than people with more cohesive self-structures (Martin & Knox, 1995).

Children and adults alike cue others to respond to their selfobject needs through *transference*. In traditional psychoanalytic theory, transference is considered irrational, deriving from unresolved developmental conflicts. However, self psychology views transference as a normal component of interpersonal relationships, consisting of expectations (Elson, 1986) that are not always related to developmental issues. For example, people with a secondary disorder of the self may express strong needs for mirroring or idealizing through transference even though they have a cohesive self.

ROLE OF DEFENSES

Although most people probably develop defenses designed to protect themselves from fragmentation, people with primary disorders of the self are especially likely use primitive defenses to protect their fragile self-structure. *Withdrawal* and *disavowal* are two noteworthy defenses described by Basch (1988). Withdrawal is the most primitive defense against experiencing painful affect. Infants may withdraw either by turning attention away from the source of displeasure or by falling asleep. Similarly, adults may withdraw behaviorally from social interaction in order to prevent expected injuries to their self. People utilizing disavowal unconsciously block the formation of a link between their perception of a threatening event and the development of the painful affect that would likely be associated with it. As a result, they have no awareness of unpleasant feelings associated with the event. In addition to these defenses, people with primary disorders of the self are likely to have defensive structures consisting of frequent behaviors and/or fantasies used to cover over their self-structure deficits (Elson, 1987) and prevent fragmentation. One example is a combination of social withdrawal and retreat into wish-fulfillment fantasies, and another is the use of chemical abuse and compulsive sex. In both examples the use of these defensive structures may lessen the frequency or severity of self-fragmentation episodes through behavioral, cognitive, and/or affective avoidance of threatening stimuli.

A HOPEFUL VIEW OF DEVELOPMENT

Even though self psychology considers childhood to be the most critical period of time for the development of self-structure, it regards development as a never-ending process. Kohut believed that maladaptive patterns are only "way stations on the path to health" (Elson, 1987, p. 36). In other words, disorders of the self should not be considered permanent characteristics. In a sufficiently responsive interpersonal environment, people with such disorders may progress along a developmental spiral of increasing self-esteem and competence to establish a new equilibrium (Basch, 1988).

PHASES OF HELPING

Although Kohut's theories about the self and its development have become increasingly popular, his theory of treatment is perhaps even more significant (Chernus, 1988). The concept of the *empathic mode of listening* is particularly important. Practitioners who use self psychology seek to understand clients' subjective experience of reality throughout the helping process, and they intervene from the perspective of that knowledge. They attempt to understand how and why clients feel and think the way they do, assuming that at some level even the most maladaptive and troublesome behavior must make sense. The empathic mode of listening distinguishes self psychology from other clinical models in which practitioners strive for objectivity as external observers of clients and their problems. For example, the concept of cognitive distortions, as used in cognitive therapy, is incompatible with the empathic mode because it presumes the practitioner understands objective reality better than the client.

The following description of self psychology in the social work helping process focuses on short-term interventions. Because Kohut's original theory of treatment was a theory of psychoanalysis, it must be modified in several ways in order to be useful for short-term practice. According to Martin (1993), these modifications include a selection of limited treatment goals and a decrease in emphasis on transference material.

ENGAGEMENT

Because self psychology places great emphasis on developing an empathic understanding of clients, practitioners do not challenge a client's interpretation of events during the engagement phase of the helping process. Instead, they focus on understanding how the client experiences events, as well as the affect and meaning associated with them. Practitioners attempt to support the client's subjective experience, although they may not necessarily agree with it. Attention to affect is a critical component of engaging clients for two reasons. First, affect provides the primary motivation for all behavior. Second, self psychology considers the acceptance and understanding of one's feelings a fundamental human need (Basch, 1988).

ASSESSMENT

The primary focus of assessment, according to self psychology, is clients' relative self-cohesiveness. Thus, practitioners must determine whether their clients are experiencing a state of self-fragmentation. Here, examining clients' recent history is critical. Clients who report numerous episodes of self-fragmentation may have a primary disorder of the self and/or they may live in an extraordinarily stressful environment. By contrast, clients experiencing isolated episodes of self-fragmentation are likely to have a secondary disorder of the self. In either case, practitioners must determine clients' particular selfobject needs in order to help them restore self-cohesiveness.

Kohut (1959/1978) emphasized the importance of empathy as a scientific tool used for collecting data about clients' subjective reality. Although empathy is most likely to be used this way in intensive, long-term clinical practice, it remains a component of the assessment process in short-term practice. Basch (1988) explained how practitioners obtain and use data through introspection and empathy. The first step is to focus one's awareness on the affects that are stimulated in oneself through interactions with the client. Second, practitioners attempt to view their affective reaction from an objective perspective, rather than simply experiencing it. Third, practitioners examine whether their affective reaction is related to the client's behavior and verbal message. In the fourth step, practitioners attempt to determine how the information gained through their own introspection may enhance understanding of the client's behavior and verbal message.

The most important information about clients' selfobject needs is expressed through their transference to the practitioner. The use of introspection and empathy is especially important for obtaining this information. Expressions of transference are most likely to emerge in the course of longer-term, intensive intervention. Because of self psychology's view of transference as a normal component of interpersonal relationships, practitioners should also look for it in even the briefest professional contacts with clients. In the course of short-term intervention, practitioners may also obtain information about clients' selfobject needs and defensive strategies by examining their interpersonal relationship patterns. For this reason, data concerning clients' current and past interpersonal relationships are extremely important for assessment.

INTERVENTION

When clients have a secondary disorder of the self, intervention must be oriented toward restoring self-cohesiveness so that they can resume their previous level of functioning. In some cases, a practitioner's focused empathic understanding may be sufficient for this purpose. Thus, some clients feel restored after only a single session or two, even before any formal interventions begin. In other cases, directly providing selfobject functions in response to clients' mirroring, idealizing, and/or twinship needs acts to restore their self-cohesiveness (Elson, 1986; Lazarus, 1991; Paradis, 1993).

In order to accomplish significant improvements in primary disorders of the self, practitioners must help clients to internalize self-structure that they currently lack through long-term, insight-oriented intervention. In the short term, practitioners can be helpful to such clients by focusing intervention on bolstering self-cohesiveness, but this strategy will not resolve the underlying primary disorder. To the extent that limited time and resources allow, practitioners also should help to enhance self-cohesiveness in order to reduce the frequency or severity of future fragmentation episodes. Martin (1993) described some ways in which practitioners can do so, including raising clients' consciousness about their needs for particular selfobject functions and building better strategies for getting those needs met.

When raising clients' consciousness about their selfobject needs, practitioners should avoid psychotherapeutic terminology. They can reduce client shame associated with needing other people by universalizing these needs. Adult clients may be surprised and relieved to learn that no one is entirely independent, and that we all need others to praise or support us from time to time. By using examples from clients' reported patterns of interpersonal relationships, along with appropriate use of transference, practitioners can help clients identify the selfobject functions they appear to need most in order to maintain their self-cohesiveness (Martin, 1993; Young, 1994). Practitioners also should help clients analyze the extent to which members of their current support system are responsive to their needs.

When helping clients strategize better ways to get their needs met in relationships with others, a number of options should be considered. In some cases, clients might need help in changing patterns of communication in order to express their needs more clearly or assertively. In other cases, they might need help in accepting the limitations of significant others and in identifying new sources of needed selfobject functions. As described by Young (1994), practitioners might need to intervene in the interpersonal environment in order to improve its responsiveness, especially when clients are children or adolescents. For example, they could educate parents about more effective ways of responding to their child's needs, or they could provide the opportunity for new selfobjects by drawing on appropriate community resources.

TERMINATION

Consistent with the use of the empathic mode, practitioners should focus on understanding clients' subjective experience of impending termination.

When clients experience termination as a positive transition, practitioners should not insist that they are denying negative feelings. When clients experience mild self-fragmentation as the termination date nears, practitioners should explore clients' feelings about terminating. The practitioner's focused empathic attention should help to restore cohesiveness. The longer the length of intervention, the more time practitioners should allow clients to prepare for termination. A single session might be sufficient for brief service, but as many as three or four might be needed when service lasts more than 6 months.

As part of termination, practitioners should review the extent to which clients feel they attained the goals set at the beginning of the helping process, even if objective measures were used to monitor progress. Especially when intervention is short-term, practitioners should help clients identify the extent to which they have remaining problems and strategize ways for them to work toward managing those problems in the future. Such strategies might lead to referrals for other services, including support, self-help, or therapy groups. At minimum, practitioners should encourage clients to maintain awareness of those situations or behaviors that precipitated the most recent fragmentation episode and to seek interactions with others that help enhance their self-cohesiveness.

APPLICATION TO FAMILY AND GROUP WORK

Pinsof (1995) conceptualized self psychology as the deepest of the theoretical orientations that may guide practitioners' understanding of families and their problems in that the self is "the most fundamental layer of human existence" (p. 20). When practitioners find that the fragile self-structure of a family member presents significant constraints on a family's ability to resolve its problems, they should consider referring that member for individual treatment. Solomon (1988) made similar recommendations for practitioners treating "narcissistically vulnerable" couples. Ungar and Levene (1994) described how viewing a family as a matrix of selfobjects can enhance practitioners' understanding of the family. In other words, the family, as a "supraordinate selfobject" (p. 307), may function collectively to satisfy its members' needs for mirroring, idealizing, and/or twinship. This view adds to an understanding of dyadic relationships between family members, and it may help self psychology–informed practitioners engaged in family treatment to maintain a systemic paradigm.

Several authors (Harwood & Pines, 1998; Shapiro, 1991; Stone, 1992) have examined the application of self psychology to group work. Harwood (1992) stated that self psychology may be particularly useful in group work when treating clients with narcissistic and borderline problems. Groups conducted from the perspective of self psychology focus on restoring or enhancing the self-cohesiveness of their individual members. Group members and leaders are potential sources of selfobject functions. In addition, the group as a whole—the *group self*—may serve as a source of selfobject functions for its members. Thus, a group member experiencing an episode of self-fragmentation might regain cohesiveness through participation with the group as a whole, as opposed to interactions with a particularly significant member of the group.

COMPATIBILITY WITH THE GENERALIST-ECLECTIC FRAMEWORK

The use of self psychology in direct social work practice is certainly compatible with a generalist-eclectic framework. Because self psychology is really three theories in one—a theory of development, a theory of psychopathology, and a theory of treatment—it may provide a metaframework for both understanding and treating clients while allowing for a variety of intervention techniques and strategies. In addition, practitioners using the empathic mode avoid limiting assessments to narrow theoretical preconceptions because they must subordinate any theoretical formulations to clients' subjective reality.

Finally, self psychology emphasizes the importance of client-practitioner relationships characterized by warmth, genuineness, respect, and collaboration. It puts the highest value on the practitioner's use of empathy. At the center of the theory is the assertion that empathic responsiveness resolves client problems associated with self-fragmentation (Chenot, 1998). In addition, the disciplined use of empathy is a part of the assessment process. Because self psychology emphasizes clients' subjective reality over objective reality, it is well suited for respecting and supporting client uniqueness. Because it asserts that people naturally progress toward maturity and health (Chenot, 1998), self psychology–informed treatment empowers clients by supporting and adding to their strengths and removing obstacles to progress.

CRITIQUE OF THE THEORY

As conceptualized by Kohut (1977, 1984), self psychology was intended to guide long-term, intensive interventions with individuals. Practitioners limited to brief or short-term interventions with individuals, families, or groups are likely to find self psychology unhelpful unless they make significant modifications to the theory as indicated in this chapter.

Cushman (1995) warned that clinical practitioners who ignore the political, social, and economic forces that fuel the growth of "narcissistic" clinical problems in contemporary society might unknowingly contribute to them. According to Cushman, the dominant construction of the self in contemporary American society is the "empty self," of which the feeling of existential emptiness is a primary characteristic. A main reason for this feeling is the extreme emphasis on self-contained individuality by society's institutions and the consequent destruction of family and interpersonal relationships. Today's consumerist economy contributes to this feeling of emptiness because people must purchase more and more products (including psychotherapy) in order for the economy to function well. However, people's existential emptiness cannot be relieved by a product alone, and so both the emptiness and the promotion of products to relieve it continue endlessly. Cushman argued that relying on self psychology to understand and treat people's problems might contribute to society's overemphasis on self-contained individuality and result in existential emptiness. Thus, practitioners must maintain awareness of the political, social, and economic forces affecting clients and expand their repertoire of intervention strategies beyond those designed to resolve intrapsychic problems.

The extent to which self psychology is applicable across cultural groups is not clear. By its very focus on the individual self, the theory expresses Western cultural traditions. As noted by Steele (1998), these traditions place great value on a "strong self" (p. 94), which Western psychotherapy views as a desirable goal of development. However, among Asian cultures a strong self is often considered a sign of arrested development, and the transcendence of selfhood may be a more desirable goal.

Gardiner (1987) has criticized self psychology theorists for ignoring gender as an important developmental variable. Layton (1990) went further in charging that Kohut's conception of the self was androcentric. However, Gardiner (1987) also stated that in many other ways self psychology is compatible with feminist theory. For example, it values empathy and interpersonal relatedness over rational insight and autonomy. Lang (1990) and Gardiner (1987) agreed that the methods of self psychology, especially its use of the empathic mode, could be important for developing a deeper understanding of women, their needs, and their experiences.

Self psychology is most suited to clinical social work services with clients having primary or secondary disorders of the self. The former category includes those clients with narcissistic, borderline, or avoidant personality disorders (American Psychiatric Association, 1994), whereas the latter category includes all clients experiencing a reduction in their psychological and/or social functioning. Self psychology may be less useful for treatment of clients who are actively psychotic. Although certain elements of self psychology—especially the emphasis on empathic responsiveness—may be applicable to any kind of social work service, the theory as a whole is not suited to practice situations limited to providing concrete services or making referrals.

CASE EXAMPLE

Margaret F., a 39-year-old White female, self-referred to an outpatient mental health center because of trouble managing stress associated with her marriage and other sources. She decided to seek professional help 2 weeks after she asked her husband, Thomas, for some support, and he responded by getting angry. Margaret had been married for 2 years to Thomas, age 44, but they had no plans to have children. According to Margaret, Thomas believed that people should deal with stress on their own and not rely on others. Margaret recently began a job directing a small child welfare organization, her first job in 5 years. She felt underpaid, so she was continuing to look for a better paying job.

Margaret previously was married to David for 15 years. The marriage ended 2 years ago in a difficult divorce in which she lost custody of their two daughters (current ages 7 and 11). She identified her drinking binges during the last couple of years of the marriage as the reason why David won custody of the children. However, she reported that David abused alcohol and drugs too. She felt that her attorney did not represent her well. The divorce decree allowed her to see the children two weekends every month and for 6 weeks during the summer. Because David always refused to help her, for each visit Margaret drove more than 2 hours each way to pick up and return the children. Margaret reported that Thomas had two previous marriages that both ended in divorce. He had one son, who was living on his own. Margaret grew up on a farm in rural Illinois. When she was 13 years old, her parents divorced; they both remarried. She was the oldest of three sisters, in addition to having a half brother and a stepbrother. Her relationships with both full sisters were strained.

Near the end of the first session, the social worker, Charles D., reflected that Margaret wanted support and that her life sounded very scattered. He told her that it would be difficult to work on improving her marital relationship in individual therapy and recommended couples treatment for this purpose. However, Margaret did not want couples treatment because she wanted to work on "her part" in the marital problems. Charles honored her request for individual therapy and suggested meeting nine more times, for a total of 10 sessions. They contracted to work on the obstacles that Margaret put in the way of getting the support she wanted.

In the second session, Margaret talked easily and freely. When Charles asked Margaret about sources of support in her life other than her husband, she identified her stepmother and a few women friends. However, she complained of having little time to do anything socially with them. During the session, Charles sometimes found it hard to get a word in edgewise. Although it was not yet clear, he wondered if this pattern might reflect a mirroring transference in which Margaret just wanted to be heard. During this session he also learned that her refusal to engage in marital therapy was related to a theme of not being heard or understood. She and David had engaged in marital counseling, but she felt that the therapist sided with her ex-husband and blamed her for everything. At the end of the session, Charles gave Margaret the following homework assignment: She was to make a list of specific situations she would like help in changing. They would prioritize them in the next session.

At the beginning of the third session, Charles asked Margaret about the previous week's assignment. She said that although she did it, she forgot to bring it with her. Attempting to recall the list, she talked about two types of situations that she found difficult. The first involved a co-worker who seemed hypersensitive and critical. The second involved her husband, who made it hard for her to express her own needs and stand up for herself. Charles asked what got in the way of her speaking up more with her husband. It didn't take Margaret long to identify that she was afraid—afraid of being alone. Talking about being alone made her think about not being able to make ends meet financially. Coming close to tears, Margaret recalled the poverty of her family of origin, which led to strong memories of being treated unfairly by her mother. She felt that her mother's unwillingness to spend money to buy her new clothes like other children had expressed a lack of support and understanding. Focusing on feelings was uncomfortable for Margaret. For homework, Charles asked her to continue paying attention to her feelings. She agreed, then asked if they could shift back to a more cognitive focus afterwards. Charles thought that working on a more cognitive level probably allowed Margaret to avoid some of the potent issues preventing her from getting on with her life.

Charles asked about the homework assignment at the beginning of the fourth session. Margaret reported that she did focus on her feelings during the week. She also quit her job, and her husband supported her doing so. It turned out that he was supportive, though inconsistently. Margaret also talked about problems with her mother. She always experienced her mother as lacking interest in, or understanding of, her feelings. Margaret voiced concerns that she was "too needy." Charles responded that this was not possible, because her needs were what they were. He added that the problem was not her needs, but whether other people were meeting them.

In the sixth session Margaret spent much of the session talking about her mother. She reported calling her mother to say that she wasn't angry with her anymore, adding that she was letting go of all her anger. Considering the strong feelings that Margaret had expressed about her mother in previous sessions, Charles thought this conversation had an unreal quality to it. He responded that it wasn't clear to him how Margaret could "let it go," and asked her to explain it to him. She said that she had been angry her whole life and was tired of it. The anger wasn't good for her. Charles asked her to tell him about it. As she talked about her anger, it became clear that behind it was the fear that her mother would again betray her.

Charles clarified that Margaret had certainly expressed anger at her mother over the years, but added that she had not expressed the feelings that lay behind it. He said that when she was able to do so, and resolve the issue, she would naturally move beyond the feeling of anger. He asked if this made sense to her, and she said that it did. Charles said that, in order for Margaret and her mother to have a relationship of any kind, Margaret would have to set the parameters. She would have to define the kinds of interactions they would have and the ways in which her mother would have to treat her. Although this made sense to Margaret, she said that it sounded difficult. Charles reminded her that they had only four more sessions, and it would be good to see her accomplish this change before their work ended.

At the beginning of the seventh session, Margaret reported that she called her mother and told her what she expects if they are to have any kind of relationship. She said that, although the conversation felt good, she was aware that her mother could betray her again. Margaret also talked about some recent conflicts with her husband regarding finances. Charles commented that perhaps the couple needed to work out a budget and an agreement on handling their finances.

Margaret spent most of the eighth session talking about David. She said that he "ranted and raved" on the phone after their older daughter visited her. She stood her ground with him on several areas of disagreement. She reported that this was not the first time she had done so, but it was the first time that she did not feel guilty about it. Charles drew parallels between Margaret's relationships with David, her mother, and Thomas, in which she had ignored her own feelings and needs out of fear of being betrayed. In order to be treated better, she would need to verbalize how she felt and what she wanted.

In the ninth session Margaret reported that her mother followed through on some things that she had asked her to do regarding the children. Instead of feeling pleased, Margaret felt hurt and angry because her mother didn't do everything that she asked. Charles supported these feelings as understandable, but he also encouraged Margaret to give her mother positive feedback for following through partly. He said that it seemed any attention to her needs by her mother made her more aware of what she did not get over the years. Perhaps she used anger to insulate herself from feeling hurt and disappointed. Margaret thought this made sense. Charles encouraged her to keep asking her mother for what she wanted, to keep paying attention to her own feelings, and to try not to remain stuck in her angry/defensive posture. Near the end of the session, Margaret talked about having some positive interactions with her husband.

In the tenth session Margaret said that she spent a 4-day weekend with her mother, sister, and daughters. She felt emotionally and physically depleted from the long weekend. She tried to explain to her sister how she felt about their mother, but her sister didn't understand. Margaret made a point to thank her mother for helping with the children, and asked her to go a step further. Because her mother didn't respond, it wasn't clear if she would follow through. Charles told Margaret that it sounded as if her family did not support her feelings or respond to her needs for attention or confirmation regarding her unique worth, which left her feeling disappointed, hurt, and angry. He told her that these needs were normal, and so were the feelings of disappointment, hurt, and anger. He encouraged her to keep trying to get the kind of understanding she wanted and deserved from her family, while realizing that she might not always get it. He also encouraged her to develop other sources of support, including her husband. Margaret said that she had accomplished the goal that she set at the outset of treatment. She thought that discovering her fear, and how her feelings were important and valid, was the most valuable lesson that she learned. However, she identified reaching an agreement with her husband about their finances and the possibility of her older daughter coming to live with her as challenges yet to be faced.

SUMMARY

Disorders of the self may be some of the most common problems encountered in clinical practice today (Cushman, 1995; Lasch, 1978; Martin, 1993), and self psychology is uniquely relevant for understanding and treating them. Although self psychology originated as a form of psychoanalysis, the above case illustrates how it may be applied to short-term social work practice. Its focus on clients' subjective experience helps them to feel understood, and it may help to reduce the potential for treatment biases according to ethnicity, gender, sexual orientation, and other aspects of client diversity. However, there is little written about the use of self psychology in treatment of ethnic minorities, gay men and lesbians, or children. Few articles describe short-term applications of self psychology, and none report on its effectiveness in treatment. These are important areas for continued development.

REFERENCES

American Psychiatric Association. (1994). *Diagnostic and statistical manual of mental disorders* (4th ed.). Washington, DC: Author.

Bacal, H. A. (1985). Optimal responsiveness and the therapeutic process. In A. Goldberg (Ed.), *Progress in self psychology* (Vol. 1, pp. 202–227). New York: Guilford.

Bacal, H. A., & Newman, K. M. (1990). *Theories of object relations: Bridges to self psychology*. New York: Columbia University Press.

Basch, M. F. (1988). *Understanding psychotherapy: The science behind the art*. New York: Basic Books.

Chenot, D. K. (1998). Mutual values: Self psychology, intersubjectivity, and social work. *Clinical Social Work Journal, 26,* 297–311.

Chernus, L. A. (1988). Why Kohut endures. *Clinical Social Work Journal, 16,* 336–354.

Cushman, P. (1995). *Constructing the self, constructing America: A cultural history of psychotherapy*. Reading, MA: Addison-Wesley.

Elson, M. (1986). *Self psychology in clinical social work*. New York: Norton.

Elson, M. (Ed.). (1987). *The Kohut seminars on self psychology and psychotherapy with adolescents and young adults*. New York: Norton.

Fosshage, J. L. (1998). Self psychology and its contributions to psychoanalysis: An overview. *Journal of Analytic Social Work, 5*(2), 1–17.

Gardiner, J. K. (1987). Self psychology as feminist theory. *Signs: Journal of Women in Culture and Society, 12,* 761–780.

Gardner, J. R. (1991). The application of self psychology to brief psychotherapy. *Psychoanalytic Psychology, 8,* 477–500.

Gardner, J. R. (1995). Supervision of trainees: Tending the professional self. *Clinical Social Work Journal, 23,* 271–286.

Goldmeier, J., & Fandetti, D. V. (1991). Self psychology in child welfare practice. *Child Welfare, 70,* 559–570.

Goldmeier, J., & Fandetti, D. V. (1992). Self psychology in clinical intervention with the elderly. *Families in Society, 73,* 214–221.

Goldstein, E. G. (1997). To tell or not to tell: The disclosure of events in the therapist's life to the patient. *Clinical Social Work Journal, 25,* 41–58.

Hartmann, H. (1939). *Ego psychology and the problem of adaptation.* New York: International Universities Press.

Harwood, I. H. (1992). Advances in group psychotherapy and self psychology: An intersubjective approach. *Group, 16,* 220–232.

Harwood, I. H., & Pines, M. (1998). *Self experiences in group: Intersubjective and self psychological pathways to human understanding.* London: Jessica Kingsley.

Kohut, H. (1977). *The restoration of the self.* New York: International Universities Press.

Kohut, H. (1978). Introspection, empathy and psychoanalysis: An examination of the relationship between mode of observation and theory. In P. Ornstein (Ed.), *The search for the self: Selected writings of Heinz Kohut, 1950–1978* (Vol. 1, pp. 205–232). New York: International Universities Press. (Original work published 1959)

Kohut, H. (1984). *How does analysis cure?* Chicago: University of Chicago Press.

Kohut, H., & Wolf, E. S. (1978). Disorders of the self and their treatment. *International Journal of Psychoanalysis, 59,* 413–425.

Lang, J. A. (1990). Self psychology and the understanding and treatment of women. *Review of Psychiatry, 9,* 384–402.

Lasch, C. (1978). *The culture of narcissism.* New York: Norton.

Layton, L. (1990). A deconstruction of Kohut's concept of the self. *Contemporary Psychoanalysis, 26,* 420–429.

Lazarus, L. W. (1991). Elderly. In H. Jackson (Ed.), *Using self psychology in psychotherapy* (pp. 135–149). Northvale, NJ: Jason Aronson.

Martin, J. I. (1993). Self psychology and cognitive treatment: An integration. *Clinical Social Work Journal, 21,* 385–394.

Martin, J. I., & Knox, J. (1995). HIV risk behavior in gay men with unstable self esteem. *Journal of Gay and Lesbian Social Services, 2*(2), 21–41.

Martin, J. I., & Knox, J. (1997). Self-esteem instability and its implications for HIV prevention among gay men. *Health and Social Work, 22,* 264–273.

Miller, J. P. (1996). *Using self psychology in child psychotherapy.* Northvale, NJ: Jason Aronson.

Mishne, J. M. (1993). *The evolution and application of clinical theory: Perspective from four psychologies.* New York: The Free Press.

O'Connor, D. (1993). The impact of dementia: A self psychological perspective. *Journal of Gerontological Social Work, 20*(3–4), 113–128.

Paradis, B. A. (1993). A self-psychological approach to the treatment of gay men with AIDS. *Clinical Social Work Journal, 21,* 405–416.

Pinsof, W. M. (1995). *Integrative problem-centered therapy.* New York: Basic Books.

Shapiro, E. (1991). Empathy and safety in group: A self psychological perspective. *Group, 15,* 219–224.

Shreve, B. W., & Kunkel, M. A. (1991). Self psychology, shame, and adolescent suicide: Theoretical and practical considerations. *Journal of Counseling and Development, 69,* 305–311.

Solomon, M. F. (1988). Treatment of narcissistic vulnerability in marital therapy. In A. Goldberg (Ed.), *Learning from Kohut: Progress in self psychology* (Vol. 4, pp. 215–230). Hillsdale, NJ: Analytic Press.

Steele, S. (1998). Self beyond ego: A new perspective. *Journal of Humanistic Psychology, 38*(1), 93–100.

Stolorow, R. (1983). Self psychology—a structural psychology. In J. D. Lichtenberg & S. Kaplan (Eds.), *Reflections on self psychology* (pp. 287–296). Hillsdale, NJ: Analytic Press.

Stolorow, R., Brandchaft, B., & Atwood, G. (1987). *Psychoanalytic treatment: An intersubjective approach.* Hillsdale, NJ: Analytic Press.

Stone, W. N. (1992). The place of self psychology in group psychotherapy: A status report. *International Journal of Group Psychotherapy, 42,* 335–350.

Ungar, M. T., & Levene, J. E. (1994). Selfobject functions of the family: Implications for family therapy. *Clinical Social Work Journal, 22,* 303–316.

Winnicott, D. W. (1965). *The maturational processes and the facilitating environment: Studies in the theory of emotional development.* New York: International Universities Press.

Wolf, E. S. (1988). *Treating the self: Elements of clinical self psychology.* New York: Guilford.

Young, T. M. (1994). Environmental modification in clinical social work: A self-psychological perspective. *Social Service Review, 62*(2), 202–218.

SECTION B

Cognitive-Behavioral Theories

9

Cognitive-Behavioral Theory

Cheryl Regehr

In this chapter, cognitive-behavioral therapy (CBT) is construed as a broad approach to counseling that encompasses a range of more specific therapy models that are based on cognitive and behavioral theories. CBT has become one of the most commonly used models of treatment for social work practitioners and our colleagues in other mental health disciplines. A recent survey (Earle, 1997) of 53 outpatient social workers at eight public psychiatric hospitals in the United States indicated that CBT was the second most commonly reported intervention approach (a problem-solving approach to therapy was the most common). Similarly, a survey of clinical social workers in private practice found that CBT approaches were utilized by 67% of the respondents, exceeded only by psychodynamic treatment approaches (Strom, 1994). The widespread use of the model is understandable in light of the simplicity, brevity, and demonstrated efficacy of the approach.

AN OVERVIEW OF COGNITIVE-BEHAVIORAL THEORY

Behavioral and cognitive theories used to be considered more distinct; however, increasingly they are grouped together. Although cognitive theory emphasizes the influence of beliefs about the self and the world on behavior and emotional states, and behavioral theory focuses on the environmental conditions or stimuli that induce and maintain behaviors (Edwards, Colby, Garcia, McRoy, & Videka-Sherman, 1997), the common factor that ties them together is adherence to a learning model of human functioning.

Broadly speaking, CBT incorporates cognitive, behavioral, and social learning perspectives and explains functioning as a product of reciprocal interactions between personal and environmental variables. Thus, CBT is a purposeful attempt to preserve the demonstrated effectiveness of behavior therapy within a less doctrinaire context and to incorporate consideration of the cognitive activities of the client in attempting to understand problems and produce therapeutic change (Kendall & Hollon, 1979).

The various models of CBT place differential emphasis on cognitions or behaviors; however, almost all acknowledge the usefulness of assessing and intervening in both domains. Hollon and Beck (1994) have classified some cognitive-behavioral models according to differential emphasis on cognition and behavior. They suggest that more behaviorally oriented approaches include Meichenbaum's (1977) cognitive-behavior modification and D'Zurilla and Goldfried's (1971) problem-solving training, whereas more cognitively oriented approaches include Ellis's (1962) rational-emotive therapy (RET) and Beck's (1967, 1976) cognitive therapy (CT) of depression. Other influential cognitive-behavioral models include Marlatt and Gordon's (1985) relapse prevention (RP) treatment for addictions and Linehan's (1993) dialectical behavior therapy (DBT) for borderline personality disorder.

Because Beck's CT is one of the most widely used and empirically validated models of CBT, it will be referred to frequently in this chapter as an example of a cognitive-behavioral approach to counseling. Although CT is, by virtue of its name, more cognitively than behaviorally focused, on closer inspection it clearly represents an integrated set of cognitive and behavioral interventions. As will become evident later in this chapter, in CT clients are trained to identify, evaluate, and modify negative beliefs, but in this process behavioral experiments are used for assessment and intervention.

HISTORICAL DEVELOPMENT

The roots of behavioral therapy can be traced to the work of Ivan Pavlov in the early 1900s. Through the use of animal experiments, Pavlov (1941) developed the concept of classical conditioning, whereby behavioral responses can be produced by pairing consequences with stimuli. Thus, in humans, the sound of an ice-cream truck bell can result in cravings for ice cream. Or, more pertinent to clinical work, in traumatized individuals, stimuli that remind them of the traumatic event (e.g., as returning to the place the event occurred) can result in emotional and physiological stress responses.

A second major contribution to the development of behavior therapy was the work of B. F. Skinner (1953), who observed that much of human behavior is not elicited involuntarily by stimuli, but is rather elicited or controlled by the consequences (or operants) that follow. The theory of operant conditioning suggests that the likelihood of a person engaging or not engaging in a particular behavior is contingent upon whether the outcomes of such behavior in the past were positive or negative. For example, a person who has been successful in establishing new relationships is more likely to risk meeting new people.

Observational or social learning theory (Bandura, 1977) represents a third theoretical contribution to the evolution of behavior therapy. Social learning theory suggests that individuals learn not only from the consequences of their own behaviors, but also from observing the consequences of others' behavior. Thus, cognitive understanding and coding of an event that is observed influences future behavior. For instance, children witnessing assaultive behavior are more likely to emulate that behavior if the aggression goes unpunished (Bandura, 1965).

A central element of social learning theory is the notion of self-efficacy or competence. Bandura (1983) suggests that expectations of competence or personal self-efficacy, triggered by the contextual factors in any situation, arise from diverse sources of information, including judgments of past performance and previous responses from others. These judgments of efficacy, in turn, affect the outcomes of situations and thereby confirm or modify existing cognitive structures. For example, people who judge themselves to be inefficacious in managing potential threats approach such situations anxiously and experience disruptive arousal. This arousal, in turn, negatively affects their performance and confirms feelings of inadequacy (Bandura, 1983). Individuals who repeatedly perceive their efforts to be ineffective can develop "learned helplessness" (Peterson & Seligman, 1983). The "learned helplessness" model has been used to explain the behavior of women in long-term abusive relationships. That is, women who have learned to expect battering as a way of life subsequently believe that they cannot influence its occurrence (Walker, 1979).

The development of social learning theory set the stage for the integration of cognitive and behavioral models. Piaget's (1952) theory of cognitive development focused on the formation of basic cognitive structures or schemas. He hypothesized that cognitive structures were formed as a combined consequence of heredity and the environment, and they, in turn, affected the functional adaptation of persons in their environments. Similarly, Beck (1967), the originator of cognitive therapy, suggested that attempts to organize, summarize, or explain one's own behavior in a particular domain result in the development of cognitive structures, or schemas, about the self. Schemas assist an individual in organizing and simplifying diverse information from complex interactions. They provide the basis on which individuals determine their expectations and beliefs about their own ability to manage any situation and about the response they are likely to get from others.

CENTRAL THEORETICAL CONSTRUCTS

It is beyond the scope of this chapter to review the central theoretical constructs of classical conditioning, operant conditioning, and the range of cognitive-behavioral models. Thus, the author has chosen to focus on explicating the main concepts in Beck's (1967, 1976) cognitive therapy.

> Puddleglum's my name. But it doesn't matter if you forget it, I can always tell you again. . . . I'm trying to catch a few eels to make an eel stew for our dinner. . . . Though I shouldn't wonder if I didn't get any. And you won't like them much if I do. . . . All the same, while I'm catching them, if you two could try to light the fire—no harm trying! The wood's behind the wigwam. It may be wet. You could light it inside the wigwam, and then we'd get all the smoke in our eyes. Or you could light it outside, and then the rain would come and put it out. Here's my tinderbox. You won't know how to use it, I expect. (Lewis, 1953, pp. 58–59)

Beck's (1967) original work in cognitive therapy began with observations of people suffering from depressive illnesses. From these observations, Beck described a triad of depressive cognitions: (1) the self as inadequate, (2) the environment as not reinforcing, and (3) the future as devoid of hope. These three types of cognitions can be found in the above quotation of C. S. Lewis's character Puddleglum. Individuals who hold negative cognitions are less likely to engage in behaviors that discount the beliefs. For example, if a person believes that he or she is not intelligent and that others will not offer assistance, he or she is less likely to pursue further education, thereby eliminating the possibility of success in that sphere. Furthermore, if the person believes that the future holds no promise, the effort required to attempt new behaviors appears useless. These behavioral responses to the negative beliefs reinforce feelings of worthlessness and intensify depressive feelings (see Figure 9.1).

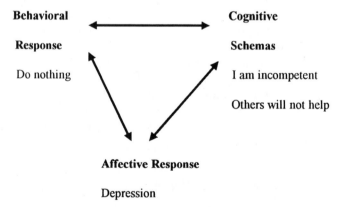

FIGURE 9.1   Cognitive-behavioral-affective interactions.

The central tenets of cognitive therapy can thus be summarized as follows:

1. Individuals acquire beliefs or cognitive maps of the world from previous experiences. These beliefs become filters through which all information about subsequent interactions must pass.
2. Beliefs or assumptions that individuals hold about themselves, others, or the world in general may accurately reflect their own skills and abilities and the environment in which they live. At times, however, these beliefs become distorted reflections of reality. Below are some examples of cognitive distortions:

   Catastrophic thinking: Small problems are always the beginning of a disaster.
   Filtering: Attending only to negative information and ignoring positives.
   Overgeneralization: Seeing one setback as a never-ending pattern of defeat.
   Polarization: Viewing others as all good or all bad.
   (Adapted from Beck, Rush, Shaw, & Emery, 1979)

   Cognitive distortions can then lead to persistent intrusive thoughts of such things as low self-worth and negative views of others.
3. Cognitions influence how individuals feel about themselves or a situation and how they will approach it. The manner in which a person deals with any situation affects the outcome and thereby confirms or modifies existing cognitive structures. For example, people who believe they will fail a driving test may approach the situation with significant anxiety, which will impede their performance. Similarly, people who believe they will be abandoned in interpersonal relationships may approach a new relationship with hostility or overly clinging behavior, thereby pushing new partners away.
4. Individuals can be taught to identify, evaluate, and challenge negative assumptions. These negative beliefs are then reframed in a positive or neutral light. Concurrently, individuals are encouraged to modify their behavioral responses in order to maximize the possibility of positive outcomes. These positive outcomes will modify cognitions and influence affect.

Perhaps the most commonly cited examples of CBT are in the series of children's books about Winnie-the-Pooh. One story, entitled "In Which Eeyore Loses a Tail and Pooh Finds One" (Milne, 1925), begins as follows:

The Old Grey Donkey, Eeyore, stood by himself . . . and thought about things. Sometimes he thought sadly to himself, "Why?" and sometimes he thought, "Wherefore?" and sometimes he thought "Inasmuch as which?"—and sometimes he didn't quite know what he was thinking. So when Winnie-the-Pooh came stumping along, Eeyore was very glad to be able to stop thinking for a little, in order to say "How do you do?" in a gloomy manner to him. (pp. 44–45)

Winnie-the-Pooh reframes Eeyore's general sense of malaise into a singular, manageable problem. Eeyore's tail is missing. He then sets about to find the tail. This definition of the problem and concrete action begin to shift Eeyore's affective state to one of hope. When the tail is successfully replaced, Eeyore's negative mood is resolved for the time being. If Winnie-the-Pooh truly hopes to be successful in helping Eeyore change his mood states, he must begin to help Eeyore identify negative cognitions himself, then evaluate and reframe the cognitions and engage in behavioral change.

PHASES OF HELPING

Phases of helping in CBT are similar to those in most other treatment approaches. Therapists and clients generally proceed through processes of engagement, data collection/assessment, intervention, and evaluation/termination. As in most practice, these phases often overlap and blend together in CBT.

ENGAGEMENT AND DATA COLLECTION/ASSESSMENT

As with other forms of treatment, the characteristics of a therapist that facilitate CBT are warmth, empathy, and genuineness. Without these therapist attributes, this model of therapy can appear gimmicky and can ignore the importance of the therapist-client interaction. One of the cardinal principles of CBT is facilitating an atmosphere of collaboration and trust (Beck & Freeman, 1990). The client must come to believe that the social worker is interested in his or her situation and willing to work cooperatively to solve the problem. The first task, therefore, is to establish rapport with the client, which will serve as the basis for the therapeutic alliance. Another related, early task is to contract with the client for a specified number of sessions—usually between 6 and 20.

In CBT the processes of engagement and data collection/assessment are intertwined. Rapport is established as the worker and client proceed with the assessment process in which the client is asked to describe the problem situation and its emotional consequences. In the assessment, the therapist is also seeking information about the client's strengths and successes on which to base reframing of negative beliefs and behavioral interventions. In addition, the identification of such strengths allows the therapist to express confidence about working together cooperatively toward a solution.

The therapist may choose to assign homework as early as the first session, which would commonly involve having the client identify situations in which the problem becomes worse. For instance, the therapist might say, "During the next week, I would like you to make some notes about when you are feeling most angry/depressed/anxious and what is occurring at those times." This marks an early beginning of the behavioral interventions and the client's first step toward exercising control over the problem. Toward the conclusion of the assessment process, the therapist summarizes the issues identified by the client and works with the client to develop a problem list, which includes identifying situations when the problems are most severe. The therapist should provide reassurance that while these problems are experienced by the client as overwhelming, they are manageable.

INTERVENTION

CBT has a strong emphasis on psychoeducation. An important part of therapy involves educating the client with regard to cognitive-behavioral concepts. Drawing and discussing with clients the cognitive-behavioral-affective triad (Figure 9.1) and the spiraling effects of cognitive-behavioral-affective interactions (see Figure 9.2) can be helpful in illustrating the theory. Many therapists augment information provided in therapy with reading material such as *The Feeling Good Handbook* (Burns, 1989) and *The Relaxation and Stress Reduction Workbook* (Davis, Eshelman, & McKay, 1988). Understanding of the theory empowers the client to engage fully in the process of determining targets of intervention and cognitive and behavioral prescriptions.

After a problem list has been developed, the next step is to identify beliefs that correspond to the list of situations the client has provided about when the problem is at its worst. Clients frequently will assume that environmental factors cause their affective and behavioral responses, as illustrated in the following example:

1. My boss didn't thank me.
2. He made me angry.
3. I quit.

In cognitive therapy, the therapist identifies the beliefs related to negative affects and maladaptive behaviors. This can be a slow process because the intervening beliefs are often not readily accessible to the client. For instance,

1. My boss didn't thank me.
2. I felt used and undervalued again.
3. I got angry.
4. I quit.

The next important step is for the client to evaluate the accuracy of his or her beliefs using three criteria: (1) What is the evidence that supports

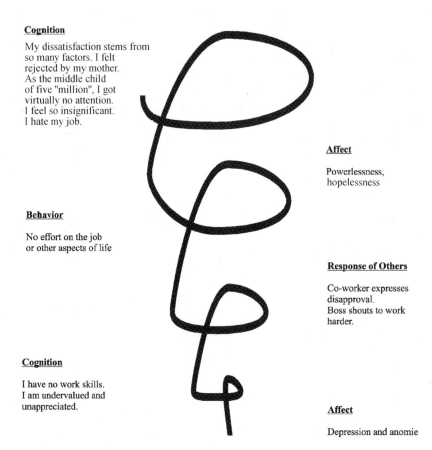

Cognition

My dissatisfaction stems from
so many factors. I felt
rejected by my mother.
As the middle child
of five "million", I got
virtually no attention.
I feel so insignificant.
I hate my job.

Affect

Powerlessness,
hopelessness

Behavior

No effort on the job
or other aspects of life

Response of Others

Co-worker expresses
disapproval.
Boss shouts to work
harder.

Cognition

I have no work skills.
I am undervalued and
unappreciated.

Affect

Depression and anomie

FIGURE 9.2   Spiraling effects of cognitive-behavioral-affective interactions. Woody Allen's recent animated movie ANTZ (1998) provides an example of the negative spiral associated with depression. In it, Woody Allen is a worker ant who is dismayed about his lot in life.

or refutes this belief?, (2) Is there an alternative explanation for the event?, and (3) What are the real implications if the belief is true? (Hollon & Carter, 1994). In the above example, therefore, the client must consider whether the boss exhibited a pattern of dismissive behavior toward her and/or others, or whether this was an isolated event that could be attributed to other causes, such as the boss simply being tired and overworked. Finally, if it is true that the client is undervalued in her job, are there other ways of increasing satisfaction with the job, short of quitting? Once clients begin to understand the concept of negative thoughts, they are asked to keep a record of these thoughts between treatment sessions (see Table 9.1).

The process of changing the thoughts involves identifying them, questioning them, and making a conscious effort to reframe negative cognitions.

TABLE 9.1 Daily Record of Thoughts, Feelings, and Behaviors

Date	Situation	Emotional response	Beliefs or thoughts	Behavioral response	Alternative response

Adapted from Beck, A., Rush, J., Shaw, B., & Emery, G. (1979). Cognitive therapy of depression. New York: Guilford Press, p. 403.

For example, "Losing my job does not represent the end of my career, but rather an opportunity to use my skills in new and creative ways." Some automatic thoughts, however, may continue to interfere with a person's ability to function. In these cases, additional behavioral techniques, such as thought-stopping, rehearsal, and externalizing the thoughts, may be of assistance.

In the thought-stopping technique, clients are encouraged to think about the maladaptive belief and experience the emotional and physical sensations that accompany it. For example, persistent thoughts about a failed relationship may bring about feelings of sadness or anger. These thoughts also may contribute to a tightening of the stomach or other muscle tension. Once clients are aware of these phenomena, they are taught how to control them. For example, when such negative thoughts, feelings, and reactions occur, clients can be directed to set a timer for 3 minutes. When the timer goes off, they must force the negative thoughts from their mind and replace them with a positive reframing of the situation or positive self-talk. As clients develop mastery of this technique, they can develop more subtle ways of stopping the thoughts, such as shaking their head slightly or snapping an elastic band on their wrist.

The technique of rehearsal is illustrated in the example of a famous golfer who envisions a good shot in his mind 1,000 times before actually swinging a club. Similarly, clients can be encouraged to rehearse events that they negatively anticipate and to imagine positive results.

Finally, externalizing intrusive thoughts that repeatedly interfere with activities or sleep can be an effective strategy. Clients can be encouraged to externalize a negative thought by writing it down, telling someone about it, or speaking it into a tape recorder. Once the thought has been dealt with in this manner, it often loses its power.

An additional technique is to coach clients to follow the advice "Begin each day by eating a frog." This behavioral technique encourages clients to begin the day with the most dreaded task, rather than putting it off and allowing negative cognitions to multiply.

While clients are focusing on and identifying negative situations and affects, it is beneficial to increase their exposure to situations that provide positive reinforcement. Consequently, the therapist works with clients to identify situations that provide them with a sense of mastery and pleasure. Clients are then encouraged to overcome negative cognitions and increase their positive activities. This may involve simple self-care, such as exercise, purchasing favorite bath salts, or going for a massage. It also may involve making time to meet with people who value them and make them feel good. Finally, clients may decide to engage in more major life changes that are personally reinforcing, such as returning to work after staying home with the children.

The final and most complex task of CBT involves ensuring that the process of treatment changes not only self-statements but also deep-rooted negative beliefs (Hollon & Carter, 1994). In part, reducing negative self-talk will improve the client's self-image. In addition, the client's engagement in more rewarding activities will alter beliefs about the self and affective responses. However, patterns frequently will emerge that represent underlying themes. In such instances, it is necessary to explore with the client the origin of these beliefs and determine whether the assumptions that have arisen are still valid. For example, people with learning disabilities may have experienced multiple failures in school, as well as ridicule from peers and family. Their consequent belief systems may be that they are failures and worthless. However, although they may not have been able to manage grade 12 algebra, they may now show tremendous skill and aptitude in another area. Acknowledging the painful historic roots of beliefs can provide the freedom to begin considering new information about successes.

EVALUATION/TERMINATION

Because CBT is time-limited, issues associated with termination are usually not as complex as those encountered in long-term forms of treatment. Nonetheless, benefits of treatment can be lost through inappropriate or abrupt closure (Beck & Freeman, 1990).

In CBT the process of termination begins in the first interview when the social worker and client agree to work together on the problems identified for a specified number of sessions. Throughout the process of therapy, the therapist and client review the treatment goals and the progress made toward these goals. Client strengths and accomplishments are acknowledged continually, and through this process the client is encouraged to become independent and self-reliant. As therapy progresses, the client plays an increasingly active role in identifying target problems and choosing strategies, thereby reducing the reliance on the therapist.

The psychoeducational nature of CBT helps clients to understand therapy as a process of learning new skills for dealing with problems. Clients are taught that, as with the acquisition of skills and knowledge in any realm, their growth and development are not expected to end with the termination of therapy. Clients are encouraged to continue to work on skills independently but may return to treatment should new situations arise that overwhelm their ability to cope and adapt.

APPLICATION TO FAMILY AND GROUP WORK

FAMILY WORK

Many of the techniques of CBT can be adapted easily to work with couples and families. Difficulties in family interactions frequently arise from cognitive distortions regarding the intentions of other family members. Kayser and Himle (1994), for example, identify dysfunctional beliefs that hinder the development of intimacy in couples. These include the belief that intimacy leads to loss of power and control in the relationship and the belief that conflict leads to loss of intimacy. Examining and revising dysfunctional beliefs can lead to higher levels of understanding, trust, and intimacy in couples and families.

The use of CBT in family work also has been described with special populations, such as juvenile offenders (Rose, Duby, Olenick, & Weston, 1996) and families suffering the aftermath of war (Rabin & Nardi, 1991). Techniques used with families of troubled youth include situational analysis, modeling, and role playing. In families of Israeli war veterans, CBT was helpful in addressing avoidance responses of the husbands and enhancing assertiveness and cognitive coping skills in the wives.

GROUP WORK

Group treatments using CBT are reported in the literature and include such diverse populations as gay and bisexual men with HIV (Roffman, Downey, Beadnell, & Gordon, 1997), those with major mental illnesses (Albert, 1994), chronic pain sufferers (Subramanian, 1991), rape victims (Resick & Schnicke, 1993), and offenders (Marshall & Eccles, 1996; Rose et al., 1996).

A common approach to group therapy with sexual offenders provides a good example of the application of cognitive-behavioral principles. Such groups are based on the theoretical premise that cognitive distortions contribute to assaultive behavior. Distortions include the belief that the assault was not really nonconsensual, was not really sex, or did not really harm the victim (Segal & Stermac, 1990). These groups focus on challenging distorted beliefs through confrontation and information about the nature of sexual assault, including the negative impact on victims. Offenders are often encouraged to demonstrate their awareness of distortions through some behavioral means. For example, they may be asked to write letters describing the impact of the assault from the victim's perspective and present these to the group (Marshall & Eccles, 1996). Other behavioral approaches address the issue of arousal. Covert sensitization requires that the offender develop a scenario of events leading to a sexual assault. The offender then must develop a list of negative consequences and review this list several times a day, including each time he begins to experience arousal. Masturbatory reconditioning is aimed at enhancing appropriate sexual behaviors and reducing deviant interests (Marshall & Eccles, 1996). Perpetrators must identify potentially dangerous situations in their offense cycle and ensure that they do not encounter them. For example, child molesters must not visit playgrounds or video arcades, but rather must develop a repertoire of other destinations.

COMPATIBILITY WITH THE GENERALIST-ECLECTIC FRAMEWORK

From the above descriptions, the compatibility of CBT with many aspects of a generalist-eclectic framework for social work practice is immediately apparent. First, the focus on individual-environmental interactions is highly consistent with the person-in-environment perspective of generalist social work practice. Second, it is clear that CBT emphasizes a collaborative relationship between the therapist and the client, client strengths, and client empowerment. In this model, the social worker and the client identify goals for change and existing strengths, work together to understand cognitive structures that perpetuate maladaptive behaviors and emotional responses, and develop a joint strategy for altering both cognitions and behaviors. Third, although eclecticism is not inherent in CBT, in the professional literature practitioners and researchers frequently advocate for the integration of CBT with other approaches, including psychodynamic treatment (Heller & Northcut, 1996; Martin, 1993), family therapy models (Kolko, 1996; Simons & Miller, 1987), and pharmacology (Kaplan & Sadock, 1995).

CRITIQUE OF CBT

STRENGTHS

One of the major strengths of CBT is the extent to which its efficacy has been validated empirically. The well-developed theoretical foundations of this model and the structured approach have made CBT highly amenable to evaluations of outcome. Although reviews of psychotherapy outcome studies frequently have led to the conclusion of equal outcomes for the different types of therapy, many of these reviews have noted the superior results for CBT with regard to difficult problems, such as panic, phobias, and compulsion (Lambert & Bergin, 1994).

Empirical studies of CBT can be found regarding many specific client populations. The effectiveness of Beck's cognitive therapy for depression has been validated extensively (Hollon & Beck, 1994). In addition, various types of CBT have been found to be effective in treatment of sexual offenders (Marshall & Eccles, 1996), individuals with posttraumatic stress disorder (Rothbaum & Foa, 1996), enuretic children (Ronen & Wozner, 1995), agoraphobic women (Burke, Drummond, & Johnson, 1997), juvenile delinquents (Hawkins, Jenson, Catalano, & Wells, 1991), and chronic pain sufferers (Subramanian, 1991).

A great strength of CBT lies in its relative simplicity and transparency. The theoretical constructs hold intuitive appeal for clients and social workers alike. Complex processes are described in a manner that is accessible and understandable. Clients are informed about the theoretical concepts and participate fully in identifying problems, modifying belief systems, and changing behaviors. Changes are noted, recorded, and often measured. This leads to a sense of empowerment and success. For new therapists, the model offers clear guidelines and techniques. The social worker is expected to share responsibility for change with the client and is not expected to encourage strong transference reactions or make miraculous interpretations about client inner processes.

LIMITATIONS

Although the simplicity and transparency of this model are considerable strengths, they can become weaknesses if the model is applied inappropriately. Inexpert therapists may experience several pitfalls. For instance, a novice therapist may become so intent on following techniques, that he or she ignores the importance of establishing a therapeutic relationship as the crucial vehicle for change. Similarly, an overreliance on cognitive understanding or behavioral change may overshadow the affective experiences of the client. If the client does not feel that the therapist understands the nature and consequences of the problem and the obstacles to change, he or she will not be able to engage in the change process. In addition, short-term behavioral and affective change can be maintained only if the client has an understanding of his or her belief systems and the etiology of these beliefs. As such, the social worker must ensure that he or she not only has addressed the symptoms of distress but also has taken time to explore the origins of such symptoms, including past experiences that have led to longstanding beliefs about self and others.

CASE EXAMPLE

To illustrate the use of CBT, the case of a victim of sexual assault will be described. Mandy was 15 when she was first raped by a former boyfriend and became pregnant. A few years later, she was beaten and sexually assaulted on several occasions within the context of a common-law relationship. In individual therapy, after she had left the abusive relationship, Mandy described her experiences in the following way:

> It sounds like a movie made for TV. He'd give me flowers, see me every night, call me every 10 minutes. I ended up moving in with him and living in this relationship that was just a nightmare. He alienated me from all my friends, all my family. He just had me. I don't even know who that person is now. I couldn't think at all. And when I tried to pull away, he became just unbelievably physically aggressive. He would do what he wanted with my body, with all of me. Kicking, hitting, punching, sexual assault whenever he felt like it.

McCann, Sakheim, and Abrahamson (1988) proposed a model for understanding trauma that considers cognitive appraisals of self and others, called schemas. They suggested that people develop self-other schemas within five areas: safety, trust, power, esteem, and intimacy. Negative schemas within any of these areas can lead to maladaptive functioning following a traumatic event. For example, negative schemas related to safety may include the belief that one is incapable of protecting oneself from harm, injury, or loss, which may in turn lead to feelings of helplessness. Regehr (1996) has adopted this model to conceptualize the impact of self-schema on recovery from rape trauma (see Table 9.2).

TABLE 9.2 Impact of Self-Schema on Recovery from Rape Trauma

Element of self-schema	Factors that enhance recovery	Factors that inhibit recovery
Safety, trust	Ability to develop and sustain relationships with others	Fear of others Lack of critical judgment of others
Esteem, self-efficacy	Confidence in personal coping based on previous successful coping	Insufficient opportunity to learn coping skills Previous experiences of poor coping
Power, control	Acceptance that events happen beyond one's control Belief in ability to control outcome of crisis	Unrealistic belief in own ability to control all outcomes View of self as powerless victim

From Regehr, C. (1996). *Do not go gentle into that good night: Strengths in sexually assaulted women.* Unpublished doctoral dissertation, University of Toronto.

Mandy described her traumatic childhood in a violent, alcoholic family. She learned that men were to be feared and that women were to acquiesce to men's demands in order to maintain peace. She felt she was responsible for assaults perpetrated against her: "He said, 'I'm sorry, I'm sorry,' and I remember saying, 'It's OK. I deserved it.' " Fear became a constant aspect of her life, and she had no confidence in her ability to overcome hardships that befell her: "I feel doomed. . . . I am afraid that something terrible will happen. It always does. I can't win for losing." Mandy would even explain away her successes as an act that she put on for the benefit of others: "I am so good at putting up a front. I am not really strong."

Cognitive-behavioral therapy, when applied to assaulted women, involves examining negative beliefs and challenging assumptions (McCann & Pearlman, 1990; Resick & Schnicke, 1993). Work with Mandy involved understanding the origins of her beliefs about men and challenging her assumption that all men were abusive. Part of this work included looking at her choices of men and her assumptions about what type of treatment she deserved from men. In the end, she was able to challenge the assumption that she deserved to be assaulted. She realized that she was not a bad child who had deserved to be beaten, nor a bad woman who should have been punished. Mandy began to see that her ability to cope was not a hoax. This encouraged her to take further risks.

Behavioral interventions were employed to reduce intrusive symptoms of nightmares and flashbacks. During the sessions, Mandy was encouraged to recount traumatic aspects of the assaults. This helped to reduce the intrusive imagery that is often associated with unresolved trauma (Briere, 1996). In addition, she was encouraged to write down the nightmares that awakened her at night. This reduced her anxiety and allowed her to return to sleep.

Although the brief CBT interventions did not change all negative aspects of Mandy's life, she did experience significant reduction of affective distress and increased confidence in her ability to manage the world. She was encouraged to return to treatment if she had a recurrence of symptoms or encountered new challenges in life that seemed beyond her ability to cope.

SUMMARY

In this chapter, CBT has been defined broadly to include many different treatment models, with differential emphasis on cognition and behavior. CBT, as a general model of treatment, holds much appeal for social workers and clients alike. The model is intellectually accessible and makes intuitive sense. Many common examples elucidating the model can be drawn from everyday life and pop culture. This accessibility is an advantage both for training therapists new to the approach and for allowing clients to engage fully in the process of treatment. Clients are empowered to (1) set their own goals, (2) identify and modify destructive beliefs and behaviors, and (3) chart their own progress and successes. In times of economic constraints in social service programming, this model can boast cost-effectiveness both in terms of demonstrated efficacy and in terms of treatment duration, which is frequently shorter than traditional models of psychotherapy.

REFERENCES

Albert, J. (1994). Rethinking difference: A cognitive therapy group for chronic mental patients. *Social Work with Groups, 17,* 105–121.

Bandura, A. (1965). Influence of models' reinforcement contingencies on the acquisition of imitative responses. *Journal of Personality and Social Psychology, 1,* 589–595.

Bandura, A. (1977). *Social Learning Theory.* Englewood Cliffs, NJ: Prentice-Hall.

Bandura, A. (1983). Self-efficacy determinants of anticipated fears and calamities. *Journal of Personality and Social Psychology, 45,* 464–469.

Beck, A. (1967). *Depression: Clinical, experimental, and theoretical aspects.* New York: Hoeber Press.

Beck, A. (1976). *Cognitive therapy and emotional disorders.* New York: International Universities Press.

Beck, A., & Freeman, A. (1990). *Cognitive therapy with personality disorders.* New York: Guilford Press.

Beck, A., Rush, J., Shaw, B., & Emery, G. (1979). *Cognitive therapy of depression.* New York: Guilford Press.

Briere, J. (1996). *Therapy for adults molested as children.* New York: Springer.

Burke, M., Drummond, L., & Johnson, D. (1997). Treatment of choice for agoraphobic women: Exposure or cognitive-behavioural therapy. *British Journal of Clinical Psychology, 36,* 409–420.

Burns, D. (1989). *The feeling good handbook.* New York: Morrow.

Davis, M., Eshelman, E., & McKay, M. (1988). *The relaxation and stress reduction workbook.* Oakland, CA: New Harbinger Publications.

D'Zurilla, T. J., & Goldfried, M. R. (1971). Problem-solving and behavior modification. *Journal of Abnormal Psychology, 78,* 107–126.

Earle, K. (1997). Models used by experienced social workers in the treatment of mental illness. *New Social Worker, 4,* 8–9.

Edwards, R., Colby, I., Garcia, A., McRoy, R., & Videka-Sherman, L. (1997). *Encyclopedia of Social Work* (19th ed.). Washington, DC: NASW Press.

Ellis, A. (1962). *Reason and emotion in psychotherapy.* New York: Lyle Stuart.

Ellis, A. (1980). Rational emotive therapy and cognitive behavior therapy: Similarities and differences. *Cognitive Therapy and Research, 4,* 325–340.

Hawkins, D., Jenson, J., Catalano, R., & Wells, E. (1991). Effects of a skills training intervention with juvenile delinquents. *Research on Social Work Practice, 1,* 107–121.

Heller, N., & Northcut, R. (1996). Utilizing cognitive-behavioral techniques in psychodynamic practice with clients diagnosed as borderline. *Clinical Social Work Journal, 24,* 203–215.

Hollon, S. D., & Beck, A. T. (1994). Cognitive and cognitive-behavioral therapies. In A. E. Bergin & S. L. Garfield (Eds.), *Handbook of psychotherapy and behavior change* (4th ed., pp. 428–466). New York: Wiley.

Hollon, S., & Carter, M. (1994). Depression in adults. In L. Craighead, W. Craighead, A. Kazdin, & M. Mahoney (Eds.), *Cognitive and behavioral interventions* (pp. 89–104). Toronto: Allyn & Bacon.

Kaplan, H., & Sadock, J. (1995). Depressive disorders. In H. Kaplan & J. Sadock, *Comprehensive textbook of psychiatry* (6th ed., pp. 516–572). Baltimore: Williams & Wilkins.

Kayser, K., & Himle, D. (1994). Dysfunctional beliefs about intimacy. *Journal of Cognitive Psychotherapy, 8*, 127–140.

Kendall, P., & Hollon, S. (1979). *Cognitive-behavioral interventions: Theory, research and procedures.* San Francisco: Academic Press.

Kolko, D. (1996). Individual cognitive-behavioral treatment and family therapy for physically abused children and their offending parents. *Child Maltreatment, 1*, 322–342.

Lambert, M. J., & Bergin, A. E. (1994). The effectiveness of psychotherapy. In A. E. Bergin & S. L. Garfield (Eds.), *Handbook of psychotherapy and behavior change* (4th ed., pp. 143–189). New York: Wiley.

Lewis, C. (1953). *The chronicles of Narnia: The silver chair.* London: Harper/Collins.

Linehan, M. M. (1993). *Cognitive-behavioral treatment for borderline personality disorder.* New York: Guilford.

Marlatt, G. A., & Gordon, J. (1985). *Relapse prevention: Maintenance strategies in the treatment of addictive behaviors.* New York: Guilford.

Marshall, W., & Eccles, A. (1996). Cognitive-behavioral treatment of sex offenders. In V. Van Hasselt & M. Hersen (Eds.), *Sourcebook of psychological treatment manuals for adult disorders* (pp. 295–332). New York: Plenum Press.

Martin, J. (1993). Self-psychology and cognitive treatment: An integration. *Clinical Social Work Journal, 21*, 385–394.

McCann, L., & Pearlman, L. (1990). *Psychological trauma and the adult survivor: Theory, therapy and transformation.* New York: Brunner/Mazel.

McCann, L., Sakheim, D., & Abrahamson, D. (1988). Trauma and victimization: A model of psychological adaption. *The Counseling Psychologist, 16*, 531–594.

Meichenbaum, D. (1977). *Cognitive-behavior modification: An integrative approach.* New York: Plenum.

Milne, A. (1925). *Winnie-the-Pooh.* Toronto: McClelland & Stewart.

Pavlov, I. (1941). *Lectures on conditioned reflexes* (Vol. 2). New York: International Publishers.

Peterson, C., & Seligman, M. (1983). Learned helplessness and victimization. *Journal of Social Issues, 2*, 103–116.

Piaget, J. (1952). *The origins of intelligence in children.* New York: International Universities Press.

Rabin, C., & Nardi, C. (1991). Treating post-traumatic stress disorder couples: A psychoeducational program. *Community Mental Health Journal, 27*, 209–224.

Regehr, C. (1996). *Do not go gentle into that good night: Strengths in sexually assaulted women.* Unpublished doctoral dissertation, University of Toronto.

Resick, P., & Schnicke, M. (1993). Cognitive processing therapy for sexual assault victims. *Journal of Consulting and Clinical Psychology, 60*, 748–756.

Roffman, R., Downey, L., Beadnell, B., & Gordon, J. (1997). Cognitive-behavioral group counseling to prevent HIV transmission in gay and bisexual men. *Research on Social Work Practice, 7*, 165–186.

Ronen, T., & Wozner, Y. (1995). A self-control intervention package for the treatment of primary nocturnal enuresis. *Child and Family Behavior Therapy, 17*, 1–20.

Rose, S., Duby, P., Olenick, C., & Weston, T. (1996). Integrating family, group and residential treatment: A cognitive-behavioral approach. *Social Work with Groups,* *19,* 35–48.

Rothbaum, B., & Foa, E. (1996). Cognitive-behavioral therapy for posttraumatic stress disorder. In B. van der Kolk, A. McFarlane, & L. Weisaeth (Eds.), *Traumatic stress: The effects of overwhelming experience on mind, body, and society* (pp. 491–509). New York: Guilford Press.

Segal, Z., & Stermac, L. (1990). The role of cognition in sexual assault. In W. Marshall, D. Laws, & H. Barbaree (Eds.), *Handbook of sexual assault* (pp. 161–174). New York: Plenum Press.

Simons, R., & Miller, M. (1987). Adolescent depression: Assessing the impact of negative cognitions and socio-environmental problems. *Social Work, 32,* 326–330.

Skinner, B. (1953). *Science and human behavior.* New York: The Free Press.

Strom, K. (1994). Social workers in private practice: An update. *Clinical Social Work Journal, 22,* 73–89.

Subramanian, K. (1991). Structured group work for the management of chronic pain: An experimental investigation. *Research on Social Work Practice, 1,* 32–45.

Walker, L. (1994). *Abused women and survivor therapy: A practical guide for the psychotherapist.* Washington, DC: American Psychological Association.

10

The Crisis Intervention Model

Karen Knox and Albert R. Roberts

Crisis intervention is one of the models that is essential for competent social work practice. Social workers must be prepared to handle acute crises of various types and causes, because clients typically are experiencing difficulties or obstacles in effectively resolving such crises without intervention. Social work practitioners working in the fields of suicide prevention, gerontology, hospice care, medical/health care, child abuse, family violence, criminal justice, sexual assault, school-based services, mental health services, and family counseling need to be knowledgeable about and skilled in dealing with crises, which result from an acute stressor, a pileup of stressors, or a traumatic event.

This chapter presents an overview of the historical development of crisis intervention and its contributions to generalist social work practice. Thus, we link the past to the present in order to better prepare social workers for practice in the 21st century. The basic assumptions and theoretical constructs of crisis theory are explained to educate students on the major tenets and goals of crisis intervention. Descriptions of the types and stages of crises, different practice models, intervention strategies, and evaluation methods are provided.

OVERVIEW OF CRISIS INTERVENTION

TWO CASE ILLUSTRATIONS OF CRISIS REACTIONS

Judy B., a 27-year-old surgical nurse, was a survivor of wife battering. She had two children with Ray, and they had been married for 6 years. As his drinking increased, so did his beatings. The final straw was a violent attack when he punched her many times in the face. The day after this last assault, after Judy looked at her swollen face in the mirror, she went to a gun store and purchased a Smith and Wesson handgun. As she drove home, glancing at the gun by her side, she finally decided to seek help. She called the battered women's shelter hotline and said, "I'm afraid that I'm going to kill my husband." The crisis worker immediately realized the volatility and dangerousness of the situation and gave Judy directions to the shelter outreach office.

Mary R. was a 22-year-old college freshman when she was raped. It was 11:00 P.M., and Mary had just left the university's main library and was walking the three long blocks to the parking lot where her car was parked. She recalls her reactions a week later:

> I was sort of in shock and numb. It was a terrifying, painful, and degrading experience. It was something you don't expect to happen. I had terrifying nightmares the past week. But it could have been much worse. He held a knife to my throat while raping me. I thought he was going to kill me afterwards. I'm glad to be alive. (Roberts, 2000, p. 4)

These case illustrations highlight the crises reactions of violent crime victims in the aftermath of traumatic victimization. Victims of violent crimes usually experience a series of physiological and psychological reactions. Some common symptoms and reactions include intense fears, heightened anxiety, hypervigilance and startle reactions, intrusive thoughts and flashbacks, despair and hopelessness, irritability, terror, sleep disturbances, shock and numbness, extreme distrust of others, and shattered assumptions that the community where they reside is not safe (Roberts, 2000).

BASIC PRINCIPLES IN CRISIS INTERVENTION

Persons experiencing traumatic events usually can benefit from rapid assessment and crisis intervention. Crisis counseling shares many principles and strategies with brief, time-limited, task-centered, and solution-focused practice models. Crisis intervention is one of the action-oriented models that is present-focused, with the target(s) for intervention being specific to the hazardous event, situation, or problem that precipitated the state of crisis. Therefore, this model focuses on problems in the here and now, and addresses past history and psychopathology only as they are relevant to the current conditions.

Crisis theory postulates that most crisis interventions can be limited to a period of 4 to 8 weeks (Hepworth, Rooney, & Larsen, 1997; Roberts, 1996, 2000). Crisis intervention is time-limited, in that the goal is to help the client mobilize needed support, resources, and adaptive coping skills to resolve or minimize the disequilibrium experienced by the precipitating event. Once the client has returned to his or her precrisis level of functioning and homeostasis, any further supportive or supplemental services are usually referred out to appropriate community agencies and service providers.

For example, a sexual assault victim may receive emergency crisis intervention services from several crisis intervention programs over a period of time. Crisis counselors and victim advocates employed by a victim-witness assistance program may work with the client through the initial investigation and rape exam. Hospital emergency room social workers also may provide crisis stabilization and crisis counseling during the medical examination, and rape crisis programs typically have emergency response services for rapid intervention at the hospital and afterwards. Most rape crisis centers provide short-term individual counseling services and time-limited (6- to 12-week) groups. The client should have stabilized and returned to a level of adequate functioning within this time frame. Any longer-term treatment needs would then be referred to other public or private sector services.

Time frames for crisis intervention vary depending on several factors, including the agency mission and services, the client's needs and resources, and the type of crisis or trauma. Crisis intervention can be as brief as one client contact, which is typical with 24-hour suicide prevention or crisis hotlines. Some crisis situations may require several contacts over a few days of brief treatment, whereas others may provide ongoing and follow-up services for up to 10 or 12 weeks. Additional crisis intervention services may be needed in the future. With the example of a sexual assault survivor, another critical time for crisis reactions is experienced when any court proceedings are conducted. This may require client involvement or court testimony that triggers memories and feelings about the rape, which can produce crisis reactions and revictimization.

The immediacy and action orientation of crisis intervention require a high level of activity and skill on the part of the social worker. They also require a mutual contracting process between the client and the social worker, but the time frame for assessment and contracting must be brief by necessity. People experiencing trauma and crisis need immediate relief and assistance, and the helping process must be adapted to meet those needs as efficiently and effectively as possible.

Therefore, some of the tools and techniques used in the assessment and contracting phases, such as intake forms, social history gathering, engagement of the client, and intervention planning, must be used in ways or formats that differ from longer-term practice models. The assessment, contracting, and intervention stages may need to be completed and implemented on the very first client contact. Clients in an active state of crisis are more amenable to the helping process, and this can facilitate completion of such tasks within the rapid response time frame.

With a rape survivor, the investigation and medical needs must be assessed and intervention initiated immediately. After this, safety issues are addressed. The victim may not feel safe at home, if the rape occurred there or if there is concern that the offender would not be arrested and could find the person there. Crisis intervention counseling would be implemented simultaneously while addressing these other needs, with the police and/ or hospital social worker providing multiple crisis services during this first contact. This process could take several hours, depending on the response time by law enforcement and medical professionals, as well as the client's coping skills and resources. The crisis social worker would need to follow through until the client had stabilized or had been contacted by another collateral provider of crisis services.

The social worker must be knowledgeable about the appropriate strategies, resources, and other collateral services to initiate timely intervention strategies and meet the goals of treatment. Specialized knowledge about specific types of crises, traumatic incidents, or client populations may be necessary for effective intervention planning. For example, crisis intervention with victims of family violence requires education and training on the dynamics and cycle of battering and abuse, familiarity with the community agencies providing services to this client population, and knowledge about the legal options available to victims. Similarly, social workers dealing with bereavement and loss in hospice settings need to be knowledgeable about the grief process, medical terminology, specific health problems or conditions, and support services for family survivors. Due to the diversity of crisis situations and events, the basic models and skills of crisis intervention must be supplemented by continued professional education and experience with specialized client populations or types of trauma encountered in generalist practice.

Another characteristic of crisis intervention models is the use of tasks as a primary change effort. Concrete, basic needs services, such as emergency safety, medical needs, food, clothing, and shelter, are the first priority in crisis intervention. Mobilizing needed resources may require more direct activity by the social worker in advocating, networking, and brokering for clients, who may not have the knowledge, skills, or capacity to follow through with referrals and collateral contacts at the time of active crisis.

Of course, the emotional and psychological trauma experienced by the client and significant others are important considerations for intervention. Ventilation of feelings and reactions to the crisis are essential to the healing process, and the practice skills of reflective communication, active listening, and establishing rapport are essential in developing a relationship and providing supportive counseling for the client. The social worker may find that intervention strategies and activities must target all levels of practice simultaneously to be effective in meeting the goals of treatment.

HISTORICAL DEVELOPMENT OF THE CRISIS INTERVENTION MODEL

Although crisis intervention has developed into a cohesive treatment model only in the past 50 years, human beings have been dealing with crises from antiquity. In ancient Greece, the word *crisis* came from two root words—one meaning "decision" and the other "turning point." Similarly, the two symbols in Chinese language for *crisis* represent danger and opportunity (Roberts, 1995). These definitions imply that crisis can be both a time for individual growth and an impetus for behavioral change, as well as an obstacle and risk for harm and unhealthy reactions.

Historically, family and religious systems helped people in crisis. The roots of crisis intervention developed in the 1940s and 1950s from several sources, including physicians, psychologists, psychiatrists, sociologists, social workers, and the military. Much of the work was done by multidisciplinary teams involving these disciplines in various settings, such as public health agencies, hospitals, family counseling centers, and disaster response programs.

One of the pioneers in crisis intervention was Dr. Eric Lindemann, who was associated with the Harvard School of Public Health and Massachusetts General Hospital. His pioneering study on loss and bereavement with 101 survivors and family members of the victims of the Coconut Grove nightclub fire in Boston was one of the first efforts to develop a more systematic way of helping people in crisis (Lindemann, 1944). From his research, theories of the grief process and typical reactions to the crisis of losing a close family member were developed. He also noted the duration and severity of grief postponement and continued bonding to the deceased and maintained that without intervention, individuals experiencing denial and grief postponement were likely to develop pathology and morbid reactions (Roberts, 1995, 2000).

Other developments in psychiatry in the 1940s and 1950s contributed to the knowledge and research base of crisis intervention. From ego psychology, Erikson's (1950) stages of human development included key psychosocial crises that had to be resolved over the course of life. He postulated that crisis and major life transitions are normal in human and social development, and can help individuals develop coping skills to successfully resolve both maturational and situational crises.

Suicide prevention services were another type of community-based mental health program that developed to respond to those in crisis. Much of the pioneering work was done at the Los Angeles Suicide Prevention Center in the late 1950s and 1960s (Dublin, 1963; Farberow & Schneidman, 1961; Roberts, 1975; Schneidman, Farberow, & Litman, 1970). As the suicide prevention movement developed, the National Institute of Mental Health Center for Studies of Suicide Prevention (now defunct) was established in 1966, and by 1972, almost 200 such suicide prevention programs had been established across the country (Roberts, 1995).

The Victim Witness Assistance Act of 1982 and the Victims of Crime Act of 1984 established federal funding and state block grants for crisis intervention programs and victim advocacy services in the criminal justice system. These comprehensive programs are located at police departments, prosecutors offices, and not-for-profit agencies. Victim advocates focus on helping crime victims and family members with court-related advocacy, medical, mental health, and financial assistance (Roberts, 1990). States and local communities have been able to develop family violence, sexual assault, and victim services programs as a result of this federal assistance. As a result, thousands of statewide, county, and city victim service and domestic violence programs expanded to help individuals resolve particular crime-related problems and crises (Roberts, 1990, 1997).

Since the 1970s, the focus for research and development of crisis intervention services and skills has been on specialized client populations and groups, such as victims and survivors of sexual assault, child abuse, domestic violence, and violent crime. The effectiveness of crisis intervention programs in various community-based social service, law enforcement, and mental health agencies has been another focus of research and program evaluation. There has been a proliferation of journal articles and books dealing specifically with crisis intervention models, skills, and intervention strategies for particular client groups.

In 1994, the co-author of this chapter (Roberts) founded a new journal, entitled *Crisis Intervention and Time-Limited Treatment.* A review of peer-reviewed articles in the journal shows diversity across crisis intervention programs and services, including school-based programs, models for working with sexual assault and incest survivors, substance abuse programs, emergency services for disaster victims, family violence models, hospital-based programs run by emergency room social workers, crisis intervention counselors in health and mental health settings, forensic mental health and homicide classification, and suicide prevention by e-mail (Boes, 1997; Burgess & Roberts, 1996; Dziegielewski & Resnick, 1995; Liese, 1995; Meyer & Ottens, 1995; Schoenfeld & Kline, 1994; Thomas, 1996; Webb, 1995; Wilson & Lester, 1998).

THEORETICAL BASE AND CENTRAL THEORETICAL CONSTRUCTS OF THE CRISIS INTERVENTION MODEL

The major tenets of crisis intervention derived originally from ego psychology and ecological systems theory. Central ideas borrowed from ego psychology include life development stages, psychosocial crises, coping skills, and defense mechanisms. From the systems/ecological perspective, concepts such as homeostasis, disequilibrium, and interdependence are basic principles of crisis intervention.

Cognitive-behavioral models, such as reality therapy, rational-emotive-behavioral therapy, and neurolinguistic programming, share many characteristics with the basic assumptions and techniques of crisis intervention. These are all action-oriented models, with a present focus and time-limited treatment. The cognitive-behavioral principle that an individual's perceptions and cognitions affect his or her beliefs, feelings, and behaviors in an interactive way is essential to crisis theory. The critical incident or precipitating event has to be perceived as a crisis by the client. Individuals involved in the same crisis situation may have very different perceptions, feelings, reactions, and coping skills.

Two other newer practice models have contributed to or been included as part of a repertoire of techniques used in crisis intervention. The solution-focused model has been used in crisis intervention with diverse client populations and is particularly suited to managed care policies, which have institutionalized time-limited treatment in most public sector agencies, such as mental health clinics, medical or hospital settings, employee assistance programs, and health maintenance organizations (Dziegielewski, 1996; Greene, Lee, Trask, & Reinscheld, 2000; Greene, Lee, Trask, & Rheinscheld, 1996; Polk, 1996).

Another model that has been used in crisis intervention is eye movement desensitization and reprocessing, which was developed by Francine Shapiro (1995). This model is also time-limited and espouses that if trauma can produce immediate symptomologies, then healing can also be accomplished in the same time frame by using this model's techniques. This approach has been used and researched with clients who suffer from post-traumatic stress disorder, such as war veterans and sexual assault and incest survivors (Forbes, Creamer, & Rycroft, 1994; Wilson, Becker, & Tinker, 1995).

Crisis intervention models have evolved over the past four decades to incorporate a wide variety of techniques and skills from many different theoretical approaches. This is important in order to intervene with diverse client populations in various crisis situations and settings. However, the basic principles and assumptions of crisis theory provide a foundation knowledge base from which more specialized strategies and techniques can be learned and developed. Two other important concepts in crisis intervention—types of crisis and stages in crisis—are discussed below.

TYPES OF CRISIS

Although each crisis and each individual's subjective experience of a crisis is unique, six main types of crises have been identified (Burgess & Baldwin, 1981).

Dispositional Crises

This type of crisis involves situational problems, such as health problems, relationship conflicts, and chemical dependency issues, that cause disequilibrium in the individual's life.

Anticipated Life Transitions

These crises are normal life tasks or activities that are very stressful, such as the loss of a job, bankruptcy, divorce, and relocation. The individual may have little or no control over the situation and may be unable to cope effectively.

Sudden Traumatic Stress

These crises are unexpected, accidental, and outside the individual's locus of control. They include disasters, crime victimization, family violence, child abuse, and sexual assault.

Maturational/Developmental Crises

This group of crises involves stressful psychosocial issues that are an expected part of the life span development. This involves being faced with difficult existential life issues such as identity, purpose, responsibility, independence, and commitment.

Crises Resulting from Psychopathology

This type of crisis stems from a preexisting psychopathology, such as schizophrenia or major depression, that can cause severe difficulties in adaptation for both the affected individual and the members of his or her family/support system.

Psychiatric Emergencies

These crises involve the acute onset of a major mental illness and/or suicidal attempts or threats.

STAGES OF CRISIS

The stages of crisis are similar to those of the grief process. These stages do not always follow a linear process—individuals can skip stages, can get stuck in a stage, or can move back and forth through successive stages. Although there are many theoretical frameworks for crisis intervention, most of them include the following four stages.

Outcry

This stage includes the initial reactions after the crisis event, which are reflexive, emotional, and behavioral in nature. These reactions can vary greatly and include panic, fainting, screaming, shock, anger, defensiveness, moaning, flat affect, crying, hysteria, and hyperventilation, depending on the situation and the individual.

Denial or Intrusiveness

Outcry can lead to denial, which is the blocking of the impacts of the crisis through emotional numbing, dissociation, cognitive distortion, or minimizing. Outcry also can lead to intrusiveness, which includes the involuntary flooding of thoughts and feelings about the crisis event or trauma, such as flashbacks, nightmares, automatic thoughts, and preoccupation with what has happened.

Working Through

This stage is the recovery or healing process in which the thoughts, feelings, and images of the crisis are expressed, acknowledged, explored, and reprocessed through adaptive, healthy coping skills and strategies. Otherwise, the individual may experience blockage or stagnation and develop unhealthy defense mechanisms to avoid working through the impacts, issues, and emotions associated with the crisis.

Completion or Resolution

This final stage may take months or years to achieve, and some individuals may never complete the process. The individual's recovery leads to integration of the crisis event, reorganization of his or her life, and adaptation and resolution of the trauma in positive meanings of growth, change, or service to others in crisis. Many crisis survivors reach out to support and help others who suffer similar traumas through volunteer work and service organizations, for example, Compassionate Friends, which offers support groups and counseling services to parents and family who have lost a child through death.

PHASES OF HELPING IN THE CRISIS INTERVENTION MODEL

The phases of helping in various models of crisis intervention (e.g., Gilliland & James, 1997; Golan, 1978; Hepworth et al., 1997) are similar to each other and to the phases of the problem-solving process. This chapter will focus on Roberts' (1991, 1995, 1996, in press) seven-stage crisis intervention model (see Figure 10.1), because it is the only model that focuses explicitly on the need to assess lethality, particularly when clients present because of a life-threatening (e.g., diagnosis of HIV positive) or dangerous and violent (e.g., woman battering or robbery victim) precipitating event. This model can be used with a broad range of crises and can facilitate the psychosocial/lethality assessment and helping process for effective crisis intervention across diverse types of clients and trauma situations (Roberts, 1996, in press).

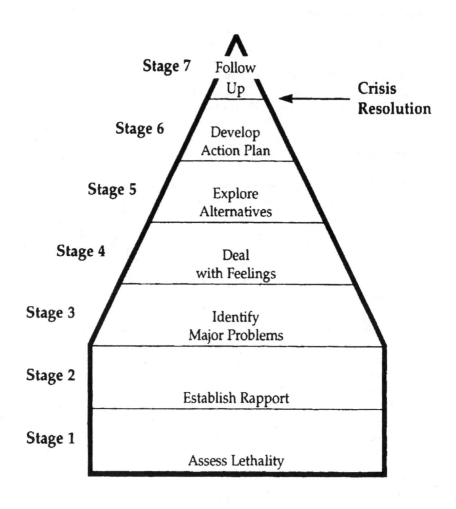

FIGURE 10.1   Roberts' (1991) seven-stage crisis intervention model.

STAGE 1: ASSESS LETHALITY

Assessment in this model is ongoing and critical to effective intervention at all stages, beginning with an assessment of lethality and safety issues for the client. With depressed or suicidal clients, it is critical to assess the risk for attempts, plans, or means to harm oneself at the current time, as well as any previous history of suicidal ideations or attempts. With victims of rape, family violence, child abuse, or assault, it is important to assess if the client is in any current danger, and to consider future safety concerns in treatment planning. In addition to determining lethality and the need for emergency intervention, it is crucial to maintain active communication with the client, either by phone or in person, while emergency procedures are being initiated (Roberts, 1998, 2000).

To plan and conduct a thorough assessment, the crisis worker needs to evaluate the following issues: (1) the duration and severity of the crisis, (2) the client's current emotional status, (3) the client's immediate psychological and social needs, and (4) the client's current coping strategies and resources. In the initial contact, assessment of the client's past or precrisis level of functioning and coping skills is useful; however, past history should not be a focus of assessment, unless related directly to the immediate traumatic event.

The goals of this stage are assessing and identifying critical areas of intervention, while also recognizing the hazardous event or trauma and acknowledging what has happened. At the same time, the crisis survivor becomes aware of his or her state of vulnerability and initial reactions to the crisis event. Thus, it is important that the crisis worker begin to establish a relationship based on respect for and acceptance of the client, while also offering support, empathy, reassurance, and reinforcement that the client has survived and that help is available.

STAGE 2: ESTABLISH RAPPORT AND COMMUNICATION

Survivors of trauma may question their own safety and vulnerability, and trust may be difficult for them to establish at this time. Therefore, active listening and empathic communication skills are essential to establishing rapport and engagement of the client. Even though the need for rapid engagement is essential, the crisis worker should try to let the client set the pace of treatment (Roberts, 2000). Many crisis victims feel out of control or powerless and should not be coerced, confronted, or forced into action, until they have stabilized and dealt with the initial trauma reactions.

Trauma survivors may require a positive future orientation, with an understanding that they can overcome current problems, and with hope that change can occur (Roberts, 1996). During this stage, clients need unconditional support, positive regard, concern, and genuineness. Empathic communication skills, such as minimal encouragers, reflection of thoughts and feelings, and active listening, can reassure the client and help establish trust and rapport with the client. The crisis worker needs to be attentive to the tone and level of the verbal communications to help the client calm down or deescalate from the initial trauma reactions.

The crisis worker must also pay attention to his or her body language and facial expressions, because trauma survivors may have been violated physically and be hypersensitive to physical space and body movements, which can frighten or startle the survivor. Facial expressions can be difficult to monitor due to their automatic nature, but this is especially important when working with disaster or trauma victims when physical damage and destruction are evident.

Being observant of the survivor's physical and facial reactions can provide cues to the worker's level of engagement with the client and can help to gauge the client's current emotional state. It is important to remember that delayed reactions or flat affect are common with trauma victims, and to not assume that these type of reactions mean that the survivor is not in crisis.

STAGE 3: IDENTIFY THE MAJOR PROBLEMS

The crisis worker should help the client prioritize the most important problems or effects by identifying these problems in terms of how they affect the survivor's current status. Encouraging the client to ventilate about the precipitating event can lead to problem identification, and some clients have an overwhelming need to talk about the specifics of the trauma situation. This process enables the client to figure out the sequence and context of the event(s), which can facilitate emotional ventilation, while providing information to assess and identify major problems for work.

Other crisis clients may be in denial or unable to verbalize their needs and feelings, so information may need to be obtained from collateral sources or significant others. It is essential to use a systems framework during the assessment and identification of problems, because crisis situations may impact at all levels of practice. Family members and significant others may be important to intervention planning in supportive roles or to ensure the client's safety. However, they may be experiencing their own reactions to the crisis situation, and this should be taken into consideration in contracting and implementing the intervention plan.

The crisis worker must ensure that the client system is not overwhelmed during this stage, and the focus should be on the most immediate and important problems needing intervention at this time. The first priority in this stage is meeting the basic needs of emotional and physical comfort and safety. After these have stabilized, other problems for work can then be addressed (Roberts, 1998).

STAGE 4: DEAL WITH FEELINGS AND PROVIDE SUPPORT

It is critical that the crisis worker demonstrate empathy and an anchored understanding of the survivor's experience, so that his or her symptoms and reactions are normalized and can be viewed as functional strategies for survival (Roberts & Dziegielewski, 1995). Many victims blame themselves, and it is important to help the client accept that being a victim is not one's fault. Validation and reassurance are especially useful in this stage, because survivors may be experiencing confusing and conflicting feelings.

Many clients follow the grief process when expressing and ventilating their emotions. First, survivors may be in denial about the extent of their emotional reactions and may try to avoid dealing with them in hopes that they will subside. They may be in shock and not be able to access their feelings immediately. However, significant delays in expression and ventilation of feelings can be harmful to the client in processing and resolving the trauma.

Some clients will express anger and rage about the situation and its effects, which can be healthy, as long as the anger does not escalate out of control. Helping the client calm down or attending to physiological reactions such as hyperventilation are important activities for the crisis worker in this situation. Other clients may express their grief and sadness by crying or moaning, and the crisis worker needs to allow time and space for this reaction, without pressuring the client to move along too quickly. Catharsis and ventilation are critical to healthy coping, and throughout this process, the crisis worker must recognize and support the client's courage in facing and dealing with these emotional reactions and issues. Crisis workers must also be aware of their own emotional reactions and level of comfort in helping the client through this stage.

STAGE 5: EXPLORE POSSIBLE ALTERNATIVES

In this stage, effective crisis workers help clients to recognize and explore a variety of alternatives for restoring a precrisis level of functioning. Such alternatives include (1) using *situational supports*, which are people or resources that can be helpful to the client in meeting needs and resolving problems in living as a result of the crisis; (2) developing *coping skills*, which are behaviors or strategies that promote adaptive responses; and (3) developing *positive and constructive thinking patterns*, which can lessen the client's levels of anxiety and stress (Gilliland & James, 1997).

The crisis worker can facilitate healthy coping skills by identifying client strengths and resources. Many crisis survivors feel they do not have a lot of choices, and the crisis worker needs to be familiar with both formal and informal community services to provide referrals. For example, working with a battered woman often requires relocation to a safe place for her and the children. The client may not have the personal resources or financial ability to move out of the home, and the crisis worker needs to be informed about the possible alternatives, which include a shelter program, a protective order, and other emergency housing services.

The crisis worker may need to be more active, directive, and confrontive in this stage, if the client has unrealistic expectations or inappropriate coping skills and strategies. Clients are still distressed and in disequilibrium at this stage, and professional expertise and guidance could be necessary to produce positive, realistic alternatives for the client.

Stage 6: Formulate and Implement an Action Plan

The success of any intervention plan depends on the client's level of involvement, participation, and commitment. The crisis worker must help the client look at both the short- and long-range affects in planning intervention. The main goals are to help the client achieve an appropriate level of functioning and maintain adaptive coping skills and resources. It is important to have a manageable treatment plan, so that the client can follow through and be successful. Do not overwhelm the client with too many tasks or strategies, which may set the client up for failure (Roberts, 1996, 2000).

Clients must feel a sense of ownership in the action plan, so that they can increase the level of control and autonomy in their lives, and to ensure that they not become dependent on other support persons or resources (Gilliland & James, 1997). Obtaining a commitment from the client to follow through with the action plan and any referrals is an important activity for the crisis worker that can be maximized by using a mutual process in intervention planning. Ongoing assessment and evaluation are essential to determine whether the intervention plan is appropriate and effective in minimizing or resolving the client's identified problems. During this stage, the client should be processing and reintegrating the crisis impacts to achieve homeostasis and equilibrium in his or her life.

The action plan should include attention to the four central tasks of crisis intervention (Slaikeu, 1984): (1) physical survival (maintaining physical health through adaptive coping skills and taking care of oneself through proper nutrition, exercise, sleep, and relaxation), (2) expression of feelings (appropriate emotional expression/ventilation and understanding how emotional reactions affect one's physiological and psychological well-being), (3) cognitive mastery (developing a reality-based understanding of the crisis event; addressing any unfinished business, irrational thoughts, or fears; and adjusting one's self-image/concept with regard to the crisis event and its impacts), and (4) behavioral/interpersonal adjustments (adapting to changes in daily life activities, goals, or relationships due to the crisis event and minimizing any long-term negative effects in these areas for the future).

Termination should begin when the client has achieved the goals of the action plan or has been referred for additional services through other treatment providers. Many survivors may need longer-term therapeutic help in working toward final crisis resolution, and referrals for individual, family, or group therapy should be considered at this stage.

Stage 7: Follow Up

It is hoped that the sixth stage has resulted in significant changes and resolution for the client, with regard to his or her postcrisis level of functioning and coping. This last stage should help determine whether these results have been maintained, or if further work remains to be done. Typically, follow-up contacts should be done within 4 to 6 weeks after termination. Final crisis resolution may take many months or years to achieve, and survivors should be aware that certain events, places, or dates can trigger emotional and physical reactions to the previous trauma. For example, a critical time is at the first anniversary of a crisis event, when clients may reexperience old fears, reactions, or thoughts. This is a normal part of the recovery process, and clients should be prepared to have contingency plans or supportive help through these difficult periods.

APPLICATION OF CRISIS INTERVENTION TO FAMILY AND GROUP WORK

Roberts' (1995) seven-stage model is applicable to family and group crisis intervention, although there are certain considerations in relation to these levels of practice. "It has been said, only partly facetiously, that families are either part of the problem or part of the solution" (Golan, 1978, p. 110). Certain crisis situations, such as shifts in family structure and developmental changes, can affect family members differently, so the crisis worker may have to assess who in the family is experiencing crisis and who will be participating in treatment.

Other crisis events, such as child abuse, family violence, and criminal offenses, involve demands from community agencies that a family member change certain behaviors or ways of coping (Bonnefil, 1980). Then there are traumatic situations that may affect all family members involved in the critical incident, such as disasters, accidents, and death.

During assessment, the family structure, dynamics, relationships, communication patterns, and support systems need to be evaluated as to potential strengths and areas in need of treatment. How the crisis affects the family system as a whole and the individuals, amount of family cooperation, and consideration of the family's support system in terms of local community resources is important in assessment and intervention planning.

Group crisis work is used with clients experiencing similar types of trauma, such as sexual assault and child abuse survivors, individuals in community or institutional disasters, persons with chemical dependency, and individuals dealing with loss and bereavement. Having the support of others who have shared similar crisis events is an important benefit of group therapy. Group work also allows members to learn from each other about ways to cope.

As in families, group members may have different reactions, experiences, feelings, and coping skills, so intervention has to be directed at the individual level, as well as with the group as a working system. The need for individual treatment in addition to group work should be part of the assessment and action plan. Self-help and time-limited groups are also excellent resources for more long-term crisis or grief resolution work.

COMPATIBILITY WITH A
GENERALIST-ECLECTIC FRAMEWORK

Crisis intervention has many things in common with a generalist-eclectic framework for direct social work practice. First, it is grounded in an eclectic orientation and theory base. This approach has incorporated the basic principles and perspectives from systems theory, ego psychology (including life cycle/human development theory), and cognitive-behavioral theories into a holistic framework for crisis intervention with diverse client populations and types of crises. Most crisis workers recognize that (1) there is no single theory that explains all clinical phenomena, (2) different treatment approaches work well with different clients, and (3) different combinations of approaches may be used with the same client (Parad & Parad, 1990).

Second, crisis intervention places an emphasis on client strengths and empowerment. A strengths approach is inherent in the crisis intervention strategy of building on the client's own coping skills and natural support system. Client empowerment is a natural outcome of this approach, because the focus in crisis work is to provide the support and resources for clients to resolve any negative effects through their own growth and development, and not to become dependent on others in their social environment to meet those needs.

Third, crisis intervention emphasizes holistic assessment within an ecosystemic perspective. Burgess and Roberts (2000) stress that crisis intervention must address the biological, psychological, and environmental damage and trauma, from both a macrosystemic and individual perspective. This is particularly true for catastrophic events. Current electronic media technology and its instant coverage of disasters has brought these events into our homes, and coverage of traumatic events has had ripple effects in the global community. This has helped to develop awareness of the importance of having large teams of experts in a variety of human and environmental specialties trained and available as rapid response teams to restore equilibrium to the total ecosystems environment in the event of catastrophes.

CRITIQUE OF CRISIS INTERVENTION

One of the strengths of crisis intervention is its effectiveness across diverse types of crises and client populations. However, although there is research and literature on specialized clients/crises, there is not much literature on cultural, gender, or age differences among crisis client populations. It is important that crisis workers be culturally competent and tailor crisis intervention practices to different ethnic and racial groups.

Another strength is the time-limited nature of crisis intervention that makes it conducive to the current realities of managed care and can permit crisis programs to reach larger numbers of clients for brief treatment. However, one of the drawbacks is that crisis workers usually don't see the end results of the initial interventions they have provided, and it may seem like a "Band-Aid" approach. Although crisis resolution may take much longer than the 4- to 6-week time frames of most crisis services, professionals must realize that a small amount of help at this critical time in a person's life can make a great difference in the long-term effects that might be experienced otherwise.

CASE EXAMPLE

Maria is a sexual assault victim who has just called 911 to report a rape by an intruder in her home. As the police officers rush to the scene, the victim services crisis counselor is requested as part of a team approach. When the police arrive, they begin the investigative work, and the victim services counselors begin the crisis intervention. The police get an initial report from Maria, and request backup at the scene to search for the suspect. They ask her if she is willing to go to the hospital for a rape exam to gather physical evidence. Maria is experiencing initial, postcrisis reactions, and the crisis counselors ask if they can speak with her. At this point, the focus of crisis intervention is to evaluate her medical and physical needs and to explain the investigative process to her so she can understand what is going on.

Maria is worried about leaving her home unattended, has questions about what will happen at the hospital, and is concerned about how much this will cost her, because she has no health insurance. She is concerned about telling her boyfriend, who is at work, and wants to call her parents. At the same time, she is remembering details about the rape and is experiencing shock and trauma reactions that are frightening and confusing. As the crisis counselors help her to calm down and focus on her immediate needs, they reassure her that they will be there to support her during the investigation and medical exam, will help her contact her loved ones, and will assist in making other necessary arrangements.

When they arrive at the hospital, the emergency room social worker is there to help during the medical exam and to answer the many medical and financial questions that worry Maria. While the police social workers contact her loved ones, they also telephone a rape crisis volunteer to assist with the case. After the police finish their initial report, they tell Maria that an investigator will be contacting her soon to take a formal statement. Maria has a lot of questions about this, which the crisis counselors answer. They also offer supportive services during the investigation and legal proceedings.

After the medical exam, the rape crisis volunteer arrives, along with Maria's family members. Plans are made for her to return to her parents' home, because she is too frightened to go to her own home. The police crisis workers then return to their duties, and the rape crisis volunteer accompanies Maria and her parents. Maria is concerned about how her boyfriend will react, and the rape crisis volunteer lets her ventilate her feelings and concerns about the sexual assault and its impact on her and her loved ones.

The rape crisis volunteer helps Maria develop a plan of how to tell her boyfriend about the rape. They also explore her immediate needs and any possible changes in her daily routine, such as whether she will go to work tomorrow, when she will return home, and what will happen if the police arrest a suspect. The volunteer also lets Maria know that counseling services are available at the rape crisis center, and that the volunteer will follow up with her tomorrow to see how she's doing and what she needs.

Maria's case will also be followed up by the police crisis counselors and by the victim-witness advocates in the court system when (and if) the case goes to trial. During this time, which can last over a year, support services will be provided through individual and group counseling at the rape crisis center. In this type of continuum of care, the different crisis counselors are responsible for various aspects of the case to ensure that the survivor receives crisis intervention services as needed.

SUMMARY

Crisis intervention is an eclectic approach that is effective across diverse types of crises, client populations, and settings. It is essential that social workers in generalist practice be knowledgeable about and trained in basic crisis intervention skills to meet the needs of their clients. Research studies, journal articles, and textbooks on both basic and specialized crisis intervention skills and models are available in a variety of disciplines and treatment areas. This chapter has provided an overview of the principles, theoretical constructs, and basic intervention skills in crisis intervention. Crisis work can be both demanding and difficult, but its rewards can be immediate and long-lasting for both clients and social workers.

REFERENCES

Boes, M. (1997). A typology for establishing social work staffing patterns within an emergency room. *Crisis Intervention and Time-Limited Treatment, 3*(3), 171–188.

Bonnefil, M. (1980). In G. Jacobson (Ed.), *Crisis intervention in the 1980s* (pp. 23–34). San Francisco: Jossey-Bass.

Burgess. A., & Baldwin, B. (1981). *Crisis intervention theory and practice: A clinical handbook.* Englewood Cliffs: NJ: Prentice-Hall.

Burgess, A., & Roberts, A. (1996). Family violence against women and children: Prevalence of assaults and fatalities, family dynamics, and intervention. *Crisis Intervention and Time-Limited Treatment, 3*(1), 65–80.

Burgess, A. W., & Roberts, A. R. (2000). Crisis intervention with persons diagnosed with clinical disorders on the stress-crisis continuum: A managed care perspective. In A. R. Roberts (Ed.), *Crisis intervention handbook: Assessment, treatment, and research* (2nd ed., pp. 56–76). New York: Oxford University Press.

Dublin, L. (1963). *Suicide: A sociological and statistical study*. New York: Ronald Press.

Dziegielewski, S. (1996). Managed care principles: The need for social work in the health care system. *Crisis Intervention and Time-Limited Treatment, 3*(2), 97–112.

Dziegielewski, S., & Resnick, C. (1995). A model of crisis intervention with adult survivors of incest. *Crisis Intervention and Time-Limited Treatment, 2*(1), 49–56.

Erikson, E. (1950). *Childhood and society*. New York: Norton.

Farberow, N., & Schneidman, E. (1961). *The cry for help*. New York: McGraw-Hill.

Forbes, D., Creamer, M., & Rycroft, P. (1994). Eye movement desensitization and reprocessing in posttraumatic stress disorder: A pilot study using assessment measures. *Journal of Behavior Therapy and Experimental Psychiatry, 25*, 113–120.

Gilliland, B., & James, R. (1997). *Crisis intervention strategies*. Pacific Grove, CA: Brooks/Cole.

Golan, N. (1978). *Treatment in crisis situations*. New York: The Free Press.

Greene, G., Lee, M., Trask, R., & Rheinscheld, J. (2000). How to work with client strengths in crisis intervention: A solution-focused approach. In A. R. Roberts (Ed.), *Crisis intervention handbook: Assessment, treatment and research* (2nd ed., pp. 31–55). New York: Oxford University Press.

Greene, G., Lee, M., Trask, R., & Rheinscheld, J. (1996). Client strengths and crisis intervention: A solution-focused approach. *Crisis Intervention and Time-Limited Treatment, 3*(1), 43–64.

Hepworth, D., Rooney, R., & Larsen, J. (1997). *Direct social work practice: Theory and skills*. Pacific Grove, CA: Brooks/Cole.

Liese, B. (1995). Brief therapy, crisis intervention, and cognitive therapy of substance abuse. *Crisis Intervention and Time-Limited Treatment, 2*(2), 11–30.

Lindemann, E. (1944). Symptomatology and management of acute grief. *American Journal of Psychiatry, 101*, 141–147.

Meyer, R., & Ottens, A. (1995). Assessment for crisis intervention on college campuses. *Crisis Intervention and Time-Limited Treatment, 2*(2), 31–46.

Parad, H., & Parad, L. (1990). *Crisis intervention book 2: The practitioner's sourcebook for brief therapy*. Milwaukee: Family Service America.

Polk, G. W. (1996). Treatment of problem drinking behavior using solution-focused therapy: A single-subject design. *Crisis Intervention and Time-Limited Treatment, 3*(1), 13–24.

Roberts, A. R. (1975). Self-destruction by one's own hands. In A. R. Roberts (Ed.), *Self-destructive behaviors* (pp. 3–31). Springfield, IL: Charles C. Thomas.

Roberts, A. R. (1990). *Helping crime victims: Research, policy, and practice*. Thousand Oaks, CA: Sage.

Roberts, A. R. (1991). Conceptualizing crisis theory and the crisis intervention model. In A. R. Roberts (Ed.), *Contemporary perspectives on crisis intervention and prevention* (pp. 3–17). Englewood Cliffs, NJ: Prentice-Hall.

Roberts, A. R. (1995). Crisis intervention units and centers in the United States: A national survey. In A. R. Roberts (Ed.), *Crisis intervention and time-limited cognitive treatment* (pp. 54–70).Thousand Oaks, CA: Sage.

Roberts, A. R. (1996). Epidemiology and definitions of acute crisis in American society. In A. R. Roberts (Ed.), *Crisis management and brief treatment* (pp. 16–33). Chicago: Nelson-Hall.

Roberts, A. R. (1997). *Social work in juvenile and criminal justice settings* (2nd ed.). Springfield, IL: Charles C. Thomas.

Roberts, A. R. (1998). *Battered women and their families: Intervention strategies and treatment programs* (2nd ed.). New York: Springer.

Roberts, A. R. (2000). An overview of crisis theory and crisis intervention. In A. R. Roberts (Ed.), *Crisis intervention handbook: Assessment, treatment, and research* (2nd ed., pp. 3–30). New York: Oxford University Press.

Roberts, A. R., & Dziegielewski. S. (1995). Foundation skills and applications of crisis intervention and cognitive therapy. In A. R. Roberts (Ed.), *Crisis intervention and time-limited cognitive treatment* (pp. 3–27). Thousand Oaks, CA: Sage.

Schneidman, E., Farberow, N., & Litman, R. (1970). *The psychology of suicide.* New York: Science House.

Schoenfeld, D., & Kline, M. (1994). School-based crisis intervention: An organizational model. *Crisis Intervention and Time-Limited Treatment, 1*(2), 155–169.

Slaikeu, K. (1984). *Crisis intervention: A handbook for practice and research.* Boston: Allyn & Bacon.

Thomas, V. (1996). Professional crisis intervention counselors: An overview of clinicians in health and mental health settings. *Crisis Intervention and Time-Limited Treatment, 2*(3), 199–212.

Webb, N. (1995). Assessment and crisis intervention with kindergarten children following a disaster: The World Trade Center Tragedy. *Crisis Intervention and Time-Limited Treatment, 2*(2), 47–60.

Wilson, G., & Lester, D. (1998). Suicide prevention by e-mail. *Crisis Intervention and Time-Limited Treatment, 4*(1), 81–88.

Wilson, S., Becker, L., & Tinker, R. (1995). Eye movement desensitization and reprocessing (EMDR) treatment for psychologically traumatized individuals. *Journal of Consulting and Clinical Psychology, 63*, 928–937.

11

The Task-Centered Model

Eleanor Reardon Tolson

The task-centered (TC) model was developed by social work educators and intended for work with social work clients including, but not limited to, those who are central to the profession's mission: the disadvantaged and disenfranchised. TC is a present-oriented, time-limited, problem-solving approach that helps clients to solve their problems as they define them. Changes in problems are secured by developing and implementing tasks. Task work is accomplished through specific, structured intervention activities called the Task Planning and Implementation Sequence. Respect for clients' rights to be self-determining is emphasized in TC.

TC is an empirical approach to practice. This means that it was developed from research findings about practice, constructed with concepts that are measurable, and includes procedures for evaluating outcomes on an ongoing basis. It has been tested and found effective.

TC can provide a structure for generalist practice that is both integrated and eclectic. This capacity results from the fact that TC is not attached to any particular theory of behavior. When explanations of behavior or alternative interventions are needed, it is possible to incorporate a wide variety of perspectives without losing the structure for intervention that the model provides. TC has been used at all system levels, including individuals, families, groups, organizations, and communities, and incorporates a strategy, work with collaterals, that makes it possible to include other systems in the intervention process.

HISTORICAL DEVELOPMENT

TC was developed in the early 1970s by Reid and Epstein (1972). One of the models for social work practice that was influential in its development was Perlman's *Social Casework: A Problem-Solving Process* (1957), which articulated the problem-solving paradigm. Studt's (1968) concept of tasks in treatment also made an important contribution. Equally influential were the research findings about practice that were being generated at that time. The findings pertained to the use of time limits, the dropout rate, and the timing of change. It was found that time-limited treatment was at least as effective as treatment of indefinite length (Reid & Shyne, 1969). This finding has been supported over time and in a large number of investigations (Gurman & Kniskern, 1981; Johnson & Gelso, 1982; Koss & Shiang, 1994; Luborsky, Singer, & Luborsky, 1975). The literature on dropouts found that a substantial number of clients terminated treatment prematurely (Beck & Jones, 1973; Garfield, 1994; Lake & Levinger, 1960; Levinger, 1960; Meltzoff & Kornreich, 1970; Silverman, 1970). It was and is believed that a major cause of dropout is a lack of congruence between client and worker about the focus of treatment. Additionally, it was found that a substantial amount of change occurred early in contact (Meltzoff & Kornreich, 1970; Orlinsky & Howard, 1986; Strupp, Fox, & Lessler, 1969).

TC can be seen as the result of integrating these influences. The work of Perlman and Studt is apparent in the concepts of target problems and tasks. The empirical findings led to the incorporation of time limits and the insistence that clients determine the focus of treatment or target problem.

During the past 25 years, TC has been continually tested and refined. It has been the subject of more than 35 published studies and doctoral dissertations, and findings have been consistently positive (Reid, 1992). Many of these studies have been controlled group experiments (Gibbons, Bow, & Butler, 1985; Gibbons, Butler, Urwin, & Gibbons, 1978; Larsen & Mitchell, 1980; Newcome, 1985; Reid, 1975, 1978; Reid & Bailey-Dempsey, 1995; Reid, Epstein, Brown, Tolson, & Rooney, 1980).

In addition to demonstrating the effectiveness of the approach, the studies have contributed to the development of the model. Perhaps the most important contribution of the research is the Task Planning and Implementation Sequence (TPIS). TPIS is a series of activities that are undertaken in the process of developing tasks. The research made it possible to identify the activities and, later, to test the effectiveness of them (Reid, 1978). Research is also beginning to help us understand what makes TC effective (Reid, 1997). Changes in target problems are associated with the amount of time spent on them. Task accomplishments are correlated with the degree of client commitment to doing the task and task preparation.

Recently, the possibility of using TC as a base for generalist practice has been explored (Tolson, Reid, & Garvin, 1994). It appears that the basic framework of TC can be adapted for work across system levels, including families, groups, organizations, and communities. A recent meta-analysis has found a greater average effect size for TC as compared to other generalist approaches (Gorey, Thyer, & Pawluck, 1998).

CENTRAL THEORETICAL CONSTRUCTS

As previously observed, TC is fundamentally an empirical approach to practice. This means that "one gives primacy to research-based theories and interventions but still maintains a skeptical attitude toward all theories and interventions" (Reid, 1992, p. 7). As a result, the theoretical base of TC is deliberately modest. The assumptions in this theoretical base pertain to the nature of problems, the nature of people, the source of motivation, and the source of change.

TC is intended to ameliorate psychosocial problems or problems in living. Problems are seen as inevitable and resulting from unsatisfied wants. Wants are shaped by belief systems, which include expectations, appraisals, and values. Unmet wants occur when life experiences fall short of expectations or are deemed deficient, unpleasant, unsatisfying, or unworthy (Reid, 1992). Unmet wants are the source for motivation. To capture this motivation, it is imperative that the clients determine the focus of treatment, which in TC is labeled the target problem. Problems are embedded in a context. The context can be the source of the unmet want, an obstacle to satisfying it, or a resource for alleviating it.

Human beings are seen as active problem-solvers who are capable of making rational choices about their wants and needs and participating in change efforts. Clients are people whose independent, problem-solving efforts have been unsuccessful. The objective of intervention is to assist the clients' efforts.

Action—in particular, client action—is believed to be the most efficient source of change and, frequently, the predecessor to attitudinal or emotional change. Furthermore, action and the ensuing feedback are critical sources of perceived self-efficacy that determine the amount and persistence of efforts an individual will expend (Bandura, 1986). Thus, successful action enhances self-efficacy, which, in turn, supports further action. This belief is manifest in the use of tasks, which are actions that clients carry out for the purpose of reducing target problems.

Although the foregoing beliefs and assumptions provide a theoretical base for TC, it must be emphasized that TC is an open and flexible framework for practice. This means that other theories and interventions can and should be incorporated as the need for them arises. In fact, it is expected that the model and its theoretical underpinnings will change as knowledge is generated. Other sources should be selected and chosen on the basis of their relevance to the situation and the extent to which they are supported by empirical research. There is one vital caveat to borrowing from theories of human behavior: They should not be used to formulate the target problems (Reid, 1992). Rather, the problem should be used to scan different theories for determining the usefulness of them.

PHASES OF HELPING

The phases of helping in TC are usually identified as initial, middle, and termination. The initial phase activities include explaining role, purpose, and treatment procedures; obtaining necessary information; identifying, prioritizing, and specifying the target problems; identifying goals; setting time limits; contracting; and assessing. All of these activities must be accomplished to some extent before any intervention can occur. The middle phase consists of employing the TPIS. TPIS is composed of a number of subactivities, which are described in the section on intervention. The last phase is termination. Relationship or rapport is seen as ongoing. Space limitations dictate a succinct summary of TC. Detailed descriptions of the procedures can be found in Reid (1992) and Tolson, Reid, and Garvin (1994).

INITIAL PHASE

Engagement

Engagement in TC is three-pronged: developing a relationship with clients, introducing them to the problem-solving process, and connecting with them through a mutual commitment to resolve client-defined problems.

The view of relationship in TC is consonant with the research on the topic, which finds that it is a mediating variable. This means that a good relationship is necessary but not sufficient to secure change (Lambert, DeJulio, & Stein, 1978; Mitchell, Bozarth, & Krauft, 1977; Orlinsky & Howard, 1986; Parloff, Waskow, & Wolfe, 1978; Patterson, 1984). Qualities stressed include warmth, empathy, genuineness, nonjudgmental acceptance, and respect for the client's right to self-determination. A relationship is developed as one engages in problem-solving; however, with children, some time usually has to be allotted for them to become familiar with the worker before problem-solving efforts begin.

Introduction to work is based on role induction or client preparation, the importance of which has been validated (Acosta, Yamamoto, Evans, & Skilbeck, 1983; Sloane, Cristol, Pepernik, & Staples, 1970; Zwick & Attkisson, 1984). It includes explaining the social worker's role (name, title, name and purpose of agency, worker's purpose within the agency, the source and reason for referral when the client is not voluntary) and treatment procedures. In TC the important issues to explain in this early stage are that the focus will be determined by the client and that work will be time-limited. Emphasis is placed on these two issues because they appear to enhance motivation, especially for nonvoluntary clients. The use of client preparation in TC is not limited to the initial session. We have found that repeating explanations is often sufficient to restart work that has bogged down.

Data Collection and Assessment

The most important activity in TC is the identification of target problems. Target problems are the aspects of the clients' lives that they most want changed. In TC it is imperative that clients choose the target problems. This does not mean that the client must be the one to identify the problem or that the worker should refrain from mentioning potential target problems. It does mean that the final choice of the focus of treatment will be determined by the client.

Identifying target problems includes two steps. First, all problems are listed. This list is usually generated by asking the client what aspects of his or her life the client would like to be different. In some cases, the client does not readily identify problems, and it is necessary to engage in a problem search that consists of reviewing the various arenas (work, school, personal relationships, health, mood, etc.) of the client's life. First, the client is encouraged to identify an inclusive list of concerns. Second, the client is asked to prioritize these potential problems. Usually no more than three target problems are worked on simultaneously. Problems include feelings, behaviors, attitudes, circumstances (including resource deficiencies), relationships, and skill deficits.

Data collection and assessment center on the target problems and entail detailed exploration. The goal of data collection is to develop a "problem specification." Problem specification consists of two activities: describing the manifestations of the problems and determining the frequency, duration, or severity of them. This process will be described using two different types of problems: depression and housing.

The manifestations of depression for a particular client might include crying spells, inability to sleep, and inability to perform daily chores. Manifestations are elicited by exploring how the client experiences the problem, and these will differ across clients with the same target problem. The next step concerns making the manifestations measurable so that change can be monitored. We want to know how many times the client cries each day or each week and how many hours per night he or she sleeps. Performance of chores can be indicated by the percent of chores completed or the time spent performing them on either a daily or a weekly basis.

A problem specification for acquiring resources is somewhat different. The manifestations are the characteristics that describe adequate resource provision for the particular client. Manifestations for a housing problem might pertain to the number of bedrooms, geographical location, and cost. In this case, manifestations are measured in terms of whether or not the desired characteristics have been obtained.

Problem specification enables the worker to individualize treatment by focusing on the particular manifestations of the problem as the client experiences it and to monitor changes as they occur over time. Monitoring change is necessary for making treatment decisions, as well as for assessing outcome. Problem specification is one of the unique strengths of TC, because it makes practice evaluation part of treatment.

During the process of exploring potential target problems and developing the problem specification(s), the worker will usually learn a great deal about the context of the problem. An ecosystem's framework is used for organizing this information and identifying gaps. The nature and impact of micro-, mezzo-, and macro-level systems are considered. This systemic assessment often influences decisions about how problems are to be solved and sometimes suggests modifications in the target problems. Frequently, it identifies important collaterals—people who are personally or professionally related to client in the problem areas. Collaterals are representatives of other systems and are frequently involved, provided the client gives permission. The importance of collaterals is the linkage they provide for affecting other systems.

Goals, Time Limits, and Contracts

Establishing goals, setting time limits, and contracting occur before intervention. In TC, goals are determined by the client, but the worker helps to make them measurable. Thus, if the client's goal is to "feel better," the worker would help him or her to define "feeling better." A useful way to do this is to refer to the manifestations of the problem that were identified in the problem specification. Using the specification previously described, the worker would ask the client to identify the number of crying spells, chores, and hours of sleep that are desired. When the goal is long term, the client is asked to identify conditions that indicate that it will be accomplished. The conditions for the goal of graduating from college, for example, may include passing all courses with a particular grade point average.

Time limits usually range from 6 to 12 sessions but can be as brief as 1 session. When more time is needed, contract extensions are considered, provided there is evidence that the client is working to resolve the problem. Contracts in TC are usually verbal. They include a list of the target problems and goals, the number and frequency of sessions, the participants, and fees, if applicable.

MIDDLE PHASE: THE USE OF TASK PLANNING AND IMPLEMENTATION SEQUENCE (TPIS) IN INTERVENTION

TPIS is the intervention in TC. It consists of a number of activities that are employed in developing tasks. A task is something the client does outside the session that is intended to reduce the target problem. There are two other types of tasks: practitioner and in-session tasks. Practitioner tasks are performed outside the session by the practitioner. In-session tasks, which are most frequently used in work with families, are performed during the treatment interview.

TPIS consists of the following activities: generating tasks, eliciting agreement to perform the task, planning the details of implementation, establishing the rationale and incentive for performing the task, simulating the task, identifying obstacles to task performance, summarizing the tasks, and reviewing task accomplishment and problem change. Each of these activities is briefly described. Although work will always begin with generating alternatives, the sequence in which the activities are accomplished is variable.

Generating task alternatives consists of brainstorming with the client the possible actions that could be taken to alleviate the target problem. It is important to suggest alternatives and to encourage the client to do so (see Reid, in press, for tasks for particular problems). The more alternatives, the better. Worker and client consider the advantages and disadvantages of the alternatives, and the client is asked to select the preferred one(s). The client is also asked whether he or she is willing to attempt the task. As with target problems, the client has the last word in choosing tasks.

After a task is chosen, the ways in which it will be implemented are planned. Decisions have to been made about when it is to be done, how often, for how long, where, with whom, under what circumstances, and in what manner. In addition to the common factors that must be planned, many tasks will require decisions about unique details. These are identified by thinking through what will be required to perform the task successfully. Careful planning is particularly important with tasks that are expected to be performed only once, such as asking for a raise at work. Some of the unique details might be identified when the client and worker begin to consider the obstacles that might be encountered. In this activity, potential hurdles are identified and ways to surmount them are planned. Although it is important to identify and plan for likely obstacles, it is also important to avoid raising unlikely concerns. Clients need to believe that they can do the tasks even if the tasks are challenging.

Establishing rationale refers to making sure that the client is aware of what is to be gained by performing the task. Incentives refer to concrete rewards that the client will receive for performing the task. They can be provided by the client, the worker, or collaterals. Incentives are particularly important when the task is difficult. The client whose task is to ask for a raise might plan to treat himself or herself to a nice dinner following task implementation, for example.

Simulation and guided practice involve rehearsing the task. These activities provide an opportunity for the client to practice the task and for the worker to provide feedback. Summarizing is done to ensure that the client knows what tasks are to be performed before the next session. Often clients are asked to provide the summary. When it is likely that some tasks might be forgotten, a task review schedule is provided (Rooney, 1981).

Problem and task reviews occur at the beginning of every session once task work has begun. The object is to learn the extent to which the tasks were implemented and the extent to which the target problems have changed. The problem specification developed during the initial phase can serve as a guide for problem review. Both task accomplishment and problem change can be rated on a 4-point scale. The client is praised when tasks are implemented. When they are not implemented or do not have the intended effect on problems, tasks are revised based on the obstacles that have been identified during the review. If tasks consistently are not performed, the target problems are reevaluated to check that they are conditions that the client indeed wants to change.

At each session, the client is reminded of the number of sessions that have occurred and the number that remain. Time limits can be extended when the client has been performing tasks and it is likely that problem resolution can be reached in a specified period of time.

TERMINATION

Termination in TC is usually limited to one session. Brevity is possible because clients are reminded of the time limits in each interview. During the last session, the worker and the client engage in a final problem review, make plans for maintaining or enhancing gains, review the problem-solving process, and discuss their reactions to separation. Praise for the client's accomplishments is offered liberally.

APPLICATION TO FAMILY AND GROUP WORK

FAMILY WORK

Family work in TC consists of consulting with more than one family member for the purpose of resolving problems. It is not required to see all or most family members, although it is often helpful to see the entire family once; nor is it required to see family members together for all sessions. Because the most important activity for enhancing and maintaining motivation is the accurate identification of target problems that are meaningful to family members, care is taken to secure everyone's opinion about what they would like to see changed. Each family member is asked to share concerns. Generally, the lists of problems will differ, which makes prioritizing critically important, because each member has to believe that he or she has something to gain. In some cases, the family, when asked as a group which problems are most important, will readily reach agreement. When there are disagreements, a useful procedure to facilitate prioritization is to consider, as each problem is described, whether it is shared, reciprocal, or individual. Shared concerns are those that are experienced by more than one member. Reciprocal concerns require a change in another person in the family. Individual concerns primarily affect only one member. When families do not readily agree on priorities, the worker can suggest a priority on shared problems and pairs of reciprocal problems. For example, if the parents are complaining about homework completion and the teenager is complaining about curfew, prioritizing both these problems will enable the participants to consider "trade-offs" (later curfew for more homework) during the intervention phase and will give everyone a stake in successful problem resolution.

GROUP WORK

Group work consists of working with more than one unrelated person who may share some problem area. TC group work can be used with either natural groups (e.g., several tenants in a housing project) or formed groups. Unlike the situation with families, the members will share an area of concern, such as problems in getting needed repairs to apartments or developing satisfying relationships. Group members are seen together for all treatment sessions, but the group sessions might be supplemented by individual sessions for members who need additional help. The unique challenges in group work entail developing a group culture that supports the members in their problem-solving efforts and using the model efficiently so that all members can progress.

The extent to which the individual concerns are related to the overall purpose of the group will affect progress and the attractiveness of the group to the members. Thus, individual pretreatment sessions to assess whether the person wants to participate in group work and in this particular group are strongly recommended. To expedite work and encourage participation throughout the stages of group development, members are taught the activities as they are encountered. In the initial phase, for example, members are taught to help one another identify target problems. When the members understand what is to be accomplished, they can be divided into subgroups or consulting pairs to work on a particular activity. Members who fall behind the progress of the group can be helped with individual sessions. An alternative is to pair a member who is making rapid progress with one who is struggling. Throughout the process, the worker is teaching the group member to give and receive feedback, to talk and listen to one another, to relate empathically, and to use the problem-solving method.

COMPATIBILITY WITH THE GENERALIST-ECLECTIC FRAMEWORK

PROBLEM-SOLVING STRUCTURE AND THEORETICAL OPENNESS

TC is a structure for generalist-eclectic practice. Two of the defining characteristics of generalist approaches, a problem-solving structure and theoretical openness, have been part of TC since its inception. It is a flexible, structured problem-solving approach in that it comprises a specific set of procedures that are expected to alleviate problems and to be adapted according to the needs of the client and the situation. Flexibility derives from the fact that it is not attached to a particular theory of behavior but can be shaped to include understandings from many theories, as well as interventions from other approaches. TC functions like our spines: sufficiently structured to keep us upright but sufficiently flexible to allow us to bend. Interventions from many different theories have been incorporated into TC on a case-by-case basis, including behavioral and cognitive-behavioral therapies, family systems therapies, bibliotherapy, narrative therapies, and crisis intervention strategies. Interventions borrowed from other approaches are usually incorporated as tasks. Approaches that are incompatible with TC are those in which clients do not choose the focus of intervention, those in which long-term treatment is required, and those, like many educational approaches, that do not individualize intervention.

HOLISTIC ASSESSMENT AND MULTISYSTEM FOCUS

Two other characteristics common to generalist approaches, holistic assessment and applicability to work with all levels of systems, evolved over time in TC. The concept of context as a hierarchy of multiple open systems that guides a holistic assessment of problems emerged in the mid-1980s (Reid, 1985). The use of this concept is continuing to be refined. The applications to work with other systems emerged as social workers experimented with using the model with families, groups, communities and organizations. These efforts have been synthesized by Tolson and colleagues (1994).

EMPOWERMENT, DIVERSITY, AND THE STRENGTHS PERSPECTIVE

TC also embraces the generalist-eclectic framework's commitment to empowerment and concern for those who are disadvantaged and disenfranchised, although it should be noted that such emphases extend beyond and predate generalist practice. They are central to the mission of social work and distinguish it from other helping professions. The extent to which TC reflects this mission can be seen by examining the strategies of empowerment and the populations that have been served with TC.

The techniques common to empowerment approaches include (1) accepting the client's definition of the problem; (2) identifying and building upon existing strengths; (3) engaging in a power analysis of the client's situation; (4) teaching specific skills; and (5) mobilizing resources and advocating for clients (Gutierrez, 1990, pp. 151–152). The first technique is, in fact, the golden rule of TC. Recognizing and building on strengths are implicit in that the client's judgment is trusted and tasks are developed that utilize strengths. Furthermore, care is taken to develop tasks that are likely to enhance self-efficacy. Skills are frequently taught either because a skill deficit is the target problem or because they are necessary to successful task completion. Mobilizing resources and advocating are aspects of practitioner tasks. At this time, TC does not include engaging the client in a power analysis, although engaging the client in a contextual analysis sometimes illuminates power dynamics.

TC has been used successfully in child welfare, public social services, school social work, corrections, medical settings, industrial settings, geriatric settings, family service, and mental health (Reid, 1996). Many of these settings disproportionately serve poor and ethnically diverse populations. In addition, poor and minority clients are disproportionately represented in the controlled studies of the effectiveness of TC.

THERAPEUTIC RELATIONSHIP

Similar to the generalist-eclectic framework and traditional social work practice, TC holds that the development of a good working relationship with the client is critically important. It should be noted, however, that TC eschews the phrase "therapeutic relationship," because it can be interpreted to mean that the relationship is the cause of change, a belief espoused in psychotherapy models in the past. Rather, as previously described, the relationship is viewed as necessary but not sufficient to cause change. This is consistent with research on the topic. The kind of relationship that is sought in TC is highly collaborative. Workers and clients participate in the decisions that are made as partners, with the worker contributing knowledge and assuming the responsibility for keeping the process moving and the client holding the power to choose the focus of treatment and the course of action.

Although the view of generalist-eclectic practice developed by the editors of this book and those of TC are consistent on the applied level, there may be some differences in philosophy. The driving ambition in TC is to develop a model that is effective, as demonstrated by scientific methods, in alleviating psychosocial problems. This purpose has implications for the use of knowledge and the generation of it.

CRITIQUE OF TC

The research regarding the effectiveness of TC has been referred to in preceding sections. The model has been found to be effective with a wide variety of challenging problems and populations. The controlled studies previously cited, for example, included "psychiatric patients, distressed marital couples, sick elderly patients, families seeking to regain their children from foster care, school children with academic and behavioral problems, sexual offenders, and delinquents in a residential center" (Reid, 1996, p. 635).

Based on the evidence, TC is an attractive "first-line" approach in most situations for several reasons (Tolson, 1988). First, it is likely to be effective. Second, ineffectiveness will be quickly apparent by means of problem reviews. Third, it is easier and more efficient to shift from TC to less structured and lengthier approaches than it is to shift to TC. Starting with a straightforward, time-limited approach is appealing to most clients, and, when results are unsatisfactory, clients generally are willing to participate in other approaches to alleviate the identified problems.

There are some clients for whom TC is not a good first choice. For example, mandated clients who do not want help and who are unable to identify any aspects of their lives that they wish to change are not appropriate (it is usually possible, however, to identify target problems with mandated clients). Clients who wish to explore existential concerns or who seek ongoing support of a general nature are not well served by TC. Finally, clients who do not choose or are not ready to take action to solve problems may prefer other approaches. This will be evident when tasks are reviewed.

The array of problems that has been addressed by TC has expanded. As a result, it seems premature to eliminate the application of TC to any particular problems. However, applications of TC in six problem areas have been delineated: family problems, emotional distress, problem drinking, problems of clients with chronic mental illness, health related problems, and inadequate resources (Reid, 1992). TC should not be the first choice when there is an alternative approach that has demonstrated effectiveness for a particular problem. For example, a child with obsessive-compulsive disorder (OCD) probably will be best served by the cognitive-behavioral approach of March and Mulle (1997). It is entirely possible to integrate the procedures of this approach into the task activity of TC, however, if doing so seems desirable. Because there are no comparative studies of TC and cognitive-behavioral work with children with OCD, the choice will depend on situational factors, including which approach is likely to be appealing to the client.

CASE ILLUSTRATION

Mrs. Carter, a 40-year-old African-American widow, has 10 children. Nine of her 10 children (ages 2 to 15) were placed in foster homes a year before TC was employed to help her (Rooney, 1981). Public assistance has been providing support for the past 15 years. The reason for the removal of the children is disputed. The client reports that she had agreed to place the children temporarily while she was in the hospital for surgery, whereas others report that the hospitalization was for alcoholism. Mrs. Carter has

changed her mind about both the hospitalization and temporary placement, but the child welfare agency went to court to obtain temporary
custody, citing the truancy and hygiene of the children, the client's alcoholism, and her inability to supervise her children.

Work involves a number of collaterals, including three public assistance
(PA) workers, two child welfare workers, the landlord, individuals connected with Alcoholics Anonymous (AA), various foster parents, school
personnel, the juvenile court judge and various court officials (including
several public defenders and prosecutors), and representatives of the public
housing authority. Complicating the situation is the fact that the relationships between some of the collaterals and Mrs. Carter are poor, and she
has to persuade them that she is cooperative and responsible.

At the first, brief meeting, Mrs. Carter, although inebriated and sometimes incoherent, clearly states her concern: She wants her children returned. Mr. Rooney, the social worker, is employed by a private agency
that has been subcontracted to serve some of the child welfare clientele.
During the second session, work begins on the conditions specified by the
court for Mrs. Carter to regain custody of her children. These conditions
include inadequate housing (her two pieces of furniture did not include
a stove or refrigerator, and there was no hot water), her drinking problem,
the children's school attendance, and an unkept home. Correcting these
conditions becomes the focus of treatment. Major obstacles are encountered in eradicating these conditions. For example, attempts to make the
current apartment adequate fail when the landlord refuses to make the
necessary improvements, instructs the tenants to send their rent to the gas
company, and threatens Mrs. Carter with eviction. Securing new housing
is complicated: Mrs. Carter lacks funds. PA workers have to approve the
new housing. Moving to a new area means the case will have to be transferred
to another PA office and the transfer will take 12 weeks. Another target
problem identified by Mrs. Carter: She has not seen her youngest children
for 2 months.

The following excerpt is a portion of the discussion about seeing the
children. Development of a task, consideration of an obstacle, and planning
one of the details is included.

Mrs. Carter: *I wish you'd ask them [i.e., child welfare] [to let her see her children].*
Mr. Rooney: *I would suggest this time—have you talked to her [a child welfare*
                worker] on the phone yet?
Mrs. Carter: *Nope. I never talked to nobody on the phone.*
Mr. Rooney: *Well, sooner or later you're going to have to start dealing with her*
                more often, because you know she's got to get to know you better.
                Right now, she doesn't know much about you and she doesn't trust
                you very much, and you don't trust her. What I would suggest is . . .
Mrs. Carter: *Well, I don't care nothing about her, period! I don't like her.*
Mr. Rooney: *She doesn't like you either.*

Mrs. Carter:	*She doesn't have anything to do with my kids; she's supposed to bring them in.*
Mr. Rooney:	*That's right; you have that right, so I would suggest that you—I can give you her number—you call her.*
Mrs. Carter:	*I got her number.*
Mr. Rooney:	*Ask her when it can be done—and I'll call her later—*
Mrs. Carter:	*Okay.*
Mr. Rooney:	*—to follow up. But she needs to hear from you first, I think.*

In the next excerpt, Mrs. Carter reflects movingly on her problems with alcohol. She shares her decision to attend AA meetings, a task Mr. Rooney had suggested previously.

Mrs. Carter:	*Doctor told me last year that I had to stop drinking. And I never did take him in my mind, you know.*
Mr. Rooney:	*That contributes to it [problem of high blood pressure], doesn't it?*
Mrs. Carter:	*Yeah. All that whiskey and wine and stuff. It runs your blood pressure up. See, I always did have trouble with my blood pressure; I started as a kid. And then when I started getting drunk, falling out and, you know, on the street and things, wind up in the hospital—you didn't know that, did you? (Laughs) Yeah, I did that a couple times last year. Got drunk and fell out on the sidewalk and wind up in the hospital.*
Mr. Rooney:	*All I remember is the first time I met you, you were in pretty bad shape.*
Mrs. Carter:	*(Laughs) Yeah, doctor said if I didn't stop it, I would wind up with sclerosis of the liver. The only reason that mine affects me so bad when I start it I don't—I stop eating. I don't have no appetite to eat. I just have a appetite to stay drunk.*
Mr. Rooney:	*What about now?*
Mrs. Carter:	*I don't want to drink because I might not survive next time I fall out. And I want my kids back. So I put myself to a test. I don't think it's always going to be easy, but—I guess I'm going through another phase.*
Mr. Rooney:	*A good phase.*
Mrs. Carter:	*Yup. I don't want no more. 'Cause he even told me, the doctor said you can drink some, but I don't want to drink no more, period. Alcohol has caused me everything bad that has happened to me in my life. Caused me to be drunk, get my TV stole out of here, my radio.*
Mr. Rooney:	*People take advantage of you?*
Mrs. Carter:	*Of course.*
Mr. Rooney:	*You see, that's the thing; I think that PA doesn't know . . . they have been here but once in 5 months and they don't know that you haven't been acting like the person they knew before.*

Mrs. Carter: *I know that.*

Mr. Rooney: *So what they've been trying to say to me and to you is, why should we make any special efforts for somebody who is going to, you know, not be able to hold up?*

Mrs. Carter: *They say once you do something, you always have to do it, but that's wrong. A person can change if he really wants to . . . see, I've been so weak all my life 'til I just can't stand to hurt nobody. I would let them hurt me and then I go and get drunk and forget about it, but you don't forget about it. You forget about it while you're drunk 'cause you don't know nothing else, and when you're real drunk, you're out.*

Mr. Rooney: *And then?*

Mrs. Carter: *When you get sober, it's the same thing.*

The original contract with Mrs. Carter was for 12 weeks. In fact, several 12-week extensions occurred and 55 sessions were held over a period of 14 months. The length of time consumed was largely because of the slowness of the bureaucratic agencies involved. Contract extensions had to be approved by the public child welfare agency. Extensions were normally difficult to obtain, but the careful documentation of task accomplishments was persuasive. At the end of the contract, which occurred because Mr. Rooney was leaving the area, four of Mrs. Carter's children were in her custody. They were attending school regularly and progressing satisfactorily. The cleanliness of the apartment was vastly improved. Mrs. Carter was to petition for the return of the remaining children when she was able to provide beds for them. At termination, she had saved enough money to purchase two more beds, and a petition hearing was scheduled for the following month. Work with Mrs. Carter demonstrates the usefulness of TC in some of the most challenging circumstances. It can be seen that mandated clients are not necessarily unmotivated, provided efforts are addressed to their concerns. The work also reveals a flexible use of time limits and a collaborative relationship with a client who was rightfully suspicious of professionals.

SUMMARY

Although the research supporting TC is more extensive than that of other approaches to the practice of social work, more is needed. There is a need to test the model with more systems, problems, and populations. More comparative studies are needed, as well as ones that examine long-term effectiveness. Finally, testing the relative effectiveness of separate parts of the model might identify the elements that are vital for success. There are some specific components of TC that merit additional empirical attention. All generalist approaches would benefit from more empirical information about the use of collaterals and practitioner tasks because it would enhance our ability to include the context or environment in our intervention efforts. Studies of the associations between relationship variables and outcomes would permit more specificity in the delineation of the types of relationships that are desired and the ways to achieve them. This is an ambitious agenda, and everyone is invited to participate.

REFERENCES

Acosta, F. X., Yamamoto, J., Evans, L. A., & Skilbeck, W. M. (1983). Preparing low-income Hispanic, Black, and White patients for psychotherapy: Evaluation of a new orientation program. *Journal of Clinical Psychology, 39*, 872–877.

Bandura, A. (1986). *Social foundations of thought and action: A social cognitive theory.* Englewood Cliffs, NJ: Prentice-Hall.

Beck, D. F., & Jones, M. A. (1973). *Progress on family: problems A nationwide study of clients' and counselors views on family agency services.* New York: Family Service Agency of America.

Garfield, S. L. (1994). Research on client variables in psychotherapy. In A. Bergin & S. Garfield (Eds.), *Handbook of psychotherapy and behavior change* (4th ed., pp. 190–228). New York: Wiley.

Gibbons, J., Bow, I., & Butler, J. (1985). Task-centered social work after parasuicide. In E. M. Goldberg, J. Gibbons, & I. Sinclair (Eds.), *Problems, tasks, and outcomes: The evaluation of task-centered casework in three settings* (pp. 169–257). Boston: Allen & Unwin.

Gibbons, J. S., Butler, J., Urwin, P., & Gibbons, J. L. (1978). Evaluation of a social work service for self-poisoning parents. *British Journal of Psychiatry, 133*, 111–118.

Gorey, K. M., Thyer, B. A., & Pawluck, D. E. (1998). Differential effectiveness of prevalent social work practice models: A meta-analysis. *Social Work, 43*, 269–278.

Gurman, A. S., & Kniskern, D. (1981). Family therapy outcome research: Knowns and unknowns. In A. S. Gurman & D. Kniskern (Eds.), *Handbook of family therapy* (pp. 742–775). New York: Brunner/Mazel.

Gutierrez, L. M. (1990). Working with women of color: An empowerment perspective. *Social Work, 35*, 1499–1553.

Johnson, D. H., & Gelso, C. J. (1982). The effectiveness of time limits in counseling and psychotherapy: A critical review. *Counseling Psychologist, 9*, 70–83.

Koss, M., & Shiang, J. (1994). Research on brief psychotherapy. In A. Bergin & S. Garfield (Eds.), *Handbook of psychotherapy and behavior change* (4th ed., pp. 664–700). New York: Wiley.

Lake, M., & Levinger, G. (1960). Continuance beyond application interviews at a child guidance clinic. *Social Casework, 41*, 303–309.

Lambert, M. J., DeJulio, S. S., & Stein, D. M. (1978). Therapist interpersonal skills: Process, outcome, methodological considerations and recommendations for future research. *Psychological Bulletin, 85*, 467–489.

Larsen, J., & Mitchell, C. (1980). Task-centered strength oriented group work with delinquents. *Social Casework, 61*, 154–163.

Levinger, G. (1960). Continuance in casework and other helping relationships: A review of current research. *Social Work, 5*, 40–51.

Luborsky, L., Singer, S., & Luborsky, L. (1975). Comparative studies of psychotherapy. *Archives of General Psychiatry, 32,* 995–1008.

March, J. S., & Mulle, K. (1997). *OCD in children and adolescents: A cognitive-behavioral treatment manual.* New York: Guilford Press.

Meltzoff, J., & Kornreich, M. (1970). *Research in psychotherapy.* New York: Atherton Press.

Mitchell, K. M., Bozarth, J. D., & Krauft, C. C. (1977). A reappraisal of the therapeutic effectiveness of accurate empathy, nonpossessive warmth, and genuineness. In A. S. Gurman & A. Razin (Eds.), *Effective psychotherapy* (pp. 482–502). Oxford: Pergamon Press.

Newcome, K. (1985). Task-centered group work with the chronically mentally ill in day treatment. In A. E. Fortune (Ed.), *Task-centered practice with families and groups* (pp. 78–91). New York: Springer.

Orlinsky, D. E., & Howard, K. I. (1986). Process outcome in psychotherapy. In S. L. Garfield & A. E. Bergin (Eds.), *Handbook of psychotherapy and behavior change* (pp. 311–381). New York: Wiley.

Parloff, M. B., Waskow, I. E., & Wolfe, B. E. (1978). Research on therapist variables in relation to process and outcome. In S. Garfield & A. Bergin (Eds.), *Handbook of psychotherapy and behavior change* (pp. 233–282). New York: Wiley.

Patterson, C. H. (1984). Empathy, warmth, and genuineness in psychotherapy: A review of reviews. *Psychotherapy: Theory, Research, and Practice, 21,* 431–438.

Perlman, H. H. (1957). *Social casework: A problem-solving process.* Chicago: University of Chicago Press.

Reid, W. J. (1975). An experimental test of a task-centered approach. *Social Work, 20,* 3–9.

Reid, W. J. (1978). *The task-centered system.* New York: Columbia University Press.

Reid, W. J. (1985). *Family problem solving.* New York: Columbia University Press.

Reid, W. J. (1992). *Task strategies: An empirical approach to social work practice.* New York: Columbia University Press.

Reid, W. J. (1996). Task-centered social work. In F. J. Turner (Ed.), *Social work treatment* (4th ed., pp. 617–640). New York: The Free Press.

Reid, W. J. (1997). Research on task-centered practice. *Social Work Research, 21,* 132–137.

Reid, W. J. (in press). *The task planner.* New York: Columbia University Press.

Reid, W. J., & Bailey-Dempsey, C. (1995). The effects of monetary incentives on school performance. *Families in Society, 76,* 331–340.

Reid, W. J., & Epstein, L. (Eds.). (1972). *Task-centered casework.* New York: Columbia University Press.

Reid, W. J., Epstein, L., Brown, L., Tolson, E. R., & Rooney, R. H. (1980). Task-centered school social work. *Social Work in Education, 2,* 7–24.

Reid, W. J., & Shyne, A. W. (1969). *Brief and extended casework.* New York: Columbia University Press.

Rooney, R. H. (1981). Separation through foster care: Toward a problem-oriented practice model based on task-centered casework. In A. A. Malluccio & P. Sinanoglu (Eds.), *Working with biological parents of children in foster care.* New York: Child Welfare League of America.

Silverman, P. R. (1970). A reexamination of the intake procedure. *Social Casework, 51,* 625–634.

Sloane, R. B., Cristol, A. H., Pepernik, C., & Staples, F. R. (1970). Role preparation and expectation of improvement in psychotherapy. *Journal of Nervous and Mental Disease, 150,* 18–26.

Strupp, H. H., Fox, R. E., & Lessler, K. (1969). *Patients view their psychotherapy.* Baltimore: Johns Hopkins Press.

Studt, E. (1968). Social work theory and implications for the practice of methods. *Social Work Education Reporter, 16,* 22–46.

Tolson, E. R. (1988). *The metamodel and clinical social work.* New York: Columbia University Press.

Tolson, E. R., Reid, W. J., & Garvin, C. D. (1994). *Generalist practice: A task-centered approach.* New York: Columbia University Press.

Zwick, R., & Attkisson, C. C. (1984). The use of reception checks in client pretherapy orientation research. *Journal of Clinical Psychology, 40,* 446–452.

SECTION C

Humanistic and Feminist Theories

12

Client-Centered Theory

Michael Rothery and Leslie Tutty

Social work has always given relationship a key importance when articulating its methods of helping, insisting that the professional relationship be understood as both the context and means for facilitating change (Biestek, 1957; Coady, 1999; Perlman, 1957, 1979). In a book that is rightly regarded as a classic on the topic, Biestek (1957) argued that this emphasis is so important that it serves to define us:

> This is one principal difference between social work and some of the other professions. In surgery, dentistry, and law, for example, a good interpersonal relationship is desirable for the *perfection* of the service, but it is not necessary for the *essence* of the service. The surgeon may not have a good bedside manner; the dentist may be inconsiderate of the patient's feelings; the lawyer may be cold and overly businesslike. But if the surgeon operates successfully, if the dentist heals the ailing tooth, and if the lawyer wins the case, they have performed the essential service requested. Not so the caseworker. A good relationship is necessary not only for the perfection, but also for the essence, of the casework service in every setting. (p. 19)

Mary Richmond (1899) can be credited with early efforts to understand relationship and its critical importance: "Friendly visiting means intimate . . . knowledge of and sympathy with a . . . family's joys, sorrows, opinions, feelings. . . . The visitor that has this is unlikely to blunder . . . [although] without it he is almost certain . . . to blunder seriously" (p. 180). Since Richmond's introduction of concepts such as *friendly visiting* and *sympathy*, social workers have striven for greater clarity in describing what it is about some relationships that makes them powerful tools for change. Different terms have been invoked in this effort to understand, such as *empathy* (Shaw, cited in Biestek, 1957), *rapport* and *emotional bridging* (LeRoy, cited in Biestek, 1957), *transference* (Taft, cited in Biestek, 1957; see also Garrett,

Mangold, & Zaki, 1982, which discusses the phenomenon without using the term), *engagement* (Smalley, 1967), and *therapeutic alliance* (Coady, 1999).

The focus for this chapter, client-centered theory, is largely credited as the work of Carl Rogers and is recognized as a radical development in the field of clinical psychology. For social work, it is perhaps less revolutionary; it is more accurately a useful reformulation and reaffirmation of knowledge and values that have informed our work for a century now. Nevertheless, Rogers' work continues to stimulate fresh, innovative thinking about "the rich interplay of one human mind with another" (Garrett et al., 1982, p. 4), and for this reason it deserves our ongoing attention.

OVERVIEW OF THEORY

UNDERSTANDING OF HUMAN PROBLEMS

As discussed in chapter 2, social work makes use of two broad types of theory. There are frameworks that help us understand and describe problems, and there are others that help us plan change. The client-centered model of helping rests primarily, though not entirely, on a theory of change.

With respect to descriptive/explanatory theory, Rogers did suggest that human problems generally can be understood as reflecting a state of incongruence. People experience pain when they perceive themselves falling significantly short of what, ideally, they wish to be. One of his interpreters explains this aspect of Rogers' theory:

> The client's self-image is contradicted by his life experience; thus . . . two levels of self-being are . . . constituted: one involving the . . . idealized self; the other touching on and flowing from, the actual experience of self-in-process. . . . Determined to defend his self-concept . . . the client is unable to admit into clear awareness those experiences that would interfere with his sense of self-worth. (Barton, 1980, p. 169)

However, Rogers argued vehemently that beyond this it is counterproductive to approach clients with preconceptions in the form of theories of personality, or psychopathology, or anything else that might work against our openness to the uniqueness of people and their situations:

> The more I have observed therapists, and the more closely I have studied [the] research . . . the more I am forced to the conclusion that . . . diagnostic knowledge is not essential to psychotherapy. It may even be that its defense as a necessary prelude to psychotherapy is simply a protective alternative to the admission that it is, for the most part, a colossal waste of time. (Rogers, 1957, pp. 101–102)

It is therefore fair to say that Rogers and his followers did not pursue a highly developed understanding of human problems. Instead, they worked to illuminate the interpersonal processes that represent a context within which healing naturally occurs.

CONCEPTION OF THERAPEUTIC INTERVENTION

The conditions that enable us to develop in self-actualizing ways are universal, Rogers believed. Good clinical social work is based on the same core elements as good parenting, good teaching, or the friendships that help us thrive. When we provide clinical social work services, therefore, we are paid to offer our clients the same growth-enhancing interpersonal experiences that more fortunate people receive naturally from friends and loved ones. To the extent that our clients may be especially estranged from themselves, they require us to provide those conditions in a skilled, well-attuned way, but there is nothing that distinguishes their needs from everyone else's in any formal sense.

Client-centered tenets about intervention and change have an apparent simplicity that can easily result in misunderstanding:

> Very early in my work . . . I discovered that simply listening to my client, very attentively, was an important way of being helpful. . . . Later a social worker, who had a background of Rankian training, helped me to learn that the most effective approach was to listen for the feelings. . . . I believe she was the one who suggested that the best response was to "reflect" these feelings back to the client—"reflect" becoming in time a word that made me cringe. But at that time, it improved my work as therapist, and I was grateful. . . .
>
> But this tendency to focus on the therapist's responses had appalling consequences. . . . The whole approach came, in a few years, to be known as a technique. "Nondirective therapy," it was said, "is the technique of reflecting the client's feelings." Or an even worse caricature was simply that "in nondirective therapy you repeat the last words the client has said." (Rogers, 1980, pp. 137–139)

The process of change, in the client-centered view, is at once simple and complex. Simply put, people are naturally inclined toward growth, and given the right conditions they will come to know themselves more fully, heal old wounds, and develop greater authenticity and congruence. They will become more knowledgeable and honest, first in relation to themselves, then in relation to others.

The "right conditions" that facilitate such growth are relationships with particular characteristics. These characteristics are congruence, acceptance, and empathy. If we are honest, accepting, and understanding, our clients will benefit from their relationship with us. The apparent simplicity of this prescription belies the subtlety of the processes it describes, however—

hence Rogers' concern about being so easily misunderstood. We will have more to say about the complexity of the core conditions below, in the section on central theoretical constructs.

HISTORICAL DEVELOPMENT

PRECURSORS AND ORIGINAL DEVELOPMENT

Historically, social work scholarship has enjoyed a reciprocal influence with the work of cognate disciplines, psychiatry and psychology prominent among them. Our efforts to understand the helping relationship are a case in point. The helping method identified with the University of Pennsylvania, the functional school of social work, made relationship a pivotal issue in its understanding of change, drawing heavily on the thinking of the psychodynamic psychiatrist Otto Rank. Carl Rogers, a psychologist, was a colleague to social workers imbued with functional thinking; it is likely through their influence that he came to meet Rank. This meeting was a turning point for Rogers, shaping his thinking for the rest of his life (Kramer, 1995). Rogers, in turn, did much to clarify conceptually what the elements of a helpful relationship are, and initiated a research program to measure those elements and their effects. The outcome was the client-centered school of counseling.

Completing a circle of sorts, Rogers' theoretical and empirical work were reabsorbed by social work, as familiar ideas possessed of a new clarity and force. It is doubtful if anyone has been trained in a social work program in the last two decades without learning about the Rogerian "core conditions" and their application to our work with clients.

Otto Rank and Carl Rogers, then, are two prominent theorists whose thought imbues the client-centered framework. The complementarity of their ideas and values is remarkable, given their differences in background. Rank trained as a psychoanalyst, was a former disciple of Freud, and was very much a product of European culture and education. Rogers, in contrast, was thoroughly American (Van Belle, 1980), the son of "a narrowly fundamentalist religious home" (Rogers, 1980, p. 27) and a graduate of universities in Wisconsin and New York.

Each man made an important mark by rebelling against his earlier training, looking for a way out of the limitations he experienced in the doctrines of the day. Rank replaced the rigid determinism of Freud's thinking with a theory that celebrated the human capacity for creativity and choice (Menaker, 1982). Rogers rejected the deterministic, objective psychology that prevailed when he was starting out, offering in its place a humanistic "home-grown brand of existential philosophy" (Rogers, 1980, p. 39). In fact, calling his work "client-centered" and "nondirective" constitutes an important philosophical position on Rogers' part—a commitment to the belief that the resources for healing and growth are to be found primarily in the client, not in the theories and techniques of the helper.

We have noted that Rogers' introduction to the work of Rank was a result of his collaboration with clinical social workers:

> From 1928 through 1939, Carl Rogers served as a therapist at the Society for Prevention of Cruelty to Children, in Rochester, New York. . . . On his staff at the Rochester clinic were a number of social workers trained at the University of Pennsylvania's School of Social Work . . . where Otto Rank had been lectur- ing since 1926. (Kramer, 1995, p. 58)

Of the shared interests that drew Rogers to Rank, a key was the idea of a form of helping based on the provision of a nurturing relationship, rather than on skill at analysis and interpretation:

> In June, 1936, intrigued by social workers who were telling him that *"relationship therapy"—not "interpretive therapy"*—was the emphasis of the Philadelphia School, Carl Rogers invited Otto Rank to Rochester to conduct a 3-day seminar on his new, post-Freudian practice of therapy. (Kramer, 1995, p. 59)

LATER DEVELOPMENTS AND CURRENT STATUS

Few scholars have the impact that Rogers enjoyed in his field. In the half century since he began publishing his ideas, he has stimulated an enormous response in terms of ongoing theory development and research. A perusal of influential journals, such as *Journal of Counseling Psychology*, will verify that literally thousands of academic, research, and professional careers are rooted solidly in his work.

The client-centered model as Rogers formulated it has not gone unchal- lenged, and we will indicate where problems lie toward the end of this chapter. However, it is remarkable, given the energy that has gone into its development, to note how the foundation Rogers laid—the concepts that are the primary focus of this chapter—remain essentially unaltered.

Much effort has gone into developing ways of measuring the core condi- tions (Truax & Carkhuff, 1967, is a prominent example). This has contrib- uted to some refinement of concepts, with terms such as *self-disclosure* and *immediacy* serving to focus on the specifics of what Rogers described under the more general processes of congruence and empathy. Other conditions presented appear to be actual additions to the repertoire, such as *confronta- tion* and *concreteness* (Carkhuff, 1987; Truax, 1963; Truax & Carkhuff, 1964).

The effort to translate Rogers' general process conditions into opera- tional behaviors has resulted in extensive catalogues of specific counseling skills (e.g., Ivey, 1988), and the application of these in education, industry, and other organizational domains has absorbed considerable interest and energy—as has their application cross-culturally (Sue, Ivey, & Pederson, 1996).

Beyond these generalities, the scope of this chapter prevents our doing justice to the vast body of work that has grown out of client-centered theory. The extent to which derivatives of the basic model diverge from their roots varies; however, none challenges it in any fundamental way, and most pay frank homage to Rogers as the germinal thinker on whose shoulders they stand.

CENTRAL THEORETICAL CONSTRUCTS

We have noted a seeming simplicity about the basic client-centered formula for change. Drawing on Rank and other humanistic influences, Rogers came to the view that everyone has a creative capacity to make choices and is motivated to grow. These naturally present capacities and inclinations can be blocked or distorted by experience, with psychological pain as a consequence. However, in the context of a sufficiently nurturing relationship, the client will rediscover them and return to a healthy, self-actualizing path.

Congruence, nonpossessive warmth, and empathy characterize the relational context that promotes such results. Although other ingredients have been recommended as client-centered thinking has evolved, these remain primary and, as we have emphasized, need to be understood as complex processes.

Congruence is interpersonal honesty and directness. The social worker who is self-aware, comfortable with herself or himself, and able to find ways to relate to clients that do not disguise who he or she is, is relating congruently. What is meant, however, is far from simple encouragement to give free expression to whatever one thinks and feels. Congruence means that "the feelings the therapist is experiencing are available to him, available to his awareness, and he is able to live these feelings, be them, and able to communicate them if appropriate" (Rogers, 1961, p. 61; see also Rogers, 1980, p. 115).

Garrett and colleagues' (1982) view of the requirements of social work interviewing is similarly demanding: "An interviewer's attention must continuously be directed in two ways: toward himself as well as toward his client" (p. 6). Both Garrett and colleagues (1982) and Rogers (1961), therefore, describe a disciplined effort to develop self-awareness and comfort with oneself. Furthermore, congruence implies the ability to use that awareness in the service of the client, sharing aspects of our experience as it is *appropriate* to do so, that is, in a manner that is sensitively attuned to client needs and readiness.

The second condition that we provide clients in creating a context for growth is acceptance, or "unconditional positive regard," which "involves the therapist's genuine willingness for the client to be whatever feeling is going on in him at that moment . . . [and requires] that the therapist cares for the client in a non-possessive way . . . in a total rather than a conditional way . . . and without reservations, without evaluations" (Rogers, 1961, p. 62). Thus, we work to establish with our clients a positive attitude about them as people unaffected by our reactions to how they feel or what they may have done. This implies the belief that we can (and must) cultivate a capacity for interpersonal generosity, based on a differentiated understanding of others as a complex mix of characteristics and potentials. Furthermore, we can discipline ourselves so that client behaviors, characteristics, or experiences that distress us do not undermine this capacity. There is something about each client that we value with no strings attached—and we are able to communicate that effectively.

The third and preeminent element in a relational context for growth is empathy. Again, Rogers took considerable pains to be clear that he did not see empathy as achievable in a formulaic, superficial fashion—the caricature being an expression of soulful concern and the words "I *know* how you feel!" Empathic understanding is never so simple:

> [Empathy] means that the therapist senses accurately the feelings and personal meanings that the client is experiencing and communicates this understanding to the client. When functioning best, the therapist is so much inside the private world of the other that he or she can clarify not only the meanings of which the client is aware but even those just below the level of awareness. This kind of sensitive, active listening is exceedingly rare in our lives, . . . yet [it] is one of the most potent forces for change that I know. (Rogers, 1980, p. 116)

These definitions and elaborations remain consistent in Rogers' writing over time (compare with Rogers, 1957), and there are a number of elements in them that we would highlight. First, there is a role for intelligence, insight, training, and experience: The social worker should grasp *accurately* and *sensitively* the emotional content and meanings implied in what the client is saying.

Second, empathy as Rogers defines it is not simply understanding feelings: He is inclined to emphasize emotions, but also returns constantly to words like *experiencing* and *meaning*. Thus, the point of empathic understanding is to communicate awareness of both the emotional and narrative aspects of what the client presents. Perhaps the word *experiencing* is attractive because it addresses both feelings about events and the meanings attributed to them—aspects that are always so interdependent that the wisdom of separating them is questionable.

A third point is that empathy implies a strong psychological attunement by the worker to the experience of the client, but not a loss of boundaries. The therapist "can grasp the moment-to-moment experiencing which occurs in the inner world of the client as the client sees it and feels it, *without losing the separateness of his own identity*" (Rogers, 1961, pp. 62–63, emphasis added). This is a clarification about which he was consistent:

It means to sense the hurt or the pleasure of another as he senses it and to perceive the causes thereof as he perceives them but without ever losing the recognition that it is *as if* I were hurt or pleased and so forth. If this "as if" quality is lost, then the state is one of identification. (Rogers, 1959, pp. 210–211)

Although empathy as a concept stresses engagement, clients are served best if we are fully able to step back, understanding their experience but also inviting new perspectives and options.

Why is empathy considered to be such a powerful precondition for growth? Rogers explains this by suggesting several benefits that accrue when we experience an empathic relationship:

1. Empathy "dissolves alienation" (Rogers, 1980, p. 151). Clients often feel alone in their problems, and an empathic relationship with a clinical social worker is a powerful antidote: "If someone else knows what I am talking about, what I mean, then to this degree I am not so strange, or alien, or set apart. I make sense to another human being" (Rogers, 1980, p. 151).

2. Empathic understanding has the effect of communicating to people that they are valued, and is therefore useful for repairing damaged self-esteem. It is Rogers' contention that empathy is not possible without caring, and the experience of being cared about encourages a sense of self-value.

3. Because empathy is nonjudgmental, "always free of any evaluative or diagnostic quality" (Rogers, 1980, p. 154), being empathically treated encourages self-acceptance. Aspects of ourselves from which we recoil are less corrosive to our self-esteem if we see that another person can hear about them without becoming threatened or angry—and may regard them as normal, even admirable, rather than as cause for shame and self-denigration.

4. When people receive empathic responses to their troubles, they are encouraged to self-explore, increasing their awareness and developing a richer experience of themselves. This is beneficial in and of itself, because a broader self-understanding exposes more options regarding how we can respond to situations. Furthermore, when painful aspects of our experience are "fully accepted and accurately labeled in awareness" (Rogers, 1980, p. 158), we are able to respond more creatively to those issues.

PHASES OF HELPING

Four phases of helping characterize generalist social work practice: engagement, data collection and assessment, planning and contracting, and evaluation and termination. What can we suggest the contribution of client-centered theory is to facilitating this process?

Regarding *engagement*, the argument is simple. Relating honestly, respectfully, and empathically should speed the development of trust and openness. However, it may be that client-centered theory, interestingly, puts too much responsibility for such relationships on the worker. Recent research and theory emphasizes that predispositions of the client are powerful as well; however skilled we may be, we still depend on our clients to respond positively if an effective helping alliance is to be formed (Coady, 1999; Miller, Duncan, & Hubble, 1997).

With respect to *assessment*, it is our view that the client-centered approach offers critical process skills. However, we would also argue that social workers require more of a framework enabling decisions regarding the kinds of data that are to be collected. With an abused spouse, we are trained to explore safety issues, for example, even if these do not emerge automatically in our interview. Similarly, if we suspect child maltreatment, addictions, suicidal tendencies, a significant lack of supports and resources, or any of a host of potentially relevant matters, we are trained to invite discussion of those, and this training is a good thing. This does not deny the risk of forming premature hypotheses about what is important and ceasing to listen carefully to the client—Rogers' thinking and approach are very useful protections against this possibility.

With respect to *planning and contracting*, client-centered theory does not offer as much direction as social workers and their clients may require. The assumption that appropriate goals and plans will emerge if clients have sufficient opportunity to explore their experience is very often valid, but by no means always.

The client-centered model is not prescriptive with respect to the length of treatment, and the timing of termination is similar to what we see with other models. What the client-centered model offers regarding *termination and evaluation* is, again, its understanding of process. In terminating, the opportunity for clients to reflect on their experience with the social worker and what it has meant to them is obviously very important, and an effective helping relationship is a context designed to encourage that. With respect to evaluation, the model suggests very good criteria for assessing the helping process, these being the core conditions and client-self exploration. Properly speaking, these are process rather than outcome variables; whereas outcomes independent of process have also been assessed in some client-centered research, the measures employed are familiar in research on other models as well. With respect to helping particular clients evaluate the success of their work, the model offers a process that facilitates that but does not suggest independent criteria for assessing the merits of goals achieved. Because it is not a domain-specific model, this is appropriate—outcomes to be evaluated will vary across people and client populations.

APPLICATION TO FAMILY AND GROUP WORK

If the basic thesis of client-centered theory is true, it should apply equally whether work is being conducted with an individual, family, group, or other social system. It was, in fact, Rogers (1980) position that communicational processes favoring the core conditions would make many diverse social settings more nurturing and supportive of learning and growth. A leader in the encounter group movement as it developed, he suggested applications of his work in educational settings, families, and organizations of various sizes and diverse purposes.

The direct evidence for the impact of client-centered methods in groups is not strong, perhaps due to significant methodological difficulties. To the extent that modeling takes place and group members learn effective communication skills that they can use in their efforts to support and help one another, it seems logical to think this would be beneficial. In family work, there is evidence enough to convince some reviewers that the core conditions do contribute significantly to positive outcomes (Gurman, Kniskern, & Pinsof, 1986; Nichols & Schwartz, 1991).

COMPATIBILITY WITH
A GENERALIST-ECLECTIC FRAMEWORK

Although Rogers was suspicious about explanatory theory, the process orientation of the client-centered model invites eclecticism. Practitioners who consider themselves Rogerians freely incorporate concepts from schools of thought as diverse as behaviorism and psychodynamic theory (a point we will return to below, in our case discussion).

Social workers who practice from a generalist-eclectic framework commonly recognize the contribution of client-centered thinking to their work. A powerful emphasis on the importance of relationship is one shared commitment; the deep respect in client-centered theory for the competency, personal power, and motivation toward health in the client is another commonality.

Rogers' insistence on the central importance of attunement to clients' experience has obvious relevance to work in situations where diversity is a factor. The process of achieving and communicating shared understanding across disparate frames of reference is considered part of all helping, so it is no surprise that this knowledge has been applied in work with diverse cultural groups (Rogers, 1980).

For similar reasons, the theory prescribes a process that will be helpful in work with people who are different from the social worker in terms of age or gender. However, it does not offer knowledge of general themes associated with gender or the life cycle—or a systematic understanding of social systems. Familiarity with such knowledge is important to generalist-eclectic workers, and will need to be acquired from sources other than the client-centered literature, if holistic assessments and effective use of life-cycle theories are to be achieved.

CRITIQUE: THE STRENGTHS AND LIMITATIONS OF THE MODEL

Several decades after Rogers began publishing and researching his work, there is no reason to question its profound impact on social work and other helping professions. The critical significance of relationship to the helping enterprise is now widely accepted as proven. Furthermore, there is little dispute about the relevance to helping of the core conditions; although there are ongoing discussions about how they might best be defined and measured, there is a rather impressive consensus as to their basic credibility and importance.

There are, however, qualifications to suggest in relation to this theory. In part, these derive from Rogers' insistence that the core conditions are all there is, that they are the *necessary* and *sufficient* conditions for positive change. In social work practice (and, it turns out, in other disciplines as well), they are not always necessary and are often not sufficient (Miller et al., 1997).

Like all of us, Rogers brought to his work certain professional and cultural assumptions. He grew up imbued with the values of American pragmatism and the Protestant belief in individual salvation. This history sets a context within which he developed an approach to helping that stresses (sometimes to the exclusion of all else) the need to assist clients in discovering the personal strengths and resources they possess so that they can apply them effectively in their lives. In his later years, Rogers worked for the development of better social conditions and more humane communities. However, it is still true that his theory could encourage an emphasis on the person of the client, and a lack of attention to deprivations or sources of oppression in clients' environments.

Working as they do with very difficult situations, social workers will easily recognize that a client who is hungry or is being brutalized by an abusive parent or partner will not necessarily have as a priority the need to explore the meanings of those experiences. Relief or protection from extremely damaging circumstances can come with concrete interventions rather than an intense helping relationship—and it may be that this is all that is required. Even when a helping relationship and the opportunity to self-explore are useful in important ways (as they must be in most cases), they will often not be sufficient.

Another general concern to be raised is that the client-centered model can be utopian, and this entails risks. This is not a necessary outcome of absorbing the theory, but a possible one to be guarded against—one that can be a more general problem with the humanistic approaches overall.

If the goal of intervention is to help clients achieve congruence, or complete harmony within themselves, the goal is an ideal that is never fully reached. If our responsibility is to strive for complete attunement with the experience of another, it is a foregone conclusion that we will always fall short.

We are likely to be more comfortable, honest, and competent in our work if we remember that our interventions are intended to ameliorate problems and achieve modest objectives. Self-actualization, personal congruence, authenticity, and other forms of salvation are not disparaged as goals, but they are lifelong pursuits and require guidance and supports different from what social workers normally offer.

Given an adequate degree of realistic modesty, there are compelling reasons for social workers to learn and continually practice the approach to relating that Rogers and his colleagues have described for us. This, however, is not all we need to know.

CASE EXAMPLE

Dave is a young adult (25 years old), married, successful in his job, and prone to depression. He has been seen at a mental health clinic on an outpatient basis; the transcript begins about 20 minutes into the eighth interview. His childhood history involves treatment that he describes as "sadistic" and "terroristic" on the part of an alcoholic father. Events that he recalls certainly justify those labels.

Dave has maintained relationships with his family of origin, because there is much in it that he values. However, he acknowledges that he is especially likely to become depressed before and after visits to his parents. This is what he is discussing at the point the transcript begins:

Dave:	*I don't know why I get so down . . . into such a state. I want to see them, or I wouldn't go. But I think about walking through that door and it's hard. And thinking about being in a room with him [his father] is just really awful.*
Social Worker:	*It sounds like you feel in a painful kind of bind about visiting them. Is part of that awful feeling the sense that you are . . . somehow feel trapped?*
Dave:	*Yeah! Like I have to go . . . I want to go . . . but also like I just want to get away from there.*
Social Worker:	*There's important stuff you need from your family, but you feel frightened when you go there.*
Dave:	*I can't stop myself from thinking about him taking his belt off (long pause) and yelling at me . . . screaming, really . . . about what he was going to do to me with it . . .*
Social Worker:	*So it makes sense that you're afraid. Going home triggers really*

	painful memories, awful memories . . . memories that get you feel-ing small again, and maybe helpless.
Dave:	*Helpless, yes, but . . . It's not as if I think he can treat me like that now. It's more like . . . (long pause of 30 seconds or more) . . . it's more just that he did those things to me. Why me? How could he do that? I was just a kid.*
Social Worker:	*I think you've just asked a question that is really painful for you—Why me? How could he do that? (Dave nods.) Do you have an answer, or even part of an answer?*
Dave:	*I sort of see him standing over me, whipping off his belt, waving it around. . . . And he looks really angry. (a long pause, and efforts to maintain composure) . . . But he also looks weird . . . I don't know . . . like this feels good to him or something . . .*
Social Worker:	*I imagine it would be especially hard . . . almost impossible to think that.*
Dave:	*He is scaring the shit out of me, and he thinks its fun. . . . The son of a bitch is getting off on . . . (haltingly) on making me so scared . . . and like there's nothing I can do.*
Social Worker:	*Is there a feeling humiliation in this? (Dave nods.) And that you're alone? (Dave nods again, fighting tears.)*
Dave:	*You know, I was just a kid . . . but at that time I was always thinking about running away . . . even going off to die somewhere.*
Social Worker:	*You were that desperate . . . so much so that you weren't sure you could go on. But you did. Part of you wanted to hang in.*
Dave:	*I guess so . . . I'm not sure about that one. I mean, if I'm so weak, so unimportant that he could do that to me and have fun while he was at it, what does that make me?*
Social Worker:	*Another painful, important question . . .*
Dave:	*It's like he really did prove I'm a piece of crap.*
Social Worker:	*That he could treat you that way convinced you, as a kid, that there was something terribly wrong with you. . .*
Dave:	*. . . Instead of something being wrong with his head. (Long pause) You know . . . when I'm talking to you here, I can see that it doesn't make sense to sort of sell out or walk out on myself because of him . . . of what he did. But it's really hard to hang on . . . I don't know how to hang on to that. He kind of haunts me . . . this picture of him is there, and I can't shake it.*
Social Worker:	*You learned to see yourself as weak and alone, and now you sound really unsure about whether you can feel any other way.*
Dave:	*I've done a lot, but I still can't ever push him away for long. I let him back, and I feel like crap.*
Social Worker:	*The thought that he could cause you such pain and enjoy it seems very powerful to you. (Dave nods.) I'm trying to imagine what that might mean to a 10-year-old boy. What did it mean to you then . . . or now?*

Dave:	*If I mattered a damn . . . if there was anything about me to . . . [the tape is indistinct here, and Dave is swallowing his words:*
	The gist is "anything about me to care for] . . . he would never have treated me like that.
Social Worker:	*Like you said, it's not that he can treat you like he did when you were a kid anymore. But he still has a terrible power over you—you let him tell you who you are. And you lose touch with how tough you've been, and how much you've accomplished.*
Dave:	*He is very powerful. . . . Funny thing, he's an old guy now, and he really can't hurt me. But he still seems so . . .*
Social Worker:	*What's real now is not the same as when you were 10. But it seems that what was real then is what keeps you stuck.*
Dave:	*You know, I'm trying to picture him as he is now, and I can't. I was there on the weekend, and I don't think I looked at him once, really. I can't explain it . . . I just point my eyes to other places than where he is. Or if I do have to look his way, there's a kind of tension in my brain, and I don't really see him.*

The interview then focused on Dave exploring ways he was still caught up in the past, and how this meant he has an imperfect view of his present reality—with his happy marriage, successful career, and ability to protect himself from mistreatment. It ended with a plan that was quite simple, but also very forceful, which was that he would spend time during a visit home allowing himself to see his father, taking note in small steps of how this man looked in the present, as opposed to the past. Learning to see, appreciate, and trust his own power was facilitated by taking the important first step of differentiating a past in which he truly was helpless from a present in which he possessed considerable strength.

An appreciation of relationship is not unique to client-centered intervention, and other models have been influenced by Rogers' work. This said, it is suggested that there are important features in this transcript that illustrate how client-centered intervention is distinguished from other approaches.

It would be easy for a theoretically predisposed interviewer to be more directive in guiding this discourse. For example, a psychodynamically oriented social worker might be very tempted to focus in detail on Dave's experience with his father, with more exploration of the fears associated with that childhood reality. Was he in fact afraid that his father would kill him? Did he feel abandoned by his mother? How might his distrust of his father affect the present helping relationship?

Existentialists from some of the more tough-minded schools might begin to develop themes around how Dave relinquishes personal power to his father—how this is a choice to continue permitting his father to dictate how he regards himself and how he feels. His reluctance to grow up, accepting responsibility for his life in the here and now, might become a major focus.

A cognitive-behaviorist social worker might pick up on Dave's character-ization of himself as a "piece of crap" and the image of his father as being all powerful, labeling these as pernicious and irrational beliefs, leading inexorably to depressed feelings. The focus of the interview might be di-rected toward strategies for blocking such thoughts, replacing them with an internal dialogue that is more nurturing and self-respectful.

We recognize that by being brief we can easily do a disservice to the models we have identified, and that is not the point. Each perspective has validity, and each has proven useful with some clients under some circumstances. Dave might well benefit from any one or all of them, skill-fully applied.

What client-centered social workers strive for, however, is a noninterpre-tive and nondirective style of working. The social worker in the transcript is aware of the various theoretical possibilities but chooses to set them aside in an effort to listen to how Dave is uniquely experiencing his situation. Faith is placed in *Dave* to figure out what is going on and where hope for improvement lies, rather than in the theories the social worker respects or the interventive techniques they prescribe. The goal is not to come up with an interpretation and plan on Dave's behalf; rather, it is to provide a relationship within which he develops his own awareness of himself, his situation, and his options.

Trusting our clients and the helping process in this way is a difficult discipline. In our view, it is further complicated by the belief that we do not really approach problems in a state of theoretical innocence. We cannot function (professionally or otherwise) without cognitive maps, and when client-centered practitioners imply that any theory at all is dangerous, we would suggest another viewpoint.

The social worker in the preceding transcript, for example, allows a number of beliefs to affect the questions posed and responses offered. Her experience working with clients with a history of trauma inevitably informs her work. She is sensitive to the importance of traumatic memories. She understands that when abuse is perpetrated sadistically, this has a special meaning for victims. She knows how important differentiating the past from the present can be for such clients.

A second reading of the transcript will show that knowledge, training, and experience are influencing what the social worker does. However, to the extent that client-centered principles are honored in this brief vignette, the worker's predispositions are utilized with tentativeness and care, and are not allowed to result in Dave's experience going unheard. Whereas theory can be a barrier to empathy, it can also, properly used, increase the depth and efficiency with which we become attuned to critical aspects of our clients' experience.

SUMMARY

The relationship that social workers offer their clients has always been considered the sine qua non of our helping enterprise to the extent that we may treat it overly reverentially (cf. Perlman, 1979). If we can accept a more modest position, recognizing that not all clients need a profound experience in relation to us, and that in many other cases this may not be enough, then that is progress (however disillusioning).

Modifications of the Rogerian point of view likely will be a matter of continuing to recognize its contribution and importance while adding caveats and qualifications. The relationship conditions offered by the social worker do help create a context for change. So too, however, do other factors (Coady, 1999; Duncan, Solovey, & Rusk, 1992; Miller et al., 1997). These include the social worker's techniques, "extratherapeutic" or environmental factors, and predispositions on the part of the client. Continuing to capitalize on the legacy Rogers left us will (somewhat ironically) be a matter of building a more differentiated appreciation of our clients' needs and circumstances, as well as a refined ability to tailor the relationship we offer to those realities. Perhaps, though it reintroduces the need for analytical thinking about clients, something that Rogers distrusted, it is a direction more congruent with his basic agenda than may seem, on the surface, to be the case.

REFERENCES

Barton, A. (1980). *Three worlds of therapy: An existential-phenomenological study of the therapies of Freud, Jung, and Rogers.* Palo Alto, CA: National Press Books.

Biestek, F. (1957). *The casework relationship.* Chicago: Loyola University Press.

Carkhuff, R. (1987). *The art of helping* (6th ed.). Amherst, MA: Human Resource Development Press.

Coady, N. (1999). The helping relationship. In F. Turner (Ed.), *Social work practice: A Canadian perspective* (pp. 58–72). Scarborough, Ontario: Prentice Hall Allyn & Bacon Canada.

Duncan, B., Solovey, A., & Rusk, G. (1992). *Changing the rules: A client-directed approach to psychotherapy.* New York: Guilford Press.

Garrett, A., Mangold, M., & Zaki, E. (1982). *Interviewing: Its principles and methods* (3rd ed.). New York: Family Service Association of America.

Gurman, A., Kniskern, D., & Pinsof, W. (1986). Research on marital and family therapies. In S. Garfield & A. Bergin (Eds.), *Handbook of psychotherapy and behavior change* (3rd ed., pp. 565–624). New York: Wiley.

Ivey, A. (1988). *Intentional interviewing and counseling: Facilitating client development* (2nd ed.). Pacific Grove, CA: Brooks/Cole.

Kramer, R. (1995). The birth of client-centered therapy: Carl Rogers, Otto Rank, and "the beyond." *Journal of Humanistic Psychology 35*(4), 54–110.

Menaker, E. (1982). *Otto Rank: A rediscovered legacy.* New York: Columbia University Press.

Miller, S., Duncan, B., & Hubble, M. (1997). *Escape from Babel: Toward a unifying language for psychotherapy practice.* New York: Norton.

Nichols, M., & Schwartz, R. (1991). *Family therapy: Concepts and methods* (2nd ed.). Boston: Allyn & Bacon.

Perlman, H. (1957). *Social casework: A problem solving process.* Chicago: University of Chicago Press.

Perlman, H. (1979). *Relationship: The heart of helping people.* Chicago: University of Chicago Press.

Richmond, M. (1899). *Friendly visiting among the poor.* New York: Macmillan.

Rogers, C. (1957). The necessary and sufficient conditions of therapeutic personality change. *Journal of Consulting Psychology 21*(2), 95–103.

Rogers, C. (1959). A theory of therapy, personality and interpersonal relationships as developed in the client-centered framework. In S. Koch (Ed.), *Psychology: A study of a science* (Vol. 3, pp. 184–256). New York: McGraw-Hill.

Rogers, C. (1961). *On becoming a person: A therapist's view of psychotherapy.* New York: Houghton Mifflin.

Rogers, C. (1980). *A way of being.* New York: Houghton Mifflin.

Smalley, R. (1967). *Theory for social work practice.* New York: Columbia University Press.

Sue, D., Ivey, A., & Pedersen, P. (1996). *A theory of multicultural counseling and therapy.* Pacific Grove, CA: Brooks/Cole.

Truax, C. (1963). Effective ingredients in psychotherapy: An approach to unraveling the patient-therapist interaction. *Journal of Counseling Psychology, 10*(3), 256–263.

Truax, C., & Carkhuff, R. (1964). Concreteness: A neglected variable in research in psychotherapy. *Journal of Clinical Psychology, 20,* 364–267.

Truax, C., & Carkhuff, R. (1967). *Toward effective counseling and psychotherapy: Training and practice.* Chicago: Aldine.

Van Belle, H. (1980). *Basic intent and therapeutic approach of Carl R. Rogers: A study of his view of man in relation to his view of therapy, personality and interpersonal relations.* Toronto: Wedge Publishing Foundation.

13

Existential Theory

Jim Lantz

Existential social work is a treatment orientation and model directed toward helping the client discover, actualize, and honor the meanings and meaning potentials in life (Lantz, 1993). In existential social work, as well as in existential psychiatry, existential psychology, and existential psychotherapy, there is a central concern with helping clients to utilize the problem-oriented and the mystery-centered components of existence in order to help them live more meaning-filled lives (Lantz & Kondrat, 1996; Yalom, 1980). In this chapter, the author outlines both the problem-oriented and the mystery-centered elements of existential social work and demonstrates how these two elements of treatment are both poles in a relationship of tension as well as complementary to each other. The chapter discusses existential social work with regard to historical development, central theoretical concepts, phases of helping, application to family and group work, compatibility with a generalist-eclectic approach, strengths and limitations, and offers a case illustration.

AN OVERVIEW OF EXISTENTIAL SOCIAL WORK AND CENTRAL THEORETICAL CONSTRUCTS

Existential social work is frequently presented as a treatment approach that pays close attention to the treatment encounter between social worker and client, the opportunities for growth to be found in trauma and crisis, freedom and responsibility, and the basic human desire to discover and experience a sense of meaning and purpose in life (Lantz, 1978, 1982, 1984, 1987, 1989, 1990, 1993, 1994, 1998; Lantz & Ahern, 1994, 1998; Lantz & Alford, 1995; Lantz & Gomia, 1995; Lantz & Kondrat, 1996). The approach to existential social work presented in this chapter has been developed, evaluated, and refined by Lantz (1974, 1991, 1992, 1993, 1996; Lantz & Kondrat, 1997; Lantz & Witter, 1994) over the past 30 years, and is based primarily on the concepts found in the existential philosophies of Gabriel Marcel (1948) and Viktor Frankl (1955, 1959, 1968, 1997). In the author's existential social work approach, problem-centered treatment ideas and activities are used to help the client "actualize" and/or make use of his or her meaning potentials in the present moment of time, and mystery-centered treatment ideas and activities are used to help the client "notice" meaning potentials in the future and to re-collect or "honor" meanings previously actualized and deposited into the past (Lantz, 1974, 1993, 1995, 1997). Both problem- and mystery-centered treatment activities help the client "shrink" his or her existential meaning vacuum and those symptoms and problems that develop, grow, and flourish in an existential meaning vacuum (Frankl, 1955, 1959, 1968, 1997; Lantz, 1974, 1993; Lantz & Ahern, 1994; Lantz & Gomia, 1995).

In the author's approach to existential social work, it is the social worker's responsibility to understand and utilize the treatment concepts of problem and mystery, existential treatment goals, power and participation, dynamics and freedom, encounter and the subject-object split, clarity and richness of knowledge, and primary and secondary reflection activities. An understanding of these basic existential themes should provide the reader with a good overview of the existential social work approach.

PROBLEM AND MYSTERY

Gabriel Marcel (1948) describes two basic ways of understanding life: life as a "problem to be solved," and life as a "mystery to be experienced." For Marcel, although both orientations to life are necessary and useful, each exists in a relationship of tension relative to the other. Marcel considers this tension between problem and mystery to be a necessary ingredient in "holistic" reflection and understanding. Marcel's views on problem, mystery, and holistic reflection can be used to identify two elements of existential social work—the problem-centered component and the mystery-centered component (Lantz, 1974, 1993). These components should be understood as complementary to each other and as two poles "in tension" (Lantz, 1994; Lantz & Kondrat, 1996).

EXISTENTIAL TREATMENT GOALS

In the problem-centered approach to existential social work, the goal of the therapist is to identify with clarity and precision a specific and (often) repetitive problem pattern or sequence that disrupts the client's problem-solving effectiveness and/or ability to actualize and make use of the meaning potentials in his or her life (Lantz, 1978, 1994). With such a specific understanding of how the client disrupts problem-solving and problem resolution, the therapist can develop a directive intervention and/or action plan that may help the client to modify his or her problem-resolution patterns to enhance the client's problem-solving and ability to actualize meaning potentials (Lantz, 1974, 1994, 1995). Haley (1976) and Beck (1976) have published outstanding presentations of the "science" of helping the client resolve problems and/or develop more effective problem-solving skills. In the problem-centered approach to existential social work, treatment is directed toward a search for problem resolution and meaning potential actualization in the here and now (Lantz, 1974, 1993, 1994; Lantz & Gomia, 1995; Lantz & Kondrat, 1996, 1997).

In the mystery-centered component of existential social work, the goal of treatment is to help the client discover meaning potentials in the future and to honor meanings previously actualized and deposited in the past (Frankl, 1968; Lantz, 1993). In this element of existential treatment, it is understood that a repetitive pathogenic pattern that disrupts the actualization of meaning potentials in the here and now may also be understood as a pattern that protects the person from meaning and meaning potential awareness and the two side effects of meaning, which are vulnerability and responsibility (Frankl, 1959; Lantz, 1982, 1984, 1994, 1997, 1998; Lantz & Witter, 1994).

In the mystery-centered approach to existential social work, the therapist understands that it is not wise to attempt to change a surface problem sequence without first developing a participatory and empathic understanding of the client's conscious and/or unconscious reasons for using such a problem pattern in his or her daily life (Frankl, 1955; Lantz, 1993; Yalom, 1980). From a mystery-centered point of view, it is possible that the development of a premature problem-centered action plan could be a manifestation of the therapist's failure to understand the client's fear of meaning, meaning awareness, connection, and human love (Frankl, 1968; Lantz, 1990, 1992; May, 1983; Yalom, 1980). As part of the mystery-centered component of treatment, the existential social worker maintains a deep respect for a client's will to meaning and also for a client's fear of meaning potential awareness and actualization. In existential social work, the therapist is aware of this "mysterious" fear in his or her own life and in his or her relationship with the client (Frankl, 1968; Krill, 1978; Lantz, 1974, 1993).

POWER AND PARTICIPATION

In the problem-centered approach to existential social work, it is frequently considered useful for the therapist to understand and utilize the power aspects of the treatment relationship to maximize the therapist's leverage, control, and influence over the client (Haley, 1976; Lantz, 1993). In the problem-centered approach, the therapist seeks to create rapid change to minimize the cost and length of treatment and to avoid a relationship of dependency between client and therapist, as sometimes occurs during long-term treatment (Haley, 1976; Lantz, 1978).

In the problem-centered approach to existential social work, the therapist is often directive and is not afraid to prescribe treatment behaviors and treatment activities. There is no question in the author's mind about the immediate effectiveness of such power-based treatment strategies (Lantz, 1978, 1993); such power-based action interventions can result in rapid change (Haley, 1976). However, it is not yet clear whether such action- and power-based interventions will result in lasting change (Lantz, 1993). It is also clear that such power-based action interventions may include dangers and limitations not yet completely understood or emphasized in the treatment literature (Lantz, 1993; Lantz & Kondrat, 1996).

From a mystery-centered perspective, healthy and long-lasting human change may not always result from a relationship of power, but is more likely to emerge in a relationship of participation (Lantz, 1994; Marcel, 1948). For Marcel (1948), Frankl (1968), May (1983), Krill (1978), Lantz (1993), and Yalom (1980), human participation occurs in an "I-Thou" relationship in which there is empathic connection to otherness without a loss of self. In different words (Marcel, 1948), human participation is a subjective sending of the self into the emotional life of the other that occurs without a loss of self and in a paradoxical way facilitates a strengthening of the self. Such participation results in increased knowledge and awareness of both the self and the other that is "mirrored" in the humanness of the self and the other (Marcel, 1948). Such participation results in a level of accurate understanding and empathy that often triggers the emergence of deep, profound, and lasting change for both members of the relationship experience (Lantz, 1993; Marcel, 1948; May, 1983; Yalom, 1980). In Marcel's (1948) view, only human participation can encourage human freedom and lasting human change. From the mystery-centered point of view, the use of power and control to induce change frequently disrupts and damages the emergence of human change (Lantz, 1993; Lantz & Kondrat, 1996; Marcel, 1948; May, 1983). In the mystery-centered approach, the therapist often decides to avoid strategic and power-based interventions that may disrupt human freedom and trigger change that may not last (Lantz, 1993, 1994; Marcel, 1948).

DYNAMICS AND FREEDOM

In the problem-centered approach to existential social work, there is a focus on causation and dynamics rather than on human freedom (Lantz, 1994). With this focus, the major danger is that the therapist may begin to view the client as a "machine" to fix or an object to be directed, manipulated, or shaped (Lantz & Kondrat, 1996). The advantage of a focus on dynamics is that such a focus can often help identify factors of influence that can be challenged and modified to facilitate problem resolution and change (Haley, 1976; Lantz, 1978).

In the mystery-centered approach to existential social work, the therapist is deeply impressed by the human ability to utilize freedom in responding meaningfully to the suffering, tragedies, problems, and limitations of human life (Lantz, 1974, 1993, 1994; Marcel, 1948). In the mystery-centered approach, it is understood that even during the horror of incarceration in a Nazi death camp (Frankl, 1959), the despair of living with a life-threatening illness (Marcel, 1948; May, 1983), or the continuous and repetitive near-death experiences of war (Frankl, 1959; Lantz, 1974, 1989; Marcel, 1948), the individual retains the ability to respond to such experiences freely with dignity, love, and decency or with a less than human form of response to life. In existential terminology, from the mystery-centered approach to treatment, the therapist believes in the "essence" of life but retains a strong belief in the person's ability to manifest freedom and "existence" in the face of essence (Frankl, 1959; Lantz, 1993; May, 1983). As both Marcel (1948) and May (1983) have so richly pointed out, any attempt to disrupt human freedom can rapidly become an attempt to disrupt the dignity of human life. From a mystery-centered point of view, it is generally more important to encourage human freedom in the face of problems than it is to obtain rapid change at the expense of human mastery and the exercise of human freedom and human control (Lantz, 1993; Marcel, 1948; May, 1983).

ENCOUNTER AND THE SUBJECT-OBJECT SPLIT

In the problem-centered approach to existential social work, the therapist views it as wise to maintain a degree of emotional distance from the client and develops leverages and strategies to use "on" the client to trigger change (Haley, 1976; Lantz, 1978). In the problem-centered orientation, the therapist can, at times, be considered the author or subject of treatment intervention and the client the object of treatment intervention (Lantz, 1994). The advantage of the subject-object split is that it can facilitate the development of strategies and action plan interventions that may trigger rapid change (Haley, 1976). This subject-object split is considerably different from the kind of treatment relationship that is encouraged in the mystery-centered orientation (Lantz, 1994).

In the mystery-centered approach, the treatment relationship between client and therapist is considered to be an encounter that includes empathy, fidelity, commitment, intersubjectivity, and mutual participation (Lantz, 1994; Marcel, 1948; May, 1983). In such an encounter, an empathic atmosphere is developed in which both the client and the therapist are touched, challenged, and changed in a rich and significant way (Frankl, 1959; Krill, 1978; Lantz, 1993; May, 1983; Yalom, 1980). Although it is not a goal of existential social work to provide help for the therapist, it is true that, in the mystery-centered approach, the encounter, empathy, and participation that occur between the client and the therapist powerfully and deeply affect them both (Lantz, 1993; Yalom, 1980). From a mystery-centered point of view, the only way to keep the therapist from feeling the impact of the treatment relationship is to conduct the relationship from a disconnected and distant treatment stance (Frankl, 1968; Lantz, 1974, 1978, 1993; Yalom, 1980).

CLARITY AND RICHNESS OF KNOWLEDGE

In the problem-centered approach to existential social work, it is considered possible to develop clear and precise knowledge of the client's repetitive problem sequences that disrupt problem resolution and actualization of meaning potentials (Haley, 1976; Lantz, 1978). From this problem-centered point of view, it is also considered possible to develop a "tailored" intervention plan that will result in increased client problem-solving and problem-resolution skills. From the problem-centered perspective, it is believed that such clarity can be achieved regularly by using competent observation skills, and that it makes good sense to expect such accurate assessments and tailored intervention plans from a professional mental health practitioner (Haley, 1976; Lantz, 1978).

From a mystery-centered point of view, the clear knowledge sought during problem-centered treatment is considered to be flat, surface, and superficial (Lantz, 1990, 1994; Marcel, 1948). In mystery-centered social work treatment, it is believed that every individual is unique and can be understood adequately only through deep knowledge developed over time during encounter in an empathic treatment relationship (Lantz, 1993; Marcel, 1948; May, 1983).

A strength and yet a problem experienced by the existential social worker from the mystery-centered perspective is his or her lack of confidence in rapid assessment and previously utilized problem-centered treatment activities (Lantz, 1974, 1993). From a mystery-centered point of view, the therapist is very aware that treatment activities based on clarity of knowledge and assessment that worked well with the last client seen in treatment often will not be helpful for the new client being treated now (Lantz, 1993; May, 1983; Yalom, 1980). Such a lack of confidence means that the existential psychotherapist must tolerate the anxiety of "starting fresh" with every new client (Lantz & Kondrat, 1996, 1997). On the other hand, this anxiety is helpful in that it pushes the mystery-centered therapist to develop new knowledge, deeper knowledge, and richer ideas about assessment and intervention that are more compatible with this "particular" client's "basic" and "central" treatment needs (Lantz, 1989, 1994). The mystery-centered approach to assessment and knowledge development with each client results in a more accurate and complete understanding of the client's "existential" and/or human treatment needs (Lantz, 1994). The mystery-centered social worker's willingness to experience "ignorance" about the client requesting help is of great advantage in promoting knowledge about the client that is based on empathy, encounter, and human participation (Frankl, 1968; Lantz, 1974; May, 1983; Yalom, 1980).

PRIMARY AND SECONDARY REFLECTION TREATMENT ACTIVITIES

In existential social work, both primary and secondary reflection treatment activities are used to help the client notice meaning potentials in the future, actualize meaning potentials in the here and now, and honor and re-collect meaning potentials previously actualized and deposited in the past (Lantz, 1993, 1994, 1995; Lantz & Gomia, 1995). In existential social work, primary reflection treatment activities are considered to be problem-solving activities directed toward objective solutions that are universal, abstract, and verifiable (Lantz, 1978, 1994; Marcel, 1948). Primary reflection thought and treatment activities are directed toward confronting, breaking down, and reducing problems (Lantz, 1978, 1994; Marcel, 1948). The major drawback in using primary reflection treatment activities is that they often facilitate the development of a treatment relationship that is overly distant, objective, and technological (Lantz, 1994). Marcel (1948) reports that "techno mania" is the major "risk" when using primary reflection to understand "human" life. In the author's view, Haley (1976) and Beck (1976) have both developed effective treatment systems that are based on what Marcel (1948) describes as primary reflection thought.

From Marcel's (1948) point of view, primary reflection is used to gain clarity about problem development and problem resolution, whereas secondary reflection is used to gain a richer, wider, deeper, more inclusive, and more holistic understanding of the meanings and meaning potentials in life (Lantz, 1993, 1994, 1995). For Marcel (1948), secondary reflection and secondary reflection treatment activities are the path toward mystery and a mystery-centered awareness of the meanings and meaning potentials in life to be discovered, re-collected, and honored. Secondary reflection treatment activities often involve circular questions, art, Socratic reflection, poetry, prayer, meditation, life review, celebration, active imagination, confirmation, ritual, drama, literature, music, and the "I-Thou" dialogue (Lantz, 1993, 1994, 1995; Lantz & Gomia, 1995; Lantz & Kondrat, 1996). The helping orientations of Frankl (1968), Krill (1978), Lantz (1993), May (1983), and Yalom (1980) are excellent examples of treatment approaches that depend mostly on secondary reflection treatment activities.

Primary reflection social work treatment activities are best used to help a client actualize and "make use" of the meaning potentials in life, and secondary reflection treatment activities are best used to "notice" meaning potentials in the future and to remember, re-collect, and honor meaning potentials that have been actualized and deposited in the past (Lantz, 1989, 1990, 1995). In the author's view, primary reflection treatment activities are best understood as problem-centered and secondary reflection treatment activities as mystery-centered. The author believes that both forms of treatment activities are necessary in existential social work, and that it is the responsibility of the existential social worker to manage and mediate the tensions that occur between the mystery- and problem-centered elements in existential treatment (Lantz, 1974, 1993; Lantz & Kondrat, 1996). The case example presented later in this chapter illustrates how the existential social worker can use both primary-reflection (i.e., problem-centered) and secondary-reflection (i.e., mystery-centered) treatment activities during existential social work treatment.

HISTORICAL DEVELOPMENT OF EXISTENTIAL SOCIAL WORK

Like existential psychology (May, 1983) and existential psychiatry (Yalom, 1980), existential social work (Krill, 1978; Lantz, 1993) has evolved out of existential philosophy, which emerged first in Europe in the early 1900s. Important existential philosophers who have influenced existential social workers, psychologists, psychiatrists, and psychotherapists include Nietzsche, Frankl, Husserl, Sartre, Heidegger, Buber, Jaspers, Kierkegaard, Ortega y Gasset, Marcel, Camus, Tillich, Maritain, Straus, Unamuno, and Merleau-Ponty (Friedman, 1964). Existential psychologists and psychiatrists who have based their work on existential philosophy include Viktor Frankl, Rollo May, Karl Jaspers, Helen Lynd, Ludwig Binswanger, Irving Yalom, Medard Boss, J. L. Moreno, Silvano Arieti, Carl Rogers, and Leslie Farber (Friedman, 1964).

Social work practitioners and theorists who have used existential concepts in their work include Andrews (1974), Brown (1980), Curry (1967), Edwards (1982), Goldstein (1984), Krill (1978), Lantz (1993), Picardie (1980), Sinsheimer (1969), and Stretch (1967). In the author's opinion, Donald Krill (1978) is the pioneer existential social work practitioner who has most actively introduced the philosophy of existentialism into our profession. The author also has long been impressed by Howard Goldstein's (1984) efforts to integrate existentialism and cognitive theory into the field of social work practice. The author of this chapter takes credit for consistently and systematically introducing existentialism into the fields of family social work and family psychotherapy over the past 30 years (Lantz, 1974, 1978, 1982, 1987, 1990, 1991, 1992, 1993, 1994, 1995, 1996, 1997; Lantz & Ahern, 1994, 1998; Lantz & Alford, 1995; Lantz & Kondrat, 1997; Lantz & Witter, 1994).

PHASES OF HELPING

In many approaches to social work practice, the process of treatment includes engagement, assessment, planning and contracting, intervention, and evaluation-termination stages. The existential social worker considers such stage models to be useful in focusing treatment and in tailoring treatment to the client's specific needs (Lantz, 1978). Although such treatment stage models are exceptionally helpful, they do not describe adequately the process of the helping relationship as it is experienced by the client during existential social work. From an existential social work point of view, it is helpful to understand the process of client change "existentially," as it occurs in the client's life. Over the past 30 years, it has been the author's observation that clients go through a series of "growth stages" during the process of existential social work treatment. These growth stages can be called awareness, exploration, commitment, skill-development, skill-refinement, and redirection stages of human growth (Lantz, 1978).

THE AWARENESS STAGE

In the awareness stage of existential social work, the therapist helps clients understand that the development and continuation of symptoms are, at least in part, the results of their failure to notice, actualize, and honor the meanings and meaning potentials in daily life. In most instances, clients view the development of symptoms as "just" a result of stress, "just" an internal psychological conflict, or "just" a medical or biochemical problem. This "just" view is both reductionistic and a tactic clients use to distance themselves from the need and responsibility to directly reflect upon the meaning and spiritual aspects of existence. This "just" defense is understandable. As Frankl (1968) has noted, the conscious realization of meaninglessness is terrifying and often requires a crisis for people to become truly aware of it.

Specific treatment activities the existential social worker can use in the awareness stage to help clients consciously reflect upon their existential vacuum include relationship-building activities, the development of trust between the therapist and the client, secondary reflection treatment activities, and "planting the awareness seed."

The ending of the awareness stage is probably the most critical period during existential social work (Lantz, 1978, 1993). As clients begin to reflect consciously on their feelings of meaninglessness, they experience more directly the pain associated with this existential-meaning vacuum. It is a time when the existential social worker must offer a great deal of support. The helper must also direct clients toward activities and reflection experiences that help them to fill their existential-meaning vacuum with a greater sense of meaning and purpose in life. This occurs by moving into the exploration stage (Lantz, 1974, 1993).

THE EXPLORATION STAGE

In the exploration stage, the existential social worker engages clients in meaning experimentation: to discern, through exploration, experiences that may result in the discovery of attitudinal, productive, and experiential values. In this stage, the therapist uses both primary and secondary reflection treatment activities to facilitate clients' experimentation with the search for meaning (Lantz, 1978, 1993).

The existential social worker is extremely active and directive in the exploration stage, not to coerce clients into accepting the therapist's meanings, but to help clients discover their own personal values and meanings that they have repressed, covered, and/or denied. The social worker's activity is designed to free the client's existential-meaning unconscious.

Toward the end of the exploration stage, clients often feel a great sense of excitement. They have discovered new meaning possibilities and experiences of meaning. They feel an increased sense of hope. This hope, however, is often short-lived unless client and social worker can move into the commitment and skill-development stages.

THE COMMITMENT STAGE

During the commitment stage of existential social work, clients, having identified and experienced a number of new meaning potentials, are asked to decide either to terminate treatment or to continue working on a basic and lasting process of realizing meaning. Such a decision cannot be made until clients have gone through both the awareness and the exploration stage. Without sufficient awareness, they will not know that the discovery of meaning is either necessary or desirable. Without exploration, they will not know that the discovery of new meaning is possible, and they will have little understanding of the directions in which this search for meaning could or should occur (Lantz, 1978, 1993).

Pressing clients for a true commitment to existential social work treatment before completion of awareness and exploration is like asking a person to appreciate pizza before ever having tasted it. Only after completion of awareness and exploration can clients make intelligent and informed decisions toward either commitment or termination (Lantz, 1993).

THE SKILL-DEVELOPMENT STAGE

After making a commitment for continued treatment, the client and the existential social worker move into the skill-development stage. In this stage, they both identify and practice specific methods that clients will find useful in their ongoing search for meaning and meaning actualization. The social worker helps clients learn that each emerging moment provides an opportunity to discover meaning. Clients use the skill-development stage to practice some of the methods of discovery of meaning that have been introduced during the exploration stage. The skill-development stage is a time of repetition, practice, hard work, and increased recognition by clients that they must replace magical expectations of immediate success with consistent work toward hard-fought therapeutic gains (Lantz, 1978, 1993).

THE SKILL-REFINEMENT STAGE

In this stage, clients continue to produce new methods of discovering meaning. This stage is a continuation of the skill-development stage, but the social worker takes a less active role, allowing clients more opportunities to be in complete charge of refining personal skills in their discovery of meaning (Lantz, 1993).

THE REDIRECTION STAGE

In the redirection stage, clients are getting ready for termination. In this stage, they demonstrate readiness to continue to search actively for, discover, and honor meaning without the social worker's assistance. The redirection stage includes celebration. The client and the social worker celebrate the client's growth, then terminate the treatment relationship. The termination is an affirmation, by both the social worker and the client, of the client's ability to continue to grow (Lantz, 1978, 1993).

APPLICATION TO FAMILY AND GROUP WORK

In existential social work, it is understood that many different treatment modalities can be utilized to facilitate the human search for meaning (Andrews, 1974; Krill, 1978; Lantz, 1974, 1989, 1993, 1995). Individual social work intervention is often used when existential social workers wish to maximize their control over the treatment process or to maximize their treatment (Lantz, 1993). Group therapy is most frequently used when the existential social worker wishes to help the client maximize the experiential aspect of treatment to learn new and more effective methods in actualizing and making use of the meaning potentials in the client's daily world (Lantz, 1974, 1993). Marital and family treatment modalities are most frequently used when the existential social worker believes that client symptoms are a signal pointing out meaning disruption problems in the client's total social network as a whole, or when the social worker hopes to mobilize social support and network resources for the client's struggle to grow (Lantz, 1974, 1993).

COMPATIBILITY OF EXISTENTIAL SOCIAL WORK WITH GENERALIST-ECLECTIC DIRECT SOCIAL WORK PRACTICE

Existential social work is a philosophical orientation to practice that is both a focused, eclectic approach and a problem-focused approach. The philosophical orientation that lies at the core of existential social work encourages a pragmatic approach to treatment within a reflective treatment relationship that encourages client freedom, responsibility, and autonomy. The existential social worker is willing to use a wide and rich variety of treatment methods with the client in a focused manner, which is very compatible with the generalist-eclectic orientation of the editors of this book.

A CRITIQUE OF EXISTENTIAL THEORY

The major criticism that has been made against existential social work, existential psychiatry, existential psychology, and existential psychotherapy is that the theory is an orientation to treatment that facilitates a tailored, flexible, and unique treatment approach with each individual client, rather than an organized theory that facilitates the development of consistent treatment procedures that can be utilized on all clients and tested by systematic, controlled research methods (Curry, 1967; Lantz, 1993; Lantz & Kondrat, 1997). In the author's view, this criticism is, in reality, a compliment and demonstrates existential treatment's compatibility with a focused-eclectic treatment approach.

Existential social work is most useful with individuals who face problems that include the need to discover, actualize, and honor the meanings and meaning potentials in their lives. The author has effectively used existential social work practice in hospital, mental health, family service, child welfare, and private practice treatment settings, and has used the approach with diverse population groups over the past 30 years (Harper & Lantz, 1996; Lantz, 1974; Lantz & Alford, 1995; Lantz & Witter, 1994). The approach is especially useful with traumatized clients (Lantz, 1974, 1993, 1995).

CASE EXAMPLE

Mr. Jakes was a 32-year-old single man who requested service because he wanted to lose weight. Mr. Jakes reported that he had "failed" at two nationally known weight loss centers, both of which had used diet, social encouragement, and behavioral management treatment techniques. When Mr. Jakes requested treatment with the author, he was 6 feet tall and weighed 324 pounds.

When the existential social worker asked about the meanings and meaning potentials that Mr. Jakes experienced in his life, Mr. Jakes reported that "nothing is meaningful except food." Mr. Jakes did not like his work (he was a bookkeeper), did not have any friends, and never dated. He reported that the only thing he really enjoyed was food. The social worker told Mr. Jakes that in the social worker's opinion, it would be "wrong" to take away the one thing in Mr. Jakes' life that he enjoyed and viewed as "meaningful" without first helping him to add new meanings to his life. This made sense to Mr. Jakes, who developed a contract with the social worker in which he would not try to lose weight but rather would attempt to notice meaning potentials and meaning opportunities in his life other than food.

In working with Mr. Jakes, the social worker used mystery-centered treatment activities to help him notice his world and the potentials for meaning. Socratic reflection, meditation, active imagination, and confirmation experiences in the treatment relationship were secondary reflection treatment activities that Mr. Jakes found especially useful for discovering meaning potentials other than food. After Mr. Jakes had developed some new hobbies, found a new job that he considered meaningful, and started doing volunteer work at a nursing home, he "discovered" that he had lost 55 pounds "without trying."

During the initial stage of treatment, Mr. Jakes and the social worker concentrated on the use of secondary-reflection, mystery-centered treatment activities to notice meanings and meaning potentials in life. After about 16 months of treatment (and the loss of more than 50 pounds), Mr. Jakes and the therapist decided to add primary-reflection, problem-centered treatment activities to help Mr. Jakes lose additional weight as he maintained his focus on finding new sources of meaning in his life. Mr. Jakes found some of the cognitive restructuring and imagery techniques in the cognitive-behavioral approach to treatment to be useful additions to the mystery-centered approach that he and the existential social worker had been using.

Mr. Jakes eventually lost 150 pounds during treatment. At the 5-year follow-up evaluation, he reported that he had maintained his termination weight of 175 pounds. He was married to a "wonderful wife" and had two children, whom he deeply loved. Mr. Jakes reported that he was "thin in weight and heavy in meaning."

SUMMARY

Existential social work is a treatment orientation that utilizes the problem-centered and mystery-centered components of existence to help the client notice, actualize, and honor the meanings and meaning potentials in life. This helps the client "shrink" his or her existential-meaning vacuum and the symptoms and problems that flourish there. In this chapter, treatment stages, methods, and modalities have been outlined and described, and case material has been presented to illustrate the existential social work approach.

REFERENCES

Andrews, E. (1974). *The emotionally disturbed family.* Northvale, NJ: Jason Aronson.

Beck, A. (1976). *Cognitive theory and the emotional disorders.* New York: New American Library.

Brown, J. (1980). Child abuse: An existential process. *Clinical Social Work Journal, 8,* 108–111.

Curry, A. (1967). Toward a phenomenological study of the family. *Existential Psychiatry, 6,* 35–44.

Edwards, D. (1982). *Existential psychotherapy.* New York: Gardner Press.

Frankl, V. (1955). *The doctor and the soul: From psychotherapy to logotherapy.* New York: Vintage Press.

Frankl, V. (1959). *From death camp to existentialism.* Boston: Beacon Hill Press.

Frankl, V. (1968). *The will to meaning: Foundations and applications of logotherapy.* New York: New American Library.

Frankl, V. (1997). *The search for ultimate meaning.* New York: Insight Books.

Friedman, M. (1964). *The worlds of existentialism.* New York: Random House.

Goldstein, H. (1984). *Creative change: A cognitive humanistic approach to social work practice.* New York: Methuen.

Haley, J. (1976). *Problem solving therapy.* New York: Harper.

Harper, K., & Lantz, J. (1996). *Cross-cultural practice.* Chicago: Lyceum Books.

Krill, D. (1978). *Existential social work.* New York: Free Press.

Lantz, J. (1974). Existential treatment and the Vietnam veteran family. In *Ohio Department of Mental Health Yearly Report* (pp. 33–36). Columbus: Ohio Department of Mental Health.

Lantz, J. (1978). *Family and marital therapy.* New York: Appleton-Century-Crofts.

Lantz, J. (1982). Dereflection in family therapy with schizophrenic clients. *International Forum for Logotherapy, 5,* 119–122.

Lantz, J. (1984). Responsibility and meaning in treatment of schizophrenics. *International Forum for Logotherapy, 7,* 26–28.

Lantz, J. (1987). The use of Frankl's concepts in family therapy. *Journal of Independent Social Work, 2,* 65–80.

Lantz, J. (1989). Meaning in profanity and pain. *Voices, 25,* 34–37.

Lantz, J. (1990). Existential reflection in marital therapy with Vietnam veterans. *Journal of Couples Therapy, 1,* 81–88.

Lantz, J. (1991). Franklian treatment with Vietnam veteran couples. *Journal of Religion and Health, 30,* 131–138.

Lantz, J. (1992). Meaning, nerves and the urban-Appalachian family. *Journal of Religion and Health, 31,* 129–139.

Lantz, J. (1993). *Existential family therapy: Using the concepts of Viktor Frankl.* Northvale, NJ: Jason Aronson.

Lantz, J. (1994). Marcel's availability in existential psychotherapy with couples and families. *Contemporary Family Therapy, 16,* 489–501.

Lantz, J. (1995). Frankl's concept of time: Existential psychotherapy with couples and families. *Journal of Contemporary Psychotherapy, 25,* 135–144.

Lantz, J. (1996). Existential psychotherapy with chronic illness couples. *Contemporary Family Therapy, 18,* 197–208.

Lantz, J. (1997). Poetry in existential psychotherapy with couples and families. *Contemporary Family Therapy, 19,* 371–381.

Lantz, J. (1998). Re-collection in existential psychotherapy with older adults. *Journal of Clinical Geropsychology, 4,* 45–53.

Lantz, J., & Ahern, R. (1994). Meaning and the family life cycle. *Journal of Religion and Health, 33,* 163–172.

Lantz, J., & Ahern, R. (1998). Re-collection in existential psychotherapy with couples and families dealing with death. *Contemporary Family Therapy, 20,* 47–57.

Lantz, J., & Alford, K. (1995). Existential family therapy with an urban-Appalachian adolescent. *Journal of Family Psychotherapy, 6,* 15–27.

Lantz, J., & Gomia, E. (1995). Activities and stages in existential psychotherapy with older adults. *Clinical Gerontologist, 16,* 31–40.

Lantz, J., & Kondrat, M. (1996). Integration of problem-oriented and mystery-centered approaches in existential psychotherapy. *Journal of Contemporary Psychotherapy, 26,* 295–305.

Lantz, J., & Kondrat, M. (1997). Evaluation research problems in existential psychotherapy with couples and families. *Journal of Family Psychotherapy, 8,* 55–71.

Lantz, J., & Witter, M. (1994). Existential psychotherapy with fast-track, suburban couples. *Journal of Contemporary Psychotherapy, 24,* 281–293.

Marcel, G. (1948). *The philosophy of existence.* New York: Philosophical Library.

May, R. (1983). *The discovery of being.* New York: Norton.

Picardie, M. (1980). Dreadful moments: Existential thoughts on doing social work. *British Journal of Social Work, 10,* 483–490.

Sinsheimer, R. (1969). The existential casework relationship. *Social Casework, 50,* 67–73.

Stretch, J. (1967). Existentialism: A proposed philosophical orientation for social work. *Social Work, 12,* 97–102.

Yalom, I. (1980). *Existential psychotherapy.* New York: Basic Books.

14

Feminist Theories

Christine Flynn Saulnier

The greatest challenge of this chapter is to choose among the various theories, approaches, and perspectives that come under the label of feminist theory. It is not possible to sum up the whole of feminism with a set of common ideas; there are too many fundamental contradictions among the theories to attempt any such reduction. I limited the number of theories discussed in this chapter to those that I think are most likely to be useful to direct service social work practitioners. The most helpful theories are those that guide social workers in operationalizing the profession's commitment to social and economic justice. I briefly discuss liberal, socialist, lesbian, radical, and womanist theories: liberal feminism because of its wide use, more than its potential for serving the needs of social and economic justice; socialist and lesbian feminist theories because of their power to challenge fundamental beliefs about issues that are often discussed but seldom addressed in American social work (i.e., economic class and sexual orientation hierarchies as two of the foundations upon which our culture is built); and radical feminist and womanist theories because they best synthesize the interaction of psychological and sociological phenomena. Those who seek a firm grounding in feminist social work have additional reading to do—beyond the thumbnail sketches of the theories presented in this chapter, and beyond the limited number of feminist theories reviewed here. The primary sources cited in this chapter provide a next step for continuing study.

AN OVERVIEW OF FEMINIST THEORY

UNDERSTANDING OF HUMAN PROBLEMS

For this overview, analyzing the varied experiences of people from a political perspective that holds a sex-based analysis as one of the key analytical lenses

255

constitutes a feminist approach. Another way of saying this is that within feminist theoretical analyses, many distresses experienced by women—and some of those experienced by men—can best be understood in terms of sex-based social and structural restrictions, constrictions, and resource deficits, as these limitations interact with various other structural and interpersonal constraints. For example, child care arrangements continue to be woefully inadequate and unaffordable in the United States, but without a feminist perspective, a working-class or poor mother who uses substandard or no care while she works is likely to be held individually responsible for child neglect. Social and legal systems deal with her as though it is her personal adequacy as a mother, rather than American child care policy, grounded in a sex-based social structure, that is at fault. If she also happens to be lesbian or Black, or otherwise outside the mainstream, her child care arrangements might be seen as indicative of how difficult it is for members of her population to function as fit mothers. Often, a flurry of analyses will attempt to explain how she is disadvantaged by her beliefs and practices, making her culturally or constitutionally less likely to comprehend the necessity for child protection guidelines. This is the antithesis of feminist analysis.

Feminist theories, first of all, explain and suggest directions for change in social and environmental factors that create or contribute to dilemmas and problems experienced by women. Second, they explain and propose interventions for women's intrapersonal and interpersonal concerns. Third, feminist theories provide a perspective for evaluating social and environmental experiences of groups and individuals, regardless of sex or gender. The emphasis placed on each of these three areas, along with the centrality of additional factors that influence marginalization or oppression, depends on which feminist theory is used.

CONCEPTION OF THERAPEUTIC INTERVENTION

Most feminist theories call for multilevel interventions. Depending on which theory is used and which feminist social worker is practicing, intervention might be primarily at a macro level and only secondarily include microlevel interventions. The opposite may also be true, however. Many feminist social workers intervene almost entirely with individuals, families, and small groups, but few feminist practitioners would suggest that intervening on only one level is adequate. Most feminists would agree on the need for policy change, but disagree about how fundamental the change in our social fabric needs to be (Saulnier, 1996).

The utility of psychotherapy is hotly debated. It is not that feminists would necessarily dismiss empirical evidence that the goals of psychotherapy are often met. Rather, some would argue that the goals of psychotherapy—individual change in behavior and self-perception—distract feminist social workers, community members, and service users from social justice work.

Psychotherapy may even be in direct conflict with social justice work if women are encouraged to cope with, instead of change, injustice (Arches, 1984; Kitzinger & Perkins, 1993). Other feminist theorists and practitioners would argue that for women to engage fruitfully in social change, healing at the individual level is often a prerequisite, and the task is best undertaken within a feminist framework (hooks, 1993; Lewis & Kissman, 1989). Still other social workers argue that individual and social change must proceed simultaneously (Weiner, 1998).

HISTORICAL DEVELOPMENT: FEMINIST THEORIES AND SOCIAL WORK CONNECTIONS

Feminist theories vary, their historical development differs, and the relationship between feminism and social work has been mixed. Some branches of feminist thought are inextricably bound to the sociopolitical climate of the historical period in which they arose. For example, it is hard to imagine how the tenets of lesbian feminism could have emerged prior to the naming and marginalization of lesbianism. On the other hand, most of the tenets of womanism—considered a late-20th-century theoretical phenomenon—have been clearly identified in both the thinking and the activism of mid-19th-century African-American women.

The profession of social work is celebrating 100 years of practice. The history of feminist social work practice is equally long (Saulnier, 1996; Weil, 1986; Wetzel, 1976; Wise, 1988). Although not all social workers have been open to feminist thought (Abramovitz, 1978), many social work practitioners have worked within feminist frameworks (Abbott, 1994; Lewis, 1996). For example, in 1917, feminist social workers were working to eliminate the incongruity of having laws against public drunkenness, but no economic or legal recourse for women living with heavy drinking, violent husbands (Woods, 1917). During the same era, Jane Addams was working diligently for women's suffrage (Meigs, 1979). Another notable social worker, Sophonisba Breckinridge, advocated women's rights in the 1930s and 1940s from her prominent position at the School of Social Service Administration, University of Chicago. Over the last few decades feminist social work theory and practice have gained increasing academic recognition. Since 1986, *Affilia*, a major scholarly journal in social work, has published writings devoted to the theories and practice of feminist social work.

Despite significant feminist social work activities, it should be noted that discrimination against women within the profession has been well documented (Gibelman & Schervish, 1993; Kravetz, 1976), social work practices have often reflected the antiwoman biases of the larger society (Krane, 1990; Kravetz, 1976; Stout & Kelly, 1990), and social work responses to feminist critiques of society and the profession have not always been positive (Abramovitz, 1978). Some social workers have supported public policies that uphold patriarchal control within and outside of families

(Abramovitz, 1978); other social workers have written detailed accounts of welfare reform that explicitly dismiss the relationship between women's sociopolitical roles and the antiwoman stance of new welfare policies (Kost & Munger, 1996).

FEMINIST THEORIES AND THEIR THEORETICAL CONSTRUCTS

LIBERAL FEMINISM

Liberal philosophy, on which liberal feminism is based, describes society as being composed of separate individuals, each competing for a fair share of resources. Liberalism's dedication to individual liberty demands freedom from interference by the state (Donovan, 1985). Of key importance to liberal feminism is that a dividing line is drawn between the public realm, which the state is expected to regulate, and the private realm, which is expected to be free from state control (Jaggar, 1983). The traditional liberal values of independence (vs. interdependence), equality of opportunity (vs. equality of outcome), and individualism (vs. collectivism) are so ingrained in Western society that they are accepted as standard social functioning, rather than viewed as a particular ideology. These traditional liberal values are central to liberal feminist thought. Liberal feminists point out that society violates the value of equal rights in its treatment of women, primarily by restricting women as a group, rather than treating women as individuals (Jaggar, 1983). They argue that women should have the same rights as men, but they often fail to examine the de facto inequality in distribution of men's rights by race, socioeconomic, and other factors.

Liberal feminists contest such public issues as women's lack of political equality, and lack of access to certain social services needed to ensure equality between the sexes. Battles for equal education, equal employment opportunities, and equal pay for equal work have been the hallmark of liberal feminism. Often inequality is seen as being exacerbated, if not caused, by women's lack of training in the skills thought to enable men's success, for example, assertiveness. Rather than train women to dismantle structural supports of power imbalances, liberal feminists are more likely to examine interpersonal interactions and encourage women to behave more like those men who are successful in their careers. That is, liberal feminists work within the structure of mainstream society to integrate women into that structure (Moore, 1993).

SOCIALIST FEMINISM

Socialist feminism draws on the theories of Karl Marx to explain how economic or material conditions form the root of culture, social organization, and consciousness itself. Oppression of women is said to be based in the private property system that exists within capitalist social and economic structures. Although socialist feminism draws on Marx's analysis of property relations, modes of production, and changes in material relations across history, it focuses primarily on a feminist-based class analysis as the central theorizing structure (Burnham & Louie, 1985). Theoretically, socialist feminists seek to end women's oppression, in part by eliminating capitalism (Moore, 1993). A socialist economic and social system is seen as insufficient to eliminate patriarchal structures and sexual division of labor, however. The latter would require a feminist revolution in addition to a socialist one (Burnham & Louie, 1985).

More pragmatically, socialist feminists focus attention on women's role in the wage labor force, often using the labor movement as a base from which to promote more equitable redistribution of resources. They focus on organizing women as women to eliminate gender-specific aspects of oppression, such as the problems of sexual abuse, insufficient child care, and constraints on reproductive rights (Burnham & Louie, 1985). Socialist feminists draw attention to apparently gender-neutral labor issues, for example, job protection, pointing out the overrepresentation of women among temporary workers and the underrepresentation of women among the workers whose jobs have been protected against contracting out. They demonstrate that such policies have a greater negative impact on female workers than on men and reinforce sexual division of labor (Creese, 1996). The analysis also focuses on how women's labor is controlled by men both in the family and in the workplace, and the enormous economic cost to women—during the work years, after divorce, and in retirement—of sporadic employment patterns and low wages (Catlett & McKenry, 1996; Thorne, 1983). Despite considerable disagreement over whether capitalism and patriarchy are separate systems (dual systems theorists include Hartmann, 1981, and Mitchell, 1971), or a single entity (unified systems theorists include Al-Hibri, 1981, and Young, 1981), socialist feminists tend to address the connections among family, employment, and social issues along both gender and class lines (Poster, 1995).

Socialist feminists have tended to work at macro levels, addressing policy (Abramovitz, 1988, 1991) and organizing needs (Weil, 1986). In each case, they have worked toward finding collective means for solving both individual and community problems (Weil, 1986). Most recently, socialist feminists have been at the forefront of addressing the gender and economic bases of caregiving (Fredriksen, 1996; Langan, 1992). In this arena, direct practice social workers are often involved.

LESBIAN FEMINISM

Lesbian feminism is a political perspective critical of heterosexual institutions (Smith, cited in Farwell, 1992) and supportive of women's identification with women. Some argue it is only coincidentally related to sexual orientation. Charlotte Bunch's (1987) distinction is often quoted in this regard:

> A lesbian is a woman whose sexual/affectional preference is for women, and who has thereby rejected the female role on some level, but she may or may not embrace a lesbian-feminist political analysis. A woman-identified woman is a feminist who adopts a lesbian-feminist ideology and enacts that understanding in her life, whether she is a lesbian sexually or not. (p. 198)

Heterosexuality is defined by lesbian feminist theorists as both a political and a personal institution in which some members of society are given privileges that are withheld from others, based on sex, gender, and sexual orientation. Gender assignments are made in this sociopolitical context with neither gender nor sexual orientation being free from social constraint. The relationship between the prescribed social roles and stigmatization of lesbians is clear (Stevens, 1995), but the implications extend beyond the place of lesbians in society. Once gender identities and sexual orientation are exposed as socially rather than naturally created, the rationale for lesbian subordination is lost. Thus, the arbitrariness of exclusive organization of sexuality, romance, love, and marriage around the heterosexual imperative is also exposed (Calhoun, 1994). That is, lesbian feminism questions the necessity for heterosexuality as a basis on which to organize society. The invisibility and active suppression of lesbianism is seen as a gauge of how threatening lesbianism is to the ideology of gender assignments, male superiority, and female dependence.

Social service and health systems have all but ignored lesbians. The result is twofold: Lesbians' needs are unmet, and strictures on acceptable diversity are shored up as all women—regardless of sexual orientation—receive a forceful message about who and what are tolerable. That is, health and social service systems powerfully reinforce the social order that privileges, or even requires, heterosexuality. The silence about lesbians and lesbianism that theorists analyzed in the 1970s (Rich, 1979) is still reflected at macro and micro levels in health and mental health care delivery (Saulnier, in press; Saulnier & Wheeler, in press; Stevens, 1995). Heterosexuality is still thought of as the natural condition and is still strongly associated with positive attitudes toward sex-based hierarchies (Kane & Schippers, 1996).

RADICAL FEMINISM

Radical feminists argue that individual women's experiences of injustice and the miseries that women think of as personal problems are actually political issues, grounded in power imbalances. Often using the slogan "The personal is political," they argue that separating public from private issues masks the reality of male power, a system of domination that operates similarly in interdependent public and private spheres. Radical feminists hold that public-private divisions isolate and depoliticize women's experience of oppression (Nes & Iadicola, 1989). Sexism is described as a social system consisting of "law, tradition, economics, education, organized religion, science, language, the mass media, sexual morality, child rearing, the domestic division of labor, and everyday social interaction" (Willis, 1989, p. x), the purpose of which is to give men power over women. The pervasiveness of sexism necessitates fundamental social change.

Radical feminists characterize society as patriarchal. By this they mean that, historically, families have been organized according to male lines of inheritance and dependence, and also that society had been constructed in a way that accrues a disproportionate share of power to men. The patriarchal structure privileges men through the complex political manipulation of individual identity, social interactions, and structural systems of power. Formal structures such as legal systems create and reinforce the sexual hierarchy, and virtually all human interactions are permeated by male privilege (Eisenstein, 1981). Patriarchy, although varied in its manifestations, is described as a cultural universal, with all institutions reinforcing that social order (Nes & Iadicola, 1989).

Radical feminism's psychological analysis of male supremacy has two main themes: (1) Women are damaged psychologically by the internalization of oppressive patriarchal messages (Echols, 1989), and (2) psychological control of women is a significant component of patriarchal systems (Donovan, 1985). Rigid sex role prescriptions not only distort people, they also lead to sex-based oppression. The psychology of sex-role conditioning accounts for women's apparent complicity with patriarchy (Echols, 1989). Radical feminists study the prevalence of violence against women, define it as political in nature, and point out that it is men who tend to abuse women and that battering is usually woman abuse.

Because of the comprehensiveness of their demand for change, radical feminists have had an uneasy relationship with health and mental health service providers and have preferred to develop new women-focused services rather than adapt existing services to meet women's needs. A prime example is the virtual revolution in women's health services, with the Boston Women's Health Book Collective often credited as the inspiration for women taking health care into their own hands ("The Many Faces of Feminism," 1994).

WOMANISM

In addition to contributing significantly to the development of all of the divisions of feminist theory discussed here, African-American writers and theorists developed another branch of feminist theory, often referred to as womanism (Collins, 1990; Davis, 1989; Giddings, 1988; hooks, 1984; Joseph & Lewis, 1981; Lorde, 1990). Womanism starts with the perspective of Black women and centers on a complex matrix of oppressions. Womanists argue that additive models of oppression—in which oppressive systems are seen as parallel and only occasionally intersecting—hide from view, and therefore from change, interlocking systems. Because of categorical thinking, it is difficult to conceive of race, sex, and class as a single consciousness with a single struggle needed to overcome them (Brown, 1990). Womanists argue, however, that it is necessary to examine all these aspects so that neither race, nor sex, nor class is hidden or discounted (Christian, 1985). That means we cannot dismantle one system of domination, then move on to the next, without understanding their intersections and interdependencies. Working from an assumption of interlocking systems is a paradigmatic shift away from focusing on separate, interacting systems. It is a move toward an inclusive view of mutually dependent, oppressive systems (Collins, 1990). Rather than posing race and gender as contradictory opposites, where a woman is expected to identify either as Black or as a woman, womanism allows for a unified whole (Brown, 1990; Ogunyemi, 1985). (Note the title of the widely read anthology *All the Women Are White, All the Blacks Are Men, But Some of Us Are Brave*, by Hull, Scott, & Smith, 1982.)

Both action and articulation are emphasized in womanist theory (Lorde, 1984). Womanism uses racial consciousness to underscore the positive aspects of African-American life (Ogunyemi, 1985). But womanism does not focus solely on a social agenda. Self-healing is among the goals (Brown, 1990). To survive, despite racist and sexist valuations, Black women need to define themselves quite differently from the way they are viewed by those in power. Although mainstream social work does not use a womanist framework for service organization or delivery, individual social workers have (Carlton-LaNey, 1997), and social and health care services have sometimes been designed within a womanist framework (Brown, 1990; Comas-Diaz, 1994; Giddings, 1988; Saulnier, 1999). This framework takes into consideration the importance of a multifaceted sociopolitical analysis, the need for individual healing, and the importance of placing high value on racial consciousness. It is likely that many, though not all, African-American women will come to social workers with a strong racial and feminist consciousness (Wilcox, 1997) and will be interested in working within a womanist framework.

DESCRIPTIONS OF PHASES OF HELPING

In the following discussion of the application of feminism in direct practice, I will stress the commonalities across branches of feminist theory.

ENGAGEMENT

Feminist practitioners work to enable women to empower themselves as individuals and collectively. Feminists seek to minimize power differentials between service users and social workers, but they do not pretend that they have equal power with all the people who seek their services. Such a masking of power is dishonest and doesn't work (Baines, 1997). A feminist approach means engaging a person in a manner that conveys a genuine respect for the individual's perspective. Social workers bring valuable skills and knowledge to an exchange, but these are no more valuable than the knowledge that service users bring about themselves and their circumstances.

DATA COLLECTION AND ASSESSMENT

Gathering data on a micro level only is a diminishing truncation of feminist social work. Data concerning family, friends, and neighborhood and other potential social supports are important sources of information about strengths, circumstances, and perceptions. This information is necessary but not sufficient. In addition to examining individual circumstances, the influence of a person's membership in a particular socioeconomic class, ethnic group, racial category, and so on, should be considered. This too is necessary but still incomplete. Social workers using feminist theories will gather information about populations who have comparable strengths, experience similar challenges, and are affected by the same type of sociopolitical circumstances. Without this final step, it is not possible to determine whether planning and intervention should be focused on micro and/or macro levels.

Assessment starts with the service user. The person seeking help provides the most important assessment of assets, hindrances, concerns, and problems. Although it may be tempting in some situations (e.g., when working with people who have chronic mental illness or alcohol problems) to assume a social work practitioner has clearer insight into circumstances and needs, it is vital to recognize that this is a deficit approach that defines service users as less expert on their own lives than professionals.

Feminist assessment centers the perspective of the service user or community member. Skilled feminist assessment requires the ability to draw out information from another's perspective. The knowledge and skills the practitioner brings to bear are important. They are the reason people accept assistance from social workers, but it is the analysis of the service user or community member that must be the basis from which we form a picture of the whole person in context.

PLANNING/CONTRACTING AND INTERVENTION

Feminist planning/contracting means that both the worker and the service user have goals to accomplish. Meetings with service users help ground feminist social workers in the direction in which social justice work needs to proceed. One way of looking at the implications of feminist theories is that it is quite difficult to do feminist or womanist interventions. Intervention at a single level is insufficient in most cases, yet the circumstances in which many social workers find themselves require just that sort of truncation of social work intervention. Another way of viewing feminist intervention is that it is simply good social work: helping service users meet basic needs, giving service users the specific help they ask for, demystifying the work we do, and teaching skills. Changing the world is our job as social workers. Some service users will want to join social workers in the effort, some will do it on their own, and some won't want any part of it. Often this is because they are too busy trying to stay alive or because they are tired from the effort and need to back away for a while.

Feminist social workers need to be aware that a focus on process that is important to many people from middle-class backgrounds may be of no interest to people from working-class or poor backgrounds (Baines, 1997). It may be challenging for people who have been trained to use process as the primary method of intervention to put aside their predilection in favor of service user/community member preferences, but self-determination requires it.

EVALUATION AND TERMINATION

As with any social work intervention, the work with the individual is complete when the service user no longer needs a social worker. Determination of when that time has arrived and measures of outcome depend heavily on the service user's goals. Progress toward goals, satisfaction with social work help, and decrease in problems should all be evaluated regularly and systematically to ensure that the intervention helps rather than hinders. A key component is service user feedback. If process and outcomes are measured only at the individual level, however, social work will have fallen short. Social justice is a larger concept than what can be measured at the micro level. Social work practice using feminist theory also will examine social structures, organizations, and communities for improvement, with careful attention to systems of oppression, particularly sex-based oppression. For example, are more women's jobs being protected from contracting out (Creese, 1996)? Are the staff's negative attitudes toward women interfering with people getting high-quality services (Beckman & Mays, 1985)? Are intake forms heterosexist (Saulnier & Wheeler, in press)? Has progress been made toward providing an adequate amount of high-quality, low-cost child care in the community (Bergmann, 1997)?

APPLICATION TO FAMILY AND GROUP WORK

FAMILY THERAPY

Family therapy theories have been widely critiqued for their sexism (Whipple, 1996), as has family therapy practice (Werner Wilson, Price, Zimmerman, & Murphy, 1997; Wright & Fish, 1997), although many family therapists practice from a feminist perspective (Dankoski, Penn, Carlson, & Hecker, 1998; Goodrich, Rampage, Ellman, & Halstead, 1988) and feminist family therapy is being developed more extensively (Akamatsu, Basham, & Olson, 1996). Yet preference for patriarchy continues to guide some practitioners of family therapy (Ivey, 1996). For example, one self-labeled feminist family therapist (Erickson, 1996) argued that women and men are "naturally dependent" upon each other. Such feminist family therapists should avoid working with lesbians, women who choose to be single, those struggling with sexual orientation, and any other people who find the heterosexual imperative distasteful. Attitudes and beliefs contrary to feminist perspectives are often more subtle. In one published case study (Goodrich et al., 1988), several clinicians, while acknowledging that the notion of fusion in lesbian relationships often reflects homophobia, had treatment goals of separation and individuation, and took an "anthropologic" view of the lesbian foursome they chose for an illustration of feminist family therapy with lesbians.

More recently, family therapists, in general, have incorporated feminist ideas into their practice, including a critique of gender-role constraints. Incorporating feminist behaviors into practice seems to be more common among those who specifically identify themselves as feminists, however (Dankoski et al., 1998). Feminist family therapy acknowledges the changes in family forms over time and across cultures. It also takes into account our developing knowledge of the limitations of family therapy; for example, there are good reasons and good evidence that family treatment is not the treatment of choice for battered women (Walker, 1995).

GROUP WORK

Group work is common to most approaches to feminist practice (Saulnier, 1996). The groups include consciousness raising, women's self-help groups, feminist therapy groups, and woman-specific skill-building groups, where women are trained in such skills as assertiveness. Through these groups, feminists counter the sex biases that have been identified in traditional groups (Walker, 1987). As far back as 1958, researchers confirmed that women's verbal inhibition, willingness to be interrupted, and commitment to defending their ideas were all influenced by the sex composition of a group (Tuddenham, MacBride, & Zahn, 1958). Additionally, feminists defined the confrontation, conflict, and competition that they perceived to be common in traditional groups as inappropriate male-identified approaches to group work (Hagen, 1983).

One form of group work, called the structural approach (Wood & Middleman, 1991, 1992), fits well with a feminist framework. It focuses on the uneven distribution of resources among people and works toward redress by means of advocacy, consciousness raising, and training clients how to negotiate systems and how to alter social arrangements. Members are encouraged to provide mutual support while using community resources to effect political change.

Social workers have noted the parallels between feminist theory and the social action components of group work (Garvin, 1991; Lewis, 1992). Personal experience as the basis for political analysis and the potential for groups to make social change are the most obvious ways in which feminism and social group work overlap (Home, 1991; Lee, 1994; Pack Brown, Whittington Clark, & Parker, 1998). Garvin and Reed (1995) pointed out their shared historical roots, including simultaneous attention to social change and individual growth (Coyle, 1947, cited in Garvin, 1991). Kravetz (1987) noted the importance of consciousness-raising groups as a mental health resource for women. She contrasted the goals of traditional psychotherapy—changing "deviant, sick, or maladaptive" aspects of an individual and helping women to adjust—with consciousness raising's call for change in both structural-social and personal-interpersonal processes. In consciousness raising, women examine personal problems in sociopolitical context, and change is assumed to be needed in both social policy and personal attitudes and behavior. Kravetz (1987) stressed the need to counteract the internalization of cultural messages that support powerlessness and devalue women, and she argued that women's groups, particularly consciousness-raising groups, can alter internalized views, thereby challenging "one of the most basic ways that oppression is maintained" (p. 64).

Cox (1991) argued that the tendency to focus either on personal or on political aspects of a problem was misguided because a single focus contributes insufficiently to empowerment of group members, particularly their ability to change their environment. She argued that social workers should promote multifaceted groups. In her own work, Cox encouraged group members to intervene at both personal and political levels. She reported that group members succeeded in changing both their consciousness (e.g., courage, sense of power, and knowledge of bureaucratic functions) and their environments (e.g., increased safety, improved food stamp policy, and increased hours of a service availability at a facility used by participants). Social work practitioners have noted bidirectional skill development, indicating that women who were empowered as individuals were better equipped to undertake collective group action. By the same token, members developed personal skills and increased confidence when they were engaged in social action leading to more tangible outcomes, such as policy change and resource development (Regan & Lee, 1992).

COMPATIBILITY WITH THE GENERALIST-ECLECTIC FRAMEWORK

ATTENTION TO HOLISTIC ASSESSMENT AND USE OF SYSTEMS AND LIFE-CYCLE THEORIES

Systems perspectives have been used by feminists, including feminist family therapists, for a long time (Featherstone, 1996). Feminism is a systems perspective, to a large extent. With the possible exception of liberal feminism, a multilevel or holistic assessment would be essential in social work practice guided by feminist theory.

Life-cycle theories, although not necessarily incompatible with feminism, tend not to be used by feminists because they have often used a deficit model to discuss single-parent families, women who are alone, and women and children's adjustment to divorce (Candib, 1989). Family life-cycle theories are often fraught with male, White, and heterosexual biases (Rice, 1994). There are notable exceptions (Dutton Douglas & Walker, 1988; Kissman, 1991; Mirkin, 1994) in which women's development across the life cycle is centered rather than marginalized. The most prominent example is the work of The Stone Center (Jordan, Kaplan, Miller, Stiver, & Surrey, 1991), where theories of women's development are created within an explicitly feminist framework.

EMPHASIS ON THERAPEUTIC RELATIONSHIP AND FIT WITH STRENGTHS PERSPECTIVE

A strengths-based perspective is often used by feminist practitioners, including feminist group workers (Pollio, McDonald, & North, 1996). Feminist emphasis on the therapeutic relationship varies. Although it is the primary intervention used by many feminist social workers, others argue that the focus on developing a therapeutic relationship is sometimes outside the interests of people who seek our services, and that the focus on relationship building and process may be class-based (Baines, 1997). The relationship focus may mask a clinician's desire for a client to adopt the worker's worldview, rather than engage in open dialogue about the social, and often political, forces impinging on a service user's life (Kitzinger & Perkins, 1993).

ATTENTION TO ISSUES OF DIVERSITY AND EMPOWERMENT

Feminist theories have improved in their attention to diversity, although it would be a mistake to assume that the media portrayal of feminism as developed and supported only, or primarily, by White middle-class women is accurate. African-American women, Latinas, American Indian women, Asian-American women, and working-class women from many backgrounds have all been committed to feminism, under many names, for many decades (Saulnier, 1996). This said, it is also true that there has been considerable racism, classism, and heterosexism in various theoretical and activist camps of feminism. There is still much room for improvement, but many feminists have grown by exposure to multiple perspectives on women's issues, and it is much less common to see feminist theorizing or practice that fails to take diversity into account.

Empowerment is what feminism is about; however, the goal of empowerment varies from intrapsychic change to social action (Cox, 1991) and tends to depend on which feminist theory is used.

GENERALIST VERSUS SPECIALIST PRACTICE

Feminist theories support the generalist framework. The author's perspective is that specialization limits effectiveness except under particular circumstances. Those circumstances include work that is done in conjunction with other practitioners who are intervening across multiple levels, for example, as part of a task force or coalition of individuals or organizations committed to feminist/womanist social work practice. Specialists may work toward a particular goal, each using a specific method of intervention. To be compatible with feminist theories, however, the work would have to be integrated, so that positive change occurred at multiple levels.

ECLECTICISM

Given the pervasiveness of oppression of women and the negative effects on one person of diminishing another, theories that guide our understanding and dismantling of oppression can guide all our social work practice. This generalizability holds for feminist theories, as well as others that promote social justice. This does not preclude, however, the use of other theories. Depending on the branch of feminism, feminist practice can be consistent with other theories. For example, radical feminist consciousness raising could draw on cognitive theories, or liberal feminist assertiveness training might mesh well with cognitive-behavioral approaches. Also, as mentioned previously, some feminist practitioners incorporate postmodern and family therapy models into their practice.

A larger question for feminist practitioners is how to choose which feminist theory will guide their work. On the surface, it might seem that social workers should choose a feminist theory based on which systems of oppression impinge on the people with whom they are working at the time. It makes sense that the problem to be solved is the best guide to choice of theory. Some theories apply better than others to particular populations and problems. For example, given liberal feminism's concern with the glass ceiling, it would not be the best approach for women who are concerned more with the income floor—a theory that centers on class struggles would be more appropriate.

The problem in choosing which feminist theory to use is complicated by the inescapable reality that theories are value-laden. Some of us value pervasive structural change and see social justice as possible only in the context of profound redistribution of power and resources. Others value stability, predictability, and incremental change. Some theories question the very foundations of American society, for example, the heterosexual nuclear family structure upon which many social policies and services are built. For some social workers, the fundamental shake-up recommended by these theories is precisely what is needed. For others, that is taking self-definition and social justice too far, too fast. Practitioners must decide what is most in-line with their reading of the code of ethics and with social work values.

CRITIQUE OF THE THEORIES

As a whole, the major strengths of feminist theories are that they (1) explain sex-based disparities, (2) guide social workers in their efforts to dismantle structural and interpersonal restrictions and constrictions, and (3) provide an analytic lens for evaluating the various forms of oppression experienced by women. Because of feminist theories and the ways that the women's movement has used them, more services are available that meet women's needs. Some common criticisms of feminist theories include the narrowness of some branches, the limited populations to whom some branches may apply, and the lack of political viability of the more comprehensive theories.

CASE EXAMPLE

Following the example of a woman in search of child care that was introduced at the beginning of the chapter, traditional intervention might focus on helping the woman improve her ability to recognize the need for adequate supervision of her child and the need to work harder to locate and keep quality child care. Perhaps she would be referred to a child care registry for news of an opening and to county offices for a voucher to cover the cost of child care during her work hours. She may be offered counseling to help her value herself and her child and to strengthen her inner resources so she can better meet the challenges of parenting. She would not be encouraged to see herself as one of many, perhaps a class of, people who are held personally responsible for failures in social policies and social systems.

Feminist social work would approach the problem differently, although many of the concrete services would still be offered. First, the problem would be contextualized, and the woman encouraged to see the problem as a generalized need, rather than her deficit. Next, she would be supported in her struggle to provide for herself and her family. Together, she and the social worker would identify concrete needs, goals, and specific resources available. They would determine which services the woman herself should pursue and which would require advocacy or other social work intervention.

The social worker might also inform the woman of community efforts to make child care more available to low-income women, if such efforts existed. This would be in the form of information giving, not pressure to take on activism as yet another duty. However, if the woman's circumstances and interests allowed (and child care was available), the worker might help her devise ways she could contribute to the effort. If not, the social worker would still contribute in some way to the efforts of the community to provide for its children.

SUMMARY

Most feminist theories suggest ways to help eliminate misperceptions, sexual inequalities, restrictions, and oppression faced by women—goals that many writers have pointed out are shared by social workers (see review by Dore, 1994)—but the goals of each branch of feminism vary according to the perspective on the forces that impede women. If backlash is any measure of how threatened patriarchal structures are by feminist analysis and intervention, the false memory syndrome campaign suggests that feminists have hit a nerve (Park, 1997). It is important to maintain feminist theory as an important approach to social work and to not let feminism slip into gender studies. Research suggests that training in gender issues without a specifically feminist perspective does not reduce sexism in clinical decision making (Leslie & Clossick, 1996).

REFERENCES

Abbott, A. A. (1994). A feminist approach to substance abuse treatment and service delivery. *Social Work in Health Care, 19*(3/4), 67–83.

Abramovitz, M. (1978). Social work and women's liberation: A mixed response. *Catalyst (US), 1*(3), 91–103.

Abramovitz, M. (Ed.). (1988). *Regulating the lives of women.* Boston: South End Press.

Abramovitz, M. (1991). Poor women in a bind: Social reproduction without social supports. *Affilia, 7*(2), 23–43.

Akamatsu, N. N., Basham, K., & Olson, M. (1996). Teaching a feminist family therapy. In K. Weingarten & M. Bograd (Eds.), *Reflections on feminist family therapy training* (pp. 21–36). New York: Haworth Press.

Al-Hibri, A. (1981). Capitalism is an advanced state of patriarchy: But Marxism is not feminism. In L. Sargent (Ed.), *Women and revolution: A discussion of the unhappy marriage of Marxism and feminism* (pp. 165–194). Boston: South End Press.

Arches, J. (1984). Women and mental health: One step forward, one step back? *Catalyst (US), 4*(16), 43–57.

Baines, D. (1997). Feminist social work in the inner city: The challenges of race, class and gender. *Affilia, 12,* 297–317.

Beckman, L. J., & Mays, V. M. (1985). Educating community gatekeepers about alcohol abuse in women: Changing attitudes, knowledge and referral practices. *Journal of Drug Education, 15,* 289–309.

Bergmann, B. R. (1997). Government support for families with children in the United States and France. *Feminist Economics, 3,* 85–94.

Brown, E. B. (1990). Womanist consciousness: Maggie Lenna Walker and the Independent Order of St. Luke. In E. Du Bois & V. Ruiz (Eds.), *Unequal sisters* (pp. 208–223). New York: Routledge.

Bunch, C. (1987). *Passionate politics: Feminist theory in action.* New York: St. Martin's Press.

Burnham, L., & Louie, M. (1985). The impossible marriage: A Marxist critique of socialist feminism. *Line of March, 17,* 1–128.

Calhoun, C. (1994). Separating lesbian theory from feminist theory. *Ethics, 104,* 558–581.

Candib, L. M. (1989). Point and counterpoint: Family life cycle theory: A feminist critique. *Family Systems Medicine, 7,* 473–487.

Carlton-LaNey, I. (1997). Elizabeth Ross Haynes: An African American reformer of womanist consciousness, 1908–1940. *Social Work, 42,* 573–584.

Catlett, B. S., & McKenry, P. (1996). Implications of feminist scholarship for the study of women's post divorce economic disadvantage. *Family Relations, 45,* 91–97.

Christian, B. (1985). *Black feminist criticism: Perspectives on Black women writers.* New York: Pergamon Press.

Collins, P. H. (1990). *Black feminist thought: Knowledge, consciousness, and the politics of empowerment.* Boston: Unwin Hyman.

Comas-Diaz, L. (1994). An integrative approach. In L. Comas-Diaz & B. Greene (Eds.), *Women of color: Integrating ethnic and gender identities in psychotherapy* (pp. 287–318). New York: Guilford Press.

Cox, E. O. (1991). The critical role of social action in empowerment oriented groups. *Social Work with Groups, 14*(3/4), 77–90.

Creese, G. (1996). Gendering collective bargaining: From men's rights to women's issues. *The Canadian Review of Sociology and Anthropology, 33,* 437–456.

Dankoski, M. E., Penn, C. D., Carlson, T. D., & Hecker, L. L. (1998). What's in a name? A study of family therapists' use and acceptance of the feminist perspective. *American Journal of Family Therapy, 44,* 368–376.

Davis, A. (1989). *Women, culture, and politics.* New York: Random House.

Donovan, J. (1985). *Feminist theory: The intellectual traditions of American feminism.* New York: Ungar.

Dore, M. M. (1994). Feminist pedagogy and the teaching of social work practice. *Journal of Social Work Education, 30,* 97–106.

Dutton Douglas, M. A., & Walker, L. E. A. (Eds.). (1988). *Feminist psychotherapies: Integration of therapeutic and feminist systems.* Norwood, NJ: Ablex.

Echols, A. (1989). *Daring to be bad: Radical feminism in America, 1967–1975.* Minneapolis: University of Minnesota Press.

Eisenstein, Z. R. (1981). *The radical future of liberal feminism.* New York: Longman.

Erickson, B. M. (1996). Ethical considerations when feminist family therapists treat men. *Journal of Family Psychotherapy, 7*(2), 1–19.

Farwell, M. (1992). The lesbian literary imagination. In S. Wolfe & J. Penelope (Eds.), *Sexual practice, textual theory: Lesbian cultural criticism* (pp. 66–84). Cambridge, MA: Blackwell.

Featherstone, V. (1996). A feminist critique of family therapy. *Counseling Psychology Quarterly, 9,* 15–23.

Fredriksen, K. I. (1996). Gender differences in employment and the informal care of adults. *Journal of Women and Aging, 8*(2), 35–53.

Garvin, C. (1991). Barriers to effective social action. *Social Work with Groups, 14*(3/4), 65–76.

Garvin, C. D., & Reed, B. G. (1995). Sources and visions for feminist group work: Reflective process, social justice, diversity, and connection. In N. Van Den Bergh (Ed.), *Feminist practice in the 21st century* (pp. 41–67). Washington, DC: NASW Press.

Gibelman, M., & Schervish, P. H. (1993). The glass ceiling in social work: Is it shatterproof? *Affilia, 8,* 442–455.

Giddings, P. (1988). *When and where I enter.* New York: Bantam.

Goodrich, T., Rampage, C., Ellman, B., & Halstead, K. (1988). *Feminist family therapy: A casebook.* New York: Norton.

Hagen, B. H. (1983). Managing conflict in all-women groups. *Social Work with Groups, 6*(3/4), 95–104.

Hartmann, H. (1981). The unhappy marriage of Marxism and feminism: Towards a more progressive union. In L. Sargent (Ed.), *Women and revolution* (pp. 1–42). Boston: South End Press.

Home, A. (1991). Responding to domestic violence: A comparison of social workers' and police officers' interventions. *Social Work and Social Sciences Review, 3,* 150–162.

hooks, b. (1984). *Feminist theory from margin to center.* Boston: South End Press.

hooks, b. (1993). *Sisters of the yam: Black women and self-recovery.* Toronto: Between the Lines.

Hull, G. T., Scott, P. B., & Smith, B. (Eds.). (1982). *All the women are white, all the blacks are men, but some of us are brave.* New York: The Feminist Press.

Ivey, D. C. (1996). Family history and gender roles: Critical factors in practitioners' views of family interactions. *Contemporary Family Therapy, 18,* 425–445.

Jaggar, A. M. (1983). *Feminist politics and human nature.* Totowa, NJ: Rowman & Allanheld.

Jordan, J., Kaplan, A., Miller, J. B., Stiver, I., & Surrey, J. (1991). *Women's growth in connection.* New York: Guilford Press.

Joseph, G., & Lewis, J. (1981). *Common differences: Conflicts in black and white feminist perspectives.* Boston: South End Press.

Kane, E., & Schippers, M. (1996). Men's and women's beliefs about gender and sexuality. *Gender and Society, 10,* 650–665.

Kissman, K. (1991). Feminist-based social work with single-parent families. *Families in Society, 72,* 23–28.

Kitzinger, C., & Perkins, R. (1993). *Changing our minds: Lesbian feminism and psychology.* New York: New York University Press.

Koedt, A., Levine, E., & Rapone, A. (Eds.). (1973). *Radical feminism.* New York: Quadrangle Books.

Kost, K., & Munger, F. (1996). Fooling all of the people some of the time: 1990s welfare reform and the exploitation of American values. *Virginia Journal of Law and Social Policy, 4,* 3–126.

Krane, J. (1990). Patriarchal biases in the conceptualization of child sexual abuse: A review and critique of literature from a radical feminist perspective. *Canadian Social Work Review, 7,* 183–196.

Kravetz, D. (1987). Benefits of consciousness-raising groups for women. In C. Brody (Ed.), *Women's therapy groups: Paradigms of feminist treatment* (pp. 55–66). New York: Springer.

Kravetz, D. (1976). Sexism in a woman's profession. *Social Work, 21,* 421–427.

Langan, M. (1992). Who cares? Women in the mixed economy of care. In M. Langan & L. Day (Eds.), *Women, oppression and social work* (pp. 67–91). New York: Routledge.

Lee, J. A. B. (1994). No place to go: Homeless women. In A. Gitterman & L. Shulman (Eds.), *Mutual aid groups, vulnerable populations, and the life cycle* (2nd ed., pp. 297–313). New York: Columbia University Press.

Leslie, L., & Clossick, M. (1996). Sexism in family therapy: Does training in gender make a difference? *Journal of Marital and Family Therapy, 22,* 252–269.

Lewis, E. (1992). Regaining promise: Feminist perspectives for social group work practice. *Social Work with Groups, 15,* 271–284.

Lewis, E. A., & Kissman, K. (1989). Factors linking ethnic-sensitive and feminist social work practice with African-American women. *Arete, 14*(2), 23–31.

Lewis, G. (1996). Situated voices: "Black women's experience" and social work. *Feminist Review, 53,* 24–56.

Lorde, A. (1984). *Sister outsider.* Freedom, CA: The Crossing Press.

Lorde, A. (1990). I am your sister: Black women organizing across sexualities. In G. Anzaldua (Ed.), *Making face, making soul* (pp. 321–325). San Francisco: Aunt Lute.

The many faces of feminism. (1994). *Ms.,* July/August, pp. 33–64.

Meigs, C. (1979). *Jane Addams: Pioneer for social justice.* Boston: Little, Brown.

Mirkin, M. P. (1994). *Women in context: Toward a feminist reconstruction of psychotherapy.* New York: Guilford Press.

Mitchell, J. (1971). *Woman's estate.* New York: Pantheon.

Moore, C. T. (1993). *soc.feminism Terminologies.* Available online: http://www.cis.ohio-state.edu/hypertext/faq/usenet/feminism/terms/faq. html.

Nes, J. A., & Iadicola, P. (1989). Toward a definition of feminist social work: A comparison of liberal, radical, and socialist models. *Social Work, 34,* 12–21.

Ogunyemi, C. (1985). Womanism: The dynamics of the contemporary black female novel in English. *Signs, 11,* 63–80.

Pack Brown, S. P., Whittington Clark, L. E., & Parker, W. M. (1998). *Images of me: A guide to group work with African-American women.* Boston: Allyn & Bacon.

Park, S. (1997). False memory syndrome: A feminist philosophical approach. *Hypatia, 12*(2), 1–50.

Pollio, D. E., McDonald, S. M., & North, C. S. (1996). Combining a strengths-based approach and feminist theory in group work with persons "on the streets." *Social Work with Groups, 19,* 5–20.

Poster, W. (1995). The challenges and promises of class and racial diversity in the women's movement. *Gender and Society, 9,* 650–679.

Regan, S., & Lee, G. (1992). The interplay among social group work, community work and social action. *Social Work with Groups, 15,* 35–50.

Rice, J. K. (1994). Reconsidering research on divorce, family life cycle, and the meaning of family. *Psychology of Women Quarterly, 18,* 559–584.

Rich, A. (1979). *On lies, secrets, and silence.* New York: Norton.

Saulnier, C. F. (1996). *Feminist theories and social work: Approaches and applications.* Binghamton, NY: Haworth.

Saulnier, C. F. (in press). Incorporating feminist theory into social work education: Group work practice examples. *Social Work with Groups.*

Saulnier, C. F., & Wheeler, E. (in press). Social action research: Influencing providers and recipients of health and mental health care for lesbians. *Affilia.*

Stevens, P. (1995). Structural and interpersonal impact of heterosexual assumptions on lesbian health care clients. *Nursing Research, 44,* 25–30.

Stout, K. D., & Kelly, M. J. (1990). Differential treatment based on sex. *Affilia, 5*(2), 60–71.

Thorne, B. (1983). Feminist rethinking of the family: An overview. In B. Thorne & M. Yalom (Eds.), *Rethinking the family: Some feminist questions* (pp. 1–24). New York: Longman.

Tuddenham, R., MacBride, D., & Zahn, V. (1958). The influence of the sex composition of the group upon yielding to a distorted norm. *Journal of Psychology, 46,* 243–251.

Walker, L. (1987). Women's groups are different. In C. Brody (Ed.), *Women's therapy groups: Paradigms of feminist treatment* (pp. 3–12). New York: Springer.

Walker, L. E. (1995). Current perspectives on men who batter women: Implications for intervention and treatment to stop violence against women. *Journal of Family Psychology, 9,* 264–271.

Weil, M. (1986). Women, community, and organizing. In N. Van Den Bergh & L. Cooper (Eds.), *Feminist visions for social work* (pp. 187–210). Silver Spring, MD: NASW Press.

Weiner, K. M. (1998). Tools for change: Methods of incorporating political/social action into the therapy session. *Women and Therapy, 21,* 113–123.

Werner Wilson, R. J., Price, S. J., Zimmerman, T. S., & Murphy, M. J. (1997). Client gender as a process variable in marriage and family therapy: Are women clients interrupted more than men clients? *Journal of Family Psychology, 11,* 373–377.

Wetzel, J. W. (1976). Interaction of feminism and social work in America. *Social Casework, 57,* 227–236.

Whipple, V. (1996). Developing an identity as a feminist family therapist: Implications for training. *Journal of Marital and Family Therapy, 22,* 381–396.

Wilcox, C. (1997). Racial and gender consciousness among African-American women: Sources and consequences. *Women and Politics, 17*(1), 73–93.

Willis, E. (1989). Forward. In A. Echols (Ed.), *Daring to be bad: Radical feminism in America, 1967-1975.* Minneapolis: University of Minnesota Press.

Wise, S. (1988). Doing feminist social work: An annotated bibliography and an introductory essay. *Studies in Sexual Politics, 21,* 71.

Wood, G., & Middleman, R. (1991). Advocacy and social action: Key elements in the structural approach to direct practice in social work. *Social Work with Groups, 14,* 53–63.

Wood, G., & Middleman, R. (1992). Groups to empower battered women. *Affilia*, 7(4), 82–95.

Woods, A. (1917). Family life and alcoholism. *Proceedings of the National Conference of Social Work, 44*, 491–494.

Wright, C. I., & Fish, L. S. (1997). Feminist family therapy: The battle against subtle sexism. *Contemporary-Family-Therapy, 29*, 341–350.

Young, I. (1981). Beyond the unhappy marriage: A critique of the dual systems theory. In L. Sargent (Ed.), *Women and revolution: A discussion of the unhappy marriage of Marxism and feminism* (pp. 43–70). Boston: South End Press.

SECTION D

Postmodern Theories

15

Narrative Therapies

Rudy Buckman, Ann Reese, and Delane Kinney

What better way to start a chapter on narrative therapies than to recount a good story. This story is about three old umpires sitting around talking baseball when they are asked how they made their calls. The first umpire, possessing great faith in his ability to perceive reality as it is, says, "I call 'em as they are!" The second umpire, understanding the difficulties of perception, says, "I call 'em as I see 'em." The third umpire, considering the power of language to construct reality, says, "Until I call 'em, they ain't." This story provides a simple example of the difficulty in knowing what we know. The first umpire claims to be able to perceive reality as it is, whereas the second recognizes that perception is not errorless and may need cleansing. Respectfully, these two umpires represent the perspective of modernism and its faith in the efficacy of the scientific method to cleanse data of error so that an accurate picture of reality is obtained. The third umpire represents a postmodern perspective, a perspective that emphasizes the power of language to construct reality, which is at the heart of narrative approaches to therapy (Collaborative Language Systems and narrative deconstruction).

Although "narrative therapy" has come to be identified with the therapeutic approach of White and Epston (1990), we also consider the Collaborative Language Systems (CLS) therapy of Anderson and Goolishian (1988, 1992) to be a coemerging branch of narrative therapy (Neimeyer, 1995; Smith & Nylund, 1997). Both have been influenced by the philosophical assumptions of postmodernism and have similarities in their therapeutic approach; however, there are important differences between the two. Recognizing the influence of hermeneutics (Gadamer, 1975; Heidegger, 1962) on CLS and the influence of deconstruction (Derrida, 1981; Foucault, 1979, 1980) on White and Epston's therapeutic approach, Neimeyer (1995) refers to CLS as a therapy of conversational elaboration and to White and Epston's

(1990) approach as a therapy of narrative deconstruction. Finding this distinction helpful, we will discuss throughout the chapter not only the similarities in but also the differences between these two types of narrative therapy.

OVERVIEW OF NARRATIVE THEORIES

Narrative approaches to therapy challenge the hierarchy of power/knowledge that empowers professionals to marginalize clients' descriptions by imposing their allegedly objective knowledge. Narrative therapists attempt to flatten the hierarchy by positioning themselves more as co-travelers, who are willing to learn from others. Rather than diagnostic categories that measure deviance from scientifically derived norms of behavior, narrative therapists view problems as being constructed in language. As Efran and Fauber (1995) explain, "Problems are not just sets of circumstances, as objectivists would have everyone believe. They are appraisals—in words and symbols—of what should and should not be, what might or might not happen, what is fair or unfair, lucky or unlucky, malleable or fixed" (p. 279). As these words and symbols are woven into stories, there exists the possibility of making meaning from life experiences that are helpful or problematic. Problematic stories about self, others, life, and so on entrap the person in a journey filled with emotional pain and difficult relationships. Like a cyberspace nightmare that has no off switch, problem saturated stories entrap people within a linguistic virtual reality that blinds them to stories of their competence, strength, and ability to cope. Bruner (cited in Held, 1995) captures this idea well when he writes, "With repetition, stories harden into reality, sometimes trapping the storytellers within the boundaries that the storytellers themselves have helped to create" (p. 108). Consequently, therapy from a narrative perspective emphasizes an elaboration of constraining monologues to liberating dialogues and/or the deconstruction or rewriting of problem saturated stories to stories of courage, strength, and competence.

COLLABORATIVE LANGUAGE SYSTEMS THERAPY

Anderson and Goolishian (1988) describe CLS or conversational elaboration as the process of creating a safe space in which people can "participate in a conversation that continually loosens up, rather than constricts and closes down" (p. 381). This is facilitated by a therapist posture that emphasizes collaboration, openness, and curiosity (not knowing). CLS therapists are not intentionally trying to rewrite stories or externalize problems as narrative deconstruction therapists might; however, they do value elaborating dialogues from stuck monologues to more liberating dialogues. Questions from a position of curiosity, which invite the client to entertain a variety of perspectives, assist in this conversational elaboration. This conversational elaboration from the said or known to the unsaid or unknown provides "the development, through dialogue of new themes and narratives and, actually, the creation of new histories" (Anderson & Goolishian, 1988, p. 380).

NARRATIVE DECONSTRUCTION THERAPY

Narrative deconstruction emphasizes deconstruction and power in therapy. White (1991) defines deconstruction as

> procedures that subvert taken-for-granted realities and practices; those so-called "truths" that are split off from the conditions and the context of their production, those disembodied ways of speaking that hide their biases and prejudices, and those familiar practices of self and of relationships that are subjugating of person's lives. (p. 27)

These practices include questions that invite clients to consider how certain narratives shape their lives, questions that invite clients to examine times when they were able to refuse living by problem-saturated narratives, and separating the problem from the person (externalizing). Modernist theories typically place pathology "inside" clients, which White and Epston (1990) consider to be a potentially harmful cultural tradition. Externalizing is a countercultural practice that protests this tradition and is a way to invite clients to deconstruct and reauthor problem-saturated stories into stories of competence and courage.

HISTORICAL DEVELOPMENT AND PHILOSOPHICAL ASSUMPTIONS OF THE POSTMODERN PERSPECTIVE

Modernism embodies the seventeenth-century Enlightenment's faith in human progress through the accumulation of facts about the natural world (Leahey, 1987). Advances in the "hard" sciences, especially physics, had convinced the social sciences that the adoption of positivism and the scientific method to study humans would be rewarded with great progress. The assumptions of modernism maintain that (1) reality exists independent of an observer; (2) immaculate perception or objectivity is possible—any error in the objective reflection of reality is cleansed from the data by the self-correcting process of science; (3) the resulting scientific truth is universal and more legitimate than knowledge not subjected to this cleansing process; (4) universal laws of human behavior enable one to understand, predict, and control all humans regardless of culture or historical time; and (5) those who possess this scientific knowledge have a role of expert in society

(Cushman, 1990; Gergen, 1991; Hoshmand & Polkinghorne, 1992; Toulmin, 1990).

Postmodernism developed in the second half of the 20th century as a challenge to the philosophical assumptions of modernism. In contrast to modernism, postmodernism maintains that the observer constructs a reality; therefore, reality is not independent of the observer. Knowledge, rather than representing objective truth, is intersubjective and represents a perspective or linguistic construction of a group of observers. Because various groups of people during different historical periods construct and language different realities, a local and time-bound perspective is valued over a universal, decontextualized, and transhistorical objective truth. Consequently, the hope of achieving universal laws of human behavior that hold for all cultures throughout all time gives way to a curiosity about how an individual or group constructs a local and historical perspective about reality. Rather than language accurately reflecting an "immaculate perception" of reality, this view believes that language is a system of signs that only has meaning in the context of other signs (Gergen, 1985, 1991, 1992; Held, 1995; Hoshmand & Polkinghorne, 1992; Kvale, 1992; Polkinghorne, 1983, 1992; Rosenau, 1992).

Linguistic philosophy (Heidegger, 1962; Rorty, 1979; Wittgenstein, 1927/1953) and poststructural literary theory (Derrida, 1981; Foucault, 1979; Gadamer, 1975) are major contributors to postmodernism and have been very influential in the development of narrative therapy. Although modernism contends that a word actually captures the essence of and accurately reflects reality, both linguistic philosophy and poststructuralism stress that language constructs rather than reflects reality. For linguistic philosophers and poststructuralists, equating the linguistic map with reality is like looking at a blue line on a highway map and expecting to find a blue road. They argue that we exist and live our lives within these maps of socially constructed symbols and meanings rather than from a godlike position of objectivity.

Derrida (1981), in his work on deconstruction, examined how certain perspectives take center stage in a society, whereas others are excluded or marginalized. For example, in patriarchal societies, the male perspective is privileged and the female perspective is marginalized (Hare-Mustin & Marecek, 1988). Privileging the male perspective is based on men's greater influence over language, which is rooted in a history of having privileged access to education and positions of authority in social institutions. Consequently, as Hare-Mustin and Marecek (1988) point out, "The arbiters of language usage are primarily men, from Samuel Johnson and Noah Webster to H. L. Mencken and Strunk and White" (p. 26).

Foucault (1979, 1980), a major influence on the narrative therapy of White and Epston (1990), also examined how power influences which knowledge is privileged and which is marginalized. He considers power and knowledge to be inseparable, expressing this by placing the terms together as *power/knowledge.* In doing this, Foucault is drawing attention to the power of knowledge to constitute or shape our lives and the fact that we all are operating within this field of power/knowledge. He was particularly concerned with hierarchies of knowledge that placed objective reality discourses (modernism) above alternative discourses.

Another historical influence on narrative therapy, especially Collaborative Language Systems, has been the work of Heidegger (1927/1962), who proposed that hermeneutics, rather than science, is the appropriate method for studying human action. Hermeneutics comes from the Greek term *hermeneutikos,* meaning interpretation, and is a field of study that focuses on the social generation of meanings (Neimeyer & Mahoney, 1995). In studying human actions, hermeneutics attempts to do so as free as possible from prior theoretical assumptions. Heidegger (1927/1962) described this mode of engaging the world as "ready-to-hand." In the ready-to-hand mode of engagement, our immediate experience of the world is studied—our relationships to practical, everyday projects, to others, and to our pasts and futures. This mode of engagement is thought to provide the most direct access to human phenomena (Packer, 1985).

In this review of the rise of postmodern thinking and the therapeutic implications of viewing humans as actively constructing reality through language, the reader may feel that modernism is being dismissed. Dismissing modernism as invalid or useless would be inconsistent with a postmodern view that values multiple perspectives. The point is that limiting one's view of humans to the lens of modernism is similar to looking at the world through one eye; one can see, but adding the perspective of another (postmodern) eye provides the binocular experience of depth.

CENTRAL THEORETICAL CONSTRUCTS

Freedman and Combs (1996) distill the essential ideas of narrative theory down to four constructs: (1) realities are socially constructed, (2) realities are constituted through language, (3) realities are organized and maintained through narrative, and (4) there are no essential truths.

REALITY IS SOCIALLY CONSTRUCTED

A social constructionist approach assumes that all knowledge is created in community through discourse. Simply put, we develop our self-image and our view of others through the particular context of our relationships. Certainly that belief is similar to many other prevailing notions in psychotherapy; however, the narrative metaphor takes the idea of social construction of meaning as the springboard of therapeutic practice. If ideas, perceptions, and beliefs that support problems are constructed, that means they are malleable. We cannot change the events of history, but we can change the interpretation.

LANGUAGE CONSTRUCTS REALITY

Creatively using language, discourse, or conversation is the art of both branches of narrative therapy. In the narrative deconstruction approach, emphasis is placed on deconstructing problematic or oppressive meanings so that new, more empowering stories can emerge. For example, in the treatment of individuals who have experienced sexual abuse, clinicians often see people who present with life stories and self-views that are filled with shame, guilt, and secrecy. Because all sexually abused people do not develop these problematic stories, therapists recognize the importance of meanings and how these are storied within the client's context. Largely it is the relationship context of the abuse that creates problematic stories. If a child is abused and the important people in that child's life blame, ignore, or otherwise respond in a nonsupportive way, it is likely that the child will develop subsequent problems. However, if children are immediately supported by their relational contexts, it is quite possible that no problems will develop. In fact, it is possible that a child could emerge from such a trauma with an enhanced sense of self, that is, as a person who had the strength to tell the truth within a caring, protective support system.

In the conversational elaboration approach, the basic premise is that human systems are language-generating and meaning-generating systems. As such, communication is seen to define rather than being a product of sociocultural systems. The therapeutic system itself is seen as a linguistic system that has become organized around a "problem." Because the problem is socially created in language, it is also resolved in language. "The therapeutic system is a problem-organizing, problem-dis-solving system" (Anderson & Goolishian, 1988, p. 372). Therapy, then, is a conversational elaboration where new ideas emerge and new meanings are generated. Both branches of narrative rely heavily on the conversational artistry of the therapist; however, CLS allows for more "drift" in the conversation in order to make a wide path for new possibilities.

REALITIES ARE ORGANIZED AND MAINTAINED THROUGH NARRATIVE

We are born into cultural, contextual stories, and we take on personal stories through our lived experience. Therefore, new, preferred stories of self must extend beyond the therapy hour by being lived and circulated within the client's community. In subscribing to this view, Epston and White are interested in bringing forth the stories of unique outcomes into a relational context. White (1995) says, "If stories that we have about lives are negotiated and distributed within communities of persons, then it makes a great deal of sense to engage communities of persons in the renegotiation of identity" (p. 26). Questions such as Who from your past would not be surprised to know that you have overcome this difficulty?, What difference do you think this accomplishment will make in the eyes of your classmates?, If your (deceased) mother were here now, what qualities in you do you think she would recognize that helped you overcome your fears? assist in broadening and strengthening successes by moving them into a social rather than intrapsychic realm. "The hard-won meanings should be said, painted, danced, dramatized, put into circulation" (Turner, 1986, p. 37). Client victories can be reinforced by literally including family, friends, and colleagues in the conversation.

THERE ARE NO ESSENTIAL TRUTHS

Being born at a certain time as male/female; within a particular region, family, and socioeconomic level; and learning a particular language, religion, cultural values, and so on, shapes one's meanings and stories. Consequently, meanings and stories are not neutral, and the narrative work of Epston and White does not assume that one story/meaning is as good as another. They are not moral relativists and in fact are quite concerned about the real effects of these meanings. White (1995) says that "any constructionist position . . . [cannot] escape a confrontation with questions of values and personal ethics" (p. 14). What is valued and privileged are culture, gender, and class specific. Whatever is privileged in the dominant culture, whatever sexism, classism, racism, and heterosexism exists in the culture, shapes our language. Because therapists, like fish, live in the waters of their culture, they are often inducted into therapeutic practices that inadvertently collude with oppressive cultural practices. White (1995) says:

> There has been a general challenge to some of the practices of power that have incited persons to measure their lives, relationships, families, and so on, against some notion of how they should be, and some challenges over the extent to which therapists have gone about trying to fashion persons and relationships to fit with the "ideal" frames that support these notions. (p. 19)

CLS therapy, however, is not necessarily concerned with dismantling oppressive social structures that promote problems, nor is it so energetically directed at competency or empowerment. CLS certainly rests on the same foundation, which recognizes that language constructs knowledge, and knowledge is power, but it is relatively apolitical.

PHASES OF HELPING

CONVERSATIONAL ARTISTRY: GUIDING PRACTICES

Many therapies that have been influenced by modernism are often de-scribed in terms of having a beginning, middle, and end of the therapeutic process. Typically, from this perspective, the stages of engagement, assess-ment, treatment, evaluation, and termination are emphasized. From a post-modern perspective, however, narrative therapists are more interested in an ongoing collaborative conversational process of learning about clients' stories than interpreting, intervening, or imposing therapists' views or theo-ries on them. The therapeutic process begins with the first telephone contact from the client, and the process of collaborating with and learning about the client continues throughout therapy. The sessions, therefore, may appear similar, with little distinction between beginning, middle, and end of therapy. "They move from part to whole to part again, thus remaining within the circle. In this process, new meaning emerges for both therapist and client" (Anderson & Goolishian, 1992, p. 30).

ENGAGEMENT

The Initial Phone Call

Therapy begins before the client enters the therapist's office. Usually much thought has been given to the idea of therapy, and significant others may have influenced the client's decision to consider counseling. So, when a narrative therapist receives an initial phone call from a new client, it is important to remember that the therapeutic conversation has begun; it is an opportunity to begin understanding preexisting stories. How the client decided to seek counseling, who (if anyone) influenced the decision, and generally what the client's concerns are are important questions to consider during the first call. This early collaboration is helpful in sorting out who should attend the sessions, what the focus should be, and when therapy will end.

The Initial Meeting

Creating a respectful (nonjudgmental) and safe place that invites open conversation, reflection, and understanding is essential in beginning (and throughout) the process of therapy. The spirit of "[h]ow we are with people, what we ask, how we ask it, how our bodies are when we ask, the physical space in which we ask, the spirit with which we ask, and the form of the actual questions asked—all these invite some response and discourage others" (Roth, 1998, p. 1). What we say and how we say it must be genuine, and we must maintain an awareness that we can participate in creating new options or we can do harm. Constant awareness of the effect we are having is crucial in setting a scene that promotes opening space as opposed to closing space. Much significance is placed on taking the therapeutic process slowly toward a co-understanding of the client's view. The therapist listens carefully and respectfully and never understands too quickly, as this could limit conversational elaboration. There is great respectfulness for clients, their pace, their use of language, and the meaning given to the words/ stories. Also, "the therapist keeps inquiry within the parameters of the problems as the client describes" (Anderson & Goolishian, 1988, p. 14). Expertise is in conversation and opening space toward new possibilities.

In the initial meeting, central themes are established and discussed. These themes are woven throughout the therapy, so the entire process should feel connected. Some useful questions to help establish central themes and focus are (1) What is the concern that brings you here?, (2) How is it affecting you and others?, (3) What has been helpful with this situation?, (4) What has not been helpful?, (5) How long has it been a concern?, (6) What are your ideas about how the difficulties began?, and (7) How do you hope the situation changes?

Multiple Helpers: Getting Others on the Treatment Team

Many clients are involved in multiple systems: their families, friends, colleagues, neighbors, agency representatives, church members, organizations, and so on. From the beginning, we are interested in learning what systems are involved and who are the people in conversation about the problem or difficulty. Those who are in language about the situation/ problem are members of the "problem determined system" (Anderson, Goolishian, & Winderman, 1986), as is the client and therapist. Often, if mutually agreed upon, these members are invited into the therapeutic process (i.e., the therapy room, telephone conversations, or meetings at home/office/agency of others). It is helpful to remember that all involved have useful information and strengths, and we assume they are doing their best for the client: "Given the context from which they view the problem, neither the family nor the helping agents have to be thought of as wrong, crazy, or unhelpful" (Levin, Raser, Niles, & Reese, 1986, p. 64). Narrative therapists are curious about what others believe the problem is, their ideas about what may be making the situation better or worse, what solutions have been attempted and by whom, how useful the solutions were, who is most concerned, and where and when the situation improves.

It is important to be aware if there is a referring agency or person involved (e.g., child protective services, court, or church). The agency often holds more power than the client and may have specific goals for treatment. For example, if child protective services has custody of a client's children and the client hopes for their return, it is critical that the therapist and client include the referring person in the process. Again, this decision is always made in collaboration with the client. Through conversation an understanding develops as to what the agency and the client hope is accomplished in therapy. Omitting this important person could unintentionally do harm.

DATA COLLECTION AND ASSESSMENT: ONGOING CONVERSATIONS

Often traditional therapies focus on extensive information gathering and use various tools (e.g., ecomaps, genograms, and standardized scales) in this endeavor. Many therapists, in this process, are encouraged to seek the "truth" about the situation or uncover clues concerning the origin of the problem, as well as the pathology within the client. These static or convergent assessments and diagnosing tools are used to make and confirm a diagnosis and design a therapeutic plan utilizing appropriate interventions. Narrative therapists do find some of this information useful; however, they generally are more interested in an interactional relationship in which the therapist and client together develop an understanding of the situation, how it is of concern, and how the client hopes the situation will change. As therapists, we are in the position of being learners about the lives of our clients. They teach us about themselves—their concerns and hopes. Together the teacher and learner define the problem to be addressed. We learn about our clients and their concerns through a process of recursive or divergent assessment, where our questions are designed to generate new meaning, open space, and highlight change. These recursive assessment questions and the themes that have been generated in the conversation between client and therapist recur from session to session.

PLANNING/CONTRACTING AND INTERVENTION: AN OVERVIEW

Narrative therapy is about conversation, dialogue, and mutually rewritten stories. It is not about intervening. *Interventions* and *strategies* are terms that imply power and private knowledge held by the therapist, to be imposed on the client. The postmodern perspective, having shifted from scientific explanations and prescriptions to collaborative public conversation, suggests we not be expert technicians who design interventions to cure people:

> Therapy is now being seen as conversation, not as intervention. The focus of therapy is increasingly on the storied basis of human life and the social construction of meaning. Within these parameters the expertise of the therapist is no longer that of the skilled technician powerfully intervening in the family feedback system. (Goolishian & Anderson, 1992, p. 13)

Therapy is not done to the client but with the client.

Some questions toward co-creating a therapeutic focus might be (1) What do you hope to accomplish by coming to therapy?; (2) How would you know if you got what you came here for?; (3) What would that accomplishment look like in your life, to you, and to others?; and (4) If the process were successful, how would I know or what might I see?

Questions are the hallmark of both narrative approaches: deconstruction narrative and conversational elaboration. Neither approach is interventionist, but both emphasize skill in the use of questions in therapy. Although narrative therapists are not experts on their clients' lives, they do have expertise in the use of questions and guiding the process. "The therapeutic or conversational question is the primary tool that the therapist uses to express this expertise. It is the means through which the therapist remains on the road to understanding. Therapeutic questions always stem from a need to know more about what has just been said" (Anderson & Goolishian, 1992, p. 32). Countless possibilities are born from questions, offering opportunities for new narratives to be created between the therapist and the client. The goal of questioning is not to interrogate or gather information toward diagnosis. Instead, it is to learn from and attempt to understand the client. Because the specifics of the intervention process are different in the two narrative approaches, each is discussed separately below.

INTERVENTION IN NARRATIVE DECONSTRUCTION THERAPY

Epston and White (1990) indicate that people usually enter therapy dominated by "problem-saturated stories." Consequently, clients believe that the problem captures their identity ("I am manic-depressive, or she is eneuretic"). These problem-saturated stories blind clients to times when they were able to influence the problem. Epston and White (1990) describe the deconstruction of problem-saturated stories and the "bringing forth" of more empowering narratives as externalizing conversations. The process of externalizing is characterized by (1) mapping the influence of the problem on a person's life, (2) mapping the influence of the person on the life of the problem, and (3) objectifying or personifying the problem and challenging the problem's domination.

Mapping the Influence of the Problem on the Person

This process begins with questions that bring forth the oppressive internalized views of self (e.g., How did the abuse talk you into seeing yourself as a bad person?). One would also map the influence of the problem in various arenas of a person's life. For example, the clinician might ask such questions as How does the temper affect your relationship with your wife?, In what way does shame influence your relationship with God?, and How does disrespect shape your teacher's view of you? Thus, depending on the important contexts for the client (i.e., relationship with self, God, lover, friend, family, work, future, etc.), the therapist attempts to develop a broad understanding of how a problem shapes a person's life.

Mapping the Influence of the Person on the Problem

This phase of questioning focuses on bringing forth alternative meanings of an experience that contradict a dominant story. Because "life is multi-storied, not single-storied" (White, 1995, p. 27), the therapist's task is to bring forth stories that re-author a person's life. These stories of strength, small victories, and accomplishments, which have gone unnoticed, are called "unique outcomes." Examples of unique outcome questions might be How were you able to overcome the fears and join into the conversation?, How did you not give in to temptation when everyone else at the party was drinking?, and What did you do to keep your temper from getting the best of you when your boss was yelling at you? Such questions highlight times when a person exercises personal agency and is not completely controlled by the problem. As clients recognize stories and claim responsibility for these unique outcomes, they tend to feel more empowered.

Externalizing Problems and Internalizing Responsibility

White and Epston (1990) define externalization as

> an approach that encourages persons to objectify and, at times, personify the problem that they experience as oppressive. In this process, the problem becomes a separate entity and thus external to the person or relationship that was ascribed the problem. Those problems that are considered to be inherent, as well as those relatively fixed qualities that are attributed to persons and to relationship, are rendered less fixed and less restricting. (p. 38)

In other words, it is not the person who is the problem; it is the problem that is the problem. Because this process separates the problem from the person or the relationship, it allows all involved to challenge the problem's domination of their lives. In addition, the client learns that all problems exist because they are kept alive through "life support," which typically consists of understandings and actions that keep the problem going. Responsibility is internalized by each person involved by learning how each contributes to keeping the problem alive and how to cut off these contributions to the life support. Freedman and Combs (1996) wisely caution us to think of externalization as an "attitude." They say that "when people approach externalization as a technique or linguistic trick, it can come off as shallow, forced, and not especially helpful" (p. 47).

INTERVENTION IN CLS THERAPY

Not Knowing and Curiosity

The cornerstone of CLS is the stance of not-knowing (Anderson & Goolishian, 1992). Anderson and Goolishian explain that the not-knowing position is vital to facilitating the elaboration of dialogue. Unfortunately, labeling this stance "not-knowing" inadvertently created an unproductive debate that was characterized by an either-or construction of knowing versus not-knowing. This battle created between knowing and not-knowing has, at times, overshadowed Anderson and Goolishian's explanations of this stance (Buckman & Robbins, 1996). Watzlawick (1984) discussed the dangers of either-or distinctions: "The reality thus constructed reverberates from the violent clash of these opposites. No matter how long and how furious the struggle has been raging, neither side seems capable of gaining the upper hand" (p. 169). In other words, once this either-or distinction is constructed, the ongoing battle of knowing versus not-knowing never ends. In this clash, knowing becomes defined as the therapist's theoretical preunderstanding (i.e., psychological theories, DSM-IV, etc.), which is imposed upon the client's experiences. Consequently, the knowing stance undermines collaboration and curiosity, while also entitling the therapist to unilaterally guide the therapy. Unfortunately, in this either-or construction, not-knowing becomes the extinction of self through having no knowledge or by being neutral. Because this stance privileges the client's knowledge over the therapist's and entitles the client to guide therapy, collaboration and curiosity are again undermined. It is hoped that our description of self-reflexivity (below), which emphasizes the interrelationship of knowing and not-knowing (both-and), will enable a new dialogue that does not inherently lead to a clash of opposites (knowing vs. not-knowing).

A Reflexive Stance/Self Reflective Habits of Mind

Gadamer (1975), in describing the hermeneutically trained mind, stresses the importance of being sensitive to a text's quality of newness by consciously assimilating one's own biases. The both-and stance of self-reflexivity (knowing and not-knowing) recognizes that it is impossible to become a blank slate or neutral within any situation. Each person has a vast amount of knowledge shaped by educational background, gender, ethnic group, race, socioeconomic status, religion, and so on, which affects how he or she makes meaning and constructs a reality. CLS therapists, mindful of self-reflexivity, recognize that being unaware of preunderstandings can entrap one within a self-fulfilling prophecy, leading to certainty and arrogance. However, by being aware that knowledge and preunderstandings shape one's constructions of reality, the therapist is better able to construct alternative or more useful meanings. In doing so, the self-reflexive therapist is less likely to constrict the ongoing conversation and more likely to nurture an attitude of curiosity and openness to knowing more about the client's story.

Therapists express an attitude of curiosity and openness by asking questions and listening "in such a way that their pre-experience does not close them to the full meaning of the client's descriptions of their experiences" (Anderson & Goolishian, 1992, p. 30). Through questions and by listening in this way, the client is invited to participate in a conversation characterized by collaboration, curiosity, and respect.

Anderson and Goolishian (1992) have described the spirit of a therapeutic conversation:

> A therapeutic conversation is no more than a slowly evolving and detailed, concrete, individual life story stimulated by the therapist's position of not knowing and the therapist's curiosity to learn. It is this curiosity and not knowing that open conversational space and thus increase the potential of the narrative development of new agency and personal freedom. (p. 38)

Because every therapeutic interaction is shaped by knowledge socially constructed between therapist and the client, the self-reflexive process of supervision is imperative. As Hoshmand and Polkinghorne (1992) point out, "[A]pproaches aimed at the development of reflective habits of mind should be central to our professional training. Professional wisdom should include the ability to evaluate and critique one's own understanding and actions" (p. 62). Freedman and Combs (1996) and Roth (1998) have suggested useful questions in promoting self-reflection. To aid the reader in developing reflective habits of mind, the authors offer the following sets of questions:

1. How am I looking at my client? What are my theoretical preunderstandings or assumptions? Are these useful or helpful in our relationship?
2. What reality are my questions bringing forth in this relationship? Do I value my client's perspective as much as my own? Are there other views that may be more useful/helpful?
3. Am I fixed in my view of this person/problem, or am I entertaining multiple views? What assumptions about gender, ethnicity, sexual orientation, and so on are influencing my descriptions of this client or situation?

EVALUATION AND TERMINATION: NO MORE COMPLAINTS

As the late Harry Goolishian often said, therapy ends when clients no longer complain about what originally brought them into therapy. This could mean many things. Possibly the problem has been dissolved and no longer exists, or new ways of viewing the problem have emerged. For example, clients may perceive their responses to the situation differently or view themselves differently and in a more accepting light. Also, others may no longer complain about the situation. There are infinite reasons clients may no longer feel as oppressed by an issue. As the concerns are reduced, the client and the therapist together decide whether to continue sessions, end the process, or take a vacation from therapy. Typically, however, this would not be discussed in terms of termination.

APPLICATION TO FAMILY AND GROUP WORK

Wherever conversations are held, narrative theory is applicable and useful. With its emphasis on the social construction of knowledge, power, language, and multiple realities, narrative approaches to therapy are well suited to working with individuals, families, and groups within their contexts.

Narrative deconstruction and conversational elaboration approaches developed within the field of family therapy and have been used extensively with families, as well as individuals. Although these approaches have distanced themselves from some of the defining characteristics of the family therapy field (e.g., symptoms stem from family conflict, and the family system should be the focus of treatment), they still recognize that family members may be a part of and participate in the organization of a problem-determined system. As discussed previously, narrative therapists are open to involving family members, as well as others who are part of the problem-determined system, in the therapy process.

Recently, narrative ideas have been applied to groups. One example of a narrative group approach is the Teaching Empowerment through Athletic Means (TEAM) program (Redivo & Robbins, 1997). This program combines concepts from sports (e.g., teamwork, goals, rules, and cooperation), experiential activities, and participants' experiences to bring to life stories of competence and resiliency. Another example of narrative group work is the anti-anorexia/anti-bulimia league (Madigan, 1996). Through social action this group externalizes and fights against social messages that support eating disorders (e.g., by painting "FEED ME" on billboards of emaciated models). Within group meetings they support and witness each other's success in resisting unrealistic social pressures to stay thin.

COMPATIBILITY WITH THE GENERALIST-ECLECTIC FRAMEWORK

Although there are differences, we believe there is a great deal of compatibility between narrative therapy and the generalist-eclectic framework for direct social work practice. The following addresses the compatibility of narrative therapy with selected components of the generalist-eclectic framework.

USE OF PROBLEM-SOLVING PROCESS

Narrative therapy does not conceptualize therapy as a progression through stages of a problem-solving process. Adherence to an abstract professional schema of how therapy should unfold, such as the problem-solving process, would seem to undermine the collaboration between the therapist and the client. Most narrative therapists probably would be more comfortable in developing a collaborative plan of what the journey of therapy would look like for each individual, family, or group.

EMPHASIS ON A GOOD WORKER-CLIENT RELATIONSHIP

Many of the preferred or valued ways of thinking about the worker-client relationship in narrative approaches to therapy are consistent with the generalist-eclectic framework. For example, narrative therapists prefer thinking of themselves as having expertise as "conversational artists," who, through collaboration and respect, open themselves to the uniqueness of another human being. By valuing and respecting the uniqueness, strengths, and competence of each person, the therapist is encouraged to view the client as restrained or oppressed by problems (Buckman & Reese, 1999).

EMPHASIS ON HOLISTIC, MULTILEVEL ASSESSMENT

Although assessment has a different meaning in narrative therapy than in the generalist-eclectic perspective, there are similarities. Narrative therapists focus on exploring how the client's ever-changing self-stories affect the client's life, which entails a broad exploration of various client life domains. For example, in externalizing discourses, narrative therapists are interested in how a problem affects family relationships, intimate relationships, friendships, work, school, leisure time, spiritual issues, and physical well-being, as well as how it may affect the client's view of self. Equally important is assessing how the client and others have prevented the problem from dominating various life domains. Not only do narrative therapists map the effects of the problem in many domains of the client's life, but they also seek the views of multiple people in the problem-organized system. Also, particularly in the narrative deconstruction approach, importance is placed on issues of culture, diversity, and oppression. Thus, similar to the generalist-eclectic perspective, narrative therapies seek to develop a broad understanding of clients' lives.

Beyond the more specific focus on self-stories, other differences between narrative and generalist-eclectic perspectives are apparent with regard to assessment. In narrative approaches to therapy, assessment is viewed as an ongoing, self-reflexive process. Throughout the process of therapy, narrative therapists assess changes not only in their clients' views but also in their own internal dialogues. They question whether their inner conversations generate unhelpful views of clients that lead to a closing of space or helpful views that allow them to open space therapeutically. Also, despite the strengths focus of the generalist-eclectic perspective, narrative approaches place more emphasis on identifying how problems do not dominate clients' lives.

FLEXIBLE USE OF A VARIETY OF THEORIES AND TECHNIQUES

In a general sense, narrative therapies share with the generalist-eclectic perspective an emphasis on the flexible use of a variety of perspectives and approaches. Because postmodernism values multiple perspectives, any attempt toward hegemony of one perspective or approach would be distrusted. Although narrative approaches do not endorse an eclectic amalgamation of theories, they are supportive of greater dialogue across arbitrarily constructed knowledge boundaries. Therefore, postmodernism encourages therapists to be "multilingual" and able to discuss issues from a variety of perspectives. By being knowledgeable and fluent in a variety of professional perspectives and approaches, a narrative therapist may be less likely to become stuck in a less useful viewpoint. In other words, narrative therapists would never "marry" or become devoted to a theory and its techniques. Doing so could seduce therapists into too much certainty and reduce their flexibility and curiosity about a client's theory of the problem.

CRITIQUE

Postmodernism and narrative therapy share a distrust and pessimism about objective attempts to discover the universal laws of human behavior. Instead of research characterized by objectivity, experimental control methods, and efforts to develop universal laws that guide therapy, narrative therapies prefer to embrace research methods that celebrate the unique, undermine certainty, and invite the client to become a co-researcher (Neimeyer & Mahoney, 1995). Postmodernism does not shun traditional methods of modernism; it only views modernism as a partial approach to knowledge (Polkinghorne, 1991) and argues for research paradigms that focus on the meanings people make of their experiences (Guba & Lincoln, 1994; Polkinghorne, 1983). Consequently, rather than an objective research-based critique, we will address two typical questions many people ask about postmodernism and narrative therapy.

WITHOUT A FOUNDATION TO STAND ON, ISN'T ONE ADRIFT IN A SEA OF UNCERTAINTY AND MORAL RELATIVISM?

Rather than developing an "anything goes" attitude, those who dedicate ourselves to practicing from a postmodern position become more concerned about examining our beliefs, values, and choices to determine how these might influence our lives and therapeutic practice. This ongoing self-examination is conducted as part of an ongoing conversation with others as we mutually "puzzle" over how certain beliefs, values, and choices affect our lives and others. By publicly revealing our ethical decision-making process, personal responsibility typically increases. Rorty (cited in Freedman & Combs, 1996) puts it this way: "The repudiation of the traditional logocentric image of the human as Knower does not seem to us to entail that we face an abyss, merely that we face a range of choices" (p. 35).

Of course, it is interesting that few point out the dangers of having an objective foundation on which to base one's beliefs and actions. For example, psychologists have persistently claimed that they practice a "value-neutral psychology," possessing knowledge cleansed of nonepistemic values and used apolitically. In doing so, psychologists remain unaware of how successful their own socialization has been:

> For all practical purposes there is no questioning, no self-consciousness, about the forces that shaped them and their conception of society. The lack of this type of self-consciousness is no less a source of bias in the psychologist than the distortion-producing motivations that he possesses like everyone else. (Prilleltensky, 1989, p. 797)

Consequently, seemingly objective statements about psychological facts are laden with values that typically support the interests of the powerful and the status quo.

In contrast, postmodernism provides a rationale for therapists to examine nonepistemic values and encourages them to develop what Freire (cited in Prilleltensky, 1989) calls conscientization and annunciation. Conscientization "refers to the process of whereby people achieve an illuminating awareness both of the socioeconomic and cultural circumstances that shape their lives and their capacity to transform reality" (Prilleltensky, 1989, p. 800). Annunciation refers to the "act of conceiving a just social arrangement in which the well-being of the population is fostered" (Prilleltensky, 1989, p. 800). This ethical vision of social justice is noticeably absent from ethical codes that emphasize right conduct and are filled with "lawyer-driven weasel words" (Bersoff, cited in Brown, 1997, p. 452).

What's All This Stuff about the Social Construction of Reality and Problems Occurring in Language? Does This Mean Problems Aren't Real?

Salvador Minuchin (1991), the father of structural family therapy, criticizes narrative approaches for their emphasis on reality being socially constructed. He is especially concerned when poverty and other harsh conditions of life are thought to be socially constructed in language. For example, in describing a woman living in poverty, he makes the point that her reality "is not a construct; it is a stubbornly concrete world" (p. 50). His argument is based on the belief that there is a real world that impinges on and causes this person to have a certain experience. He is concerned that the idea that poverty is socially constructed minimizes and dismisses the plight of this woman. However, postmodernism does not dismiss or minimize any person's experiences and meanings of life; it promotes awareness of how important and real these constructions are. Narrative therapists would be just as concerned as Minuchin about helping this woman find and navigate programs that could assist her with food, medical services, housing, and so on. However, they would not assume that poverty unilaterally causes this woman to have an invariant experience, which is shared by each and every person who lives in poverty. Efran and Fauber (1995) write:

> Thus, there are as many different poverties as there are individuals who consider themselves poor. Even in the meanest of ghettos, it would not take long to find people who are deeply fulfilled, lead meaningful lives, and have a clear vision for their children and for the future. Alternatively, a visit to an affluent community will quickly turn up many lost souls, leading "lives of quiet desperation" amid an overabundance of creature comforts and venture capital. (p. 287)

CASE EXAMPLE OF NARRATIVE DECONSTRUCTION

At age 10 Jana kept secret that Jim, a 16-year-old male, coerced her into having sex on several occasions by telling her he wouldn't like her if she refused. Although the secret was painful, his moving away from the neighborhood brought some relief. Later, however, he moved back to the neighborhood, and all of her pain and fear returned. Jana revealed the situation to her mother, and her mother notified the police and child protective services (CPS). CPS referred them to our agency.

During an externalizing conversation, Jana, her mother, and we talked about how the abuse and secrets had affected their relationship, as well as Jana's friendships, schoolwork, and view of herself. The themes of self-hatred and fear kept coming up, and so we asked Jana: "How have you kept fear and self-hatred from completely messing up your life?" and "What or who has helped you in not letting the self-hatred and fear mess up your life?" She told a story about the time she wrote a note to a friend about how "deprest" she felt, and the friend wrote back that Jana needed to "heal her brain." As Jana continued the story, she put a hand on each side of her head and stated: "It's like ever since then I've been healing my brain."

Because many children's preferred way of communicating is through their imaginations and play, we often use drawing, singing, sculpting in clay, and role playing to encourage the objectification or personification of problems (Buckman, 1997). We asked Jana to draw a picture of her brain and she drew a brain divided into two parts. The left side was colored pink and contained an *A*, the words *best friends*, and "Good job Jana." The right side contained a girl's face and a boy's face, which she indicated was Jim, and vertical black wavy lines surrounding the two. Using this drawing to objectify her problem seemed to allow her to think about and consider her situation from a safer distance. Consequently, she seemed to have an easier time engaging questions such as: How have good friends, good grades, and doing a good job helped heal this side of the brain?, Do you have to cut this side out [the side with Jana and Jim] to heal this brain, or can you grow the healing side enough so it heals the whole brain?, Are there things you'd like to add to the healing that would help this brain heal even more?, and Does this side [with Jana and Jim] ever try to convince the healing side that it's your fault?

This drawing and others, in conjunction with curious questions, created an environment of playful seriousness where multiple viewpoints and alternative meanings could more easily be explored. Gradually, stories of Jana's courage in preventing her whole brain from being destroyed by the abuse and of ways to continue the healing of her brain began to take form. The drawings were also helpful in working with Jana's mother and CPS. Her mother would listen intently as Jana talked about her drawings and how Jana had become vulnerable to Jim's interpersonal coercion. Consequently, her mother was able to drop a great deal of her anger and blame of Jana and adopt a more compassionate/supportive attitude. The drawings and resulting conversations with the CPS worker enabled the worker to use similar language with Jana and Jana's mother; for example, she would discuss "brain healing" and relationship healing with them during home visits.

CASE EXAMPLE OF CONVERSATIONAL ELABORATION

Franky, age 12, was referred for therapy by his teacher, who was concerned because he was distracted in class and becoming interested in gangs. The teacher became concerned about gang involvement because of the baggy pants Franky wore daily to school. He had been suspended several times for wearing them. Because this was an inner-city school with significant neighborhood gang activity, these concerns were taken seriously. The mother's primary concern was that Franky maintain good grades. She did not share the teacher's view that Franky was in gangs but voiced hope in Franky's education being his ticket out of poverty.

We began slowly in our work with Franky, and he told us about his friends and favorite school subjects. In response to broad questions, he discussed his teacher's concern about gang affiliation. Although he thought this was funny and denied any gang involvement, he was worried about being perceived as "crazy" and being "sent away to a home." After explaining that our role was not to send him away, he felt more comfortable talking to us. He agreed that distraction was a difficulty for him in class. He also said that his mother thought therapy sessions would improve his grades. Franky wore the baggy pants to the first session and most subsequent meetings.

In the second meeting, Franky taught us that besides improving his grades, he wanted to ease his mother's and teacher's worries. This opened up space for conversation about how to help his mother and teacher not worry. His primary concern, of which his teacher was unaware, was the sadness he was feeling over the recent death of his father. The majority of dialogue concerned this profound loss, how he was coping, and how he kept his father alive in his life at home and at school. From this point on, Franky brought photos of his father to sessions and began keeping photos in his notebook. He used them for guidance and would consult his father on how to handle tough situations.

Franky quickly taught us, once he had disclosed his loss, that the primary way of comforting himself was by wearing his father's pants. With this revelation, the baggy pants, symbolizing gang affiliation, suddenly "dissolved" into the comforting presence of his father. This transformation in meaning allowed everyone in Franky's life to reconsider their views and practices around him. The teacher no longer reprimanded him for wearing the baggy pants, his distractibility and grades improved, his sadness lightened, and his teacher and mother worried less.

A commitment to collaboration, curiosity, respect, and opening space to multiple views enabled us to avoid privileging the teacher's concerns about gangs or the mother's concerns about grades. Limiting therapy to these concerns and our preconceived ideas about gang styles could have limited conversations and closed space. By staying open to different voices, we were able to open space and collaborate with Franky. Franky's baggy pants became a reminder to be wary of tightly fitting or constraining ideas.

SUMMARY

In this chapter, we have presented two narrative therapies: narrative deconstruction and CLS, both of which have been influenced by postmodernism. Both approaches emphasize that humans, through social linguistic interactions, develop stories about self, others, and life. These stories are problematic when they entrap a person, family, or group in a journey filled with pain. Both approaches envision therapy as a process of curiosity, collaboration, and respect. The narrative deconstruction approach emphasizes deconstruction of narratives through the process of externalization and questions that invite clients to examine not only how stories shape their lives but also how they have refused to be dominated by problem-saturated narratives. The narrative deconstruction approach also focuses on the relationship between power and knowledge and the use of power to privilege some perspectives while marginalizing others. CLS therapy emphasizes the "not-knowing" (self-reflexive) posture of the therapist and the development of new stories that are more liberating and supportive of competence and strength. CLS therapists are not, however, as directive or intentional in terms of externalizing problems or rewriting stories. It is our sincere hope that readers will use this chapter to encourage and support their ability to provide respectful, collaborative, and competency-based therapy.

REFERENCES

Anderson, H., & Goolishian, H. A. (1988). Human systems as linguistic systems: Preliminary and evolving ideas about the implications for clinical theory. *Family Process, 27,* 371–393.

Anderson, H., & Goolishian, H. A. (1992). The client is the expert: A not-knowing approach to therapy. In S. McNamee & K. Gergen (Eds.), *Social construction and the therapeutic process* (pp. 25–39). Newbury Park, CA: Sage.

Anderson, H., Goolishian, H. A., & Winderman, L. (1986). Problem-determined systems: Toward transformation in family therapy. *Journal of Strategic and Systemic Therapies, 5,* 1–13.

Brown, L. (1997). The private practice of subversion: Psychology as Tikkun Olam. *American Psychologist, 52,* 449–462.

Buckman, R. (1997). Using art to externalize and tame tempers. In T. Nelson & T. Trepper (Eds.), *101 interventions in family therapy* (Vol. 2, pp. 437–439). New York: Haworth Press.

Buckman, R., & Reese, A. (1999). Therapeutic loving: Opening space for children and their families. *Journal of Systemic Therapies, 18*(2), 5–19.

Buckman, R., & Robbins, J. (1996). *Knowing/not-knowing: A new dialogue.* Unpublished manuscript.

Cushman, P. (1990). Why the self is empty: Toward a historically situated psychology. *American Psychologist, 45,* 599–611.

Derrida, J. (1981). *Positions* (A. Bass, Trans.). Chicago: University of Chicago Press.

Efran, J., & Fauber, R. (1995). Radical constructivism: Questions and answers. In R. Neimeyer & M. Mahoney (Eds.), *Constructivism in psychotherapy* (pp. 275–304). Washington, DC: American Psychological Association.

Foucault, M. (1979). *Discipline and punish: The birth of the prison.* Middlesex, England: Peregrine Books.

Foucault, M. (1980). *Power/knowledge: Selected interviews and other writings.* New York: Pantheon Books.

Freedman, J., & Combs, G. (1996). *Narrative therapy: The social construction of preferred realities.* New York: Norton.

Gadamer, H. (1975). *Truth and method* (D. Linge, Trans.). Berkeley: University of California Press.

Gergen, K. J. (1985). The social constructionist movement in modern psychology. *American Psychologist, 40,* 266–275.

Gergen, K. J. (1991). *The saturated self: Dilemmas of identity in contemporary life.* New York: Basic Books.

Gergen, K. J. (1992). The postmodern adventure. *The Family Therapy Networker, 16*(2), 52–57.

Goolishian, H. A., & Anderson, H. (1992). Strategy and intervention versus nonintervention: A matter of theory. *Journal of Marital and Family Therapy, 18,* 5–15.

Guba, E., & Lincoln, Y. (1994). Competing paradigms in qualitative research. In N. Denzur & Y. Lincoln (Eds.), *Handbook of qualitative research* (pp. 105–117). London: Sage.

Hare-Mustin, R., & Marecek, J. (1988). The meaning of difference: Gender theory, postmodernism, and psychology. *American Psychologist, 43,* 455–464.

Heidegger, M. (1962). *Being and time* (J. Macquarrie & E. Robinson, Trans.). New York: Harper & Row.

Held, B. (1995). *Back to reality: A critique of postmodern theory in psychotherapy.* New York: Norton.

Hoshmand, L., & Polkinghorne, D. (1992). Redefining the science-practice relationship and professional training. *American Psychologist, 47,* 55–66.

Kvale, S. (Ed.). (1992). *Psychology and postmodernism.* London: Sage.

Leahey, T. (1987). *A history of psychology: Main currents in psychological thought.* Englewood Cliffs, NJ: Prentice-Hall.

Levin, S., Raser, J., Niles, C., & Reese, A. (1986). Beyond family systems—toward problem systems: Some clinical implications. *Journal of Strategic and Systemic Therapies, 5,* 62–69.

Madigan, S. (Ed.). (1996). *Revive: The Magazine of the Vancouver Anti-anorexia/Antibulimia League, 2*(1), 1–14. Vancouver, BC.

Minuchin, S. (1991). The seductions of constructivism: Renaming power won't make it disappear. *The Family Therapy Networker, 15*(5), 47–50.

Neimeyer, R. (1995). Constructivist psychotherapies: Features, foundations, and future directions. In R. Neimeyer and M. Mahoney (Eds.), *Constructivism in psychotherapy* (pp. 11–38). Washington, DC: American Psychological Association.

Neimeyer, R., & Mahoney, M. (1995). *Constructivism in psychotherapy.* Washington, DC: American Psychological Association.

Packer, M. (1985). Hermeneutic inquiry in the study of human conduct. *American Psychologist, 40,* 1081–1093.

Polkinghorne, D. (1983). *Methodology for human sciences: Systems of inquiry.* Albany, NY: State University of New York Press.

Polkinghorne, D. (1991). Two conflicting calls for methodological reform. *Counseling Psychologist, 19,* 103–114.

Polkinghorne, D. (1992). Postmodern epistemology of practice. In S. Kvale (Ed.), *Psychology and postmodernism* (pp. 146–165). Newbury Park, CA: Sage.

Prilleltensky, I. (1989). Psychology and the status quo. *American Psychologist, 44,* 795–802.

Redivo, M., & Robbins, J. (1997). *Teaching empowerment through athletic means.* Unpublished manuscript.

Rorty, R. (1979). *Philosophy and the mirror of nature.* Princeton, NJ: Princeton University Press.

Rosenau, P. M. (1992). *Post-modernism and the social sciences: Insights, inroads, and intrusions.* Princeton, NJ: Princeton University Press.

Roth, S. (1998). *Questions and ways of being in therapeutic conversation.* Unpublished manuscript.

Smith, C., & Nylund, N. (1997). *Narrative therapies with children and adolescents.* New York: Guilford Press.

Toulmin, S. (1990). *Cosmopolis: The hidden agenda of modernity.* New York: The Free Press.

Turner, V. (1986). Life not death in Venice: It's second life. In C. White & D. Denborough (Eds.), *Introducing narrative therapy* (p. 24). Adelaide, Australia: Dulwich Centre Publications.

Watzlawick, P. (1984). *The invented reality: How do we know what we believe we know.* New York: Norton.

White, M. (1991) Deconstruction and therapy. *Dulwich Centre Newsletter, 3,* 21–40.

White, M. (1995). *Re-authoring lives: Interviews and essays.* Adelaide, Australia: Dulwich Centre Publications.

White, M., & Epston, D. (1990). *Narrative means to therapeutic ends.* New York: Norton.

Wittgenstein, L. (1953). *Philosophical investigations* (G. Anscombe, Trans.). New York: Macmillan. (Original work published 1927)

16

Constructivist Theory[1]

Donald K. Granvold

Constructivism represents the first major "evolution" within the cognitive revolution of the 1960s and 1970s. Constructivism has been described as more a philosophical context of practice than a technique (Anderson, 1990). As will be evident in this chapter, however, there are rich and varied practice implications to be drawn from the constructive school of thought. Currently, constructivism is one of the most exciting, provocative developments in psychological thought. The scholar/practitioner who is open to postmodern thinking will find the movement to be ripe with possibilities. Although this chapter does not specifically address social constructionism, this parallel movement shares many philosophical and practice similarities with constructivism. (For information on social constructionism see chapter 15, as well as Combs & Freedman, 1990; Franklin, 1998; Gergen, 1985, 1991; Goolishian & Anderson, 1987; Hoyt, 1994, 1996, 1998; Watzlawick, 1984; and White & Epston, 1990.)

AN OVERVIEW OF CONSTRUCTIVISM

What is constructivism? To seek an answer to this question is no less formidable than to attempt a succinct definition of other psychotherapeutic approaches, such as behaviorism, cognitivism, and psychoanalytic psychotherapy. Entire books have been devoted to the definition of constructivism and its psychotherapeutic applications (cf. Franklin & Nurius, 1998; Guidano, 1987, 1991b; Guidano & Liotti, 1983; Kuehlwein & Rosen, 1993; Mahoney, 1991, 1995a, in press; Martin, 1994; G. Neimeyer, 1993; R. Neimeyer & Mahoney, 1995; Rosen & Kuehlwein, 1996; Sexton & Griffin, 1997). Although a narrow consensus does not exist, as evidenced in the varied content presented in these volumes, common features can be heard among the diverse voices.

Constructivist psychotherapy is based on the premise that humans attach unique meanings to life experience. These constructions are formulated individually or are co-constructed interpersonally. Rejected is the view that a fixed, external reality exists from which absolute, immutable meanings are drawn. Functioning as a learned collaborator, the therapist guides the client in the articulation, explication, elaboration, evaluation, and ultimate revision of his or her constructions toward ends that appear to promote greater personal and interpersonal well-being, long-term personal development, and social good. Meaning making is ascribed a central role in the promotion and continuation of human problems. Furthermore, it is held that many life problems, both personal and interpersonal, can be eliminated or ameliorated through the modification of meaning constructions. Human potential and client strengths are emphasized in the elaboration of meanings, and possibilities are sought with the objective to obviate and eliminate limitations and barriers to greater self-actualization, well-being, and social responsibility.

HISTORICAL DEVELOPMENT

The cognitive revolution began in the mid-1950s with the pioneering works of George Kelly (1955) and Albert Ellis (1955, 1958, 1962), followed shortly thereafter by Aaron T. Beck (1963, 1967, 1976). When the cognitivists entered the debate, the behaviorists and psychodynamicists were in a fervent struggle for psychotherapeutic supremacy. By the mid- to late 1970s the cognitive revolution was mounting full strength, and by the mid-1980s the revolution could be considered a success—a majority of the behaviorists and a substantial number of psychodynamicists recognized the legitimate strength of cognitive intervention and began to align themselves with the movement.

The cognitive revolution initially was predominated by a logical positivist view of human functioning in which individuals were appraised as evidencing "rational" or "irrational" cognitive functioning. Logical positivism emphasizes a scientific view of reality in which factual knowledge is connected with experience in a way that direct or indirect confirmation is possible. Therapists assisted their clients in determining the faulty thoughts, beliefs, and/or information processing considered to be etiologically accountable for their emotional responses, maladaptive behaviors, and other consequential cognitive responses.

Constructivism evolved from traditional cognitivism as scholar/clinicians began challenging the logical positivist philosophy undergirding established cognitive treatment procedures. The most notable pioneers in the movement include Michael Mahoney (1980, 1985, 1991) and Vittorio Guidano (1987, 1991b; Guidano & Liotti, 1983), followed soon by Robert Neimeyer (1987, 1993a, 1993b). This development began in the early 1980s in concert with the postmodernism movement under way in the intellectual world, including art, philosophy, and the humanities. Postmodernity challenges the belief in obdurate truths and universal models in favor of multiple perspectives, contradiction, and change. Postmodern thought holds that reality is subjective and that language constitutes the structures of social reality (Kvale, 1992; Maturana & Varela, 1987). Both constructivism and social constructionism represent developing clinical perspectives from postmodern consciousness.

THE PHILOSOPHICAL AND METATHEORETICAL FOUNDATIONS OF CONSTRUCTIVISM

CONSTRUCTIVIST ONTOLOGY

Although constructivism is a fairly recent development, its philosophical roots can be traced to the works of Vico, Kant, and Vaihinger, and more recently to the writings of Hayek (Mahoney, 1991, 1995b). Consistent with the views of these learned scholars, constructivists consider humans to be active participants in the creation of their own reality. This ontological position stands in contrast to realism and objectivism, which contend that a fixed, verifiable, external reality exists. The implications of such a fixed, absolutistic view are that it is possible to achieve a "reality check" and that "truth" exists objectively. R. A. Neimeyer (1993a) notes that, according to this correspondence theory of truth, "the validity of one's belief systems is determined by their degree of 'match' with the real world, or at least with the 'facts' as provided by one's senses" (p. 222). The constructivist view is that "reality" is a co-creation between the individual and the external stimuli to which he or she is responding. The human mind is not a tabula rasa (clean slate), but rather each individual's meaning structures are uniquely and independently forged. Prior experiences, images, sensations, conceptualizations, and associations mutually interact and collectively operate to effect each individual's unique brand of meaning making. "Reality," thus, is highly influenced by idiosyncratic human mentation. Based on this understanding of human functioning, constructivists abandon validity in favor of *viability*. Here the viability of any construction (conceptualized personal reality) "is a function of its consequences for the individual or group that provisionally adopts it (cf. von Glasersfeld, 1984), as well as its overall coherence with the larger system of personally or socially held beliefs into which it is incorporated (Neimeyer & Harter, 1988)" (R. A. Neimeyer, 1993a, p. 222). Human mentation necessarily results in the development of unique meanings for each individual.

CONSTRUCTIVIST EPISTEMOLOGY

The constructivist view of human knowing (epistemology) is based on a motor theory of the mind. That is, the mind has the capacity to create meanings beyond the mere information processing of sensory data. This proactive and generative feature of human mentation is a cardinal principle of constructivism. The locus of reality and knowledge development is *within* the individual. Furthermore, not only is the mind considered to be proactive and generative, but human systems are considered to be *autopoietic*—self-organizing and active in determining their own evolution (Maturana & Varela, 1980). This motor theory view of the mind stands in contrast to sensory theories that assert that information from the external world flows inward through the senses to the mind, where it is maintained. Popper (1972) refers to this view as the "bucket theory of the mind." Behaviorism and information-processing models are examples of psychological approaches based on this sensory theory.

Constructivist epistemology further holds that knowledge processing is performed at both tacit and explicit levels. In this two-level model, unconscious processes are accorded a central role in the formulation of cognitive structures necessary for ordering everyday experience. The contention is that there can be no meaning independent of an abstract order, that to perceive particulars requires abstract ordering.

It is particularly noteworthy that these tacit ordering rules are considered to govern the individual's conscious processes and operate to constrain the individual's sense of self and the world. In this central/peripheral knowledge-processing duality, core or nuclear processes are change-resistant. It is theorized that the self-system "protects" core ordering processes in order to preserve the integrity of the system (Mahoney, Miller, & Arciero, 1995). Change in these core ordering processes involves system *perturbation*—challenge, disorganization, and distress—leading to emerging complexity and differentiation. Humans evolve through an ongoing recursion of perturbation and adaptation. Although core structures must be relatively stable and change resistant in order to maintain the integrity of the self-system, it is necessary that they be challenged in order to promote the very changes that keep the individual alive as an adapting, evolving self.

METATHEORETICAL BASES

No singular, succinct theory can be delineated to describe constructivism. Rather, several established theories are drawn upon by constructivists and integrated to formulate an understanding of human functioning and human change processes. Below, the most common theories evident in the clinical formulations of constructivists are discussed briefly.

Systems Theory

Constructivists ascribe to systems theory (see chapter 4), which posits that the human system seeks to sustain its integrity while continuing to evolve.

Constructivist Theory

Evolution inherently involves an ongoing recursion of adaptation. Disorganization and distress lead to emerging differentiation (Granvold, 1996b). The human system se balance between the comfort of maintenance and the drive

Life-Span Development Theory

Another contemporary trend that has had a remarkable impact on the theory and practice of counseling is the focused interest on human psychosocial development across the life span (see chapter 5, as well as Guidano, 1987, 1991b; Guidano & Liotti, 1983; Kegan, 1982; Mahoney, 1991; Mahoney & Lyddon, 1988). This dynamic evolutionary process takes place in and is a part of a social/ecological context. Guidano (1991b) notes that life-span human development is regulated by periods of systemic relative stability punctuated by growth periods in which the self-system experiences upheaval, resulting in a more complex and highly differentiated self. Ever-expanding knowledge of self, the world, and one's place in it relies on this lifelong process.

Attachment Theory

Both constructivists and traditional cognitivists consider attachment theory (see chapter 6) to be a viable way of conceptualizing the impact of early developmental experiences on identity, personality development, and psychopathology. In cognitive terms, early attachment experiences result in the formation of self-schemas—relatively inflexible, general rules or silent assumptions (beliefs, attitudes, concepts) about self and one's relationship with others and the world. Early maladaptive self-schemas are considered by both constructivists and traditional cognitivists to be significantly accountable for psychological disturbance and, furthermore, effective psychotherapy is highly contingent upon accessing and modifying them (Beck, 1976; Beck, Rush, Shaw, & Emery, 1979; McGinn & Young, 1996; Rush & Beck, 1978; Young, 1990).

CENTRAL THEORETICAL CONSTRUCTS AND THERAPEUTIC PROCESSES

Constructivists hold that human evolution inherently involves disorder. Disorder is not construed as pathology or the enemy of mental health or personal well-being (Mahoney, in press). To the contrary, complex, human living systems maintain their "aliveness" and progression through the experience of personal disorganization with its concomitant emotional expressions. In short, constructivists do not share the assumptions upon which the pathology perspective is based. Correspondingly, diagnostic labeling is

..)proached with caution and skepticism due to its characteristic negative, deficit meanings (descriptions of negative traits, behaviors, and cognitive and emotive functioning) and the implication that an external, knowledgeable expert can possibly narrowly classify another human being. For most constructivists, the *Diagnostic and Statistical Manual of Mental Disorders (DSM)* represents an invented model of abnormality in which mental disorders are viewed as naturally occurring, objective entities (Raskin & Lewandowski, 2000). Exception is taken with the use of such psychiatric nosology in which clients are objectified and their complexities of self obviated.

The constructivist's normalization (depathologization) of human disturbance and distress has remarkable clinical conceptualization and intervention implications. Drawing on individual uniqueness and human creative potential, "problems" are construed as opportunities for constructive change. An empowerment agenda is sought in which the client gains greater agency over internal discovery and differentiation, interpersonal relationships and satisfaction, and the achievement of life goals. Treatment is ideally focused on the client's core meaning structures (self-schemata) and overall evolutionary objectives.

GOAL OF THERAPY: FOCUS ON PROCESS VERSUS PROBLEM RESOLUTION

Constructivists lean toward process-focused treatment goals rather than problem resolution. Conceptualizing the human condition from a systems and developmental theory perspective, "problems" and other forms of human discomfort may be considered to be disequilibrating perturbations to the individual self-system. A problem is conceptualized as a discrepancy between a client's current capacity and the developmental challenges being experienced. A perturbation is an opportunity to explore new meanings and to consider creative change possibilities. Ongoing evolution and higher order differentiation of self derive from the process of adaptation and change (preferably proactive). Intervention tends to emphasize a variety of historical, developmental (e.g., attachment), and self-organizational (self-identity) themes. The cognitive focus is on defining the client's meanings and meaning-making patterns, followed by the elaboration of these meanings toward more viable representations of experience (Lyddon, 1990). For example, a client who presents with nonendogenous clinical depression and is free of suicidal risk may adopt the perspective through constructivist treatment that the depression exists as a catalyst for change in one or more key areas of life (including self-identity). To consider the depression a "problem" to be eliminated or remarkably reduced could interfere with the preferable, albeit painful, change process. By taking a problem focus and treating the depression, the client could experience short-term relief but sustain long-term untoward or negative consequences for failing to make effective change in self, his or her social relationships, or life circumstances. This is not to say that treating the depression could *not* effect profound and pervasive change in the individual, but rather the likelihood of such change is considered to be greater through constructivist means.

UNCONSCIOUS PROCESSES

The complexity of human cognitive functioning necessarily relies on abstract operations. Unconscious processes are considered to have a strong influence on cognitive, emotional, and behavioral functioning. They are accorded a central role in the ordering of everyday experience (Guidano, 1988; Mahoney, 1991). As noted earlier, core ordering processes are critical to the integrity of the human system; therefore, it is theorized that they are heavily protected against challenge. Even though they may promote disadvantageous outcomes for the individual, they remain relatively immutable. Their change resistance prevents the human system from becoming highly unstable. The abstract ordering capabilities of these deep structures are considered to govern the individual's conscious processes and operate to constrain the individual's sense of self and the world. The therapeutic challenge is to access and produce modification in the core meanings operating to negatively influence the client's sense of self, interpersonal interactions, and view of the world and his or her self-actualization possibilities.

EMOTIONS AS CHANGE AGENTS

In the cognitive-behavioral tradition, therapists have applied methods to control, alter, or terminate emotions considered to be maladaptive in effect: anxiety, anger, worry, guilt, sorrow, sadness, and the like. Such emotions typically have been labeled "negative" and have tended to be conceptualized as intrusive, maladaptive, debilitating, and generally unpleasant to experience. Constructivists contend that meaningful change inherently involves experiencing intense emotions, and, therefore, measures to limit or eliminate emotive responses may actually inhibit the change process.

Another conceptualization with which constructivists take exception is the contention that emotions are postcognitive or epiphenomena of cognition. On the basis of this postcognitive assumption, affective change most commonly has been sought through cognitive change methods. Constructivists argue that "emotion and cognition operate within partly independent systems and that, contrary to the common view, affective reactions often occur prior to cognitive reactions" (Safran & Greenberg, 1991, p. 4). Humans are universally emotionally reactive, and this reactivity represents an immediate "knowing response" to environmental threat in which effective self-interest, self-protection, and survival strategies are enacted (Guidano,

1991a). Furthermore, emotions are considered to be essential elements of human knowledge processing, and constructivists contend that to produce change in core emotional themes requires new emotional experiences (Guidano, 1991a).

Constructivists encourage clients to explore, experience, and express their emotions through the use of experiential treatment procedures. Disequilibrium resulting from emotional intensity is considered to be a viable means of accessing core beliefs and state-dependent cognitions (Greenberg & Safran, 1989; Lyddon, 1990). Methods to access affective states and stimulate emotional arousal include guided discovery, imagery, imaginary dialogues (empty-chair technique), and therapeutic rituals.

SELFHOOD PROCESSES

Constructivist conceptualizations reflect a view of self as an evolutionary, epistemological, self-organizing, autopoietic (self-producing or self-renewing) system rather than as a fixed entity (Guidano, 1987, 1991b, 1995; Guidano & Liotti, 1983; Mahoney, 1991; Maturana & Varela, 1987). The self is not singular or fixed, but rather is a multifaceted and ever-changing "system" of identity meanings. Selfhood is a process reflecting a history of development and accumulated meanings forged through tacit and explicit cognitive operations (Guidano, 1988). The beliefs, memories, and patterns of processing information that make up the individual's core sense of self provide "a set of basic expectations that direct the individual's patterns of self-perception and self-evaluation" (Guidano, 1988, p. 317). During childhood, these core ordering structures (Mahoney, 1991) or deep cognitive structures (Guidano, 1987) "develop into highly stable and enduring themes" and "are elaborated upon throughout an individual's lifetime," ultimately serving as "templates for the processing of later experience" (Young, 1990, p. 9). For many, early experiences result in the development of maladaptive schemas. These self-schemas tend to be highly change-resistant, self-perpetuating, and activated by events in the environment, and lead to psychological distress (Young, 1990).

Nurius and Berlin (1994) note that, because schemata are seldom "purged" from our memory system, we have ever-increasing sets of self-conceptions. Due to cognitive limitations, only a partial set of self-schemata can be activated at a given time. The activated "self" is the one that "reflects meaningful links between the demands of the situation and self-conceptions related to those cues" (p. 255). Thus, the socially embedded nature of self-schemata plays a powerful role in the activation of one set of self-conceptions over another. From the above conceptualization, it can be concluded that multiple "possible" selves exist among stored schemata (Markus & Nurius, 1986). One's "active" sense of self is *never* a complete representation of one's being. Furthermore, one's sets of self-conceptions are continuously expanding as the experience of life is translated into selfhood development.

PHASES OF HELPING

The relationship between client and therapist is recognized as the most meaningful ingredient in the helping process. Constructivists assume a nonauthoritarian role with their clients for the most part. Knowledge-based authority is recognized, but information is shared in a nonabsolutistic, nonauthoritarian manner. Research findings, clinical conceptualizations and interpretations, approaches to change, and the like are not presented as absolute, inexorable, or inviolate, but rather as understandings, perspectives, or one of several ways to construe experience. Clients' meaning constructions are given paramount importance. It is the therapist's task to access those meanings as opposed to telling the clients what they are experiencing and why.

ENGAGEMENT

The engagement process involves a determination of the client's purposes for seeking treatment, expectations of the therapeutic relationship and the treatment process, and motivation for change. Initial attention is given to structuring the roles of client and therapist. Role structuring requires gaining answers to many questions from the client, as well as imparting information as a means of clarifying the treatment process. Ultimately, the effective engagement of the client is accomplished by joining the client's unique meaning-making processes through mutual inquiry. Achieving this end and progressing to the elaboration of client constructions relies heavily on the use of the Socratic method (Beck et al., 1979; Beck & Emery, 1985; Ellis, 1994; Granvold, 1994). The therapist assumes an active role in the process of illuminating deeply held, often "inarticulate constructions" considered highly operative in the client's life experience (R. A. Neimeyer, 1995a). On the basis of therapist behavior, the client should become aware early on that the client retains ultimate control over access to his or her constructions. It is the client's awareness of this potential and his or her trust in the therapist that will allow access to and constructive elaboration of these constructs toward the client's greater well-being. This critical awareness and the outcomes identified above represent the operations of constructivist engagement of the client in treatment.

ASSESSMENT

Consistent with the reciprocal determinism model of human functioning (Bandura, 1978), assessment includes consideration of social/environmental forces, overt behavior, and internal dispositions. Although all of these phenomena are considered to be active determinants of behavior, construc-

tivists consider cognitive functioning to be highly influential in the maintenance and modification of human disturbance and dysfunction. Hence,
the primary focus of assessment is on meaning-making activity.

The assessment of meaning-making is focused on (1) peripherally held
beliefs, views, and conceptualizations; (2) relationships between and among
constructs; and (3) core ordering processes or tacitly held constructs (about
self, others, and the experience of life). Surface held cognitions are much
easier to access and are considered to be much less influential in their
impact on functioning than core meaning structures. They may, however,
serve as a point of entry to the process of excavating for core schemata.
Furthermore, isolating surface constructs may allow for meaningful cognitive elaboration important to desired, more immediate behavioral and
emotional activation.

In contrast to assessment procedures in the tradition of many therapies
where the objective is to proceed unobtrusively, constructivist assessment
is inherently change-stimulating. Constructivist assessment involves the client in the discovery of meanings, an enterprise that cannot be pursued
passively. There are no constructivist standardized tests that are "objectively"
administered and interpreted, resulting in a static "expert opinion" of the
client by the therapist. Should a constructivist access psychological test
results, single responses, response "patterns," and composite results would
be utilized to access peripherally held cognitions and ideally to provide
preliminary direction to the discovery of core meaning structures. (See
the following for information on constructivist assessment: Feixas, 1995;
Mahoney, 1991; G. Neimeyer, 1993; G. Neimeyer, Hagans, & Anderson,
1998; G. Neimeyer & Neimeyer, 1981; Safran, Vallis, Segal, & Shaw, 1986.)

PLANNING/CONTRACTING AND INTERVENTION

Although constructivist treatment is looser in form than orthodox cognitive
intervention, the therapist sets an agenda with the client and exercises an
active role in guiding the course of treatment. Early in treatment, attention
is focused on defining goals. Presenting problems set the initial direction
in treatment. They may serve as incremental steps in a more grand developmental undertaking, or, alternatively, the process utilized in the treatment
of these dilemmas may become the client's blueprint for future self-directed
or therapist-guided personal development. In either case, once treatment
goals are identified, the client and the therapist engage collaboratively in
planning a change strategy.

The negotiation of a therapeutic contract may be done more or less
formally. The contract involves agreement on the goals, methods, and
course of treatment (scheduling, frequency rate, payment, etc.). Although
the contract may be maintained tacitly, prudent practice standards call for
the consummation of a written contract (signed by both the client and
the therapist) as soon as clinically feasible in which treatment goals and

indicators of progress and outcomes are set forth (Bernstein & Hartsell, 1998; Houston-Vega, Nuehring, & Daguio, 1997).

Consistent with the multiplicity of constructivism, there is no narrowly formulated treatment technology for universal application to clients. To the contrary, there has been resistance to the development of a proliferation of techniques (Guidano, 1991b; Mahoney, 1986, 1991; Rosen, 1993). Despite the reluctance to promote treatment technologies, this section on intervention would be incomplete without the inclusion of a listing of intervention options that constructivists have used to promote change. The following list is a sampling of techniques: cognitive elaboration (Granvold, 1996b; Mahoney, 1991; G. Neimeyer, 1993; R. A. Neimeyer, 1996); movieola (Guidano, 1991a); stream of consciousness, journaling, life review, mirror exercises, bibliotherapy (Mahoney, 1991); repertory grid, downward arrow, laddering, the "bow tie" technique (G. Neimeyer, 1993); narrative writing (Goncalves, 1995; Hoyt, 1998; White & Epston, 1990); externalizing the problem (White & Epston, 1990); symptom prescription (Watzlawick, 1984); enactments (role plays, empty-chair technique) (Greenberg & Safran, 1987; Safran & Greenberg, 1991); journaling (Mahoney, 1991); imagery and guided discovery (Safran & Segal, 1990); embodiment exercises (promoting sensory and physical awareness) (Mahoney, 1991); and therapeutic ceremonies or rituals (Mahoney, 1991; R. A. Neimeyer, 1993a). The clinical example at the end of this chapter will give the reader insight into cognitive elaboration, an intervention method frequently used by constructivists to promote client meaning constructions that promote client well-being, interpersonal satisfaction, and personal development.

EVALUATION

The most profound question with regard to evaluation is, What are the specific, salient indicators of change? For those wedded to an empirical practice model, change is reflected in measurable outcome criteria, such as scores on standardized psychological tests, and records of discrete cognitive or overt behavior. Constructivists tend to consider such quantitative measurement to be reductionistic and an inadequate means to explain the complexities and idiosyncratic nature of the human experience. Daniels and White (1997) contend that to understand therapeutic change, therapists must understand "what 'change' means *to the actual people who are undergoing counseling,* rather than looking at the nature of change merely through the perspectival lens of a particular psychological theory" (p. 177). In a effort to seek this understanding, constructivists have shifted focus from outcome research to an exploration of the process of psychotherapeutic change. Questions are being asked about what kinds of intervention strategies at what moments in therapy produce what effects (Greenberg, 1986, 1992; Martin, 1994; R. A. Neimeyer, 1995b; Rennie, 1995; Rice & Greenberg, 1984; Toukmanian & Rennie, 1992). The conduct of process research takes many forms, including the "change events" perspective in which observable markers of change within therapy are delineated and analyzed, and narrative research focused on such phenomena as retrospective client or therapist accounts of their intentions at specified points in the narrative (Rennie, 1992; Rennie & Toukmanian, 1992).

TERMINATION

Termination of the change effort is a collaborative process, as are all other aspects of constructivist treatment. Determining timely termination is ideally associated with the achievement of client-generated outcomes. Exceptions to this protocol are those circumstances in which treatment has been mandated for clients exhibiting socially irresponsible, unethical, or unlawful behavior. In those situations, termination decision making is biased toward the therapist. Despite the client's inclination to terminate, the therapist may sustain treatment until treatment goals have been satisfactorily satisfied in his or her judgment. With voluntary clients, termination is sought as the client exercises a desire for "time-out" following incremental change or upon satisfactory completion of the change effort. The decision to terminate is preferably jointly made by client and therapist. As the final session approaches, relapse prevention strategies (preferably infused throughout treatment) are addressed specifically (Granvold & Wodarski, 1994; Greenwald, 1987; Laws, 1989; Marlatt & Gordon, 1985).

APPLICATION TO FAMILY AND GROUP WORK

Constructivist practice methods have been applied with couples, families, and groups. The constructivist (and social constructionist) conceptualization of couples and families as social systems along with the emphasis on development from infancy across the life span are highly relevant in the assessment and treatment of family system dilemmas. Constructivists focus on the possibilities for mutual (couple) or collective (family) enhancement, enrichment, and achievement through the promotion of the synergystic constructive potential of the family system. Creative avenues for systemic change are sought for the benefit of family members individually and interpersonally.

Constructivist approaches to treatment are also suitable for group treatment. The group has been advanced as a valuable context in which to develop an awareness of constructivist thinking for the promotion of individual change and to learn of group processes (Brower, 1998). Group members' unique perceptions and cognitive elaborations may provide meaningful inroads into rigid, narrow, or judgmental thinking on the part of group members. The established advantages of group process are as highly relevant for constructivist psychotherapy as for other interventions.

COMPATIBILITY WITH GENERALIST-ECLECTIC FRAMEWORK FOR SOCIAL WORK PRACTICE

Constructivist treatment is highly compatible with a generalist-eclectic social work practice perspective. Constructivism emphasizes the client's strengths and possibilities (Saleebey, 1992). A collaborative relationship is sought with the client in which the therapist assumes a nonauthoritarian, albeit knowledgeable, stance. Although the primary focus of constructivist assessment and intervention is on the meaning-making process (internal dispositions), in the social work tradition, environmental conditions and social factors are considered in the promotion of the client's immediate goals and ultimate personal development. Treatment strategies are varied, flexible, adjustable as treatment proceeds, and uniquely tailored to the client. There is a priority on the therapeutic relationship in recognition of the powerful role relationship factors play in efficacious treatment.

Constructivist voices are highly evident in the psychotherapy integration movement (Granvold, 1999; Mahoney, 1991, 1995c; R. A. Neimeyer, 1993c, 1995b). This movement honors contributions of various schools of psychotherapy in the formulation of potentially viable theories of human behavior and human change processes. Change is considered possible through multiple avenues, and the cross-fertilization of schools of thought is believed to be worthy of active and on-going consideration.

CRITIQUE OF CONSTRUCTIVIST PRACTICE

Constructivism is not a closely bound construction of postulates and techniques. Consistent with the essence of postmodernism, there are as many forms of constructivism as there are constructivists. Within the movement, "internal tensions" exist around issues such as (1) the *centrality of the self*, ranging from an "evolving self" to a self-less psychology; (2) the *locus of meaning*—more internally generated versus socially constructed languaging; (3) acceptance or rejection of *ontological realism* and the degree of importance placed on ontology; (4) the *therapist's degree of directiveness* and vigor in promoting therapeutic change; and (5) the endorsement of empirical versus qualitative process *research* (R. A. Neimeyer, 1995b). There is such diversity within constructivism that specifying the defining features is somewhat problematical. The metatheoretical assumptions and theoretical developments discussed above represent interrelated conceptualizations more or less reflected in the theoretical bases and clinical interventions of constructivists. The range of diversity that constructivism allows is creditworthy in terms of therapeutic freedom, flexibility, and creativity, and simultaneously poses challenges to those interested in learning the praxis of constructivism. From student to experienced practitioner, the "how to's" are fuzzy.

Constructivism is clearly far more highly developed philosophically than methodologically. Temptation exists to develop definitive treatment manuals outlining and demonstrating constructivist practice. There is a strong bias within the movement against "technologizing" constructivist practice (Guidano, 1991b; Mahoney, 1986, 1991; Rosen, 1993). The explication of practice methodologies, however, may serve to clarify, inform, expand, and refine the spiny constructions of human change processes. The positive potential of clear, demonstrative treatment exemplars presented in the form of "a" way, vis-à-vis "the" way to intervene with clients merits strong consideration.

It is interesting to note that, although constructivists tend to reflect a research bias away from traditional empirical exploration, empirical research findings serve constructivists with clinically viable content. These findings represent organizing themes that both shape the therapist's understanding of a given category of human experience (e.g., loss) and inform practice decisions. The therapist's ways of exploring subjective meanings is through avenues that likely have been drawn from empirical research. For example, a line of questioning regarding parallel parenting expectations of a divorced parent may be drawn from empirical research on postdivorce parenthood. Furthermore, specific subjective meanings expressed by a client "make sense" to the therapist based on a cognitive structural meaning matrix into which the content is integrated. This meaning matrix is, for the critically informed therapist, likely infused with empirical knowledge. The very research that constructivists tend to discount or devalue in meaning is likely to be having a remarkable impact on praxis. Although the range in methodological forms of inquiry justifiably should be expanded, perhaps the valuation of empirical research findings by constructivists deserves revisiting.

Constructivism has come under sharp criticism for the appearance of failing to hold people accountable for cruel, unfair, abusive, socially insensitive, selfish, and irresponsible conduct (see Held, 1995; Pittman, 1992). Bandura (1986, 1996) notes that, despite our commitment to idiosyncratic meanings, therapists must be wary of client "mechanisms of moral disengagement" that serve to obscure or minimize the client's agentive role in irresponsible and unconscionable conduct. When clients evidence socially irresponsible, unethical, or illegal behavior and maintain corresponding beliefs, attitudes, and viewpoints supportive of such behavior, the therapist must assume the role of agent of social responsibility (Granvold, 1996a). Social workers in particular, but helping professionals from all disciplines, come into contact with clients whose behavior fits the above criteria. It is consistent with the *intent* of constructivist philosophy and praxis for therapists to promote client self-regulatory processes (self-monitoring, self-evaluation, and self-sanction) and humane conduct, and when there is evidence of client despicable or unconscionable behavior, to challenge the mechanisms of moral disengagement such as denial, gross distortions and misattributions, and rationalization. Constructivism does not endorse an "anything goes" solipsism in which personal meanings are maintained independent of a social order. Constructivists are charged with the dual responsibility to facilitate personal development and well-being and to guide clients in making choices that satisfy and uphold moral standards. Where there is bona fide evidence that the client has failed to self-govern in a socially conscionable manner, the therapist is to intervene to establish or restore the mechanisms of humane agency.

CASE EXAMPLE

Constructivist treatment methods invite the client to explore, examine, appraise, experience, define, and redefine themselves, their life experiences, and their directions in life both inside and outside the session (Mahoney, 1991). In the example that follows, I have tried to explicate the use of cognitive elaboration to promote this process in some measure.

Blake presented for therapy approximately 1 year after the death of his only son. Throughout the preceding year, Blake had been experiencing intense grief and severe depression. Despite his emotional state, he continued his senior management position but reported the ability to perform his responsibilities only minimally. His marital relationship with Jeana (his second wife and not the mother of his deceased son) was suffering from his "protracted" grief. Blake explained that he and his 28-year-old son, James, were to have gone hunting together last year on the weekend that James was killed in an auto accident. Blake and Jeana were scheduled to take a weeklong trip beginning the weekend following the hunting trip. Blake (who has cancer in remission) withdrew from the trip with his son on the advice of his physician. The doctor believed that Blake needed to rest prior to his vacation based on symptomatic evidence. Blake maintained that he was responsible for his son's death because he withdrew from the hunting trip.

The first session was devoted to understanding his views of what happened and empathizing with Blake's pain. No effort was made to involve him in construct elaboration while attempting to empathetically join him. In the second session, I decided to seek a better understanding of the consequences (viability) of his constructs surrounding his son's death and to promote an elaboration of constructs.

Blake: *I was perfectly aware of James' drinking problem. If I had gone hunting with him, I am convinced that he would be alive today.*

Don: *I see, Blake. So, you feel responsible for his death—that had you been with him, you could have prevented the accident from happening.*

Blake: *Yes. It's my fault.*

Don: Blake, when you think "It's my fault," what thoughts and images cross your mind?

Blake: Oh God . . . I feel a terrible feeling in the pit of my stomach. I hear myself saying things like, "Why didn't you go with him?" "You knew that this might happen!"

Don: You have a sick feeling in your stomach, and you sound critical of yourself. What other feelings can you identify as you concentrate on "It's my fault?"

Blake: I feel overwhelming loss . . . regret, pain, and helpless. It's depressing; the whole bundle is depressing.

Don: So you experience many intense feelings, and they've lasted for approximately a year now; is that correct, Blake?

Blake: Yes, that's right.

Don: How would you say that these feelings have served you, Blake?

Blake: I'm not sure that I understand what you mean.

Don: Can you think of any benefits you have derived from feeling this array of feelings?

Blake: I guess that they are just part of my grief.

Don: Yes, I believe that they are an important part of your grief, and also grieving is a very important part of dealing with loss—especially one as great as the loss of your son. (Pause) Blake, while these emotional reactions and their effects are to be expected as part of grieving, do you have any thoughts about how you might reduce the intensity of your grieving at this time?

Blake: If you are getting at "Have I grieved long enough?" I really don't know. I do know that I think I need to perform better at work like I used to, and my relationship with Jeana is suffering from my depression. I don't want to lose her. I really don't know, though, how I can get a better handle on my feelings.

Don: Blake, in a sense, I believe that you're saying that your grieving has fit your views of proper or acceptable grieving. You appear to be saying now, however, that change needs to happen so that the grief doesn't create other problems for you. And furthermore, you are uncertain how to go about change. Have I fairly accurately captured your views?

Blake: That's it. You pretty much understand the situation I think.

Don: Blake, perhaps you can continue to honor the memory of James, accept that you could likely have prevented his death had you gone with him that weekend, and yet, modify your grieving so that other problems don't get created in the process.

Blake: That sounds good to me, and I think that's really why I'm here.

Don: And I am really pleased that you are here, Blake. . . . Since focusing specifically on blaming yourself for James' death appears to result in other problems, suppose you expand your thoughts about James' death in addition to "It's my fault." What other thoughts do you have about James' life or his premature death?

Blake: Well, not to be too hard on the kid, but he did have a drinking problem, and, ultimately, I guess that you could say he was responsible for the accident that took his life. He was drunk!

Don: Yes, I agree with you that James was responsible for his drinking and the accident. It is somewhat a question of when does a parent quit protecting his child. Blake, can you function with both of these beliefs, "It's my fault" and "James was responsible for his drinking"?

Blake: Even though they seem contradictory, I think I can.

Don: So it is possible to maintain multiple views or beliefs about a situation.

Blake: Yes, I think it is.

Blake continued to elaborate the meanings of his son's life and ultimate death through this session and several subsequent sessions. My role was to prompt the generation of a variety of meanings through Socratic questioning and to guide Blake in appraising the various meanings in terms of their consequences. For example, Blake concluded that James' death would have been a "waste" if he didn't do something in James' name that would have a positive impact on the problem of drinking and driving in our society. That meaning-making process resulted in Blake's active involvement in and financial support of Mother's Against Drunk Driving. Blake also reconciled that had the roles been reversed and *he* was killed under the same circumstances as was James, he would want James to enjoy happiness and joy in life despite the loss. This role reversal contemplation was particularly significant to Blake. Further elaborations included the following: Depression will not bring James back. Had I prevented the accident that night, it would not have ensured that James would not have a fatal accident on another occasion. Focusing on self-blame is likely to bring many unwanted consequences, including poor work performance, marital unhappiness, and potentially an end to the remission state of my cancer. I can focus on James' *life* through more active devotion of time and energy to my grandson (James' only child).

Blake arrived at the above elaborations and many more. He learned to appraise meanings in terms of their various consequences and he attempted to translate the meanings into more productive (by his definition) actions. The elaboration of meanings, rather than the restructuring of the belief that "It's my fault," allowed Blake to hold on to an important, and in some ways viable, view of self-responsibility for the tragic death of his only son. Challenging that belief would have been, I believe, less effective than allowing it to stand as one of many meanings in the matrix of constructs surrounding Blake's loss. The emotions that comprise grief will be lifelong visitors in Blake's experiencing of life. He accepted this as both normal and reasonable and remained committed to making "use" of his grief for the benefit of himself and others.

SUMMARY

Constructivist philosophical and metatheoretical assumptions are a challenge to the theories that undergird many currently "popular" interventions. The view that distress and disorder are inherent and necessary in the enterprise of human change is at odds with the pathology and mental illness models that predominate. Constructivist ontology and epistemology represent a marked departure from well-established rationalist and empiricist perspectives. Criticism, challenge, and resistance notwithstanding, the strength of constructivism can be expected to mount as a result of internal and external developments. From within, theoretical sophistication and experientially grounded practice applications are ongoing. The broader context of these developments is the postmodernism movement, which is continuing to shape our intellectual culture across disciplines. The critical "helping professional in evolution" may well find constructivism to be viable in addressing some of the deficiencies that characterize many contemporary forms of intervention.

NOTES

[1]This chapter is dedicated to the memory of my dear friend, Vittorio Guidano, M.D. (1944–1999). Vittorio was a charismatic and exceedingly brilliant leader in the constructivism movement. As evident in this chapter, his contributions to constructivist theory and practice were remarkable. While he was highly influential worldwide, his presence was particularly powerful in Europe, Mexico, and South America. Vittorio was the founding director of the Centro di Psicoterapia Cognitiva Post-Razionalista in Rome and a founding member of the Italian Association for Cognitive Behavioral Therapies. His work will continue to enlighten students of constructivism at all levels and provide unending thrust to the constructivism movement. He had much more to give to the helping professions, and for this we are suffering a great loss. Beyond this, I shall miss his infectious joy in living the moment, the depth of intimacy he showed in our relationship and with others, and his ever-present ability to see the humor in life. Ciao mi amico, ciao.

REFERENCES

Anderson, W. T. (1990). *Reality isn't what it used to be.* San Francisco: Harper & Row.

Bandura, A. (1978). The self system in reciprocal determinism. *American Psychologist, 33,* 344–358.

Bandura, A. (1986). *Social foundations of thought and action: A social cognitive theory.* Englewood Cliffs, NJ: Prentice-Hall.

Bandura, A. (1996). Reflections on human agency: Part 1. *Constructive Change, 1*(2), 3–12.

Beck, A. T. (1963). Thinking and depression. *Archives of General Psychiatry, 9,* 324–333.

Beck, A. T. (1967). *Depression: Clinical, experimental, and theoretical aspects.* New York: Harper & Row.

Beck, A. T. (1976). *Cognitive therapy and the emotional disorders.* New York: International Universities Press.

Beck, A. T., & Emery, G. (1985). *Anxiety disorders and phobias.* New York: Basic Books.

Beck, A. T., Rush, A. J., Shaw, B. F., & Emery, G. (1979). *Cognitive therapy of depression.* New York: Guilford Press.

Bernstein, B. E., & Hartsell, T. L. (1998). *The portable lawyer for mental health professionals.* New York: Wiley.

Brower, A. M. (1998). Group development as constructed social reality revisited: The constructivism of small groups. In C. Franklin & P. S. Nurius (Eds.), *Constructivism in practice: Methods and challenges* (pp. 203–214). Milwaukee: Families International.

Combs, G., & Freedman, J. (1990). *Symbol, story, and ceremony: Using metaphor in individual and family therapy.* New York: Norton.

Daniels, M. H., & White, L. J. (1997). Applying second-generation cognitive science toward assessing therapeutic change. In T. L. Sexton & B. L. Griffin (Eds.), *Constructivist thinking in counseling practice, research, and training* (pp. 174–187). New York: Teachers College Press.

Ellis, A. (1955). New approaches to psychotherapy techniques. *Journal of Clinical Psychology* (Monograph Suppl. 2).

Ellis, A. (1958). Rational psychotherapy. *Journal of General Psychology, 59,* 35–49.

Ellis, A. (1962). *Reason and emotion in psychotherapy.* Secaucus, NJ: Citadel.

Ellis, A. (1994). *Reason and emotion in psychotherapy: A comprehensive method of treating human disturbances.* New York: Birch Lane Press.

Feixas, G. (1995). Personal constructs in systemic practice. In R. A. Neimeyer & M. J. Mahoney (Eds.), *Constructivism in psychotherapy* (pp. 305–337). Washington, DC: American Psychological Association.

Franklin, C. (1998). Distinctions between social constructionism and cognitive constructivism: Practice applications. In C. Franklin & P. S. Nurius (Eds.), *Constructivism in practice: Methods and challenges* (pp. 57–94). Milwaukee: Families International.

Franklin, C., & Nurius, P. S. (Eds.). (1998). *Constructivism in practice: Methods and challenges.* Milwaukee: Families International.

Gergen, K. (1985). The social constructionist movement in modern psychology. *American Psychologist, 40,* 266–275.

Gergen, K. (1991). *The saturated self.* New York: Basic Books.

Goncalves, O. F. (1995). Hermeneutics, constructivism, and cognitive-behavioral therapies: From the object to the project. In R. A. Neimeyer & M. J. Mahoney (Eds.), *Constructivism in psychotherapy* (pp. 195–230). Washington, DC: American Psychological Association.

Goolishian, H., & Anderson, H. (1987). Language systems and therapy: An evolving idea. *Psychotherapy, 24,* 529–538.

Granvold, D. K. (1994). Concepts and methods of cognitive treatment. In D. K. Granvold (Ed.), *Cognitive and behavioral treatment: Methods and applications* (pp. 3–31). Pacific Grove, CA: Brook/Cole.

Granvold, D. K. (1996a). Challenging roles of the constructive therapist: Expert and agent of social responsibility. *Constructivism in the Human Sciences, 1,* 16–21.

Granvold, D. K. (1996b). Constructivist psychotherapy. *Families in Society, 77,* 345–359.

Granvold, D. K. (1999). Integrating cognitive and constructive psychotherapies: A cognitive perspective. In T. B. Northcut & N. R. Heller (Eds.), *Enhancing psychodynamic therapy with cognitive-behavioral techniques* (pp. 53–93). Northvale, NJ: Jason Aronson.

Granvold, D. K., & Wodarski, J. S. (1994). Cognitive and behavioral treatment: Clinical issues, transfer of training, and relapse prevention. In D. K. Granvold (Ed.), *Cognitive and behavioral treatment: Methods and applications* (pp. 353–375). Pacific Grove, CA: Brooks/Cole.

Greenberg, L. S. (1986). Research strategies. In L. S. Greenberg & W. M. Pinsof (Eds.), *The psychotherapeutic process: A research handbook* (pp. 707–734). New York: Guilford Press.

Greenberg, L. S. (1992). Task analysis. In S. G. Toukmanian & D. L. Rennie (Eds.), *Psychotherapy process research* (pp. 22–50). Newbury Park, CA: Sage.

Greenberg, L. S., & Safran, J. D. (1987). *Emotion in psychotherapy.* New York: Guilford Press.

Greenberg, L. S., & Safran, J. D. (1989). Emotion in psychotherapy. *American Psychologist, 44,* 19–29.

Greenwald, M. A. (1987). Programming treatment generalization. In L. Michelson & L. M. Ascher (Eds.), *Anxiety and stress disorders* (pp. 583–616). New York: Guilford Press.

Guidano, V. F. (1987). *Complexity of the self.* New York: Guilford Press.

Guidano, V. F. (1988). A systems, process-oriented approach to cognitive therapy. In K. S. Dobson (Ed.), *Handbook of cognitive-behavioral therapies* (pp. 307–354). New York: Guilford Press.

Guidano, V. F. (1991a). Affective change events in a cognitive therapy system approach. In J. D. Safran & L. S. Greenberg (Eds.), *Emotion, psychotherapy, and change* (pp. 50–79). New York: Guilford Press.

Guidano, V. F. (1991b). *The self in process.* New York: Guilford Press.

Guidano, V. F. (1995). Constructivist psychotherapy: A theoretical framework. In R. A. Neimeyer & M. J. Mahoney (Eds.), *Constructivism in psychotherapy* (pp. 93–108). Washington, DC: American Psychological Association.

Guidano, V. F., & Liotti, G. A. (1983). *Cognitive processes and emotional disorders.* New York: Guilford Press.

Held, B. S. (1995). *Back to reality: A critique of postmodern theory in psychotherapy.* New York: Norton.

Houston-Vega, M. K., Nuehring, E. M., & Daguio, E. R. (1997). *Prudent practice: A guide for managing malpractice risk.* Washington, DC: NASW Press.

Hoyt, M. F. (Ed.). (1994). *Constructive therapies.* New York: Guilford Press.

Hoyt, M. F. (Ed.). (1996). *Constructive therapies* (Vol. 2). New York: Guilford Press.

Hoyt, M. F. (Ed.). (1998). *The handbook of constructive therapies.* San Francisco: Jossey-Bass.

Kegan, R. (1982). *The evolving self.* Cambridge, MA: Harvard University Press.

Kelly, G. A. (1955). *The psychology of personal constructs.* New York: Norton.

Kuehlwein, K. T., & Rosen, H. (Eds.). (1993). *Cognitive therapies in action: Evolving innovative practice.* San Francisco: Jossey-Bass.

Kvale, S. (1992). Introduction: From the archaeology of the psyche to the architecture of cultural landscapes. In S. Kvale (Ed.), *Psychology and postmodernism* (pp. 1–16). Thousand Oaks, CA: Sage.

Laws, D. R. (Ed.). (1989). *Relapse prevention with sex offenders.* New York: Guilford.

Lyddon, W. J. (1990). First- and second-order change: Implications for rationalist and constructivist cognitive therapies. *Journal of Counseling and Development, 69,* 122–127.

Mahoney, M. J. (1980). Psychotherapy and the structure of personal revolutions. In M. J. Mahoney (Ed.), *Psychotherapy process* (pp. 157–180). New York: Plenum.

Mahoney, M. J. (1985). Psychotherapy and human change processes. In M. J. Mahoney & A. Freeman (Eds.), *Cognition and psychotherapy* (pp. 3–48). New York: Plenum.

Mahoney, M. J. (1986). The tyranny of technique. *Counseling and Values, 30,* 169–174.

Mahoney, M. J. (1991). *Human change processes: The scientific foundations of psychotherapy.* New York: Basic Books.

Mahoney, M. J. (Ed.). (1995a). *Cognitive and constructive psychotherapies: Theory, research, and practice.* New York: Springer.

Mahoney, M. J. (1995b). Continuing evolution of the cognitive sciences and psychotherapies. In R. A. Neimeyer & M. J. Mahoney (Eds.), *Constructivism in psychotherapy* (pp. 39–67). Washington, DC: American Psychological Association.

Mahoney, M. J. (1995c). Theoretical developments in the cognitive psychotherapies. In M. J. Mahoney (Ed.), *Cognitive and constructive psychotherapies: Theory, research, and practice* (pp. 3–19). New York: Springer.

Mahoney, M. J. (in press). *Constructive psychotherapy: Exploring principles and practical exercises.* New York: Guilford Press.

Mahoney, M. J., & Lyddon, W. J. (1988). Recent developments in cognitive approaches to counseling and psychotherapy. *Counseling Psychologist, 16,* 190–234.

Mahoney, M. J., Miller, H. M., & Arciero, G. (1995). Constructive metatheory and the nature of mental representation. In M. J. Mahoney (Ed.), *Cognitive and constructive psychotherapies: Theory, research, and practice* (pp. 103–120). New York: Springer.

Markus, H., & Nurius, P. S. (1986). Possible selves. *American Psychologist, 41,* 954–969.

Marlatt, G. A., & Gordon, J. R. (Eds.). (1985). *Relapse prevention.* New York: Guilford.

Martin, J. (1994). *The construction and understanding of psychotherapeutic change: Conversations, memories, and theories.* New York: Teachers College Press.

Maturana, H., & Varela, F. (1980). *Autopoiesis and cognition.* Boston: Reidel.

Maturana, H., & Varela, F. (1987). *The tree of knowledge.* Boston: New Science Library.

McGinn, L. K., & Young, J. E. (1996). Schema-focused therapy. In P. M. Salkovskis (Ed.), *Frontiers of cognitive therapy* (pp. 182–207). New York: Guilford Press.

Neimeyer, G. J. (Ed.). (1993). *Constructivist assessment: A casebook.* Newbury Park, CA: Sage.

Neimeyer, G. J., Hagans, C. L., & Anderson, R. (1998). Intervening in meaning: Application of constructivist assessment. In C. Franklin & P. S. Nurius (Eds.), *Constructivism in practice: Methods and challenges* (pp. 115–137). Milwaukee: Families International.

Neimeyer, G. J., & Neimeyer, R. A. (1981). Personal construct perspectives on cognitive assessment. In T. V. Merluzzi, C. R. Glass, & M. Genest (Eds.), *Cognitive assessment* (pp. 188–232). New York: Guilford Press.

Neimeyer, R. A. (1987). An orientation to personal construct therapy. In R. A. Neimeyer & G. J. Neimeyer (Eds.), *Personal construct therapy casebook* (pp. 3–19). New York: Springer.

Neimeyer, R. A. (1993a). An appraisal of constructivist psychotherapies: Some conceptual and strategic contrasts. *Journal of Consulting and Clinical Psychology, 61,* 221–234.

Neimeyer, R. A. (1993b). Constructivism and the cognitive psychotherapies: Some conceptual and strategic contrasts. *Journal of Cognitive Psychotherapy, 7,* 159–171.

Neimeyer, R. A. (1993c). Constructivism and the problem of psychotherapy integration. *Journal of Psychotherapy Integration, 3,* 133–157.

Neimeyer, R. A. (1995a). An invitation to constructivist psychotherapies. In R. A. Neimeyer & M. J. Mahoney (Eds.), *Constructivism in psychotherapy* (pp. 1–8). Washington, DC: American Psychological Association.

Neimeyer, R. A. (1995b). Constructivist psychotherapies: Features, foundations, and future directions. In R. A. Neimeyer & M. J. Mahoney (Eds.), *Constructivism in psychotherapy* (pp. 11–38). Washington, DC: American Psychological Association.

Neimeyer, R. A. (1996). Process interventions for the constructivist psychotherapist. In H. Rosen & K. T. Kuehlwein (Eds.), *Constructing realities: Meaning-making perspectives for psychotherapists* (pp. 371–411). San Francisco: Jossey-Bass.

Neimeyer, R. A., & Harter, S. (1988). Facilitating individual change in personal construct theory. In G. Dunnett (Ed.), *Working with people* (pp. 174–185). London: Routledge & Kegan Paul.

Neimeyer, R. A., & Mahoney, M. J. (Eds.). (1995). *Constructivism in psychotherapy.* Washington, DC: American Psychological Association.

Nurius, P. S., & Berlin, S. B. (1994). Treatment of negative self-concept and depression. In D. K. Granvold (Ed.), *Cognitive and behavioral treatment: Methods and applications* (pp. 249–271). Pacific Grove, CA: Brooks/Cole.

Pittman, F. (1992). It's not my fault. *Family Therapy Networker, 16*(1), 56–63.

Popper, K. R. (1972). *Objective knowledge: An evolutionary approach.* London: Oxford University Press.

Raskin, J. D., & Lewandowski, A. M. (2000). The construction of disorder as human enterprise. In R. A. Neimeyer & J. D. Raskin (Eds.), *Constructions of disorder* (pp. 15–40). Washington, DC: American Psychological Association Press.

Rennie, D. L. (1992). Qualitative analysis of the client's experience of psychotherapy. In S. G. Toukmanian & D. L. Rennie (Eds.), *Psychotherapy process research* (pp. 211–233). Newbury Park, CA: Sage.

Rennie, D. L. (1995). Strategic choices in a qualitative approach to psychotherapy process research. In L. T. Hoshmand & J. Martin (Eds.), *Research as praxis* (pp. 198–220). New York: Teachers College Press.

Rennie, D. L., & Toukmanian, S. G. (1992). Explanation in psychotherapy process research. In S. G. Toukmanian & D. L. Rennie (Eds.), *Psychotherapy process research* (pp. 234–251). Newbury Park, CA: Sage.

Rice, L. N., & Greenberg, L. S. (1984). *Patterns of change.* New York: Guilford Press.

Rosen, H. (1993). Developing themes in the field of cognitive therapy. In K. T. Kuehlwein & H. Rosen (Eds.), *Cognitive therapies in action: Evolving innovative practice* (pp. 403–434). San Francisco: Jossey-Bass.

Rosen, H., & Kuehlwein, K. T. (Eds.). (1996). *Constructing realities: Meaning-making perspectives for psychotherapists.* San Francisco: Jossey-Bass.

Rush, A. J., & Beck, A. T. (1978). Adults with affective disorders. In M. Hersen & A. S. Bellack (Eds.), *Behavioral therapy in psychiatric settings* (pp. 286–330). Baltimore: Williams & Wilkins.

Safran, J. D., & Greenberg, L. S. (1991). Emotion in human functioning: Theory and therapeutic implications. In J. D. Safran & L. S. Greenberg (Eds.), *Emotion, psychotherapy, and change* (pp. 3–15). New York: Guilford Press.

Safran, J. D., & Segal, Z. V. (1990). *Interpersonal process in cognitive therapy.* New York: Basic Books.

Safran, J. D., Vallis, T. M., Segal, Z. V., & Shaw, B. F. (1986). Assessment of core cognitive processes in cognitive therapy. *Cognitive Therapy and Research, 10,* 509–526.

Saleebey, D. (1992). *The strengths perspective in social work practice.* New York: Longman.

Sexton, T. L., & Griffin, B. L. (Eds.). (1997). *Constructivist thinking in counseling practice, research, and training.* New York: Teachers College Press.

Toukmanian, S. G., & Rennie, D. L. (1992). *Psychotherapy process research: Paradigmatic and narrative approaches.* Newbury Park, CA: Sage.

von Glasersfeld, E. (1984). An introduction to radical constructivism. In P. Watzlawick (Ed.), *The invented reality* (pp. 17–40). New York: Norton.

Watzlawick, P. (Ed.). (1984). *The invented reality: How do we know what we believe we know?* New York: Norton.

White, M., & Epston, D. (1990). *Narrative means to therapeutic ends.* New York: Norton.

Young, J. (1990). *Cognitive therapy for personality disorders: A schema-focused approach.* Sarasota, FL: Professional Resource Press.

17

Solution-Focused Therapy

Jacqueline Corcoran

Solution-focused therapy is a relatively new treatment approach with a unique focus, not on problems, but on solutions to problems and the strengths clients invariably possess. After providing a brief overview of solution-focused practice, this chapter will discuss the historical development behind the model's formulation by de Shazer (1985, 1988) and associates (de Shazer et al., 1986) and the phases of the helping process, including some of the key theoretical constructs. After a detailed explanation of the model, its compatibility with a generalist-eclectic framework will be discussed, along with a critique of the model. Finally, a case example of solution-focused therapy with a young woman suffering from social anxiety will be presented.

OVERVIEW OF SOLUTION-FOCUSED PRACTICE

In solution-focused therapy, clients are viewed as having the necessary strengths and capacities to solve their own problems (Berg, 1994; Cade & O'Hanlon, 1993; De Jong & Berg, 1998; O'Hanlon & Weiner-Davis, 1989). Because individuals are unique and have the right to determine what it is they want, the task of the practitioner is to identify strengths and amplify them so that clients can apply these "solutions." Given the lack of emphasis on problems, history taking and discussion of how symptoms manifest themselves are not detailed. Nor is there a need to understand how the problem began, because this knowledge may offer little in terms of how to solve the problem (De Jong & Berg, 1998). In general, the past is deemphasized other than times when exceptions to problems occurred. The model orients instead toward the future when the problem will no longer a problem. To this end, practitioners assist clients in eliciting "exceptions," times when the problem is either not a problem or is lessened in terms of duration, severity, frequency, or intensity (Berg, 1994; Cade & O'Hanlon, 1993; De Jong & Berg, 1998; O'Hanlon & Weiner-Davis, 1989).

The construction of solutions from exceptions is considered easier and ultimately more successful than stopping or changing existing problem behavior. When exceptions are identified, the practitioner explores with clients the strengths and resources that were used. These resources are enlarged upon through the use of questions presupposing that positive change will occur (e.g., "When you are doing better, what will be happening?" and "When therapy is successful, what will be different?") because changes in language are assumed to lead to changes in perception. When clients view themselves as resourceful and capable, they are empowered toward future positive behavior. Behavioral, as well as perceptual, change is implicated because the approach is focused on concrete, specific behaviors that are achievable within a brief time period. The view is that change in specific areas can "snowball" into bigger changes due to the systems orientation assumed to be present: Change in one part of the system can lead to change in other parts of the system (O'Hanlon & Weiner-Davis, 1989).

The systemic basis of solution-focused therapy also means that the context of a particular behavior is more influential than innate individual characteristics. In this model, the individual is depathologized; instead, the emphasis is on situational aspects—the who, what, where, when, and how of a particular behavior (Durrant, 1995).

HISTORICAL DEVELOPMENTS

Although some of the key figures associated with solution-focused therapy are social workers (e.g., Insoo Kim Berg and Michelle Weiner-Davis), the model has arisen out of the field of family therapy, with Mental Research Institute (MRI) brief therapy as a specific influence (de Shazer et al., 1986). An essential family therapy concept involves a systemic notion of causality, that a change in one part of a routine sequence will result in further change for the system. In both MRI and solution-focused approaches, the pattern around a problem is altered as opposed to discovering its underlying cause (O'Hanlon & Weiner-Davis, 1989). Where the models depart is that MRI brief therapy focuses on problems, whereas solution-focused therapy emphasizes solutions to problems.

Another major influence on solution-focused therapy is the work of the psychiatrist Milton Erickson (O'Hanlon & Weiner-Davis, 1989). Erickson believed that individuals have the strengths and resources to solve their own problems and that the therapist's job is to uncover these resources and activate them for the client. For Erickson, many times an activation of these resources involves an amplification of symptomatic behavior through the use of paradoxical directives (e.g., prescribing symptoms). Unlike MRI brief therapy, which also employs paradoxical interventions on a routine basis, solution-focused therapy relies on paradox only as a last resort when other, more direct attempts to elicit positive behavior in the client have failed.

A further theoretical influence on solution-focused therapy is social constructivism, the view that knowledge about reality is constructed from social interactions (Berg & De Jong, 1996). In other words, reality is relative to the social context. Therefore, the concept of the "expert" practitioner, who categorizes, diagnoses, and solves client problems objectively is viewed with skepticism. Sharing perceptions with others through language and engaging in conversational dialogues is the medium by which reality is shaped (de Shazer, 1994). Thus, the solution-focused practitioner uses language and questioning to influence the way clients view their problems, the potential for solutions, and the expectancy for change (Berg & De Jong, 1996).

PHASES OF HELPING

The phases of helping in solution-focused therapy are not as discrete as they are in a generalist-eclectic framework. Although "joining" in solution-focused therapy parallels the engagement process of the generalist-eclectic framework, a distinct assessment phase in which information gathering of the problem, its history, and the various ecological systems levels involved is not included. Indeed, joining occurs concurrent to helping the client formulate treatment goals. Discussion of goals leads to exception finding, identification of times when movement toward treatment goals already happens. Therefore, goal setting and exception finding involve the planning/contracting and intervention phases of a generalist-eclectic model. Evaluation in the solution-focused model most commonly involves noting progress on solution-focused scales; however, solution-focused scales are also used for goal setting, task construction, and exception finding. In addition, termination is a focus from the beginning of treatment, because goal setting and solution finding orient the client toward change in a brief time period (De Jong & Berg, 1998). Given the difficulty in trying to outline the phases of solution-focused treatment in generalist-eclectic terms, this section will be outlined in the following way: joining (engagement), assessment (assessing the client relationship, assessing pretreatment change), goal setting (the miracle question, scaling questions), the exception-finding intervention, and termination.

Joining

The therapist gains cooperation of the client in finding solutions by "joining" with the client as the initial phase of engagement. "Joining" is the clinician's task of establishing a positive, mutually cooperative relationship (Berg, 1994). The worker should convey acceptance of the client's positions and perspectives rather than becoming invested in who is "right" and who is "wrong." These strategies seen as counterproductive in that defensive clients are less amenable to working with the therapist and to change (Cade & O'Hanlon, 1993).

Strategies for enhancement of joining involve recognition of idiosyncratic phrasing the client uses and adopting this language. For example, child behavior problems may be referred to as "fussing" or "attitude problems" as the client may call them (Berg, 1994; O'Hanlon & Weiner-Davis, 1989). The assumption is that clients feel understood when their language is used by the worker.

As well as using language idiosyncratic to the client, the worker should also be vigilant for any strengths and resources to compliment, recognizing that every problem behavior contains within it an inherent strength (O'Hanlon & Weiner-Davis, 1989). This is the same principle as reframing from family therapy in which previously viewed negative behavior is considered in a positive light. For example, an individual who nags is said to be simply concerned about bringing out the best in someone (Berg, 1994). Through reframing, the client is given credit for positive aspects of his or her behavior, and the joining process is enhanced.

A related intervention, normalizing, involves depathologizing people's concerns. For example, if parents bring their children in for treatment insisting that they have "attention deficit hyperactivity disorder," the child's behavior can instead be discussed as "high-spirited" or "energetic—like many children at this age." A parent objecting to his or her teenager's dress style can be told that a normal process of adolescence involves finding an identity, and this may include experimentation with different styles. The objective is to help people view themselves as struggling with ordinary life difficulties. Normalizing makes more manageable problems previously viewed as insurmountable.

Assessment

For the purposes of describing the phases of helping, assessment comprises assessment of the client relationship and inquiry about pretreatment changes. There are three main client relationships in the solution-focused model: the customer, the complainant, and the visitor (Berg, 1994; Berg & Miller, 1992; Cade & O'Hanlon, 1993; De Jong & Berg, 1998). Most traditional therapy models assume the presence of a "customer," a person who comes in voluntarily to make changes in his or her life. The second type of client is the complainant. Complainants ostensibly come to therapy voluntarily to change, but it soon becomes apparent that they want someone or something else outside of themselves to change. These clients tend to blame other people, events, and circumstances for their problems. The third type of client, the visitor, is directed or mandated to visit a practitioner by another person or entity invested in the client's change. The visitor, therefore, is a nonvoluntary participant in treatment whose main goal is ending contact with the helping system (Berg, 1994).

The visitor and the complainant type of client are often difficult to engage in treatment because these clients are not interested in change for themselves (Berg, 1994). In the solution-focused model, strategies are used with both client types. For example, visitors can be engaged toward the goal of getting the mandating body "off their backs" ("Whose idea was it that you come to therapy?" and "What would they say you need to do so you don't need to come here anymore?"), and change can be directed toward that end. Complainants can be engaged through the use of "coping questions," which are designed to elicit the resources people use to cope with difficult circumstances ("This sounds very hard. How do you manage? How do you have the strength to go on?"). An additional intervention with complainants is to emphasize the context for behavior ("What are you doing when he is behaving?").

Another aspect of assessment involves inquiry about pretreatment changes, that is, asking clients what kind of changes they have noticed between the time they first scheduled their appointment and the first session. Some authors (Lawson, 1994; Weiner-Davis, de Shazer, & Gingerich, 1987) have reported that, when asked, over 60% of clients note pretreatment changes. Others (Allgood Parham, Salts, & Smith, 1995) who have asked the question in more neutral terms ("Have you noticed any changes?" versus "What changes have you noticed?"), and as part of a presession intake versus intake during the first session, have reported that only 30% of clients note such change. Nevertheless, Allgood and colleagues (1995) found that clients who reported pretreatment change had lower rates of dropout from therapy. They hypothesize that drawing the client's attention to pretreatment changes might bolster client motivation to stay in therapy. Furthermore, they suggest that attention to pretreatment change might have a "snowball effect" in that small changes lead to bigger changes. For example, if one person in a relationship acts more kindly, then there is a greater likelihood of a positive action on the part of the other partner, and, subsequently, a greater possibility of positive perception by both parties.

GOAL SETTING

In the solution-focused model, emphasis is on well-formulated goals that are achievable within a brief time frame. Although goal setting will be discussed as a discrete phase of helping, it is more accurate to view discussion of goal formulation as starting as soon as the client comes in contact with the practitioner: What will be different about your life when you don't need to come here anymore? The presuppositional phrasing of this question is presumed to effect the way clients view their problems and the potential for change (Cade & O'Hanlon, 1993) and underlies all solution-focused questioning. Furthermore, expectancy for change is conveyed by using words such as *when* and *will*. Examples of such questioning include *When* you are controlling your temper, what *will* you be saying? and *When* you are getting along, what *will* you be doing differently? The use of definitive phrasing to convey an expectancy for change is consistent with the solution-focused orientation toward the future. People who have experienced a negative and stressful past may easily project this past into the future and assume their lives will always be the same. Use of the "miracle question" and "scaling questions" are ways to help clients envision a more hopeful future.

The Miracle Question

In the miracle question, clients are asked to conjure up a detailed view of a future without the problem. A typical miracle question involves the following: "Let's say that while you're sleeping, a miracle occurs, and the problem you came here with is solved. What will let you know the next morning that a miracle happened?" (de Shazer, 1988). Specifics are elicited about this no-problem experience so that clients may develop a vision of a more hopeful and satisfying future (De Jong & Berg, 1998). Sometimes asking clients to envision a brighter future may help them be clearer on what they want or to see a path to problem solving. By discussing the future in a positive light, hope can be generated, and change can be enacted in the present by the recognition of both strengths to cope with obstacles and signs of possibilities for change (Cade & O'Hanlon, 1993).

Scaling Questions

After clients are encouraged to expand their futures and the possibilities (De Jong & Berg, 1998), the practitioner helps the client develop concrete, behaviorally specific goals that can be achieved in a brief time frame. Clients typically begin to discuss their goals in abstract and non-sensory-based language: "I will feel better." The task of the clinician is to encourage and develop observable correlates of these states (Cade & O'Hanlon, 1993). For example, rather than "not feeling depressed," goals might involve "getting to work on time," "calling friends," and "doing volunteer work." As this example illustrates, goals should involve the presence of positive behaviors rather than the absence of negatives (De Jong & Berg, 1998).

A useful technique for making concrete even the most abstract of goals involves scaling questions (Berg, 1994; Berg & Miller, 1992). Scaling questions involve asking clients to rank themselves on a scale from 1 to 10, with 1 representing "the problem" and 10 representing "when the problem is no longer a problem." The practitioner then develops with the client specific behavioral indicators of the 10 position.

Scales offer a number of advantages (Cade & O'Hanlon, 1993). First, a ranking will enable clients to realize they have already made some progress toward their goals ("You're already at a five? You're halfway! What have you done to get to that point?"). Any progress made can then be the basis for exception finding. (Exception finding will be covered in more detail in the following section.) Scales can also be used to guide task setting ("What will you need to do to move up to a 6?"). Clients identify specific behaviors that will help them move up one rank order on the scale. Finally, scales can be used to track progress over time.

Scales can further be used as a basis for the exploration of relationship questions (Berg, 1994). Relationship questions help clients understand the context of situations and the part they themselves play in interactions. Typical questions include "Where do you think your mother would rank you?" and "Where would your probation officer put you?" Further questioning can help the client identify the steps necessary to take so that other key people will recognize progress ("What would she say you need to do to move up a number?"). When more than one person is present in the session, relationship questions can be used to stimulate interaction, helping family members clarify their expectations of each other. Relationship questions also enable clients to become more adept at taking on the perspective of others. This ability opens up new meanings and possibilities for change as clients reflect on how they might act differently (Berg & De Jong, 1996).

FINDING EXCEPTIONS TO PROBLEMS

The central concern of solution-focused practice is identifying exceptions, times when the problem is not a problem or when the client solved similar problems in the past (Berg, 1994; Berg & Miller, 1992; Cade & O'Hanlon, 1993; O'Hanlon & Weiner-Davis, 1989). Exceptions provide a blueprint for individuals to solve their problems in their own way. When exceptions are identified, the social worker then asks about the resources that were applied to make these occur ("How did you get that to happen?" "How did you manage that?" and "How did you come up with that idea?"). Uncovering information about these resources elucidates how clients can solve their problems.

Another way to seek exceptions is for the worker to help clients identify strengths they display in other areas, such as their employment or hobbies. Here, the intent is to help clients apply existing solutions to the presenting problem. For example, potential strengths to exploit could involve patience, energy, communication skills, organizational ability, the ability to delay gratification, managerial skills, attention to detail, and so on. Inquiry is designed to elicit these resources and explore how these could be used to solve problems (O'Hanlon & Weiner-Davis, 1989).

A further way to find and build on exceptions involves an intervention borrowed from narrative therapy, called "externalizing the problem"

(White & Epston, 1990). Externalizing the problem involves using language to cast the problem as an entity outside of the client. In this way, a problem that is considered inherent or fixed can be viewed as less stable and rigid. Relative influence questions (White & Epston, 1990) are then asked of individuals to determine the extent of their influence over their problems, as well as the influence of the problem over them ("When are you able to stand up to the anger and not let it tell you what to do?" "When can you resist the urge to smoke/shoot up?" and "When are you able to overcome the temptation to just stay in bed instead of getting your kids ready for school?"). Clients discover exceptions by identifying times when they are able to exert control over their problems. Externalizing also has the benefit of freeing up people to take a lighter approach to "serious" problems. Because their problems are no longer viewed as innate, pathological qualities, they are more able to generate options.

A final way to help clients discover exceptions is to prescribe the "first formula task" for homework after the first session. Again, de Shazer (1985) pioneered the following question: "This week notice all the things that are happening that you want to have continue to happen." The purpose of the task is to have clients focus on what is already working for them. Adams, Piercy, and Jurich (1991) compared the use of the solution-focused "first formula task" and a task focusing on details of the problem. The authors found that the solution-focused task resulted in greater improvement on presenting problems and clearer formulation of treatment goals.

TERMINATION

Because change is oriented toward a brief time period in the solution-focused model, work is oriented toward termination at the beginning of treatment. Questions include "What needs to happen so you don't need to come back to see me?" and "What will be different when therapy has been successful?" (Berg, 1994). Once clients have maintained changes on the small concrete goals they have set, the therapist and the client start to discuss plans for termination, as it is assumed that achievement of these small changes will lead to further positive change in the client's life. Termination is geared toward helping clients identify strategies so that change will be maintained and the momentum developed will further change to occur. Although the practitioner does not want to imply that relapse is inevitable, the client must be prepared with strategies to enact if temptation presents itself or if the client begins to slip into old behaviors. Therefore, it is during termination that possibility rather than definitive phrasing is used. For example, "What *would* be the first thing you'd notice *if* you started to find things slipping back?" "What *could* you do to prevent things from getting any further?" and "*If* you have the urge to drink again, what *could* you do to make sure you didn't use?" might be typical inquiries to elicit strategies to use if there is a return to old behavior.

Termination also involves building on the changes that have occurred, with the hope they will continue into the future. Selekman (1995, 1997) has proposed a number of such questions, including "With all the changes you are making, what will I see if I was a fly on your wall 6 months from now?" and "With all the changes you are making, what will you be telling me if I run into you at the convenience store 6 months from now?" (Selekman, 1997). Questions are phrased to set up the expectation that change will continue to happen.

APPLICATION TO FAMILY AND GROUP WORK

FAMILY WORK

Because of the emphasis on the context of the relationship for behavior change, solution-focused therapy works well with couples and families, and, in fact, the model emerged from the family therapy field. Solution-focused questions are asked of family members so they can understand the way their behavior influences others ("What are you doing when he is behaving?"). The solution-focused orientation also redirects the blaming and attacking stance of family members into requests for the presence of positive behaviors ("What would you like her to be doing?"). Then the focus turns to times when the hoped for behavior already occurs and what is different about the context, particularly the responses of other family members, during these nonproblem times. This focus presumably leads to a more positive view of other family members, which, in turn, leads to more positive behaviors.

GROUP WORK

Surprisingly little has been written about solution-focused group work. Clinical reports have included Selekman's (1995) description of a solution-focused parent support group and Corcoran's (1998) discussion of a psychoeducational/solution-focused approach with juvenile offenders. One empirical study (Zimmerman, Prest, & Wetzel, 1997) involved a combination psychoeducational/solution-focused approach, with maritally distressed couples. Here, couples demonstrated improved marital adjustment after the 6-week intervention.

A solution-focused approach alone or in combination with another model can offer advantages for group therapy. Solution-focused therapy can empower clients who might otherwise find a group too problem-focused or complaint-driven. A solution-focused model can also build on the strengths of individuals in groups, offering inspiration and solutions to problems.

In addition, a solution-focused approach can be advantageous for nonvoluntary populations in group work, such as criminal offenders and substance abusers. As mentioned, nonvoluntary populations can be difficult to engage in traditional treatment models. One of the advantages of solution-focused treatment is that strategies can be used so that the nonvoluntary client is responsible for the work in therapy ("Whose idea was it that you come to group?" "What does your probation officer/the court need to see to know you don't need to come here anymore?" "What would they say you're doing differently?" and "What would they say is the next step you should take?"). By eliciting answers to these types of questions, nonvoluntary clients can be engaged in their main objective: to get the referral source "off their backs," so they no longer have to attend treatment (Berg, 1994).

COMPATIBILITY WITH THE GENERALIST-ECLECTIC FRAMEWORK

Solution-focused therapy shares many similarities with a generalist-eclectic framework. Solution-focused and social work practice share a systemic view, acknowledging the importance of context rather than an emphasis on individual pathology. Although both solution-focused therapy and social work address the key influence of the immediate relationship context, social work also emphasizes systems, ecological, and broader environmental levels. In both perspectives, a systemic notion of change is promoted in recognition that a small change in one part of the system can produce change in another part of the system. However, solution-focused therapy departs from a generalist-eclectic framework in eschewing a holistic assessment of the various system levels, along with information gathering about the problem and history taking. Although the generalist-eclectic framework espouses an emphasis on health, normality, and client strengths, in actuality "assessment" implies the diagnosis of a problem. The practitioner has to decide on the client's problem so that it can be solved. Hence, the assumption is that a logical link exists between the problem and the solution (De Jong & Berg, 1998). In contrast, solution-focused therapy does not emphasize the problem, nor does it assume that an understanding of a problem leads to its solution. In this approach, treatment begins with an exploration of strengths and how to target these strengths toward positive change.

Although both solution-focused therapy and a general-eclectic framework speak of a collaborative relationship between the practitioner and the client, the solution-focused approach concretely puts this into practice. First, there are specific techniques to assist in joining, such as normalizing and reframing, and specific interventions depending on the client type involved. The spirit of collaboration is seen in clients being given respect for their unique worldviews and being allowed to determine their own treatment goals. Respect is conveyed for people's individual strengths and resources, with the assumption that people are capable of solving their own problems. The task of the practitioner is to help clients identify their resources, then enlarge upon them. This approach is in contrast to a view of an "expert" practitioner who possesses specialized knowledge on life-cycle theories or minority populations. In these approaches, specialized knowledge is applied to client problems and a diagnosis is made. It appears, therefore, that although a collaborative process is touted in a generalist-eclectic framework, "expert" knowledge is still required.

Although eclecticism is not as central a feature in solution-focused therapy as it is in the generalist-eclectic framework, allowance is made for the use of other models and theories as these fit with the client's needs and goals. Cognitive and behavioral approaches are particularly compatible with solution-focused therapy, as they are all directed toward both cognitive and behavioral change. Cognitive interventions, for example, can be used to help clients identify the resources they use that are cognitive in nature ("What were you thinking about yourself/the other person when you were able to do that?" and "What were you telling yourself?"). The use of cognitively based questions can help people develop further resources for coping.

Another way that cognitive-behavioral interventions can supplement solution-focused therapy was demonstrated in a study with maritally distressed couples in which a combination psychoeducational and solution-focused group approach was used (Zimmerman et al., 1997). One assumption the authors made was that psychoeducational interventions could mediate adjustment due to the content being informative, education-based, and skill-building. In this study, couples reported improved marital adjustment after the 6-week combination approach in groups.

In regard to behavioral theory, the premise that positive reinforcement increases the frequency of behavior is similar to the solution-focused view that a focus on the positives or solutions amplifies further positive behavior. For example, through behavioral parent training, children learn that their positive behavior will gain them attention, praise, and other rewards and that their misbehavior will be ignored. For other reasons as well, child behavior problems are a logical focus of the solution-focused model. In this model, questions are designed to address the concerns of parents, who are the "complainants" of their children's behavior. Coping questions elicit the resources parents employ to deal with "such difficult circumstances." Parents are asked to consider how their own behavior affects their children's. Focus on when their children display appropriate behavior cultivates in parents a more positive view of their child and encourage future positive behavior. Solution-focused questioning further engages children, who usually represent the visitor type of relationship in developing treatment goals and in taking responsibility for the work in therapy. Despite the apparent advantages of solution-focused therapy for behavior problems, there is only beginning empirical support for its effectiveness (Corcoran & Stephenson, 1999; Lee, 1997).

In comparison, behavioral parent training has received a great deal of empirical support for decreasing negative child behavior problems (e.g., Kazdin, 1997; Serketich & Dumas, 1996). Therefore, some of the other empirically tested interventions from parent training could be used to supplement solution-focused therapy, as parents may not always have the skills or knowledge to influence their children's behavior. Such specific information may include, for example, providing labeled rather than unlabeled praise ("You did a good job in picking your toys off the floor" versus "You did a good job"), offering reinforcement immediately after appropriate behavior, and withdrawing privileges for a brief duration after misbehavior (e.g., taking away bike privileges for the misuse of a bike). The solution-focused model may be more palatable to parents because it is not didactic in nature like behavioral parent training; the occasional provision of specific, empirically tested information at key points may further assist parents in more effectively managing their children's behavior.

Other than the provision of specific information, behavioral change techniques may also be used to supplement solution-focused therapy, specifically the use of behavioral rehearsal and feedback. Rehearsing behaviors through the use of role play in session, for example, may be helpful so that clients are cued as to how they demonstrated exceptions in certain situations. In addition, clients may have to practice a situation successfully before they are able to implement the new pattern of behavior in future settings. These suggestions show that solution-focused therapy might benefit from behavioral and cognitive-behavioral interventions in helping clients discover resources (cognitive coping) or those that allow them to practice new situations (rehearsal and feedback) or focus on reinforcement of positive behaviors.

CRITIQUE OF SOLUTION-FOCUSED PRACTICE

STRENGTHS

A main strength of solution-focused practice is its compatibility with social work values, including the importance of context for behavior, a systemic perspective, client self-determination, and a focus on the strengths and resources of the individual. The focus on strengths is a particularly unique orientation because many other practice models are pathologizing (De Jong & Berg, 1998). The focus on client resources and what the client is doing right empowers and offers hope to people who are often beleaguered by the time they come for treatment. Solution-focused questioning offers a concrete way to implement these values in social work practice.

Another advantage of the solution-focused approach is that the work of treatment is placed on the client rather than the practitioner. Clients have to decide on their own goals and clarify what they want in concrete terms.

Practitioner collaboration helps clients discover and build on the resources they employ during nonproblem times. Through this process, clients are empowered to help themselves (De Jong & Berg, 1998).

Although empirical support for solution-focused therapy has not been established (see Limitations, below), several studies (e.g., De Jong & Hopwood, 1996; de Shazer, 1991; Lee, 1997) have provided some indication of the model's efficacy. De Jong and Hopwood (1996) [also reported in Berg & De Jong, 1996; De Jong & Berg, 1998], for instance, claim that for 275 clients treated at the Brief Family Therapy Center in Milwaukee, success was attained at posttest at least 60% of the time, no matter if the client-identified problem included family violence, communication problems, suicidal thoughts, or sexual abuse, among other issues. At 7- to 9-month follow-up, success was attained at least 70% of the time, except with health problems or panic attacks. However, success was defined very broadly: Almost 50% at posttest showed only 1 to 3 points of change on a scale; for follow-up, "success" was determined if goals were either "met" or "partly met."

Another study focusing specifically on family violence used a solution-focused approach with court-ordered domestic violence perpetrators and their partners, with an emphasis on times when they were able to resolve conflict in nonviolent ways (Sirles, Lipchick, & Kowalksi, 1993). Satisfaction with services was assessed during a follow-up phone intervention. Women overall were more satisfied: Eighty-four percent were positive about their experience in counseling, 6% reported mixed feelings, and 11% were dissatisfied. For men, 54% found therapy to be positive, stating they had acquired skills in controlling their drinking, arguing, and avoiding violence; 23% were mixed in their response; and 23 percent were negative toward counseling.

Some beginning empirical work has examined the effects of solution-focused therapy in a children's mental health outpatient facility (Lee, 1997). Presenting problems included those related to family relationships, school, children's behavior at home, and children's difficulties with emotional regulation. At a 6-month telephone interview, a little over half (54%) of respondents indicated that their goals had been met, with 11% stating their goals had been partly met and almost a third (32%) that their goals had not been met.

LIMITATIONS

The studies reviewed above are fairly representative of the empirical work on solution-focused therapy, and they present a number of limitations. First, global, nonstandardized ratings of change are relied upon ("goals met," "goals partly met," "goals not met") (e.g., De Jong & Hopwood, 1996; de Shazer, 1991) rather than standardized measures. Second, rarely is baseline data collected, except for solution-focused scales in some cases (e.g., De Jong & Hopwood, 1996). Third, telephone interviews have been a primary method of data collection, but they are associated with particular biases. For instance, those with stable telephone listings who can be reached at follow-up may have more resources and may also have been better served by the intervention. Fourth, the reliance of some studies on client satisfaction is questionable because the literature has indicated that most clients who are queried will report high satisfaction with services (Larsen, Attkisson, Hargreaves, & Nguyen, 1979). Because of the lack of research and its poor quality, it is difficult to know how effective solution-focused therapy is, in what areas, and with what particular populations.

Concerns can further be raised about using solution-focused therapy only when threats to safety are involved. Family violence is one particular area of concern. Despite the positive findings reported by Sirles and colleagues (1993), methodological problems call into question these results. Moreover, empirical study suggests that attitudes about violence toward women and, to a lesser extent, the ability to engage in rational thinking may need to be targeted in order to affect men's violent behavior (Eisikovits, Edleson, Guttman, & Sela-Amit, 1995).

Although a solution-focused approach might offer advantages in terms of targeting and building upon prosocial behavior when offending problems are involved, the need for rehabilitation may demand other approaches as well. A study conducted in the Swedish prison system used both solution-focused therapy and a network approach (Lindforss & Magnusson, 1997). This study was notable in that subjects were randomized to treatment and control conditions. After an average of five sessions, 60% had reoffended in the experimental group compared to 86% in the control group. In addition, the control group subjects tended to commit more serious offenses, including drug offenses.

The solution-focused model might also be limited when a client has suffered from abuse or trauma, such as sexual abuse or sexual assault. Some clinical discussions of solution-focused work with adult sexual abuse survivors have been published (Dolan, 1991; Durrant & Kowalski, 1990). Each of these approaches is quite different, even though both are described as solution-oriented. For example, Dolan (1991) integrates the processing of feelings and the impact of abuse on survivor perceptions of self and others, while also maintaining an emphasis on the resources victims have used to survive trauma. In contrast, Durrant and Kowalski (1990) argue that discussion of abuse is not necessary unless the survivor feels it is; offering choices and respecting the client's wisdom about what is needed for recovery are viewed as further empowering the survivor. With no empirical work in this area, it is difficult to know the benefits of any particular orientation over another. Similarly, with child victims of sexual abuse, it is unknown whether a solution-focused approach alone would assist in recovery. The research on child treatment suggests that, for sexual abuse issues, a targeted rather than a nondirective approach is appropriate (Celano,

Hazzard, Webb, & McCall, 1996; Cohen & Mannarino, 1996). Without empirical work on solution-focused therapy for child sexual abuse victims, it is not known how solution-focused therapy would compare with a treatment specifically focused on sexual abuse issues.

Apart from these concerns, another critique of solution-focused therapy has been its emphasis on behavior and perception rather than feelings. Kiser, Piercy, and Lipchick (1993) argue that feelings, behaviors, and cognitions are linked and that feelings cannot be ignored, as they are an inextricable facet of human existence. If feelings are ignored, they may cloud people's ability to remember the exceptions to their problems or to imagine a future without the problem. These authors suggest that the role of feelings can be integrated into solution-focused work. For example, exceptions can center on times they felt better and what was different about their behaviors and cognitions when they felt this way.

The lack of emphasis on feelings could have particular relevance for the treatment of affective disorders, such as depression and anxiety. A solution-focused approach to these problems might, however, offer certain benefits. For example, depressed individuals could be assisted to identify times when they have more of a sense of meaning about their lives. The miracle question could orient them towards a more hopeful future. The scaling question could assess progress toward a more positive state by rank ordering the different behavioral correlates associated with varying degrees of well-being. The next section will present a case example with a woman coming to treatment for social anxiety to illustrate how solution-focused therapy may be utilized with such problems.

CASE EXAMPLE

A 25-year-old woman, Sarah Matthews (fictitious name), presented in treatment because she had never had a serious boyfriend, much less a date, due to her extreme anxiety and discomfort when speaking to men. Sarah coped with this anxiety by avoiding contacts with men. When contact was inevitable, her heart would pound, and she would blush, stammer, and mumble. Sarah related she had been sexually abused as a child (a one-time incident when she was 5 years old) by a teenage uncle. Sarah had never told anyone before about the abuse and was adamant about not discussing it any further in therapy. She said she only wanted to tackle the social anxiety.

The first intervention with Sarah was the construction of a solution-focused scale. Sarah was asked specific behaviors that would indicate she was at a 10, when she didn't need to come to therapy anymore. She described that she would be able to speak to men in casual social contact and to feel comfortable in social and work situations that might include men. Sarah's description entailed a behaviorally specific goal that was achievable within a brief time period. She didn't, for example, state that she wanted to be able to date men or have a boyfriend. These objectives might have been possible only after she had been able to meet her more immediate goal, as small change can "snowball" into bigger changes.

Sarah was then asked to rank herself on the solution-focused scale. Sarah placed herself at 2, as she was able to speak to one man at her workplace. Sarah was complimented; she had made some progress toward her goal. Inquiry about the exceptions that had occurred to get her to this point were explored. Sarah said that the exception involved a delivery man who came out weekly to her work setting. Her job as office manager was to get him to sign for the order he delivered. She said at first she had avoided him, conveniently being "way too busy" when he came by, forcing a co-worker to get him to sign. However, her co-worker's job duties then changed, and Sarah had no choice but to have contact with the delivery man. She said she would experience extreme dread at the prospect of his coming to the office. When he made his weekly visit, she said that she would shake and sweat, avoid eye contact, and mutter enough of a response to get the job done. After 4 months of this, she said she was finally at the point at which she no longer dreaded his visits and could respond to him very brusquely with one-word answers, but at least she was no longer submerged with anxiety. When asked about the resources she had employed to get to this point, she said that becoming familiar with him and seeing him joke around with her co-workers had helped. She was asked how she could apply the resources she had employed in the past to current situations that were bothering her. She identified that the exception involved exposing herself to contact with a man over time, which allowed her to eventually perceive him as safe. She denied that there were any other men with whom she had contact on a regular or, even an occasional, basis.

When asked how she could make more of that happen in her life, she stated she had considered joining a church social club. She was complimented for coming up with such a creative solution and was asked how she could go about joining such a group. She said she had attended a couple of different churches in the area and had found one with which she felt comfortable and that this church offered a singles group. It was agreed that the task for the following week, which would get her to 3 on the solution-focused scale, would involve calling about meeting times for the singles group.

Sarah came to the next session smiling and pleased. She reported that not only had she called about the singles group, she had also attended a meeting on Friday night. She was asked again about the resources she had used to do this: How had she been able to face her fears and get herself to this group? She said she was just at the point at which she was sick of having her life so curtailed. She said she wanted a husband and children one day, so she needed to get past this problem if she was to achieve this. She reported that the group comprised both young women and men and that everyone was very welcoming and accepting; she felt only minor anxiety in the presence of so many men. When asked how she had been able to do this, she said that getting the courage up to call and then to attend the meeting had been the hard part. She further stated that she had been able to summon up the courage because she was so motivated to deal with this problem. She said that scheduling a therapy appointment had also meant she was serious about tackling her problem. For Sarah, calling about a therapy appointment seemed to comprise pretreatment change. It appeared as if taking such a positive step toward action motivated her to make further changes. As a result of these changes, Sarah ranked herself at 5 on the solution-focused scale.

As sessions progressed, she ranked herself at 7, 8, 9, and 10, respectively. She was able to make these changes by attending the singles group meetings on a regular basis, as well as other social events connected with the group. By hearing people disclose, Sarah learned that even the male members were no different from her in having problems and difficulties with which they struggled. Over time, Sarah became comfortable with relating to men on a social basis with none of her earlier anxiety symptoms.

SUMMARY

The case example illustrates how the solution-focused model can be used to identify and enlarge upon people's strengths in order to facilitate change. The chapter has suggested that solution-focused therapy can be used in combination with other helping models when the practitioner is faced with certain client problems. However, further empirical work is needed to establish how effective solution-focused therapy is both alone and in combination with other models for different populations and in different problem areas.

REFERENCES

Adams, J., Piercy, F., & Jurich, J. (1991). Effects of solution focused therapy's "formula first session task" on compliance and outcome in family therapy. *Journal of Marital and Family Therapy, 17,* 277–290.

Allgood, S., Parham, K., Salts, C., & Smith, T. (1995). The association between pretreatment change and unplanned termination in family therapy. *American Journal of Family Therapy, 23,* 195–202.

Berg, I. K. (1994). *Family-based services: A solution-focused approach.* New York: Norton.

Berg, I. K., & De Jong, P. (1996). Solution-building conversations: Co-constructing a sense of competence with clients. *Families in Society, 77,* 376–391.

Berg, I. K., & Miller, S. (1992). *Working with the problem drinker.* New York: Norton.

Cade, B., & O'Hanlon, W. H. (1993). *A brief guide to brief therapy.* New York: Norton.

Celano, M., Hazzard, A., Webb, C., & McCall, C. (1996). Treatment of traumagenic beliefs among sexually abused girls and their mothers: An evaluation study. *Journal of Abnormal Child Psychology, 24,* 1–17.

Cohen, J. A., & Mannarino, A. P. (1996). A treatment outcome study for sexually abused preschool children: Initial findings. *Journal of the American Academy of Child and Adolescent Psychiatry, 35,* 42–50.

Corcoran, J. (1998). *A solution-focused approach to group treatment with juvenile offenders.* Manuscript submitted for publication.

Corcoran, J., & Stephenson, M. (1999). *The effectiveness of solution-focused therapy with behavior-disordered children: A preliminary report.* Manuscript submitted for publication.

De Jong, P., & Berg, I. K. (1998). *Interviewing for solutions.* Pacific Grove, CA: Brooks/Cole.

De Jong, P., & Hopwood, L. E. (1996). Outcome research on treatment conducted at the brief family therapy center. In S. D. Miller, M. A. Hubble, & B. L. Duncan (Eds.), *Handbook of solution-focused brief therapy* (pp. 272–298). San Francisco: Jossey-Bass.

de Shazer, S. (1985). *Keys to solutions in brief therapy.* New York: Norton.

de Shazer, S. (1988). *Clues: Investigating solutions in brief therapy.* New York: Norton.

de Shazer, S. (1991). *Putting difference to work.* New York: Norton.

de Shazer, S. (1994). *Words were originally magic.* New York: Norton.

de Shazer, S., Berg, I. K., Lipchick, E., Nunnally, E., Molnar, A., Gingerich, W., & Weiner-Davis, M. (1986). Brief therapy: Focused solution development. *Family Process, 25,* 207–221.

Dolan, Y. (1991). *Resolving sexual abuse.* New York: Norton.

Durrant, M. (1995). *Creative strategies for school problems: Solutions for psychologists and teachers.* New York: Norton.

Durrant, M., & Kowalski, K. (1990). Overcoming the effects of sexual abuse: Developing a self-perception of competence. In M. Durrant & C. White (Eds.), *Ideas for therapy with sexual abuse* (pp. 65–109). Adelaide, Australia: Dulwich Centre Publications.

Eisikovits, Z. C., Edleson, J. L., Guttmann, E., & Sela-Amit, M. (1995). Cognitive styles and socialized attitudes of men who batter: Where should we intervene. In S. M. Smith & M. S. Straus (Eds.), *Understand partner violence* (pp. 69–76). Minneapolis: National Council on Family Relations.

Kazdin, A. E. (1997). Practitioner review: Psychosocial treatments for conduct disorder in children. *Journal of Child Psychology and Psychiatry, 38,* 161–178.

Kiser, D., Piercy, F., & Lipchick, E. (1993). The integration of emotion in solution-focused therapy. *Journal of Marital and Family Therapy, 19,* 233–242.

Larsen, D. L., Attkison, C. C., Hargreaves, W. A., & Nguyen, T. D. (1979). Assessment of client/patient satisfaction: Development of a general scale. *Evaluation and Program Planning, 2,* 197–207.

Lawson, D. (1994). Identifying pretreatment change. *Journal of Counseling and Development, 72,* 244–248.

Lee, M. Y. (1997). A study of solution-focused brief family therapy: Outcomes and issues. *American Journal of Family Therapy, 25,* 3–17.

Lindforss, L., & Magnusson, D. (1997). Solution-focused therapy in prison. *Contemporary Family Therapy, 19,* 89–104.

O'Hanlon, W. H., & Weiner-Davis, M. (1989). *In search of solutions: A new direction in psychotherapy.* New York: Norton.

Selekman, A. (1995). *Pathways to change: Brief therapy solutions with difficult adolescents.* New York: Guilford Press.

Selekman, A. (1997). *Solution-focused therapy with children.* New York: Guilford Press.

Serketich, W. J., & Dumas, J. E. (1996). The effectiveness of behavioral parent training to modify antisocial behavior in children: A meta-analysis. *Behavior Therapy, 27,* 171–186.

Sirles, E. A., Lipchick, E., & Kowalski, K. (1993). A consumer's perspective on domestic violence interventions. *Journal of Family Violence, 8,* 267–276.

Weiner-Davis, M., de Shazer, S., & Gingerich, W. J. (1987). Building on pretreatment change to construct the therapeutic solution: An exploratory study. *Journal of Marital and Family Therapy, 13,* 359–363.

White, M., & Epston, D. (1990). *Narrative means to therapeutic ends.* New York: Norton.

Zimmerman, T. S., Prest, L. A., & Wetzel, B. E. (1997). Solution-focused couples therapy groups: An empirical study. *Journal of Family Therapy, 19,* 125–144.

PART 4

Service Models for High-Risk Populations

18

The Wraparound Process

Ralph A. Brown

The child and family services system needs restructuring and renewal. Society can no longer afford to administer a system based primarily on agencies' mandates as opposed to clients' needs. Often, children's services focus on identification of children's, families', and communities' problems, rather than their respective strengths. The wraparound process (WP) offers a new approach to servicing children and families with complex needs that is based on their strengths, not their problems. The current status of traditional categorical services is unacceptable; changes must occur in light of ever-shrinking resources, particularly if the system is to have an impact on children (VanDenBerg & Grealish, 1996a). Efforts to reform services for children and their families are shifting away from restrictive treatment options (e.g., out-of-home care, ranging from foster care to residential treatment) toward the development of comprehensive community-based systems of care or individualized service initiatives (Burchard & Schaefer, 1992; Friedman, 1993; Tighe & Brooks, 1995; VanDenBerg, 1993; Yoe, Santarcangelo, Atkins, & Burchard, 1996). A system of care is "a comprehensive spectrum of mental health and other necessary services which are organized into a coordinated network to meet multiple and changing needs of severely emotionally disturbed children and adolescents" (Stroul & Friedman, 1986, p. iv).

Wraparound is a process; it is not a program or a type of service. The WP is conceptualized as an integral component within a system of care for the provision of individualized services for children with complex needs.

The system of care is a "philosophy about the way in which services should be delivered to children and their families" (Stroul & Friedman, 1986, p. iv); the system should be child-centered and community-based rather than driven by agency mandate or function. The system of care stresses that services should be comprehensive, individualized, and least restrictive. Families should be full participants in planning and service delivery. Service integration, case management, early identification and intervention, advocacy, and sensitivity to individual differences are key elements. (Brown & Hill, 1996, p. 37)

The WP is consistent with the move toward systems of care and represents an individualized approach to service that can enhance the overall benefits of a system of care (Rosenblatt, 1996). The term *wraparound process* refers to a specific set of principles and practices for developing individualized service plans for families with children with complex needs, based on their strengths (VanDenBerg & Grealish, 1996a). Rosenblatt (1996) has called the WP "one of the most attractive packages for children with multi-system needs" (p. 114).

WRAPAROUND HISTORY

There have been several influences that have shaped the development of wraparound services in North America. VanDenBerg (personal communication, November, 1998) credits the L'Arche movement for developing the values and principles that came to guide the WP. L'Arche, which was created in 1964 by Jean Vanier, is an international federation of small communities in which people with developmental disabilities live, work, pray, and share their lives with those who assist them (L'Arche, 1999). L'Arche emphasizes a sense of community and sharing among vulnerable peoples, particular those with disabilities. Similar to the WP, L'Arche is predicated on the values of independence, competence, choice, involvement, and decision making by all participants, and the emphasis on people's strengths rather than their weaknesses, regardless of the severity of their disabilities.

An early precursor to wraparound was the Kaleidoscope program in Chicago, which, in 1975, under the direction of Karl Dennis, began to provide individualized services to youth and families. One of the most important developments that facilitated the evolution of wraparound was the Alaska Youth Initiative. In 1985, the state of Alaska was one of the first to implement the Child and Adolescent Service System Program. The Alaska program, with leadership from John VanDenBerg, focused its efforts on returning children and youth from out-of-state institutions to community-based services within Alaska.

The label of 'wraparound' to describe a method of individualization and linkages to community was first used by Dr. Lenore Behar in 1986 (VanDenBerg, 1999). In North Carolina, a class action lawsuit pertaining to youths denied treatment precipitated a survey to identify similar children throughout the state (Behar, 1986). One finding from the survey indicated that these children's needs overlapped almost all agencies. Based on this finding, Behar (1986) observed that a child could benefit not only from individualized services within the treatment system but also from additional services (e.g., day treatment, respite care, and vocational training) that "wrapped around" the child.

A number of projects have influenced the evolution of wraparound. Naomi Tannen has worked with emotionally disturbed children and their families in New York and Vermont to develop systems of care that are responsive to families' needs and strengths (VanDenBerg, in press). The Vermont Wraparound Care Initiative is an exemplary program focused on preventing out-of-home placements and encouraging community-based services for children and adolescents experiencing severe emotional or behavioral difficulties (Yoe et al., 1996). In West Virginia, Mary Grealish and other staff of The Pressley Ridge Schools have worked to implement the WP in rural and urban therapeutic foster care (VanDenBerg, 1999).

TARGET POPULATION

One could argue that the principles and approaches of the WP are applicable to any child and family. However, throughout North America, proponents of WP have focused on children and families with complex needs. The phrase "children and families with complex needs" describes families who have "needs in many life areas which, if not met, may have a dramatic negative effect on the quality of life of the family" (VanDenBerg & Grealish, 1996a, p. 3). Often, children in these families are at risk of being removed from the home and the community to residential or institutional treatment inside or outside their communities (Duchnowski & Friedman, cited in VanDenBerg & Grealish, 1996a).

There are a number of reasons for focusing on children and families with complex needs. First, these children and families often are the most challenging for service providers and other community members. Second, the costs associated with the number and diversity of interventions with these families can be extensive, and prevention or reduction in length of out-of-home care is often a goal of the WP. Third, it is often easier for communities to attract service providers and funders to focus on and come together about children and families with complex needs. Although the target population for the WP is children and families with complex needs, the focus is on strengths rather than problems, deficits, and diagnostic labels. Wraparound service providers identify a child's and family's "unmet needs" as the intervention target.

VALUES UNDERPINNING WRAPAROUND

Three core values, compassion, voice and choice, and integration, drive the WP at the individual and community level (VanDenBerg & Grealish, 1998). Compassion emphasizes the dignity of children and their families receiving services. The central component of this value stresses nonblaming:

WP accomplishes this by focusing on the child and family's strengths and assets, not their problems. The process also focuses on how to support each child and family in as normalized a way as possible by ensuring access to ongoing supports in their local community, rather than creating dependence on more time-limited, government-funded programs. (Brown & Debicki, in press)

The value of voice and choice guides workers in listening to children and families about what they think they need and what will be helpful. This value calls for individualized services for each client, "rather than trying to fit families into programs that are the same for everybody, or 'one size fits all' " (Brown & Debicki, in press). A central component of individualizing services is service flexibility; practitioners must build services around the child and family, rather than slotting the child and family into categorical services.

The value of integration ensures that service providers and the service system combine both formal and informal services and supports for families. Services should be family-centered, not agency-centered, and emphasis should be placed on the use of informal services and supports rather than on formal programs.

PRINCIPLES AND CRITICAL ELEMENTS IN THE WP

The following principles and critical elements flow from the above values and underlie the WP. These principles should be used as benchmarks for a community to determine if it is delivering the WP. The author participated with community colleagues in Ontario in the early stages of the development of these principles. Later, the author, in collaboration with community colleagues, used these principles as a basis for designing an evaluation of the impact of the WP in Ontario (Brown & Debicki, in press).

COMMUNITY OWNERSHIP

The WP will be owned by and be reflective of the broader community, including formal and informal services, religious and spiritual groups, diverse cultural groups, business associations, service clubs, neighborhoods, churches, municipal politicians, law enforcement agencies, advocates, and parents.

COMMUNITY-BASED

The WP will be based in the community. Services and supports provided to each child and their family will be made available in the local community.

When residential treatment or hospitalization is accessed, these service modalities will be used as resources and not just as placements that operate outside of the plan produced by the child and family team (see Central Components of the WP).

INDIVIDUALIZED PLANS

Each plan will be individualized to a particular child and family. Each plan will encompass two or more areas (e.g., home, school, work, and community) of a family's life.

STRENGTH-BASED

The plan will be developed based on the strengths of the child and family (not their deficits) and the resources available through their individual child and family team. No interventions will be allowed in the plan that do not have matching child, family, or community strengths.

ACCESS, VOICE, AND OWNERSHIP

Children and families involved in the WP will have the opportunity to access services through the community effort regardless of their personal circumstances. In addition, children and families will be involved in all aspects of the development of their plan.

COLLABORATION

The WP requires system collaboration. It will be implemented through multiple involvement of and resourcing by both formal and informal systems such that planning, services, and supports cut across traditional system boundaries.

INFORMAL RESOURCES OR COMMUNITY SUPPORTS

It is important that the services and supports written into the child and family's plan will be available on a continuous basis in the community over time and for as long as they are needed by the child and family. The use of informal services will be maximized as much as possible so that the plan is sustainable, especially when formal services are no longer available to or needed by the child and family.

ACCESS TO FLEXIBLE FUNDING

The wraparound team for each child and family will have access to some funding that is not attached to a formal or categorical service. Some level of flexible funding is necessary to promote individualization in the wraparound plan for the child and family.

UNCONDITIONAL SUPPORT

Each client family is entitled to unconditional support. When things do not go well, the child and family are not blamed or excluded from receiving services; rather, the individualized services and supports will be changed.

MEASURABLE OUTCOMES

Outcomes must be observable and measured. Each wraparound plan for client families will identify individualized outcome goals. Together, families and service providers will identify goals and will determine the extent to which they have achieved these goals.

INCLUSIVITY

The initiative to implement the WP will be inclusive. Subject to the client family's approval, any sector, group, or part of the local community will be welcome to play a role in the WP.

CENTRAL COMPONENTS OF THE WP

THE COMMUNITY TEAM

Many communities that attempt to integrate the WP within their service delivery system develop a community team to guide and manage the implementation of the process. The people who control access to formal and informal services and supports within that community comprise this team. As identified above, "community ownership" is one of the principles and critical elements in the WP. Thus, a community team might commonly consist of representatives from community advocacy groups (including parents and youth), public and private agencies, schools, the business community, faith communities, universities and colleges, service clubs, neighborhoods, municipal government, and law enforcement agencies. It is

critical that a community team prevents its functioning from being dominated by agency and professional stakeholders. For a community team to
be successful, it must include a significant number of parents, youth, and
former consumers of service (Brown & Debicki, in press; VanDenBerg &
Grealish, 1996a).

Specifically, a community team ensures the following tasks are addressed
in the community: (1) definition of the target population; (2) establishment
of a mechanism for referral into the WP; (3) training of a pool of wraparound facilitators; (4) development of flexible funding; (5) creation of a
subcommittee to review wraparound plans; (6) development of a technical
assistance team—a small group of people who are responsible for training
and consultation to support the ongoing delivery and evaluation of the
WP; (7) involvement of parents, past consumers of service, and older youth
in all aspects of the initiative; and (8) measurement of outcomes at the
child and family team level and at the community level. (For detail about
these activities, see Brown & Debicki, in press.)

WRAPAROUND COORDINATOR AND FACILITATORS

The communities that have implemented the WP more quickly have allocated funding for a wraparound coordinator who is in a neutral position
relative to individual community agencies. The community team would
hire this person. The community refers potential wraparound clients
through the coordinator, who, in collaboration with the community team or
a subcommittee of the community team, determines eligibility and assigns
children and families to a wraparound facilitator. The coordinator also
manages a cross-agency pool of flexible funds that are used to support
individual wraparound plans.

Wraparound facilitators work directly with individual children and families. Given that the approach of the WP may be new in most communities,
it is important to develop a pool of trained wraparound facilitators. The
training equips these staff with the values and skills inherent in the WP.
Some communities have acquired funding to support full-time wraparound
facilitators. In other communities, social service agencies have freed up
their staff a half day per week to act as facilitators to manage one or two
wraparound cases. The latter type of arrangement has proven to be a
challenge for some communities; participants (staff, agencies, and the community team) need to protect the facilitator's time so that wraparound
work is not an addition to a full-time workload. The duties and functions
of the wraparound facilitator are described in the following subsections.

STRENGTHS DISCOVERY/STRENGTHS "CHAT"

Once a wraparound facilitator has been assigned to a child and family, his
or her first task is to conduct a strengths discovery. One of the distinguishing

characteristics of the WP pertains to the focus on children's and families' strengths. Historically, much direct practice in the helping professions, including social work, has taken a deficit-based approach. Professional schools often train practitioners to seek out and identify clients' "problems" and "weaknesses." Some assessment and intervention models emphasize the need to identify the barriers that prevent clients from improving their life circumstances. Identification of these barriers can range from individual deficits to oppressive structures within society and within existing social policies. If helping approaches remain focused only on examining and removing these barriers, one could argue that the treatment planning is deficit-based. It should be stressed, however, that a strengths approach does not mean that the problems of the child and family are ignored (VanDenBerg & Grealish, 1996a).

A strengths discovery forms a central piece in developing a wraparound plan with a child and family. The purpose of the strengths discovery is to learn about the family's strengths, values, preferences, and culture. This process usually involves the wraparound facilitator having a conversation (a "strengths chat") with the family. This chat sometimes includes friends, relatives, or professionals who are involved with the family. A strengths chat should help the family identify resources, values and preferences, and admirable qualities (VanDenBerg & Grealish, 1996a). The focus is on asking the family what works for them and what their "best qualities" are. For example, the wraparound facilitator might ask the mother what her best qualities as a mother are.

FORMATION OF A CHILD AND FAMILY TEAM

After the wraparound facilitator conducts the strengths chat with the child and family, the next step is to form a child and family team. One must stress the value of ownership; this is the *family's* child and family team, rather than the professionals' team. The facilitator asks the family to identify who they know could assist in addressing the family's needs. These people could be neighbors or relatives and the professionals involved in their lives (e.g., child welfare or children's mental health workers). A child and family team usually consists of between 4 to 10 people who know the child and family best, including the child and family members. No more than half of the team may be comprised of professionals; the remainder of the team members must represent the family and informal services. Formal services are those services or programs that are time-limited and government-funded (e.g., child welfare, education, children's mental health, child care, and young offender services). Informal services are those services, supports, and strategies that are available in a neighborhood or community over time (e.g., churches, businesses, other families, cultural groups, leagues and teams, unions, volunteer networks, recreation services, service clubs, and youth groups).

DEVELOPMENT OF THE WRAPAROUND PLAN

Once the family has identified the composition of the child and family team, the wraparound facilitator pulls together the members of the team for a meeting with the family. After a brief review of the results of the strengths chat, the team begins to address the wraparound plan. The plan must be family-centered, and the caregivers must have ownership of the plan. The plan must be based on the unique strengths, resources, values, norms, and preferences of the child and family, as identified in the strengths discovery. A central precept of the WP stresses that people who experience needs are usually the best people to define the needs (VanDenBerg, Grealish, & Debicki, 1998).

Plans address family life domain areas that include living situation, financial, educational or vocational, social or recreational, behavioral or emotional, psychological, health, legal, cultural, and safety. These life domain areas provide a central framework within which a child and family team can build a wraparound plan. The facilitator asks all team members to assess needs in each life domain. Subsequently, the team identifies the two or three most important life domains that require attention. Some teams simply collectively prioritize the life domains in order of importance, whereas others vote on each life domain. In either case, the wraparound facilitator ensures that the family has the key note (e.g., by giving them veto power or more votes). The next step involves brainstorming options to meet the family's identified needs. Finally, the team assigns tasks, roles, and responsibilities for addressing these needs, as well as a time frame within which to meet these needs.

In developing the plan, it is critical that a backup plan be identified in the event the original plan meets with some challenges and difficulties. Also, it is essential that the team ensures that there is a crisis plan available. The ideal plan has no more than 25% formal, or funded, resources. Although the plan must include a balance of categorical services (i.e., existing funded traditional services or programs) and informal community family resources, informal supports are deemed more relevant to families because they last longer and are less costly (VanDenBerg & Grealish, 1996b, 1996c). To ensure that the plan is consistent with the wraparound values, beliefs, and assumptions, the plan must demonstrate evidence of addressing the 11 principles and critical elements described above. To ensure the integrity of the use of the WP and to ensure that the plan adequately and appropriately addresses all child protection or community safety concerns, a third party, usually a subcommittee of the community team, reviews the plan.

IMPLEMENTATION OF THE PLAN

As indicated above, to provide a context for implementing a wraparound plan, the child and family team needs to ensure that the implementation addresses over time the 11 critical elements and principles. For example, as the team implements the plan, it needs to remind itself that the client family's needs drive the plan. It is critical to reemphasize that throughout the implementation of the plan the partnership among client families, informal resources, and service providers is central. This process is necessary to guarantee program fidelity. It is necessary to check and document that interventions are consistent with the values and beliefs of the WP.

Within this context, the child and family team meets periodically (usually every few weeks) to review progress in implementation of the wraparound plan and to make any necessary adjustments based on the client family's needs (VanDenBerg & Grealish, 1996a). It is important to incorporate in this review the initial goals identified by the team and some indication of ongoing outcomes (i.e., to what extent the team is achieving these goals). This review may require adjustments to the initial goals and strategies or the formulation of new goals and strategies. It is not unusual for a child and family team to go through several plans over the course of a number of months.

CASE EXAMPLE[1]

The following case example provides an overview of the WP up to and including the development of the wraparound plan.

BACKGROUND INFORMATION

At the time of referral to the Anywhere Residential Treatment Center (ARTC), Ben was an 11-year-old male only child of a single mother, Mary. Mary had quit high school at the age of 17 to live with Jerry, Ben's father. She was 3 months' pregnant and subsequently delivered Ben 2 months prematurely. She and Jerry moved away from their families to Anywhere, 5 hours away, where Jerry obtained a position as an apprentice electrician.

Ben was a very cranky baby and as a toddler was into everything. His father, Jerry, was not ready for parenthood and regularly beat Ben when he misbehaved, or locked him in a closet. When Mary tried to intervene, they argued until Jerry became enraged and began to hit her. When Ben was 7, Jerry beat Mary so badly that she was hospitalized. With her minister's help, she decided to leave Jerry.

Unfortunately, leaving Jerry meant leaving the family home that they had bought with money saved from Jerry's job. Consequently, Mary moved into subsidized housing on social assistance. Because she had not completed high school, she could not find employment. As Ben's emotional/behavioral needs became more complex, other parents in the housing complex increasingly isolated Mary.

Ben has always been a difficult child. The difficulties emerged when he entered the educational system. He had frequent and severe temper tantrums as a toddler. He experienced aggression toward peers and adults within the school environment. He has had no significant friendships. He does not initiate interactions appropriately with his peers at school or in the neighborhood. Instead, Ben will often grab other children by the throat and tell them he wants them to be his friend. Nor does it help him to ingratiate himself with their parents. His mother has become totally fed up with dealing with irate parents and generally feels ashamed in the process.

The school placed Ben in a segregated classroom for children with emotional/behavioral problems 4 years ago. The school is not planning reintegration into mainstream education soon. The school repeatedly suspended Ben for progressively longer periods for his defiant and aggressive behavior. Over the years, Ben has received individual and group therapy, and Ben and Mary have attended family therapy a number of times—all to no avail. Recently, when the school sent him home, he became aggressive toward his mother.

REFERRAL

The school personnel recommended to Mary that Ben needs an out-of-home placement and probably long-term treatment in the ARTC. Both they and Mary don't know what else to do. Mary took Ben to the ARTC and told them her story. The intake worker, Colleen, suggested that a referral to the WP might be a more helpful step than placing Ben in an out-of-home placement for long-term residential treatment. Mary agreed to try it; Kate became Mary's wraparound facilitator.

STRENGTHS DISCOVERY

Kate met with Mary and Ben in their home. She did a strengths inventory and discovered the following about Mary. Despite the current conflict, Mary is very committed to staying together with Ben as a family. Mary loves to read and watch educational television shows and is an incredible cook. She is a great budgeter and has learned to make do on the little money she receives on social assistance. She is very giving with others and has attended church since she was a young child. Currently, she attends an inner-city church that has a strong community outreach component.

Kate found Ben to be an enjoyable child on a one-to-one basis. He opened up to Kate when he discovered how well he could beat her at computer games, something at which he is very good. Ben is very strong-willed (as his teachers will attest) and usually follows through with things that he commits to doing. He is eager to play sports but has not been given the opportunity, given his acting out behavior. Ben would very much like to have one special friend, as he often feels very lonely. Kate found Ben's room to be neat and clean, and, when asked, Mary stated that Ben could be very helpful around the house.

CONFIGURING A CHILD AND FAMILY TEAM

When asked who is, has, or could be a support to them, Mary identified the following group of people, who subsequently agreed to be on their wraparound team. Mary said that Ernie, the minister at the church with whom she has developed a relationship, was helpful. Mary had developed a strong friendship with a woman, Wendy, who lives in the housing complex. Wendy has two teenage sons who are active in basketball and baseball. Joe, the child and youth worker from Ben's class, agreed to join the team, as did Colleen, the intake worker from ARTC. Ernie nominated the youth group leader, Alex, who also agreed to be on the team.

DEVELOPMENT OF THE WRAPAROUND PLAN

Over the next month, the wraparound team helped Ben and Mary to identify their major needs and to develop a plan to meet these needs. The first step was to consider all the life domain areas within which Ben and Mary had unmet needs. This included social, recreational, crisis/safety, emotional, behavioral, educational, and vocational areas. In consultation with their team, Ben and Mary picked three life domain areas to focus on in the development of their plan. These were (1) a blend of educational and crisis/safety, for Ben; (2) education, for Mary; and (3) social/recreational, for Ben. Following this, the team helped Ben and Mary to identify the top need in each life domain that would have the greatest positive impact on their lives. The following specific needs were identified:

1. Ben needed to succeed within the segregated classroom. This would lead to reintegration in the mainstream educational system. In order to do this, plans for crisis/safety were needed.
2. Mary needed to go back to school part-time to work toward her high school diploma. This would enable her to get a job to support herself and Ben.
3. Ben needed to develop at least one peer friendship. This would help meet his social/recreational needs.

Once these needs were prioritized, the team considered the strengths and resources of the family, the community, and the team in order to develop a detailed plan. The following plan was developed for each of the identified needs.

Plan for Need #1

In order to deal with crisis/safety issues and optimize the likelihood for Ben to have a successful experience in the classroom, the following proactive strategies were developed.

1. Joe will develop a motivational plan within the classroom to build on Ben's strength with computer games and his sports interest.
2. If Ben begins to feel angry, he will be allowed to leave the classroom and go outside to do some chores for cash. Joe will arrange this with the caretaker at the school.
3. If Ben chooses not to do this, the principal has agreed that Joe will spend time with Ben on a one-to-one basis to help Ben resolve the issue that is upsetting him.

In addition, the following reactive strategies were developed to address this need.

1. If Ben becomes aggressive, Joe will take him home to cool off for the rest of the day.
2. If Ben needs to be taken home, Joe will go to Ben's home the next morning to resolve the issue with Ben before bringing him back to school.
3. If Ben becomes out of control at school or at home, the police will be called to help ensure safety. Colleen obtained approval from ARTC's director to admit Ben for 24 hours in such a circumstance. Again, depending on with whom the aggression occurred (e.g., Joe or Mary), the person involved will come to ARTC to resolve the issue with Ben before he returns home or to school. In developing this strategy, the team realized that it would be important to have a police department youth officer as an ex-officio member of the wraparound team. They subsequently asked one to join the team.

The team agreed that the desired outcome for this first need would be for the physical aggression at home and at school to cease and for the amount of time out of the segregated classroom to decrease over time. Joe and Mary will chart Ben's progress within these two areas on a daily basis for review at the wraparound team meetings.

Plan for Need #2

The following strategies were developed to support Mary in her goal to attend school part-time to work on her high school diploma.

1. Ernie will help Mary get into an adult education program. Mary initially will work on one course until she feels ready to try two at a time.

2. Ernie will tutor Mary if she needs help in any subject she takes.
3. Wendy will take Ben to her house one evening a week to play sports with her two teenage boys to allow time for Mary to study. Wendy also offered to take Ben if he is returned home from school early due to aggression or defiance.
4. In exchange for Wendy's help, Mary will cook supper for Wendy, her two sons, and Ben. Mary will take supper to Wendy's in advance on evenings that Ben spends time there.

The team agreed that the desired outcome is for Mary to earn her high school diploma. They will measure this by the number of courses she completes. Kate will check with Mary every few weeks to ensure that she is getting enough time to do her schoolwork on a regular basis.

Plan for Need #3

The following strategies were developed to help Ben meet his need for peer friendship.

1. Alex, the youth group leader, will have Ben help him set up for the youth group he runs every Sunday night at the church. In exchange, he will play basketball or baseball with Ben (for at least a half hour) until the group begins. Initially, Ben will not attend the youth group.
2. Joe, Alex, and Ernie will each provide Ben one-to-one instruction on how to initiate play appropriately and how to share.
3. Ben will practice these skills in his play with Alex, as well as in his play with Wendy's two sons when he at their house.
4. When the team thinks that he has had sufficient practice in initiating play and sharing, Ben will join the youth group. Alex will ask one peer with similar interests as Ben's to pair up with Ben with the hope that, with support, they may become friends over time. If this strategy does not work with that peer, Alex will try it with another.

The team agreed that the desired outcome is for Ben to develop appropriate skills with which to initiate play and eventually to share in playing with another peer. The adults involved in this strategy will measure this through direct observation.

RESEARCH AND EVALUATION CHALLENGES

The proponents of the wraparound approach argue that measuring outcomes is essential for sound practice.

If you don't measure the results of your wraparound process efforts, you never really prove that what you are doing actually works. If you don't measure the results of your efforts, your innovations are forever classified as "fads." Most programs or communities never measure the outcomes of their system innovations. It is no longer enough to just know in our hearts that what we are doing is effective: we must measure what we do. Unfortunately, very few innovations are ever evaluated. (VanDenBerg & Grealish, 1998, p. 77)

Unfortunately, these same proponents do not provide sufficient direction for measuring effectiveness. One recent wraparound training manual devotes only 3 out 110 pages to consider outcome measurement. This may be one reason that there has not been sufficient evaluation studies to determine the effectiveness of the wraparound approach.

Another reason for the lack of evaluation efforts with wraparound may be related to the newness of this approach. In a discussion about systems of care (within which the WP is a component), Stroul, McCormick, and Zaro (1996) observe: "[B]ecause systems of care are fairly recent innovations, evaluation and research efforts related to them are in early stages of development" (p. 333).

The author is the principal investigator in an ongoing evaluation of the WP in eight communities in Ontario. This research project has two components: (1) an examination if practice will change in response to WP training, and (2) an evaluation of the impact of wraparound with families and children. For families with children (0–18 years) with complex needs, the study is measuring the following variables: child psychosocial functioning, child emotional and behavioral strengths, child and family functioning, level of out-of-home placement intrusiveness, service history, and client satisfaction. The research design is a combination of randomization and matched comparison. (For more information about this study, see Brown & Debicki, in press, or contact the author.)

One challenge in conducting this type of community-based research pertains to the different objectives and perspectives that practitioners and researchers bring to the task. Practitioners are focused on the service delivery and the lobbying of funding sources to provide resources to support the continued wraparound effort. Researchers focus their attention on documenting and accounting for the effectiveness of the wraparound initiative. Although the practitioners' and researchers' objectives are not mutually exclusive, in order to integrate intervention and research initiatives, a high degree of cooperation is necessary among practitioners, community partners, funders, and researchers. It has been an exciting challenge in our current research initiative to ensure that each of these stakeholders actively participates and influences the research. Others wishing to provide wraparound services and to evaluate this process may benefit from attending to this challenge.

The strength-based focus of wraparound creates another interesting challenge for service providers and researchers alike. In our current research effort, we have been struck by the lack of strength-focused evaluation instruments. Most evaluation instruments available in the field could be considered deficit- or problem-based. These instruments tend to identify struggles and conflicts children and families experience, and often they slot children and families into categories that determine a diagnostic label. Wraparound facilitators report a value conflict when they ask families to identify their strengths, then ask families to complete questionnaires that seemingly focus on problems and deficits. One exception that we have found and that we are using in our study is the Behavioral and Emotional Rating Scale (Epstein & Sharma, 1997), which measures the emotional and behavioral strengths of children and adolescents.

A CRITIQUE OF THE WP

STRENGTHS

In many respects, the WP appears simply to represent good social work practice. Concepts that the WP incorporates have been included within traditional social work teaching and practice. Both wraparound and traditional social work practice value an approach to working with clients that is collaborative and focused on strengths and empowerment. Similarly, both the WP and social work practice value community-based practice, as well as coordination and cooperation among programs, services, and agencies.

The WP is compatible with many other practice approaches and theoretical perspectives that are common in social work practice. It shares with feminist theory (e.g., Valentich, 1984) an emphasis on a nonexpert approach and equality in a helping relationship wherein both the practitioner and the client are treated with dignity and respect. The WP shares with empowerment theory (Gutierrez & Rappaport, cited in Hancock, 1997) an emphasis on "accepting the client's definition of the problem; identifying and building upon existing strengths; teaching specific skills; and finally, mobilizing resources and advocating for the client" (p. 235). The WP also has much in common with solution-focused, narrative, and other approaches that are influenced by social constructionism. Similar to these approaches, the WP deemphasizes reliance on professional experts as the only source of knowledge. Also, the WP emphasizes the construction of meaning and the social context. In particular, the WP alerts social workers to the fact that they cannot assume their contexts, realities, and experiences are the same as those of their clients.

WEAKNESSES

On a less positive note, one could argue that wraparound's call for changes to the structure and funding of social services, as well as its emphasis on informal supports, could be used to rationalize recent, regressive social policy trends in North America. Restructuring with regard to service delivery and funding has been used as a guise for cutting funding levels to social services. Similarly, money saved through deinstitutionalization and closing of residential facilities is often not funneled into community-based services. As Aronson and Neysmith (1997) have pointed out, "The suggestion in the efficiency-driven policy discourse that costs have been or can be better managed and cut out is, in large part, a deception. Many are not eliminated but, rather, shifted to the 'community'—a euphemistic and insubstantial concept" (p. 42). Although there is the potential to use the WP to rationalize funding and service cuts, it should be noted that this would not be supported by proponents of the WP.

Another weakness of the WP, noted above, is the lack of an empirical base for its effectiveness. Rosenblatt (1996) notes that research to date on the WP is limited by small sample sizes and methodological problems. He concludes that more and better designed evaluation studies are needed to ascertain its effectiveness.

SUMMARY

The wraparound process is offering something new. From a practice context, the WP has the potential for mobilizing formal and informal resources to help meet the needs of children and families that they identify. The WP described in this chapter places the child and family at the center of the service delivery system. It encourages all stakeholders, including the family, to participate in making the lives of social work clients better. In the author's experience, in communities in which the WP is occurring, there is a sense of hopefulness and excitement in service delivery, even within the context of downsizing and realignment of services. Families and service providers alike are experiencing this positive energy. The WP has been a vehicle to bring partners (i.e., families, individual agencies, individual workers, and funders) together to plan and move services forward.

NOTE

[1]The author wishes to thank Andrew Debicki, manager of Program Services, Lynwood Hall Child and Family Centre, Hamilton, Ontario, Canada, for supplying the wraparound case example for this chapter.

REFERENCES

Aronson, J. & Neysmith, S. (1997). The retreat of the state and long-term care provision: Implications for frail elderly people, unpaid family carers and paid home care workers. *Studies in Political Economy, 53,* 37–66.

Behar, L. (1986). A state model for child and mental health services: The North Carolina experience. *Children Today, 15*(3), 16–21.

Brown, R. A., & Debicki, A. (in press). The wraparound process: Strength-based practice. In M. Callahan (Ed.), *Valuing the field: International perspectives.* Southhampton, England: Ashgate Press.

Brown, R. A., & Hill, B. A. (1996). Opportunity for change: Exploring an alternative to residential treatment. *Child Welfare, 25,* 35–57.

Burchard, J. D., & Schaefer, M. (1992). Public mental health services for children and families and graduate training in psychology: Bridging the gap. In M. Kessler, S. E. Goldston, & J. M. Joffe (Eds.), *The present and future of prevention: In honor of George W. Albee* (pp. 138–154). Newbury Park, CA: Sage.

Debicki, A., Simpson, K., Pouyat, S., Nicoloff, N., McClure, C., Prendergast, L., & Finlayson, B. (1998). Wraparound Ontario eh! Representatives of seven Ontario communities describe practice change, lessons learned, and the challenges of implementing the wraparound process in Ontario, Canada. *Child and Family: A Journal of the Notre Dame Child and Family Institute, 2*(2), 3–15.

Epstein, M. H., & Sharma, J. (1997). *Behavioral and emotional rating scale: A strength-based approach to assessment.* Austin, TX: PRO-ED.

Friedman, R. M. (1993). Preparation of students to work with children and families: Is it meeting the need? *Administration and Policy in Mental Health, 20*(4), 297–310.

Hancock, M. R. (1997). *Principles of social work practice: A generic practice approach.* New York: Haworth.

L'Arche. (1999). *What is L'Arche?* (available online: www.larchecanada.org/aaccueil.html).

Lourie, I. S., Katz-Leavy, J., & Stroul, B. A. (1996). Individualized services in a system of care. In B. A. Stroul (Ed.), *Children's mental health: Creating systems of care in a changing society* (pp. 429–452). Baltimore: Brookes.

Pozatek, E. (1994). The problem of certainty: Clinical social work in the postmodern era. *Social Work, 39,* 396–403.

Rosenblatt, A. (1996). Bows and ribbons, tape and twine: Wrapping the wraparound process for children with multi-system needs. *Journal of Child and Family Studies, 5,* 101–117.

Stroul, B. A., & Friedman, R. M. (1986). *A system of care for severely emotionally disturbed children and youth.* Washington, DC: Child and Adolescent Service System Program Technical Assistance Center, Georgetown University Child Development Center.

Stroul B. A., McCormick, M., & Zaro, S. M. (1996). Measuring outcomes in systems of care. In B. A. Stroul (Ed.), *Children's mental health: Creating systems of care in a changing society* (pp. 313–336). Baltimore: Brookes.

Tighe, T. A., & Brooks, T. (1995). Evaluating individualized services in Vermont: Intensity and patterns of services, costs, and financing. In C. Liberton, K. Kutash, & R. Friedman (Eds.), *The 7th annual research conference proceedings, a system of care for children's mental health, expanding the research base* (pp. 47–52). Tampa: Florida Mental Health Institute.

Valentich, M. (1984). Feminism and social work practice. In F. J.Turner (Ed.), *Social work treatment: Interlocking theoretical perspectives* (pp. 564–589). New York: The Free Press.

VanDenBerg, J. (1993). Integration of individualized mental health services into the system of care for children and adolescents. *Administration and Policy in Mental Health, 20,* 247–257.

VanDenBerg, J. (1999). History of the wraparound process. In B. J. Burns & S. Goldman (Eds.), *Promising practices wraparound for children with serious emotional disturbance and their families* (pp. 19–26). Washington, DC: Center for Effective Collaboration and Practice, American Institutes of Research.

VanDenBerg, J., & Grealish, E. M. (1996a). Individualized services and supports through the wraparound process: Philosophy and procedures. *Journal of Child and Family Studies, 5,* 7–21.

VanDenBerg, J., & Grealish, E. M. (1996b). *The wraparound process: Balancing informal and formal resources* (handout). Burlington, Ontario: Wraparound Process Training.

VanDenBerg, J., & Grealish, E. M. (1996c). *What is the wraparound process?* (handout). Burlington, Ontario: Wraparound Process Training.

VanDenBerg, J., & Grealish, E. M. (1998). *The wraparound process training manual.* Pittsburgh, PA: The Community Partnerships Group.

VanDenBerg, J., Grealish, E. M., & Debicki, A. (1998). *The wraparound process and the development of a wraparound plan video.* Hamilton, Ontario: The Community Partnership Group and Lynwood Hall Child and Family Centre.

Yoe, J. T., Santarcangelo, S., Atkins, M., & Burchard, J. D. (1996). Wraparound care in Vermont: Program development, implementation, and evaluation of a statewide system of individualized services. *Journal of Child and Family Studies, 5,* 23–29.

19

Family Preservation Services

Scottye J. Cash

Family preservation services (FPS) focus on short-term, intensive, in-home services to families to help avoid the unnecessary placement of children in out-of-home care. Although FPS have been used predominantly with child welfare clients, they have been adapted for use with juvenile justice (e.g., Henggeler & Borduin, 1995) and children's mental health (e.g., Seelig, Goldman-Hall, & Jerrell, 1992) clients. This chapter provides an overview of FPS in the field of child welfare, with a primary focus on the most prevalent model of these types of services—the Homebuilders model (Kinney, Haapala, & Booth, 1991).

CHARACTERISTICS AND PRINCIPLES OF FAMILY PRESERVATION SERVICES

FPS began to develop as a response to the concern that a large number of children were being placed in foster care with little hope of ever being reunified with their families (Lindsey, 1994). The Homebuilders program and other FPS were developed with the intention of doing whatever it takes to avoid unnecessary out-of-home placements of children. Despite this emphasis, proponents of FPS recognize that "some placements will always be necessary because some families will never be able to raise their own children safely and productively" (Kinney et al., 1991, p. 9).

FPS were designed to be delivered very differently than traditional child welfare services. The defining features of FPS are that they are (1) home-based and directed at the entire family; (2) crisis-oriented (available 24 hours a day, 7 days a week); (3) time-limited (4 to 6 weeks in the Homebuilders model compared to 6 months in other models); (4) intensive (10 hours per week or more—hence, caseloads are small); (5) community-oriented and focused on building families' connections with formal and informal resources; and (6) focused on client strengths, self-determination, and empowerment (Kinney et al., 1991; Schuerman, Rzepnicki, & Littell, 1994).

Certain principles and values of FPS differentiate them from traditional services and change the ways that workers perceive and work with clients. The following principles and values underlie the Home-builders model (Kinney et al., 1991) and are an integral part of most family preservation services.

1. *It is the worker's job to instill hope.* Many clients who come to the attention of FPS have been involved in the social service system for long periods of time. Many of these clients have experienced multiple stressors and losses, and many have had negative experiences with professionals and the system. A sense of hopelessness is often the result for such clients. Consequently, this principle asserts that one of the prime responsibilities of family preservation workers is to instill hope in their clients, particularly by recognizing and pointing out strengths and resiliency. This might involve demonstrating to clients that they can have a more positive experience with the social service system and teaching them how to navigate and influence the system to better meet their needs. A corollary of this principle is that workers cannot know ahead of time if a family's situation is hopeless, and that therefore they should feel as hopeful as possible about every family they work with.

2. *Clients are our colleagues and should be given as much power as possible.* Kinney and associates (1991) contend that "clients will want to form partnerships with us if they perceive that we are trying to give them something rather than taking something away" (p. 63). Furthermore, they state that "we think clients will warm up to us and loosen up much faster if we show we are interested in and sincerely care about them" (p. 65). This principle speaks to the importance of clients' active participation in the helping process in terms of providing information and problem solving. The ultimate goal is empowerment: "[O]ur job is to help clients take control of their lives rather than to take control of their lives for them . . . that is the whole point: to empower them to handle their problems" (Kinney et al., 1991, p. 65). A corollary of this principle is that "not knowing can be valuable" (Kinney et al., 1991, p. 66). Being honest with clients about the fact that we often don't know what the solutions to problems are helps to make the work collegial and to keep the power in the hands of clients.

3. *We can do harm.* It is important to remind ourselves that good intentions don't necessarily lead to good outcomes and that we can do harm to clients. Gibbs and Gambrill (1999) argue that the "history of the helping professions demonstrates that caring is not enough

to protect people from harmful practices and to insure that they receive helpful services" (p. 5). They note that common mistakes in helping include offering the wrong types of services (e.g., offering psychological counseling when clients need material resources), withdrawing intervention too soon or continuing it too long, increasing client dependency, and overlooking client assets. This principle holds that it is imperative to evaluate our practice on an ongoing basis so that we can understand when to stop a treatment that isn't working and when to change treatments (Berlin & Marsh, 1993; Bloom, Fisher, & Orme, 1999). One strategy is to select interventions that have been found to be effective with certain populations or problems. Still, because every client is unique (with regard to culture, ethnicity, socioeconomic status, etc.), we need to factor in the unique characteristics and circumstances of each client in formulating our assessments and interventions. Furthermore, we need to check with clients regularly to be sure that our services are helpful rather than harmful.

HISTORICAL DEVELOPMENT

The impetus for the development of FPS came from a number of demonstration projects in the 1970s that focused on the problems of the child welfare system. The problems that were examined included lack of permanent placement for children who had been removed from their homes, foster care drift (i.e., multiple foster care placements for a child), and lack of tracking of children who were in the system (Lindsey, 1994). The demonstration projects found that when services were intensive, used cognitive-behavioral treatments, and involved biological families in the treatment, the children were more likely to be reunified with their biological family or experienced fewer placements (Lindsey, 1994).

FPS developed gradually in response to such child welfare demonstration projects. One particularly notable FPS, the Homebuilders program (Kinney et al., 1991), emerged in 1974 in Tacoma, Washington, and quickly gained national and international attention. The reason for this attention was the short length of service time (this was especially attractive to funding sources and legislators, as the cost-benefit ratio was much lower for the Homebuilders program than for institutional care) and success rates of 85% to 95% (Blythe, Salley, & Jayaratne, 1994). It should be noted that the success rates, although very positive, were not based on rigorous research designs (Berry, 1997; Gelles, 1996; Schuerman et al., 1994). Few studies incorporated comparison or control groups, and many studies were one group, posttest only, with placement of the child as the only dependent variable. Thus, it was difficult to establish with any certainty that FPS were more effective than traditional services.

Despite methodological shortcomings, the early research results and the impetus for providing more effective and efficient services to children at risk of being removed from the family led to the creation of new policies. The Adoption Assistance and Child Welfare Act was passed in 1980 and created a set of priorities for outcomes for children who were in the child welfare system. These priorities were ordered as follows: (1) children should be with their natural families; (2) when preservation of the family isn't possible, the next alternative is for termination of parental rights and the adoption of children; (3) legal guardianship for the child should be the next preferred outcome; and (4) if foster care is the only alternative, the placement should be long-term. Although these were the priorities as set by the federal government, monetary support to achieve these was not provided until 1993, with passage of the Family Preservation and Family Support Act (amended in 1996). This act finally provided states with the funding necessary to work toward the four priorities established in the 1980 Adoption Assistance and Child Welfare Act.

During the past decade family preservation programs have proliferated throughout North America and Australia. Although many programs have claimed to follow the Homebuilders model, few have demonstrated treatment fidelity. Instead, new programs usually modify the Homebuilders model to meet their agencies' and client populations' needs. Thus, there are now many diverse forms of FPS, some of which do not adhere to the strict time limits of the Homebuilders model, to the intensive nature of the interventions, or to the requirement that families need to be at imminent risk of child placement.

Recent research on FPS and concerns for the safety of children have led to controversy about the effectiveness of FPS and their suitability for some families (see Critique section of this chapter). Such controversy has led to some policy and program changes. On the policy end, one result of such controversy was the passing of the 1998 Safe Families Act, which decreased the waiting period for the termination of parental rights following foster care placement from 18 to 12 months. Programmatic changes that have ensued from such controversy have centered on a greater emphasis on reliable and valid assessment of familial risk (in order to determine better when the risk of child maltreatment precludes the goal of family preservation).

THEORETICAL FOUNDATIONS

FPS are based generally on an ecological model (Bronfenbrenner, 1979; Garbarino, 1991; Germain & Gitterman, 1980; Kemp, Whittaker, & Tracy, 1997; see also chapter 4) of human functioning. The ecological model provides a comprehensive way of understanding and helping families because it recognizes the interdependence between people and their environments. As Berry (1997) explains: "There are layers of interaction within ever-widening circles of the environment, much like the layers of an onion, and effective social intervention (understanding and helping) will assess the contribution of each layer to a situation and attempt to bolster or influence each layer" (p. 52). An ecological model takes into account not only the individual and interpersonal factors in a family's situation but also aspects of the social and physical environment—and the adequacy (or "goodness of fit") of the links between the family and its environment. Furthermore, the ecological model incorporates not only the risk factors present within the family and the family's environment, but also the factors that help families and exhibit resiliency. Thus, the ecological model is consistent with the strengths perspective (Cole, 1995; Saleebey, 1996; Weick & Saleebey, 1995) that has gained popularity in social work theory. The ecological model conceives the situation of a family at risk of child maltreatment as one in which the stresses and demands on a family outweigh their strengths and resources (Darmstadt, 1990; Fraser, 1997; Moncher, 1995; Thomlison, 1997). Whittaker, Schinke, and Gilchrist (1986) note that the ecological model suggests that "effective service programs and policies for children, youths, and families will be those that attend to both skill acquisition and the provision of social support" (p. 492). In keeping with the ecological perspective and the reality of poverty for many families, FPS also stress the importance of helping families to procure basic resources (e.g., shelter, food, and clothing).

Theoretical perspectives on social support and stress and coping (see chapter 4) also inform FPS. Research has established that parental stress and social isolation are factors associated with child maltreatment and out-of-home placement (Moncher, 1995; Thomlison, 1997). Social support and positive social networks have been found to be key mediating factors in a person's (or family's) ability to adapt to stressful situations and cope positively (Lovell & Richey, 1991). FPS endeavor to help families connect to sources of social support in their informal social networks not only to help them deal with their immediate concerns but also to create a safety net that they can rely on in times of crisis or need (Darmstadt, 1990; Lovell & Richey, 1991; Moncher, 1995).

FPS also draw on a wide variety of clinical theories and techniques. Foremost among these are cognitive-behavioral, client-centered, and crisis theories. A study of the interventions used by Homebuilders workers (Lewis, 1991) illustrates the use of techniques from these theories. Lewis (1991) found that there were nine core interventions used in most Homebuilders cases. Four of these "involved activities that tended to be used to establish and facilitate therapeutic relationships" (Lewis, 1991, p. 95), which is illustrative of client-centered theory. The other core techniques were clarifying problems, setting treatment goals, reframing, using reinforcements, and identifying natural consequences, which illustrates use of cognitive-behavioral and crisis theories.

PHASES OF HELPING

The description of the steps in the helping process provided in this section is adapted from the Homebuilders model (Kinney et al., 1991). Although the Homebuilders model does not use the same terminology, the description of the phases of helping in this model have been organized according to the stages in the problem-solving process (i.e., engagement, data collection and assessment, contracting and intervention, and evaluation and termination). It should be noted that due to the short-term and intensive nature of FPS, these stages of helping overlap and blend together more than in traditional counseling approaches.

ENGAGEMENT

The engagement phase involves establishing trust and forming a partnership with a family. This usually begins with the first phone call to the client, which Kinney and colleagues (1991) call "getting to know you: chitchat therapy on the phone" (p. 55). In initial phone calls workers should try to avoid direct questioning and instead actively listen to clients' concerns. The goal is to allow clients to talk about any feelings of anger and to feel understood. This helps to calm clients and lays the foundation for a positive relationship. Safety issues need to be explored, and, if there are concerns, safety plans should be established. Some negotiation about services the family would like to receive should take place, and the first face-to-face meeting should be arranged. Talking on the phone is a safe way to first meet the family and to defuse negative emotions and expectations.

The first face-to-face meeting with the family usually takes place in the family's home, but if there are concerns about safety, it is advisable to meet in a public environment, such as a restaurant. Workers should act as gracious guests in families' homes and should endeavor to put family members at ease by relating to them person-to-person (e.g., using social chitchat) before moving into a helper-helpee relationship. The goal in the first meeting is to encourage clients to tell their stories and to listen, understand, and build trust.

Inherent in forming a working partnership is the notion that social workers should actually like their clients and be able to see them as real people who are at times expert in their own lives. Kinney and colleagues (1991) outline beliefs necessary for achieving trust with families. These include that (1) there are many similarities between us and the clients we work with; (2) families are doing the best they can, and they have in the past coped with difficult situations; (3) families have optimism and inherent strengths; and (4) most of the time, family members really do care about each other.

Engagement with child welfare families can be difficult. Because of previous negative experiences, clients may find it hard to believe that a social worker views them positively and wants to form a working partnership. Nevertheless, workers need to help clients like them. In addition to maintaining positive beliefs about families, workers need to act in ways that will make families want to spend time with them and to share thoughts and feelings that make them vulnerable. The cardinal rule in the Homebuilders model is "when in doubt, listen" (Kinney et al., 1991, p. 68). (For further information on issues in and strategies for working with involuntary clients, see Kinney et al. [1991] and Rooney [1992].)

DATA COLLECTION AND ASSESSMENT

This aspect of the helping process is intertwined with the engagement process. As with the engagement process, active listening is key to data collection and assessment. Workers need to allow clients to tell their stories and to hear the whole story from each family member's point of view. Sometimes, due to family conflict, it may be best to talk with each family member individually. Kinney and colleagues (1991) describe the essence of data collection and assessment as follows:

> The priority now is understanding, withholding judgments on the specifics, trying to feel compassion, and engaging with each family member. This is imperative. The more compassion family members can feel from us, the more they will trust us. The more they trust us, the more information they will give us. The more information we have, the better the assessment we can formulate. (p. 81)

There are a number of important principles to data collection and assessment in FPS. First, workers need to check to see if they really understand what clients have told them. Second, assessments need to focus on strengths and abilities, as well as on problems and deficits. Third, assessment is an ongoing process that tracks the evolution of problems and strengths and that is continually updated until the conclusion is reached that the family is functioning satisfactorily and there is no further need for services (in the Homebuilders model, this means only that there is no longer a threat of placement) (Kinney et al., 1991).

With regard to the ongoing assessment process, Kinney and colleagues (1991) suggest a number of strategies: (1) minimize blame and labeling, (2) help the family members to reach consensus about the facts (either by clarifying very specifically about the details in question or by finding very general statements that family members can agree on), (3) help family members to interpret each other's behavior in less negative ways, and (4) define problems in terms of skill deficits—this avoids blaming individuals and implies hope about learning necessary skills.

Although Kinney and colleagues (1991) prefer natural observation and conversation to formal procedures and tests for assessment purposes, other authors have suggested integrating standardized measures into the assessment process. Pecora, Fraser, Nelson, McCrosky, and Meezan (1995) urge FPS workers to "consider the possibility of building an assessment protocol that combines demographic and clinical data with measurement of family and individual functioning" (p. 96). Toward this end, the authors suggest a number of measures that can be useful for family assessment. They also caution, however, that families should be consulted about the practicality and meaningfulness of standardized tests and that assessment of family functioning should be individualized enough to incorporate the family's specific needs, desires, and cultural values.

CONTRACTING AND INTERVENTION

Once the worker has gathered enough information to understand the family's situation and family members feel understood, the next step is to prioritize problems and goals. This contracting process involves a balance between letting the family members set their own priorities and ensuring that such priorities address important safety issues and don't contravene ethical standards. Workers also need to help families be realistic about the number of goals and the scope of the goals (i.e., small, achievable goals) that they choose to focus on. Once goals are set, workers help families to use Goal Attainment Scaling (Kiresuk & Sherman, cited in Kinney et al., 1991), so that behaviors or events are specified for each potential outcome level (e.g., a 3-point scale might specify the best, expected, and worst outcomes for a goal). The worker then reviews with family members on a weekly basis the progress on goals and helps them to make necessary adjustments to goals or strategies to achieve them.

Intervention in FPS involves helping clients not only to solve their particular problems but also to problem-solve in general. Kinney and colleagues (1991) talk of helping their clients to become "personal scientists . . . to learn to observe their problems and systematically vary ways of dealing with these problems until they come up with one that fits for them" (p. 93). They also specify three ways by which they teach clients: (1) direct instruction (e.g., teaching skills), (2) modeling (specific skills as well as productive attitudes), and (3) contingency management (i.e., rewarding positive behavior either informally or through a behavior management program).

Workers in FPS use many different strategies for dealing with various types of problems. For problems involving basic needs, workers may help families obtain food, shelter, income assistance, employment, furniture, clothing, child care, and/or medical services. Workers also help clients develop skills (e.g., budgeting, housework, home repair) so that they can better meet their basic needs. Lewis (1991) suggests that providing clients with concrete services early in the helping process helps to engage and demonstrate to them the worker's commitment to helping the family. For intrapersonal problems, workers use cognitive, behavioral, and reflective listening/supportive strategies to help clients learn to manage and change their feelings. For interpersonal problems, workers may teach communication, assertiveness, problem-solving, and/or parenting skills. Berry (1997) argues that a focus "on modeling life skills, such as parenting skills, and teaching and practicing with family members the positive and constructive communication and negotiation skills . . . will contribute to a more positive and less abusive family environment" (p. 144).

Homework is frequently assigned to families in an effort to help them become actively involved in the change process and to stay focused on their goals even when the worker is not available. Workers also help families to develop and maintain daily routines with regard to getting up in the morning, cooking meals at specified times, and getting kids to bed on time. Kinney and colleagues (1991) contend that "the more family members are preoccupied with productive pursuits, the less time they will have for getting in trouble" (p. 74).

It is important to keep in mind that most FPS are crisis-oriented, intensive, and short-term. Crises do not always occur between 9:00 A.M. and 5 P.M. and cannot always be dealt with quickly; thus, workers must be accessible and have flexible schedules. Also, because FPS are time-limited, the goals of intervention must be realistic.

EVALUATION AND TERMINATION

As discussed previously, in FPS termination usually occurs within a relatively short period of time. In the Homebuilders model, services continue "only until the threat of out of home placement has been averted" (Kinney et al., 1991, p. 139). As mentioned earlier, it is increasingly common for this to be determined not only by worker judgment but also by the use of standardized assessment measures. Termination decisions are also influenced by periodic goal-attainment scaling reviews. Although termination usually occurs within 4 to 6 weeks in the Homebuilders model, extensions are allowed if circumstances warrant this. If the family has problems and goals that they want to continue to work on after the threat of placement has been averted, they are referred to other services.

There must be a process to termination, and it should begin at the first session. Families are told at the outset that services are limited to a short time period. As the weeks go by, workers should "count down" with families to help them anticipate termination. Workers should also help families anticipate how they will cope with problems that arise later and help them build in necessary supports (formal and/or informal). When families are referred to other services, it is often helpful if the family preservation worker goes with them to the first meeting. Many workers will celebrate a final session with a family with a meal or some other ritual. Although follow-up contacts with families are not usually formally planned, workers do tell families that they are welcome to call. Kinney and colleagues (1991) state that "it is not uncommon . . . to maintain minimal and informal contact with clients for years" (p. 156).

COMPATIBILITY WITH THE GENERALIST-ECLECTIC FRAMEWORK FOR DIRECT SOCIAL WORK PRACTICE

FPS are very compatible with the generalist-eclectic framework. The principles and values of family preservation practice are congruent with those of the profession of social work. These principles and values include a genuine respect for clients, a commitment to self-determination and empowerment, a recognition of clients' strengths, a focus on the worker-client relationship and working in partnership with clients, and a person-in-environment perspective. It should be acknowledged that our profession's adherence to these principles and values has waxed and waned over the years, and at times we have become identified more closely with psychiatry than with the roots of social work (Specht & Courtney, 1994). FPS represent a move to reembrace traditional social work practice values and principles.

Family preservation services are compatible with the generalist-eclectic approach in a number of other ways. These include (1) commitment to holistic, multilevel assessment that is informed by ecological systems theory, (2) use of a problem-solving framework to help clients learn how to deal with current and subsequent problems, and (3) the flexible use of a wide variety of theories and techniques.

CRITIQUE OF FAMILY PRESERVATION SERVICES

The family preservation model has been scrutinized and has raised heated debate perhaps more than any other approach to practice. The concerns and questions about FPS have centered on two issues: (1) the overall effectiveness of the model and (2) the appropriateness for its use with families that are at high risk for child maltreatment.

EFFECTIVENESS OF FPS

As mentioned earlier, although the results of early research on FPS were very positive, recent, more methodologically sound studies of FPS have produced less positive results. Summary reviews of the research on FPS (Blythe et al., 1994; Rossi, 1992; Schuerman et al., 1994; Wells & Biegel, 1992) note the conflicting results of studies and conclude that skepticism about effectiveness remains and that there is a need for larger, better designed studies. Thus, the field anxiously awaited the results of Schuerman and colleagues' (1994) research on the Illinois Family First program, because it was recognized as the "most scientifically credible evaluation of any family preservation program" (Epstein, 1997, p. 46).

The results of the study by Schuerman and colleagues (1994) were disappointing to the advocates of FPS. This study found no significant differences in outcome with regard to rate or duration of child placement or subsequent reports of child maltreatment between families who received FPS and those who received traditional child welfare services. There was some evidence of better family and child functioning in the FPS group; however, this difference was not sustained over time. There was evidence that the clients who received FPS were more satisfied with their services and had more positive views of the relationships with their workers. Despite their overall negative findings, Schuerman and colleagues (1994) note study limitations and are cautious about drawing firm conclusions. In particular, they point out that, as in many previous studies, the rates of placement and maltreatment were low for both the experimental (FPS) and the control (traditional services) groups—and thus, the probability of detecting differential effects was low.

This landmark research has generated a number of debates in the field with regard to the effectiveness of FPS and directions for research. With regard to conclusions about the overall effectiveness of FPS, Courtney (1997) notes that "whereas the results of the Family First evaluation should temper uncritical enthusiasm for family preservation services, they should not be considered prima facie evidence that service approaches to preserving families are doomed to failure" (p. 73). Furthermore, Nelson (1997) has argued that "the universally high satisfaction both families and workers express with the services" (p. 111) represents some evidence of effectiveness and that the negative finding to date with regard to more objective criteria "may represent a failure of the research to detect the successes of the program" (p. 105).

With regard to directions for research, a number of authors (e.g., Berry, 1997; Cash, 1998) have pointed out that, to date, studies have focused almost exclusively on outcomes and have ignored process variables. This neglect of process variables in the research has resulted in a dearth of information about the types of services provided, the characteristics of the target populations, and how such factors influence outcomes. The assessment of the overall effectiveness of FPS is particularly difficult because there is such a wide range of family preservation models that differ from one another in many important ways. Although some recent studies (e.g., Schuerman et al., 1994) have begun to incorporate consideration of such variables, additional research is warranted to determine the associations among client characteristics, service factors and processes, and outcomes.

CONCERNS ABOUT PLACING CHILDREN AT UNNECESSARY RISK

Some authors (Gelles, 1996; McDonald, 1994) have raised the concern that family preservation services place children at unnecessary risk. Gelles (1996) argues that assessment strategies and tools are not reliable and valid enough to warrant making decisions to keep a child in a home that may be dangerous. McDonald's (1994) critique of FPS offers a similar view; however, she goes further in arguing that family preservation services may reward a family that does not deserve help. She points out, for example, that a family that benefits from family preservation services often receives concrete services such as housecleaning and child care. McDonald argues that this rewards the family for negative behaviors and amounts to money wasted. Although, McDonald's latter argument is clearly simplistic, concerns for the safety of the child are legitimate. This and other critiques do not, however, deny the potential utility of family preservation services. Research is needed to determine the types of services that are needed to help different types of families while ensuring a safe environment for the child.

CASE EXAMPLE

The Trowell family was referred to the state child protective services department for physical abuse of their 5-year-old son. It was reported that the father had severely bruised the child by hitting him with a belt numerous times. Upon intake, it was determined that physical abuse did occur, and the case was opened by the investigation unit. The investigating worker's assessment determined that the child was at imminent risk of being placed into foster care. The Trowell family was given the option of participating in family preservation services, which they accepted.

The family preservation worker, Kelley, received the referral on a Thursday afternoon. That afternoon, Kelley contacted (via telephone) the mother, Heather, to arrange a time to meet with the whole family. During the initial phone conversation, Kelley explained to Heather what was involved in family preservation services and what some of the initial steps would be. Also during the conversation, Kelley worked on trying to establish rapport with Heather by showing interest in learning more about the family and empathizing with struggles and stresses. Heather seemed to open up on the telephone and seemed more trusting than she did initially. It was agreed that Kelley would come over on Saturday morning to meet the whole family.

Kelley arrived at the Trowells' house at the agreed upon time. She noticed that the screens on the windows were ripped and that the front steps to the house were somewhat dangerous (nails sticking out, rotted boards, etc.). Kelley was greeted at the door by Heather. Upon entering the home, Heather introduced Kelley to her husband, Matt, and her son, Steven. Kelley noted that Matt seemed suspicious of her, so she began their conversation by discussing the reason that she was involved in the case. After a few minutes of discussing the basics of family preservation services, Kelley "chitchatted" with both Heather and Matt about their week and what they enjoyed doing. Through this conversation, Kelley discovered that they enjoyed camping, bowling, and playing ball in the front yard. Kelley also found out that Matt was a plumber by trade but enjoyed painting and metal sculpting. Throughout the time that Kelley was at the house, Steven was watching cartoons and at times became noisy and would run around the house, thus irritating both Heather and Matt. Before the end of the first visit, Kelley discussed with Heather and Matt that she would like to help them, and the best way for her to help was for all of them to work together as a team. Kelley then initiated a serious discussion with Heather and Matt about the abuse and the importance of calling her if they ever felt as it they were losing control. During this time, Kelley discussed with them that she would be available to the family 24 hours a day, 7 days a week, and if an emergency arose, they were to call her immediately. Kelley stressed that a key to receiving family preservation services was to contract that they would work on the problems that brought them to the attention of the child welfare system and would agree not to physically abuse Steven. Kelley arranged another visit with the family on Monday morning.

On Monday morning, Kelley again came to the family's home. From her previous discussions with the family, she learned that they all love jelly-filled donuts, so, on her way to the house, she stopped by the local donut store and bought some. The family was very pleased to see that she had remembered what they liked, and they all sat around the dinner table and ate the donuts together. During this visit, the importance of setting goals was discussed with the family. Together with Kelley, the family developed several goals that they would like to work toward. For each goal listed, they outlined who was responsible for completing the goal and what steps were necessary to achieve it. They also wrote beside each goal what resources and strengths they had to meet that goal. The three goals that they created were (1) to maintain control (i.e., refrain from emotional and physical abuse) when Steven got into trouble, (2) to learn and use positive parenting skills, and (3) to better manage their finances and the upkeep of the home.

The first two goals were associated with the physical abuse report that had brought the family to the attention of the child welfare system. The third goal was related to fixing the broken screens and porch so that the home was physically safe and to helping the family with budgeting so that they could better meet their basic needs (their utilities had been shut off at times due to failure to pay bills). This last goal also related to helping the family feel better about themselves and their home, as well as more hopeful about their future.

During the first visit, each of the goals was broken down into tasks and target dates were set. The first two goals were going to be accomplished by the parents attending a parent training class offered in their neighborhood, and also by Kelley teaching and modeling positive parenting skills to the family in their own home. It was arranged that Kelley would have at least 8 hours per week of contact with the family in their home, and additional time if necessary. If the parents needed transportation to the grocery store or to do other errands (they did not have a car), either Kelley or an aide would try to provide this assistance.

It was agreed that the third goal would be a family-type project to be worked on during some of Kelley's visits. Kelley would provide the necessary materials to fix the house, and they would work on it together. If a project was beyond their capabilities, Kelley was allocated a certain amount of concrete services money that she could use to hire someone to help complete the job.

The focus of subsequent visits by Kelley was varied and dictated by the needs and interests of the family. Kelley bought some board games that were appropriate for Steven's age, and at times all of them played together so that Kelley could model and coach Heather and Matt how to interact in a more positive manner with Steven. Some visits focused on fix-it projects around the house, whereas others focused on teaching parenting or budgeting skills and problem solving ongoing family issues. Kelley became a trusted friend of the family and would sometimes help cook and then eat dinner with the them. Informal counseling and support were integrated naturally into social/recreational and practical activities.

Heather and Matt attended the parent training group and not only learned skills and gained knowledge but also made several friends. They exchanged phone numbers with some of the group members and began to establish a positive social network that they could call upon during times of crisis. Kelley also referred Heather to other community agencies and organizations in an effort to connect her with needed resources and sources of formal and informal support.

Over the 6-week period, the family made many gains in the areas of parenting, budgeting, and getting along with each other. They began to feel much better about themselves and their home. At times, the family still had difficulties, and Kelley had to go to the house to help mediate crisis situations. But, as the course of treatment progressed, the number of "unscheduled" visits decreased, and the family seemed to be coping better. The family seemed appreciative of the services that were provided and gained a level of trust not only with Kelley but also with the child welfare agency.

Kelley closed the Trowell case about 7 weeks after the case was opened. She determined, based on her own observations as well as a formal assessment of risk (the Family Assessment Form; Meezan & McCroskey, 1996), that the case was appropriate to close. The family had achieved all three of the goals and had created support systems, both formal and informal, to rely upon in times of crisis or need. At a 6-month follow-up, the family was still intact, and no subsequent reports had been filed with the child welfare system.

SUMMARY

Family preservation services are not a panacea for all of the problems that families face, but they are an important part of a continuum of child welfare and other social work services. Although the model is not without its flaws, and the jury is still out on whether the FPS are more effective than traditional services, the principles and values associated with the model are sound and congruent with those of the social work profession. The model is neither dogmatic nor static—it pushes the boundaries of traditional clinical practice, encourages creativity, and continues to evolve.

REFERENCES

Berlin, S., & Marsh, J. (1993). *Informing practice decisions.* New York: Macmillan.

Berry, M. (1997). *The family at risk: Issues and trends in family preservation services.* Columbia: University of South Carolina Press.

Bloom, M., Fischer, J., & Orme, J. G. (1999). *Evaluating practice: Guidelines for the accountable professional.* Boston: Allyn & Bacon.

Blythe, B. J., Salley, M. P., & Jayaratne, S. (1994). A review of intensive family preservation services research. *Social Work Research, 18,* 213–224.

Briar, K. H., Broussard, C. A., Ronnau, J. R., & Sallee, A. (1995). Family preservation and support: Past, present and future. *Family Preservation Journal, 1*(1), 5–23.

Bronfenbrenner, U. (1979). *The ecology of human development: Experiments by nature and design.* Cambridge, MA: Harvard University Press.

Cash, S. J. (1998). *Family preservation services: Predicting service usage and subsequent outcomes.* Unpublished doctoral dissertation, University of Texas, Arlington.

Cole, E. S. (1995). Becoming family centered: Child welfare's challenge. *Families in Society, 76,* 163–172.

Courtney, M. E. (1997). Reconsidering family preservation: A review of Putting Families First. *Children and Youth Services Review, 19,* 61–76.

Darmstadt, G. L. (1990). Community-based child abuse prevention. *Social Work, 35,* 487–493.

Epstein, W. M. (1997). Social science, child welfare, and family preservation: A failure of rationality in public policy. *Children and Youth Services Review, 19,* 41–60.

Fraser, M. W. (1997). The ecology of childhood: A multisystems perspective. In M. W. Fraser (Ed.), *Risk and resilience in childhood: An ecological perspective* (pp. 1–9). Washington, DC: NASW Press.

Garbarino, J. (1991). *Children and families in the social environment* (2nd ed.). New York: Aldine de Gruyter.

Gelles, R. (1996). *The book of David.* New York: Basic Books.

Germain, C., & Gitterman, A. (1980). *The life model of social work practice.* New York: Columbia University Press.

Gibbs, L., & Gambrill, E. (1999). *Critical thinking for social workers: A workbook.* Thousand Oaks, CA: Pine Forge Press.

Henggeler, S. W., & Borduin, C. M. (1995). Multisystemic treatment of serious juvenile offenders and their families. In I. M. Schwartz & P. AuClaire (Eds.), *Home-based services for troubled children* (pp. 113–130). Lincoln: University of Nebraska Press.

Kemp. S. P., Whittaker, J. K., & Tracy, E. M. (1997). *Person-environment practice.* Hawthorne, NY: Aldine de Gruyter.

Kinney, J., Haapala, D., & Booth, C. (1991). *Keeping families together: The homebuilders model.* New York: Aldine De Gruyter.

Lewis, R. E. (1991). What are the characteristics of intensive family preservation services? In M. W. Fraser, P. J. Pecora, & D. A. Haapala (Eds.), *Families in crisis:*

The impact of intensive family preservation services (pp. 93–107). Hawthorne, NY: Aldine de Gruyter.

Lindsey, D. (1994). *The welfare of children.* New York: Oxford University Press.

Lovell, M. L., & Richey, C. A. (1991). Implementing agency-based social-support skill training. *Families in Society, 72,* 563–573.

McDonald, H. (1994). The ideology of "Family Preservation." *Public Interest, 115,* 45–60.

Meezan, W., & McCroskey, J. (1996, Winter). Improving family functioning through family preservation services: Results of the Los Angeles experiment. *Family Preservation Journal,* pp. 9–29.

Moncher, F. J. (1995). Social isolation and child-abuse risk. *Families in Society, 76,* 421–433.

Nelson, K. E. (1997). Family preservation—What is it? *Children and Youth Services Review, 19,* 101–118.

Pecora, P. J., Fraser, M. W., Nelson, K. E., McCroskey, J., & Meezan, W. (1995). *Evaluating family-based services.* New York: Aldine de Gruyter.

Rooney, R. H. (1992). *Strategies for work with involuntary clients.* New York: Columbia University Press.

Rossi, P. H. (1992). Assessing family preservation programs. *Children and Youth Services Review, 14,* 77–97.

Saleebey, D. (1996). The strengths perspective in social work practice: Extensions and cautions. *Social Work, 41,* 296–305.

Schuerman, J. R., Rzepnicki, T. L., & Littell, J. H. (1994). *Putting families first: An experiment in family preservation.* New York: Aldine de Gruyter.

Seelig, W. R., Goldman-Hall, B. J., & Jerrell, J. M. (1992). In-home treatment of families with seriously disturbed adolescents in crisis. *Family Process, 31,* 135–149.

Specht, H., & Courtney, M. (1994). *Unfaithful angels.* New York: Free Press.

Thomlison, B. (1997). Risk and protective factors in child maltreatment. In M. W. Fraser (Ed.), *Risk and resilience in childhood: An ecological perspective* (pp. 50–72). Washington, DC: NASW Press.

Weick, A., & Saleebey, D. (1995). Supporting family strengths: Orienting policy and practice toward the 21st century. *Families in Society, 76,* 141–149.

Wells, K., & Biegel, D. E. (1992). Intensive family preservation services research: Current status and future agenda. *Social Work Research and Abstracts, 28,* 21–27.

Whittaker, J. K., Schinke, S. P., & Gilchrist, L. D. (1986). The ecological paradigm in child, youth, and family services: Implications for policy and practice. *Social Service Review, 60,* 483–503.

20

Interactive Trauma/ Grief–Focused Therapy with Children

Kathleen Nader and Christine Mello

Disasters, violence, and severe accidents may result in symptoms of posttraumatic stress disorder (PTSD) and/or a number of adverse and prolonged effects (e.g., disturbed mental health, anguish, fear, distrust, and poor health) (Nader, 1996a). Most notable are the posttraumatic reenactments, altered impulse control, and disturbed thought patterns that result in violence (e.g., previously traumatized school snipers). In general, violence has increased following traumatic events that affect an entire populous (e.g., after war or floods) (Ibrahim, 1992; Kohly, 1994). Thus, the cycle of trauma and of violence may be perpetuated by individuals whose traumatic reactions or traumatic grief remain unresolved (Nader, 1996b).

The treatment model that will be discussed in this chapter represents an eclectic approach that draws on psychodynamic, cognitive-behavioral, and various other theories. Although it has been used primarily after exposure to single incidents of trauma, it has been adapted for use after multiple traumas (e.g., sexual abuse). In this chapter, the focus will be on the use of this treatment with traumatized children. In lieu of presenting a separate case example at the end of the chapter, the application of the treatment model is illustrated by references to case material throughout the chapter.

AN OVERVIEW OF THE MODEL

Understanding Traumatic Response

Psychic trauma occurs when an individual is exposed to an overwhelming event and is rendered helpless in the face of intolerable danger, anxiety, or instinctual arousal (Pynoos & Eth, 1986). The *Diagnostic and Statistical Manual of Mental Disorders* (*DSM-IV*; American Psychiatric Association [APA], 1994) describes the reexperiencing, avoidance, increased arousal, and social dysfunction of PTSD that may occur after exposure to these events. There is significant evidence that failure to resolve moderate to severe traumatic reactions may result in long-term consequences that interfere with the child's ability to function adequately (socially, academically, professionally, and personally) (Wilson & Raphael, 1993). In addition, there is evidence that individuals who experience traumas are more likely to have children who experience traumas (Nader, 1998).

CONCEPTION OF THERAPEUTIC INTERVENTION

The goals of treatment for traumatized children include both repair of the injured aspects of the child and recovery of healthy aspects that may have been eclipsed by traumatic response and changes (Nader, 1994). Effective individual intervention goals include (1) to hear everything, including the worst, and to help the child see more clearly the minute details of the experience (Nader, 1994; Pynoos & Nader, 1993); (2) to recognize distortions, omissions, spatial misrepresentations, and distractions, along with their emotional meaning for the child (Nader, 1997b; Pynoos & Nader, 1989a; Terr, 1979, 1991); (3) to recognize and address the many intense impressions (e.g., multiple visual and perceptual experiences) before, during, and after a traumatic event (Nader, 1997b; Pynoos & Nader, 1989a); (4) to discover the emotional meaning that becomes embedded in the details of the event (Nader & Pynoos, 1991; Pynoos & Nader, 1989a, 1993); (5) to correct underinflation or overinflation of important aspects of the event; (6) to identify fantasies/desires or urges to act (Nader, 1994; Nader & Pynoos, 1993a; Pynoos & Eth, 1986; Pynoos & Nader, 1989a, 1993); (7) to facilitate facing emotional moments with the associated affect and reenter the fantasy/moment with the child/adolescent resulting in release, reprocessing, and redefinition (Levy, 1938; Nader & Pynoos, 1991; Pynoos & Eth, 1986); (8) to provide a sense of resolution and reorientation so that a healthy ego is returned to a normal developmental path (Nader & Pynoos, 1991; Pynoos & Nader, 1993); and (9) to enhance recognition of the successful self through recognition of good choices, successful actions, right thinking, and personal strengths.

Of primary importance is uncovering the truth and examining it clearly without distortions engendered by fears, horrors, confusions, avoidances, and/or a sense of helplessness. The method includes a process of reviewing and reworking specific aspects of the event toward that end. This process is designed to elicit a thorough account from the child of his or her experience, including affective, sensory, and physiological experiences; sources of traumatic anxiety; traumatic reminders; early coping processes; and trauma-related life stresses. The clinician's recognition of the following aspects of the traumatic situation is essential for effective intervention: all details of the event (Nader, 1994; Pynoos & Eth, 1986; Pynoos & Nader 1989a), the phases of response (Nader 1994, 1996a), cultural differences (Marsella, Friedman, Gerrity, & Scurfield, 1996; Nader, Dubrow, & Stamm, 1999), the phase of the traumatic event (e.g., ongoing war or violence vs. the initial or later aftermath; Nader, 1996a), and the needs and recovery of others in the family or community (Nader, 1997b; Nader & Pynoos, 1993b; Pynoos & Nader, 1988a).

This treatment method is directive while observing the child/adolescent's timing and need for closure. The degree of directiveness is adjusted to the tolerance and needs of the child (Nader, 1994). During sessions, in order to face fully and in detail each traumatic moment, the clinician must be unhindered by personal distractions (including unresolved traumas). For example, traumatized clinicians have become stalled or have over- or under-focused on aspects of trauma, thereby hindering a survivor's progress (Nader & Pynoos, 1993b). Trauma recovery is often characterized by progress and periodic exacerbation of symptoms. Each child establishes his or her own rhythms of review and focus on the issues of trauma and bereavement (Nader, 1994). Success in using this method requires a good sense of timing: knowing when to push the child or when to permit things to unfold. For example, in the case of Susan, described in Nader (1997b), the clinician recognized that Susan had both loving and angry feelings toward her dead sister. In the right way and at the appropriate moment, the clinician pushed Susan to express her anger and to act on her concern for her sister. This freed her to honor both emotions fully on her own. The clinician assists the child through treatment sessions skillfully, in order to provide a sense of resolution, closure, and reorientation. Achieving the proper closure at the end of each session prevents leaving the child with renewed anxiety and an unnecessary avoidance of the therapeutic situation (Nader, 1994; Pynoos & Eth, 1986).

THEORETICAL BASE

Therapeutic approaches to PTSD nearly all incorporate cognitive and emotional reprocessing of traumatic memories (Pynoos, Nader, & March, 1991). The techniques of this treatment cross psychotherapeutic boundaries and include principles found in a number of clinical theories. For example, directed and spontaneous symbolic or actual reenactments of traumatic episodes may find their precursors in the psychodrama of Gestalt therapy or spontaneous play of play therapy (Amster, 1943; Axline, 1947); bringing subconscious traumatic impressions to clear consciousness and permitting the assignment of new meaning is found in the cathartic abreactions of psychoanalytic treatment, the hypnotic elicitation and reframing of Milton Ericksonian therapies (Erickson, Rossi, & Ryan, 1985), and Levy's abreactive therapy (Levy, 1938); and emphasis of intense traumatic moments prior to redefinition are similar to the review, flooding, redefining, and sometimes desensitization of cognitive-behavioral therapies.

CENTRAL PREMISES OF TREATMENT

ASSISTING CHILDREN'S ACCURATE TRAUMATIC RECALL

Intense impressions, desires to act, imagined actions, and role identifications are deeply imprinted into children's traumatic memory representations and, if unresolved, can result in major changes in behavior and personality (Nader, 1997b). In remembering life-threatening events, children's recall is not organized as a single episode, but rather as multiple traumatic episodes within a single event (Pynoos & Nader, 1989b). Children's memories are context-specific. When children have initial difficulty in accurate recall, rather than memory impairment, it is often because they lack an adequate retrieval strategy (Johnson & Foley, 1984). In the initial interview, the clinician provides children with a strategy of recall that permits retrieval of accurate descriptions of subjective experiences (Nader, 1994).

Prohibiting or misleading recall instructions may limit memory and thereby introduce distortions. Instructing a child to forget what happened or progressing only to a certain point in recalling an incident may restrict future memories (Pynoos & Nader, 1989). Therefore, the initial interview and the clinician's ability to explore the traumatic experience thoroughly may be key to the overall intervention with a traumatized child.

EACH INDIVIDUAL'S EXPERIENCE IS UNIQUE

Although there are similarities in response to traumatic events, experiences are different for each individual enduring these events. Each of the 200 people in the room where a tornado hit has a unique experience. Each individual brings to a traumatic experience different backgrounds, strengths, cognitive and personality styles, reactions to stress, and expectations that influence perceptions and reactions. For example, children who have been traumatized previously (e.g., those who have been abused or exposed to intermittent violence) often respond differently to the initial interview that is focused on a recent, single traumatic incident. Resistance and avoidance are more prominent; trust is more difficult. For these children, trust building may precede other trauma work. It is essential to treat the individual in context. This means understanding the personal experience of trauma; the individual's culture and personality; and his or her family, school/job, and community needs.

This treatment recognizes the need for changing levels of numbing and periods of avoidance as ego strength and trust are restored. Treatment may become more directive as tolerance increases. Inasmuch as a child's personal rhythms and timing are respected, the clinician recognizes an individual readiness to regress, express traumatic emotions or desires, or engage in repetitive play of the trauma with appropriate interpretations (Nader, 1997b). As ego strength returns, with direct focus, forgotten traumatic memories representing moments too horrible to recall initially are often recovered and thoroughly addressed. These moments may be addressed as they become relevant to recovery, or as they are identified by the child. Directing the focus of treatment to the full force of traumatic rage and/or helplessness may have to wait until some recovery has been accomplished (Nader, 1994). Over time, aspects of the trauma take on new meaning for the child as he or she enters a new developmental phase or as life and treatment unfold. These issues are then worked through in the context of this new meaning or reappraisal (Nader & Pynoos, 1991; Pynoos & Nader, 1993).

THE IMPORTANCE OF ADVOCACY

Clinicians or their appointees need to act as advocates and to enlist the support of family, friends, teachers/employers, and the community for the child/adolescent in order to minimize secondary adversities and promote recovery (Nader, 1994; Nader & Pynoos, 1993b). In the immediate aftermath of the event, children need protection from unnecessary reexposure to traumatic scenes (e.g., injury). Inappropriate media coverage or courtroom pictures that exhibit corpses or mutilated bodies may also have a harmful effect (Nader, Pynoos, Fairbanks, Al-Ajeel, & Al-Asfour, 1993). In enlisting the aide of the personal and community milieu, the therapist mobilizes people in the child's life to protect the child from clumsiness, confusion, lack of concentration, and/or compulsions that may lead to injury or hazard (Nader, 1994/1995, 1997b).

DOING NO HARM

Appropriate training and supervision are essential to trauma interventions. Failure to understand trauma treatment (Nader & Pynoos, 1993a) or cultural customs can lead to mishap (e.g., misdirection of rage) and even death (e.g., murder or suicide) (Nader, 1996a; Swiss & Gilder, 1993). This understanding is crucial to assuring accurate assessment and protection of those affected by the event (Nader, 1996a; Nader, in press).

Understanding the interaction of trauma and grief reactions is essential to treatment and the prevention of harmful reactions and behaviors by the bereaved (Eth & Pynoos, 1985; Nader, 1997a, 1997b). This interaction includes but is not limited to recognizing trauma and grief reexperiencing, traumatic rage and helplessness, and the intensification and complication of reactions (Nader, 1997a).

In the course of successful traumatic treatment, intense traumatic emotions (e.g., rage and helplessness) and strong wishes to act (e.g., to fight or flee) emerge. These emotions and desires must be dealt with appropriately within the session and in a manner that prevents their dangerous or harmful expression in the external world (Nader, 1997b). Moreover, abreactive experiences are not just giving permission or encouraging the expression of feelings. For example, there is the story of the rageful man who was taught in Gestalt treatment to bring his anger to the surface and beat on a mattress. Later, he beat an elderly woman to death when frustrated by her slowness.

When traumatic emotions are reawakened, it is essential that there be some sense of resolution or closure. A school psychologist reported having read numerous articles on trauma/grief-focused therapy, but when she and her colleagues tried the techniques, students felt worse instead of better afterwards. Reviewing an experience with a traumatized individual must be done skillfully and only when the goals of a session can be achieved (e.g., processing of traumatic thoughts and emotions, a new view of aspects of the experience, or repairing the self-concept).

HISTORICAL DEVELOPMENT

ORIGINAL DEVELOPMENT

This interactive trauma/grief-focused therapy began as a semistructured research interview. The interview included a draw-a-picture/tell-a-story method and a set of research questions developed by Drs. Ted Shapiro, Karen Gilmore, and Robert Pynoos (personal communications: K. Gilmore, August 1994; R. Pynoos, 1985; T. Shapiro, August 1994). This research interview initially was used at Payne Whitney Medical Center (Cornell University) with children whose parents had attempted suicide and later in Los Angeles as a diagnostic interview with children exposed to violence (Eth & Pynoos, 1985). The initial specialized interview for traumatized children, with innovations by Drs. Pynoos and Eth and additions by Dr. Nader, was first published in detail in 1986 (Pynoos & Eth, 1986). It has continued to evolve in its clinical diagnostic and therapeutic use in response to the needs of traumatized children (Nader, 1994, 1997b; Nader & Pynoos, 1991; Pynoos & Nader, 1993; Pynoos, 1993).

LATER DEVELOPMENTS AND CURRENT STATUS

In addition to use after individual exposure to trauma, this treatment has been used nationally and internationally (Goenjian et al., 1997; Nader, 1997b) in (1) school or community settings following acts of violence and disasters resulting in multiple deaths and injuries (Nader, 1997b; Nader & Pynoos, 1993b; Nader, Pynoos, Fairbanks, & Frederick, 1990) and (2) the aftermath of war (Nader et al., 1993). Adaptations are made depending on the circumstances of the precipitating event and the culture and community in which it is used.

When provided by Dr. Nader, training in the use of this specialized treatment involves didactic training sessions with opportunities for trainees to observe and to be observed in sessions with children. Continued training over time addresses the progression of treatment and provides continued feedback regarding the progress of the children and the progress of the clinician in applying this treatment.

PHASES OF HELPING

ENGAGEMENT

A format that is essentially equal to that described in Pynoos and Eth (1986) is used both as a diagnostic and an initial treatment interview. Initial contact acknowledges that the interview is prompted by an actual event in the child's life. One method of establishing rapport is to have the child draw a picture and tell a story about it. The interviewer's genuine interest in the picture and the story have been observed to assist in establishing a comfortable relationship between the interviewer and the child (Nader, 1993). Moreover, the visual and perceptual episodes of children's experiences become embedded and transformed in their drawings and play (Nader, 1993; Nader & Pynoos, 1991; Pynoos & Eth, 1986; Pynoos & Nader, 1993). The child provides clues to important psychodynamic issues in initial drawings.

DATA COLLECTION AND ASSESSMENT

The potential results of unresolved traumatic response underscore the need for accurate assessment (Wilson & Keane, 1996). In our work, initial assessment has included the use of the Childhood Posttraumatic Stress Reaction Index (CPTS-RI; Frederick, Pynoos, & Nader, 1992), the Pynoos Brief Grief Inventory (Pynoos, 1984), and an exposure and coping questionnaire (Nader, 1993). Multiple issues affect the accuracy of such instruments, including the selection and training of interviewers, interviewer style, trauma intrinsic issues (e.g., briefing, phase of response), and child intrinsic issues (e.g., culture, age) (Nader, 1996a). For further information on instruments that directly measure childhood traumatic reactions, the reader is directed to Carlson (1997), Nader (1996a), and Stamm (1996).

Preliminary briefing is an essential part of preparation for assessment with children following traumatic events. Knowing the details of the traumatic event enables the clinician to recognize aspects of symptomatic response and variables affecting response. For example, following a hostage taking in which the assailant dictated a suicide note, then killed herself, children's worry about their peers was most highly associated with severity of response (Nader, 1997b). Questions regarding the child's fear for others' safety were based on an understanding that the woman had waved her guns around and had accidentally fired a shot just missing one child.

The initial clinical interview is both diagnostic and therapeutic. It permits assessment of specific traumatic moments, their effects, and grief. It provides a strategy of recall that helps enable future treatment, including delayed treatment. Done well, it provides the child with an initial sense of relief and often reinstates a sense of self-control. The initial interview can provide a measure of progress and recovery at specific checkpoints. Further information with regard to risk and protective factors can be assessed through interviews with parents and teachers, or through school records (Nader, 1996b). In this treatment model, assessment is an ongoing process that is intertwined with intervention. Thus, many of the principles and techniques discussed in the next subsection on intervention relate to assessment as well.

PLANNING/CONTRACTING AND INTERVENTION

The length of treatment for traumatized children varies depending on the severity of traumatic response and other factors (e.g., personality, previous experience of trauma, emotional health, and family circumstances). Children who are mildly to moderately traumatized may benefit from 2 to 16 sessions. Moderately to severely traumatized children may need 1 to 3 years of treatment. Life events may prompt the need for additional sessions over the course of the child's development.

When there have been dual or multiple individual traumas or a trauma and a loss, attention to relevant aspects of each event may be necessary. Depending on the emotional impact of each event, some children may need to address a previous trauma before attending to the current event; others may be reminded over time of the previous trauma and undergo symptoms related to each. Additionally, issues that were of relevance in the earlier trauma or traumatic sequence (e.g., abandonment, betrayal, and victimization) are likely to appear as issues in the current trauma or traumatic episode (Nader, 1997b).

Several principles and techniques (see below) are used to help children review, express, and resolve traumatic emotions and memory impressions. Using these techniques assumes a trusting relationship between the clinician and the child. Reworking traumatic memories may include reentering a moment or fantasy toward abreaction or completion of a desired act. The availability of a variety of toys, including those representative of aspects of the event, permits restoration of the anxiety-provoking situation in play and reentering the experience or fantasy associated with the event (Levy, 1938; Nader & Pynoos, 1991).

Orienting to the Trauma and Reorienting to the Present

At the beginning of treatment, the trauma survivor must be oriented to the trauma. Introducing oneself as a trauma therapist, at the first session, is the beginning of this process. Children who have been traumatized repeatedly or who become easily entranced with some aspect of a personal traumatic experience may need orientation away from the trauma at the beginning and end of the session, as well as closure (e.g., noticing the beautiful day/view/picture before addressing the trauma and after closure). For these children, reorientation to the present may prevent mishap after the session.

Recognizing Clues to Content

Children's play, drawings, initial comments or verbalizations, and the reports of others give clues to the portion of the traumatic event that needs resolution during the session. A child may give clues to specific moments of importance by gesture or expression. For example, Sandy, a third-grade student who, 18 months after a tornado disaster, appeared to be functioning well, was asked to review again her experience just prior to the destruction and her injury. At one point, the clinician observed that Sandy kept her visual focus on the corner of the room. Attention to what she saw in a corner, where the trauma had occurred, revealed a continued deep sadness about her helplessness to move herself and friends to safety once the debris began to fly.

Information from teachers, parents, or friends may also suggest the traumatic content that has engaged the child's mind during the week. For example, when a boy who had been molested was heckled about his effeminate haircut, he flashed the other children to prove his manhood. In session, he dressed a female doll in clothes like his own and cut her hair like his. The session focused on his anger at and destruction of this helpless, feminine/masculine form. He was not ready to focus on his molestation for many months afterward.

Using Play and Drawings

Play and drawings invariably signify in some way the child's unconscious preoccupation with memories of the trauma. The use of play and drawings in the assessment and treatment of trauma can (1) provide an opportunity for reexamination of an experience in order to give it new meaning, (2) indicate the child's processing and eventual resolution of traumatic elements, (3) allow the child an opportunity to be active in completing a desired or fantasied act within a safe therapeutic setting, (4) reveal the details of the event that remain in the child's active mind, (5) reveal elements of the child's continuing internal experience of the event, and (6) display the child's spatial representation of the event. Details revealed may become a part of review and re-review of aspects of the event (see below). Both play and drawings permit the interpretation or the linking of the play/drawings to aspects of the traumatic episode. The traumatic link is most often identified after completion of the story or segment of the play. If the drawings or play are interpreted or addressed too early, the child often stops (Nader & Pynoos, 1991).

Recognizing Symbolism

There is no standard symbolism for trauma. What is important is the child's own symbolism, history, and personal traumatic experience. After a traumatic death, children have often used balloons as a way to send a message (perhaps of love) to the deceased (Nader & Pynoos, 1991). For one child, recognizing that each of three different colored balloons represented a particular girl gave meaning to a series of pictures with colored balloons in them. Although it has been interpreted as a maternal figure, with individual traumatized children the sun has been used, for example, to represent father; deity; or the contrast of a beautiful, now empty, day against the gloom of sudden, tragic death. After seeing his mother stabbed with a barbecue fork, a boy included a two-pronged item in each of his drawings (e.g., adjacent buildings, unidentifiable objects, "sticks" on the ground, and pointed hills).

Working Through the Intensity of Traumatic Impressions

As a consequence of physiological (e.g., increased pulse) and psychological (e.g., horror) phenomena during traumatic events, multiple impressions register or imprint themselves with intensity and may become interlinked (Nader, 1997a). They include sensory impressions (e.g., touch, images, sounds, and smells), strong desires (e.g., to fight, flee, hide, rescue, or find), attempts to understand (e.g., feelings or actions of others; "Why me?"), senses of injustice (e.g., bad things happen to good people; bad people have success), senses of betrayal (e.g., the unwelcomed actions of known others), rejection of self (e.g., disdain for the helpless or ineffectual self), and changes of focus (e.g., prominence of ineffectual self or of negative events over positive). These deeply ingrained impressions, desires to act, imagined interventions, and role identifications become embedded in children's traumatic memory representations and will become evident over time in the course of treatment. Even the smallest details may become carved solidly into the child's memory (Nader, 1997a).

When children's impressions and desires to act during an event go unresolved, the result can be major changes in behavior and personality. For example, ongoing intervention fantasies include the child's fantasies during and after the event of preventing or stopping harm, of challenging the assailant, or of repairing damage. Lack of resolution of a revenge fantasy (see Nader & Pynoos, 1991), traumatically imprinted desire for retaliation, or identification with the aggressor may result in increased aggression or inhibition (Nader, 1997b).

Intense traumatic impressions—wishes, urges and emotions—remain in the psyche as strong urges to express and must be intensely expressed. Consequent repeated behaviors may endanger or frustrate. In the treatment session, these wishes, urges, and emotions can be expressed with intensity and without harm.

Traumatically imprinted thoughts and images repeat themselves until they are properly processed or become suppressed, remaining influential in the child's life. This can result in an increase in arousal symptoms or in readiness to arousal (Nader & Fairbanks, 1994; van der Kolk & Sapporta, 1991) or in a variety of other troubles (Herman, 1992; Nader, 1996a; Terr, 1991). Some of these unresolved thoughts and images, as well as many of the urges to act or desires that occur in the intensity of a traumatic moment, endure as compulsions to act. For example, memories of his mother's horror when as an infant a boy had fallen on his head resulted in repeated head banging in elementary school. He told the therapist that, although he did not know why, he had to show his mother that it didn't hurt.

In treatment, a child's embedded impressions from various traumatic moments represent themselves in play or drawings. The playing out of these moments to the desired completion is facilitated. The therapist allows the denial in fantasy (e.g., healing the mutilated or shot father; stopping the harm to self or others) and addresses the feeling (e.g., "I'll bet you wish you could have patched up your father and that he could have talked to you like that"). These interpretations often lead to an expression of sadness, to a sense of relief, or to an examination of heretofore unstated feelings (e.g., self-blame), fantasies (e.g., jumping up and punching the assailant), or desires (e.g., to be protected from seeing the mutilation).

If, at the end of treatment, the clinician and the child have not uncovered and resolved specific traumatic moments or emotions, these emotions may translate into repeated complexes of behavior and emotions (behavioral patterns, life scripts, or dramas). For example, unexpressed depression over not assisting an injured child across the room may result in the repeated need to rescue others, an ongoing depression over a sense of ineffectualness, or a sense of hurting others somehow. The cause of these scripts, patterns, or disorders, having been undiscovered in relation to the event, may remain unrecognized. A girl molested by her father and others until age 12 remembered only his rubbing against her body. Under stress she experienced tightness of throat, nausea, fatigue, a sense of aloneness, and feelings of being trapped and of being caretaker to everyone else. She did not remember the forced oral copulation until treatment sessions in her 50s (Nader, 1996b). Even unresolved curiosity may become a part of reenactments (e.g., curiosity about what death feels like; see Nader, 1994).

Recognizing Roles

Some intense impressions (e.g., desires to take action, understand, or change things) may result in assuming specific roles over time. Consequently, children may take one of several roles in their play and actions following traumatic events based on their experiences and what they witnessed during the event. These include most prominently aggressor, rescuer, or victim. They may include other roles dictated by the experience such as witness (or mobilized witness), assistant to the perpetrator, soother/calmer, aggravator, or searcher. The child may change role or identification over the course of treatment (in and out of session). Remaining in one of the roles without resolution may lead to changes in personality and/or life choices and to dangerous or troublesome behaviors (Nader, 1997a, 1997b; see example of Ralph in Nader, 1997b).

Understanding Developmental Differences

Children differ developmentally in the ways in which they approach and respond to danger (Eth & Pynoos, 1985; Nader, in press; Nader & Pynoos, 1991; Pynoos & Nader, 1988b). Issues such as trust, protection, and ability to intervene change. For example, preschool children may look to external sources for protection. School-age children may become involved in fantasies of rescue and exile and may envision special powers to intervene or be rescued. Preteens may become more specific in the manner in which they would intervene, such as the 11-year-old boy who wished he had used his martial arts training to stop his mother's rapist and who proceeded to further perfect his martial arts skills (Pynoos & Nader, 1988b). Adolescents may be especially troubled by a sense of their own physical ineffectualness and vulnerability or their aggressive impulses. For example, a 12-year-old girl had a difficult time expressing, in play, her revenge fantasy toward a sniper who shot her in the neck, until the therapist helped her to understand that she would not really be hurting anyone.

Understanding Aspects of Rage

Successful anger is never unleashed upon another person. It is used to do something productive. For example, in the traumatic situation, it mobilizes self-protection, escape from danger, fending off the aggressor, and making things right (e.g., calling medics, moving people out of harm's way). After a traumatic situation/experience, anger may facilitate good efforts, such as sticking with treatment, working toward the protection of others (e.g., court testimony), or a creative work (e.g., that informs others, honors the deceased, or shows strength of spirit).

When facilitating expression of rage or anger, it may be important for children to know that you believe in their goodness and self-control. This can be done, for example, by acknowledging that the child would never really hurt anyone, and that hurting the doll/picture will not really hurt anyone. For some traumatized children, expression of rage (even in fantasy) has frightening implications for a morality challenged by recent events.

Recognizing Spontaneous and Ongoing Regression

Childlike behaviors are common under normal circumstances—for example, during playfulness, anger, or endearment. Moreover, regression may be as subtle as returning to an old desire for a person (e.g., old friend), place (e.g., a place representing happier times), or situation that signifies good feelings (e.g., a sense of safety). Regressions such as loss of skills (e.g., at school) may be complicated or exaggerated by other trauma symptoms (e.g., changed biochemistry, cognitive difficulties, lack of sleep, and/or preoccupations). Consequently, regression may be difficult to recognize. In children, it may be interpreted as defiance, laziness, sloppiness, or attention getting. It is important that clinicians, parents, and teachers learn to identify a child's specific regressive tendencies.

Reviewing and Re-reviewing of Trauma

Over time the clinician and the child may go over a specific issue or trauma segment many times as it takes on new meaning in the course of development or treatment. Additionally, with progress, children lose levels of their numbness and become more aware of the issues and aspects of a traumatic episode.

Children may have partial amnesia for details that are regained in the process of review and re-review in a single session. Backing up and moving forward in slow motion allows the child to recapture details (Nader, 1997a) and the emotions that go with them (see example of Susan in Nader, 1997b). If done without skill, purpose, and good timing, this technique can distress and/or add to a tendency toward psychological numbing and avoidance. Timing is essential in recognizing how to go over and over in finer detail.

Recognizing Successes

When successes during a traumatic event are recognized, it can be emotionally freeing: (1) skills become more prominent, failures less prominent;

(2) overall functioning may improve; and (3) some forms of guilt or self-recrimination may cease. For example, a boy in Kuwait watched as the Iraqi soldiers beat a man to death. He stood motionless behind a TV to save himself, yet felt like a failure and as if he had betrayed the man who was killed. In session, it was necessary to go over, in detail, his silent conversation with himself while the soldiers beat the man. This revealed a strong desire to help his friend and an accurate assessment that both would die if he intervened. His analytic skills were noted. Relief was observable in the session, and afterward he was able to lift his head and gaze in his interactions with others.

EVALUATION AND TERMINATION

In working with traumatized children, the therapist requires ample debriefing and sufficient self-care in order to work effectively. Without this, the therapist may terminate cases prematurely. This can occur as a result of a reduction in thoroughness in discovering and exploring the child's individual emotion-laden moments and intense traumatic impressions (Nader, 1994).

One measure of recovery is whether the child can function without fear, has regained parts of lost self, and can experience joy. During treatment, it is important that clinicians be thorough in review and re-review in order to assess resolution and reorientation of all significant "moments" and impressions of traumatic experience. The semistructured interview used in the initial consultation can be readministered at intervals to assess progress. In the example of Sandy, cited earlier, it was in re-reviewing prior to termination that the clinician noted the child's fixed visual focus as a clue to the need to further resolve feelings of sadness and helplessness.

Other life issues, unresolved developmental issues, or a sense of success may bring trauma work to an apparent stopping point or diversion (Nader & Pynoos, 1991). Children and adults often save the deeper levels of some traumatic emotions (e.g., rage or helplessness) until other issues have been resolved in treatment. After significant improvement in their levels of functioning, they may wish to leave treatment prematurely both to avoid the intensity of the unresolved issues and because it no longer seems urgent to resolve anything. In the event that termination is premature, it is of help to prepare the child for the kinds of issues (e.g., unresolved anger) that may occur in the future and to leave the door open for return to treatment.

APPLICATION TO FAMILY AND GROUP WORK

Family and group work can provide important supplemental supports to this individual treatment method. Moreover, it is essential to work collaboratively with the child's family and school.

FAMILY WORK

Even if only one family member has been subjected to a trauma, the entire family is affected. Whole-family sessions generally are held to help families to understand the differences in their courses of recovery, to aid their abilities to help rather than hinder each other's recovery, and to address specific posttrauma family issues. For example, a mother and two young daughters entered treatment after the shooting death of the husband and father. Individual treatment addressed the personal traumatic and grief reactions of each family member; occasional family sessions permitted the discussion of, for example, why Sally became so upset when her mother wanted to visit the grave regularly. Sally was still contending with traumatic, intrusive images of her father's bloody body and not yet ready to grieve. Her mother and sister had not seen the body (Pynoos & Nader, 1993). In cases such as this, when more than one family member is in treatment, weekly communication between clinicians is also essential.

Conjoint work has proved helpful to children and other family members when there has been intense worry about a family member during the traumatic event. After a sniper attack, a preschooler began checking on her brother in the night and became anxious when he was away from home. Another young girl was very angry with her brother, who had run for safety, leaving her behind. Joint sessions with the pairs of children allowed expressions of both anger and worry (Nader, 1997b).

GROUP WORK

Group work is especially pertinent when a traumatic event has affected a group or community. When addressing the needs of a community following a catastrophic event, a comprehensive mental health program includes periodic groups for administrators, for school personnel, and for parents; individual treatment for identified adults and children; and small groups for grieving and for injured children. Cooperative efforts, at all phases of intervention, between clinicians and intervention teams is essential to prevent working at cross-purposes and divisiveness (Nader, 1997b; Nader & Pynoos, 1993). Although childhood traumatic response occurs primarily in relationship to exposure to traumatic phenomena regardless of adults' experiences, recovery of the adult community affects the recovery of children (see Nader, 1997a, 1997b).

Initially after a traumatic event, a large group meeting for parents and school personnel generally includes the following: (1) discussion of the event and correcting rumors, (2) discussion of the adults' reactions to the event, (3) question-and-answer period about the children's reactions and discussion about the possible course of traumatic and grief reactions, (4) information about the psychological first aid that parents can provide, and (5) descriptions of planned services. Helping adults to discuss and understand their own reactions assists them in understanding their children's reactions (Nader, 1997b; Pynoos & Nader, 1988a).

When working with a school community, a classroom exercise and general discussion have been used to normalize the spectrum of the children's reactions, to screen for posttraumatic stress and other symptomatic reactions, and to address issues of dying and loss (Nader, 1997b; Pynoos & Nader, 1988a). These techniques in the group setting must be psychologically sound; for example, we do not engage children in their revenge fantasies in this group setting.

Child Groups

Group work can be helpful in addressing issues, such as injury or grief and loss, and in providing peer support and general coping strategies. For example, grief groups can help children establish a support system and permit open discussion of reactions and difficulties related to their losses. Children who previously have resolved their own grief reactions are an asset to these groups.

Adult Groups

Periodic meetings with parents and teachers are important to a child's progress. We have conducted parent groups and periodic teacher groups when the event has affected a community. Parents may need assistance to adjust to regressions and other changes in the child and to establish a rhythm with the child that enhances recovery. For example, severely traumatized or retraumatized children may need to reestablish a sense of trust, especially toward adults. A child who trusts is often easier to like than a child who distrusts. Distrustful behaviors may result in the discomfort, rejection, or annoyance of others. These reactions may contribute to or perpetuate the distrust. Parents may need assistance in recognizing that some traumatized children's behaviors are both measures of self-protection and cautious attempts to regain love and trust. The distrustful and annoying conduct is the noise that covers an intense desire to be loved and protected, combined with an intense fear of continued betrayal and harm (Nader, 1997b).

COMPATIBILITY WITH THE GENERALIST-ECLECTIC FRAMEWORK

Interactive trauma/grief–focused therapy is compatible with the main tenets of the generalist-eclectic framework for practice. First, it emphasizes the need to consider the child in context and to conduct a holistic assessment that considers factors such as family relationships, school adjustment, peer relationships, and culture. The model also promotes the use of environmental resources (e.g., support of family and school) in treatment. Second, this approach emphasizes the importance of a strong therapeutic relationship in order to enable children to work through the trauma. Third, with regard to a strengths perspective, the model focuses on successes and recognizes that high levels of personal strength can coexist with fragility in individuals who are moderately to severely traumatized. Fourth, the goal of the treatment is to replace a sense of helplessness with a sense of empowerment. Fifth, the model is eclectic and stresses flexibility in using techniques that fit the individual.

CRITIQUE OF THE MODEL

This treatment model has assisted children exposed to a variety of traumatic events (e.g., witness to suicide, violence, and natural disasters) and has been adapted for work with adults. The method works best with individuals who have been exposed to single or multiple incidents of trauma and who have an ability to develop trust. There is statistical evidence of the effectiveness of the direct screening interview (Nader, 1996a; Nader et al., 1990). Preliminary findings suggest significant reduction in trauma symptoms and improved functioning after use of this method. Moreover, the reports of children and adults who have undergone treatment suggest improvement in the quality of life. For example, close adult friends have observed that children were happier after treatment than before the traumatic incident. Adults and adolescents have suggested the same results for themselves.

Like other methods, this treatment model requires knowledge of trauma, child development, and psychotherapeutic principles. Personal strength, courage, confidence, sensitivity, and skilled timing are essential to the trauma clinician. If a clinician has been exposed to a personal traumatic experience, any unresolved traumatic symptoms or themes may hinder the giving of treatment. For widespread traumatic events (e.g., war or disaster), mental health professionals must have addressed their own traumatic responses prior to assisting others.

This treatment method can be more difficult to apply when the trauma is in the distant past and its aspects are well buried and/or distorted. When trust has been badly damaged, some individuals require trust building and slower paced treatment, perhaps less strongly directive in the beginning or during phases over the course of treatment. It may be more difficult to use this treatment with adults or adolescents who have adopted a successful and ingrained style of avoidance (e.g., use of drugs).

SUMMARY

During traumatic events multiple traumatic impressions become embedded in memory. If unresolved for children, these intense impressions may result in repeated patterns of thought, emotion, and/or behavior (e.g., traumatic reenactments), disturbances in thought or conduct (e.g., disturbed morality, violence), or chronic mental disorders (e.g., major depression, PTSD). Interactive trauma/grief–focused therapy enables reprocessing and resolution of traumatic memory impressions and restoration of self-esteem, joy, and a normal developmental path.

REFERENCES

American Psychiatric Association. (1994). *Diagnostic and statistical manual of mental disorders* (4th ed.). Washington, DC: Author.

Amster, F. (1943). Differential use of play in treatment of young children. *American Journal of Orthopsychiatry, 13,* 62–68.

Axline, V. (1947). *Play therapy.* Boston: Houghton-Mifflin.

Carlson, E. B. (1997). *Trauma assessments.* New York: Guilford Press.

Erickson, M., Rossi, E. L., & Ryan, M. O. (Eds.). (1985). *Life reframing in hypnosis: Seminars, workshops, and lectures of Milton Erickson* (Vol. 2). New York: Irvington.

Eth, S., & Pynoos, R. S. (1985). Developmental perspectives on psychic trauma in children. In C. Figley (Ed.), *Trauma and its wake* (pp. 35–52). New York: Brunner/Mazel.

Frederick, C., Pynoos, R. S., & Nader, K. (1992). *The childhood posttraumatic stress reaction index* (CPTS-RI). A copyrighted inventory.

Goenjian, A., Karayan, I., Pynoos, R. S., Minassian, D., Najarian, L. M., Steinberg, A., & Fairbanks, L. A. (1997). Outcome of psychotherapy among early adolescents after trauma. *American Journal of Psychiatry, 154,* 536–542.

Herman, J. L. (1992). Complex PTSD: A syndrome in survivors of prolonged and repeated trauma. *Journal of Social Issues, 40,* 33–50.

Ibrahim, Y. M. (1992, August 4). Iraqis left coarse scars on the psyche of Kuwait. *The New York Times,* p. A3.

Johnson, M. K., & Foley, M. A. (1984). Differentiating fact from fantasy: The reliability of children's memory. *Journal of Social Issues, 40,* 33–50.

Kohly, M. (1994). *Reported child abuse and neglect victims during the flood months of 1993.* St. Louis, MO: Missouri Department of Social Services, Division of Family Services, Research and Development Unit.

Levy, D. M. (1938). Release therapy in young children. *Psychiatry, 1,* 387–390.

Marsella, A. J., Friedman, M. J., Gerrity, E. T., & Scurfield, R. M. (Eds.). (1996). *Ethnocultural aspects of posttraumatic stress disorder.* Washington, DC: American Psychological Association.

Nader, K. (1993). *Childhood trauma: A manual and questionnaires.* Costa Mesa, CA: Two Suns.

Nader, K. (1994). Countertransference in treating trauma and victimization in childhood. In J. Wilson & J. Lindy (Eds.), *Countertransference in the treatment of Posttraumatic Stress Disorder* (pp. 179–205). New York: Guilford Press.

Nader, K. (1994/1995). *Psychological first aid for trauma, grief and traumatic grief.* Costa Mesa, CA: Two Suns.

Nader, K. (1996a). Assessing traumatic experiences in children. In J. Wilson & T. Keane (Eds.), *Assessing psychological trauma and PTSD* (pp. 291–348). New York: Guilford Press.

Nader, K. (1996b). Children's exposure to traumatic experiences. In C. A. Corr & D. M. Corr (Eds.), *Handbook of childhood death and bereavement* (pp. 201–222). New York: Springer.

Nader, K. (1996c). Children's traumatic dreams. In D. Barrett (Ed.), *Trauma and dreams* (pp. 9–24). Cambridge, MA: Harvard University Press.

Nader, K. (1997a). Childhood traumatic loss: The interaction of trauma and grief. In C. R. Figley, B. E. Bride, & N. Mazza (Eds.), *Death and trauma: The traumatology of grieving* (pp. 17–41). London: Taylor & Francis.

Nader, K. (1997b). Treating traumatic grief in systems. In C. R. Figley, B. E. Bride, & N. Mazza (Eds.), *Death and trauma: The traumatology of grieving* (pp. 159–192). London: Taylor & Francis.

Nader, K. (1998). Violence: Effects of parents' previous trauma on currently traumatized children. In Y. Danieli (Ed.), *International handbook of multigenerational legacies of trauma* (pp. 571–583). New York: Plenum.

Nader, K. (in press). *Treatment methods for childhood trauma.* In J. P. Wilson, M. Friedman, & J. Lindy (Eds.), *Core treatment approaches for PTSD.* New York: Guilford Press.

Nader, K., Dubrow, N., & Stamm, B. H. (1999). *Cultural issues in the treatment of trauma and loss. Honoring differences.* Philadelphia: Taylor & Francis.

Nader, K., & Fairbanks, L. (1994). The suppression of reexperiencing: Impulse control and somatic symptoms in children following traumatic exposure. *Anxiety, Stress and Coping: An International Journal, 7,* 229–239.

Nader, K., & Pynoos, R. S. (1991). Play and drawing as tools for interviewing traumatized children. In C. Schaeffer, K. Gitian, & A. Sandgrund (Eds.), *Play, diagnosis and assessment* (pp. 375–389). New York: Wiley.

Nader, K., & Pynoos, R. S. (1993a). The children of Kuwait following the Gulf Crisis. In L. Lewin & N. Fox (Eds.), *Effects of war and violence in children* (pp. 181–195). Hillsdale, NJ: Laurence Erlbaum.

Nader, K., & Pynoos, R. S. (1993b). School disaster: Planning and initial interventions. *Journal of Social Behavior and Personality, 8,* 299–320.

Nader, K., Pynoos, R. S., Fairbanks, L., Al-Ajeel, M., & Al-Asfour, A. (1993). Acute posttraumatic stress reactions among Kuwait children following the Gulf Crisis. *British Journal of Clinical Psychology, 32,* 407–416.

Nader, K., Pynoos, R. S., Fairbanks, L., & Frederick, C. (1990). Children's PTSD reactions one year after a sniper attack at their school. *American Journal of Psychiatry, 147,* 1526–1530.

Pynoos, R. S. (1984). *Brief grief inventory.* An unpublished inventory.

Pynoos, R. S. (1993). Traumatic stress and developmental psychopathology in children and adolescents. In J. M. Oldham, M. B. Riba, & A. Tasman (Eds.), *American psychiatric press review of psychiatry* (Vol. 12, pp. 205–238). Washington, DC: American Psychiatric Press.

Pynoos, R. S., & Eth, S. (1986). Witness to violence: The child interview. *Journal of the American Academy of Child Psychiatry, 25,* 306–319.

Pynoos, R. S., & Nader, K. (1988a). Psychological first aid and treatment approach for children exposed to community violence: Research implications. *Journal of Traumatic Stress, 1,* 445–473.

Pynoos, R. S., & Nader, K. (1988b). Children who witness the sexual assaults of their mothers. *Journal of the American Academy of Child and Adolescent Psychiatry, 27,* 567–572.

Pynoos, R. S., & Nader, K. (1989a). Prevention of psychiatric morbidity in children after disaster. In D. Schaffer, I. Philips, & N. B. Enzer (Eds.), *Prevention of mental disorders, alcohol and other drug use in children and adolescents* (pp. 225–271). Rockville, MD: U.S. Department of Health and Human Services.

Pynoos, R. S., & Nader, K. (1989b). Children's memory and proximity to violence. *Journal of the American Academy of Child and Adolescent Psychiatry, 28,* 236–241.

Pynoos, R. S., & Nader, K. (1993). Issues in the treatment of posttraumatic stress in children and adolescents. In J. P. Wilson & B. Raphael (Eds.), *International handbook of traumatic stress syndromes* (pp. 535–549). New York: Plenum.

Pynoos, R. S., Nader, K., & March, J. (1991). Post traumatic stress disorder in children and adolescents. In J. Weiner (Ed.), *Comprehensive textbook of child and adolescent psychiatry* (pp. 339–348). Washington, DC: American Psychiatric Press.

Stamm, B. H. (Ed.). (1996). *Measurement of stress, trauma and adaptation.* Lutherville, MD: Sidran Press.

Swiss, S., & Gilder, J. E. (1993). Rape as a crime of war: A medical perspective. *Journal of the American Medical Association, 270,* 612–615.

Terr, L. (1979). Children of Chowchilia: Study of psychic trauma. *Psychoanalytic Study of the Child, 34,* 547–623.

Terr, L. C. (1991). Childhood traumas: An outline and overview. *American Journal of Psychiatry, 148,* 10–20.

van der Kolk, B., & Sapporta, J. (1991). The biological response to psychic trauma: Mechanisms and treatment of intrusion and numbing. *Anxiety Research, 4,* 199–212.

Wilson, J., & Keane, T. (Eds.). (1996). *Assessing psychological trauma and post-traumatic stress disorder.* New York: Guilford Press.

Wilson, J., & Raphael, B. (Eds.). (1993). *International handbook of traumatic stress syndromes.* New York: Plenum Press.

PART 5

Summary and Conclusion

21

Revisiting the Generalist-Eclectic Approach

Nick Coady and Peter Lehmann

The first three chapters (i.e., Part 1) of this book dealt with the major elements and basic principles of the generalist-eclectic approach to direct social work practice. Given the fact that the last 17 chapters have focused on various theoretical perspectives for direct practice, for purposes of review and integration it is important to revisit the generalist-eclectic approach in this final chapter. In the first part of this chapter, we review conceptualizations of levels of theory (high-, mid-, and low-level theory) and broad classes of mid-level practice theory (psychodynamic, cognitive-behavioral, humanistic and feminist, and postmodern) that were discussed in chapter 2 and consider how these conceptualizations can facilitate an eclectic use of theory in practice. Second, the compatibility between the various mid-level practice theories reviewed in Part 3 (chapters 6 to 17) of the book and the generalist-eclectic approach is considered. The third part of the chapter revisits how the problem-solving model is a useful framework for integrating the eclectic use of theory with the artistic, intuitive-inductive elements of practice. Finally, some of the practical challenges to generalist-eclectic practice are identified and strategies for dealing with these challenges are suggested.

THE USEFULNESS OF CONCEPTUALIZING LEVELS AND CLASSES OF THEORY TO FACILITATE ECLECTICISM

Reflecting on the array of theoretical perspectives that are re
chapters in this book raises the potential for feeling overwhe
sheer number of theories and their different perspectives on hu

lems and the helping process. This potential for "theoretical overload" becomes probable when one considers that over 200 separate theories of counseling have been identified (Herink, cited in Garfield & Bergin, 1994). Given this confusing array of theories, many of which feature rather esoteric and mystifying language, one can understand why practitioners might retreat to the structure, safety, and certainty that can be provided by a narrow allegiance to one approach to counseling. As understandable as this tendency may be, we are convinced of the arguments for eclecticism that were reviewed in the first chapter. In order to make eclecticism feasible, however, strategies for simplifying and demystifying the vast array of theoretical perspectives is necessary. It is our hope that the organization of this book reflects two helpful strategies in this regard: (1) differentiating among high-, mid-, and low-level theoretical perspectives; and (2) classifying the vast array of mid-level practice theories into like categories and providing general descriptions of the commonalities within each broad category.

DIFFERENTIATING AMONG THE LEVELS OF THEORY

A consideration of the differential function and usefulness of the various levels of theory can be a helpful first step in dealing with "theoretical overload." Chapter 2 presented a discussion of three levels of theory for direct practice (see Figure 2.1 in chapter 2 for an overview). The chapters on theory in this book were grouped into three parts corresponding to the three levels of theory identified. Part 2 (chapters 4 and 5) of the book contained chapters on high-level or metatheories (ecological systems and human development theories, respectively) that provide general ways of looking at and understanding a broad range of human behavior. These theories represent foundational knowledge for generalist-eclectic practice, and their main value is in providing broad, normative lenses for data collection and assessment. Although these high-level theories can provide general ideas for intervention, they do not prescribe interventions to the extent that lower-level theories do.

Part 3 (chapters 6–17) of the book was devoted to mid-level practice theories (the usefulness of the subclassifications of these theories will be considered later). In general, this level of theory provides more specific ways of understanding human behavior and is also prescriptive with regard to the change process. Historically, most of these theories have laid claim to being universally applicable to understanding and intervening with the entire range of human problems. A generalist-eclectic approach maintains, however, that each of these theories may be relevant for understanding and intervening with some clients' problems but not with others. Workers should use these theoretical perspectives tentatively in the data collection and assessment phases and take care not to force-fit clients' experience into theoretical boxes. These theories can be used individually or in combination to guide intervention, based on a determination of their relevance to the client's problem situation and their fit with client factors (e.g., coping style).

Examples of low-level theories (i.e., wraparound services, family preservation services, and interactive trauma/grief–focused therapy with children) were provided in Part 4 (chapters 18–20) of the book. These theories provide much more concrete understanding of and intervention guidelines for specific problems and populations. These models and therapies usually apply concepts and strategies from one or more of the mid-level theories to a specific client problem (e.g., grief, child abuse and neglect, addictions, or psychiatric disorder). Thus, this level of theory can be viewed as a subset or derivative of the mid-level theory. In many respects, low-level theory that incorporates concepts and strategies from a number of different mid-level theoretical perspectives can be viewed as a logical extension of the generalist-eclectic approach, as long as it is not rigidly prescriptive, allows for individualized interventions based on holistic assessment, and embraces basic social work values and principles. For example, interactive trauma/grief–focused therapy (chapter 20) is consistent with a generalist-eclectic approach in that it not only incorporates therapeutic strategies from a number of theories (e.g., psychodynamic, cognitive-behavioral, and humanistic/Gestalt) in the treatment of trauma, but also values broad-based assessment, tailors intervention flexibly to individual clients, and recognizes the need for clinical judgment or a "good sense of timing" with regard to decisions about intervention.

The conceptualization of levels of theory is one way of bringing order to the overwhelming number of theoretical perspectives for practice. The three levels of theory can be viewed as complementing rather than competing with each other. High- and low-level theories can be construed as providing support to the use of mid-level theories. High-level theories provide a broad lens for viewing human behavior and ensure that a broad range of factors (e.g., biological, personal, interpersonal, environmental, and sociocultural) are considered in the effort to understand clients' problem situations. These theories ensure that the big, person-in-environment picture is entertained in data collection and assessment and they guard against the danger of tunnel vision or myopia that exists with mid- and low-level theories. On the other end of the spectrum, the type of in-depth knowledge that low-level theories provide about specific client problems can be seen as a valuable resource to support the use of more general, mid-level theory. For example, even if one is drawing eclectically from a range of mid-level theory in working with a client, if a specific clinical issue (e.g., grief or trauma) surfaces, it would be helpful to refer to low-level models (e.g., interactive trauma/grief–focused therapy) for more specific ideas for understanding and treating such issues.

CONCEPTUALIZING AND CHARACTERIZING CLASSES
OF PRACTICE THEORY

A second useful way of simplifying and demystifying theoretical perspectives is to group the vast array of mid-level practice theories, models, and therapies into like groupings. In this book, we have grouped mid-level clinical theories into one of four classifications: (1) psychodynamic, (2) cognitive-behavioral, (3) humanistic and feminist, and (4) postmodern (which are the four subsections in Part 3 of this book). Chapter 2 provided an overview of the central characteristics of each of these four groupings of theory. Table 21.1 summarizes this information. The reader should note that although humanistic and feminist theories have similarities (see chapter 2) and are grouped together as one of our four classifications of practice theory, their distinctness merits separate consideration (see chapter 2).

The broad characterization of the major classes of direct practice theory found in Table 21.1 allows for identifying the commonalities among theories in each of the four groups, as well as for pointing out differences across groups. This description helps to bring order and clarity to the confusing array of theories within the field and allows for the identification of the strengths and weaknesses of the various classes of theory, both of which facilitate the eclectic use of theory. The concepts in the left-hand column of the table represent some of the important dimensions by which to compare theoretical perspectives. It should be emphasized that the characterizations of the classes of theory with regard to these dimensions are very general and should be construed as descriptions of central tendencies. For example, although the primary focus in most cognitive-behavioral and humanistic therapies is on the present, this is not to say that such therapies do not focus at all on the past. The same caution applies to the characterization of the classes of theory with regard to focus on affect, cognition, and behavior; focus on symptoms or general growth/development; and degree of structure and directiveness. The dangers of such broad characterizations include the potential to minimize differences within groups of theory and to overlook similarities across groups. An example of the danger of minimizing differences within groups of theory is found in some of the major differences between solution-focused therapy and the other types of postmodern theory. As pointed out in chapter 2, solution-focused therapy concentrates more on specific symptoms and behaviors and is more directive, compared to narrative and constructivist theories. With regard to the danger of exaggerating differences across groups of theory, integrative theorists have demonstrated how seemingly antithetical theories are not as different and incompatible as one might suppose (e.g., see discussion in chapter 2 of Wachtel & McKinney's [1992] and Safran and Segal's [1990] integrative models).

With these limitations in mind, a general consideration of how the concepts in the left-hand column of Table 21.1 are construed by or manifested

TABLE 21.1 Characterization of Classes of Direct Practice Theories

	Psychodynamic	Cognitive-behavioral	Humanistic	Feminist	Postmodern
View of causation of human problems	Traumatic experiences or inadequate nurturance in childhood lead to unconscious internalization of conflict or developmental deficits	Maladaptive behaviors and/or cognitions are learned through conditioning, reinforcement, and/or modeling	Defenses against painful aspects of experience lead to losing touch with authentic experiencing in the present	Institutionalized system of male privilege results in exploitation and oppression of women and other disadvantaged groups	Negative interpretation of self and of life experience and/or internalization of toxic cultural narratives that oppress marginalized groups
Goal of intervention	Develop emotional/cognitive understanding of connection between early and current problems	Learn more adaptive thoughts and behaviors	Develop new awareness of and meaning about experiences in the present	Raise consciousness of oppression and empower for personal and social change	Develop more positive views of self and of life experience and/or develop freedom from oppressive cultural assumptions
Primary focus on past or present	Past and present	Present	Present	Present and past	Present and past

(continued)

409

TABLE 21.1 (*continued*)

	Psychodynamic	Cognitive-behavioral	Humanistic	Feminist	Postmodern
Primary focus on affect, cognition, or behavior	Affect and cognition	Cognition and behavior	Affect	Affect, cognition, and behavior	Cognition
Primary focus on specific symptoms or general growth/development	General growth/development	Specific symptoms	General growth/development	General growth/development	General growth/development
Degree of structure and directiveness (low, medium, high)	Low-medium	Medium-high	Low-medium	Low-medium	Low-medium

Note. The characterizations in this table are broad generalizations that do not hold for all of the more specific approaches within these classes (see discussion in this chapter and in chapter 2).

in each class of theory can help the practitioner to consider which class of theory might best suit particular clients at particular points in the counseling process, as well as to consider which classes of theory might be used simultaneously to address clients' concerns more holistically. For instance, a client who wants to focus on specific symptoms in current day-to-day functioning, to avoid exploration of painful feelings, and to have a high degree of structure and direction in counseling may be best served, at least initially, by a cognitive-behavioral approach. Once this client learns to cope more effectively with presenting symptoms, however, he or she and the worker may decide that a focus on feelings (i.e., affect) may be helpful to consolidate and further gains. If client issues seem to be connected to early problematic relationships with caregivers, a psychodynamic approach might then be used to explore the link between affective difficulties in the present and the past and to work through such feelings. If a connection to earlier intimate relationships is not apparent, or if the client is adverse to exploring such connections, a humanistic approach may be more appropriate for dealing with affective issues. If the client is a woman whose issues seem to be connected to a history of abuse or oppression, consideration should be given to integrating a feminist approach with any of these other approaches. Also, a postmodern approach could be integrated with any of the other theoretical approaches or used as a follow-up to other approaches in order to integrate changes into more empowering views of one's self and one's life story.

To summarize, a general characterization of the broad classes of direct practice theories can be helpful to demystify the confusing array of approaches to counseling and to facilitate considerations involved in the eclectic use of theory. It is imperative, however, to keep in mind the limitations of such a general characterization and to pursue a more in-depth understanding of a wide variety of theories, including knowledge of the similarities and differences among specific theories within and across classifications.

THE COMPATIBILITY BETWEEN THE GENERALIST-ECLECTIC APPROACH AND THE VARIOUS DIRECT PRACTICE THEORIES

All of the chapters in Part 3 of this book included at least a general consideration of the compatibility between the particular practice theory under consideration and the principles of the generalist-eclectic approach, as outlined in chapter 1. Although there were differences in emphasis noted by some authors, there was a strong endorsement of the generalist-eclectic approach to practice by the authors of these chapters. Overall, there was consensus about the importance of (1) a person-in-environment perspective and comprehensive and holistic assessment that includes attention to issues of diversity and oppression; (2) a therapeutic relationship marked by collaboration, empathy, warmth, and genuineness; and (3) an eclectic use of a wide range of theories and techniques. A cynic could suggest that the authors might have felt compelled to endorse such principles and values, to conform either to the wishes of the editors or to the social work profession's growing commitment to the generalist perspective; however, we do not think that this was the case. Instead, it seems to us that this convergence in thinking reflects the relatively recent trend in the clinical field toward valuing a person-in-environment perspective, worker-client collaboration, and eclecticism. We think that this is a major and healthy shift in thinking, because the historical legacy of the clinical field has been marked, to a large degree, by rigid adherence to single models of therapy that tended to have narrow, mostly psychological, views of human problems and noncollaborative, expert orientations.

It is particularly noteworthy that the older, more traditional theoretical perspectives (i.e., psychodynamic and cognitive-behavioral theories) have undergone significant changes in emphasis over the years. In general, psychodynamic theories have broadened their intrapsychic focus to include much greater consideration of environmental factors; have moved away from a rather distant, expert-oriented therapeutic stance toward a much more collaborative and empathic approach; and have become more open to the value and usefulness of other theories and their techniques. It should be noted, however, that we chose to include in this book the psychodynamic theories that had moved furthest in these directions. There are still psychodynamic theories that do not embrace these trends. Similarly, cognitive-behavioral theories, particularly the more behaviorally oriented ones, have not always embraced generalist principles. Over time, these theories have broadened their focus of assessment beyond stimulus-response patterns to include cognitive and social factors; have embraced the importance of a good therapeutic relationship, at least as a facilitating factor for change; and have become more open to eclecticism. Again, for the cognitive-behavioral section of the book, we selected theories that were most compatible with the generalist approach. In particular, readers should be reminded that the task-centered and crisis intervention models have a strong connection to social work and are perhaps better conceptualized as atheoretical and eclectic models, respectively (see chapter 2 for a fuller discussion of this point). There are still many traditional behavioral theories that would not endorse generalist principles.

Beyond the general endorsement of the values and principles of the generalist-eclectic approach by the contributing authors of the practice theory chapters in this book, there are other, more specific similarities between some theories in the book and elements of generalist-eclectic practice. First, in many ways, the task-centered model (TC) could be construed as part of our generalist-eclectic approach. Although this model borrows mostly from cognitive-behavioral theory, it is in essence a problem-solving model that provides structure for the eclectic use of the entire range of theory. Tolson, Reid, and Garvin (1994) have argued that TC is "an ideal base for generalist practice . . . [and] for eclectic practice" (p. 22). Furthermore, similar to our recognition of the intuitive-inductive elements of practice (see chapter 2), TC incorporates the recognition that theory is not always used in practice. Although the TC literature does not refer to intuition or inductive theory building, it refers to the related idea of commonsense reasoning: "We rely, when possible, on explanations based on reasoning. When a theoretical explanation is needed, we are free to apply the theory or combination of theories that best explain the problem encountered" (Tolson et al., 1994, p. 22).

Second, a number of other theories reviewed in this book also have similarities to the intuitive-inductive elements of practice that we endorse as part of our generalist-eclectic approach. Most noteworthy in this regard are client-centered theory (chapter 12); existential theory, particularly the mystery-centered approach (chapter 13); and the Collaborative Language Systems variety of narrative therapy (chapter 15). These approaches emphasize the importance of suspending theoretical thinking, entering into the phenomenological world of clients, building genuine and collaborative personal relationships with clients, and developing felt understanding of their lives. In chapter 12, Rothery notes the client-centered disdain for "preconceptions in the form of theories of personality, or psychopathology, or anything else that might work against our openness to the uniqueness of people and their situations" (p. 224). In chapter 13, Lantz explains that existential theory involves tolerating "the anxiety of 'starting fresh' with every new client" (p. 245) and "developing a participatory and empathic understanding" (p. 242). In discussing collaborative language systems therapy in chapter 15, Buckman, Reese, and Kinney describe "a therapeutic posture that emphasizes collaboration, openness, and curiosity (not knowing)" (p. 280). Although each of these theories have somewhat different emphases, they share with each other, and with the intuitive-inductive approach to practice, an emphasis on the artistic and humanistic elements of practice. This is not to say that other theoretical approaches do not also allow for artistic and humanistic factors (e.g., attachment, self-psychology, feminist, and constructivist theories do so clearly), but that other theories do not emphasize them to the same extent.

Despite the overall compatibility between the variety of practice theories presented in this book and the generalist-eclectic approach to practice, it would be remiss to not make a closer examination of differences. The only direct contrast that we noted between a central principle of generalist-eclectic practice and a theoretical perspective is solution-focused therapy's dismissal of the value of holistic assessment. In chapter 17, Corcoran states that "solution-focused therapy departs from a generalist-eclectic framework in eschewing a holistic assessment of the various system levels, along with information-gathering about the problem and history taking" (p. 335). This and other conflicts between solution-focused therapy and mainstream social work principles have been noted by others (Stalker, Levene, & Coady, 1999). This suggests that social workers should be particularly mindful of following generalist social work principles when using solution-focused therapy as part of their eclectic approach.

Although we have noted only one direct contrast between the practice theories reviewed in the book and the generalist-eclectic approach, there are certainly differences in the degree to which various theories emphasize central social work principles and values. It should be pointed out that despite the general endorsement of a person-in-environment perspective and holistic assessment by all but one practice theory represented in the book, specific practice theories, by definition, have more preconceptions and are less comprehensive than a generalist perspective. Every practice theory has preconceived ideas about the cause of human problems (e.g., see Table 21.1). For example, psychodynamic theories may give consideration to environmental and sociocultural factors in assessment, but focus is directed to intrapsychic issues and their connection to inadequate or traumatic experiences in childhood. Despite a commitment to broad-based assessment, the preconceptions that exist for all practice theories can function as blinders. Furthermore, most practice theories are far more psychologically oriented and pay much less attention to issues of diversity and oppression than a generalist social work perspective. Of the practice theories reviewed in this book, only task-centered and feminist theories devote considerable attention to broad social issues (e.g., poverty), and only feminist theories and the social deconstruction variety of narrative therapy focus considerably on issues of diversity and oppression. Also, despite an openness to eclecticism, by virtue of their primary theoretical orientation, all practice theories are less theoretically and technically "open" than the generalist-eclectic approach. Thus, despite the general compatibility between many theoretical perspectives and the generalist-eclectic approach, we believe that, when drawing on theories, clinical social workers need to consciously integrate the central principles and values of generalist social work into their practice.

REVISITING THE IMPORTANCE OF THE PROBLEM-SOLVING MODEL AS A FRAMEWORK FOR INTEGRATING THE ARTISTIC AND SCIENTIFIC ELEMENTS OF PRACTICE

As discussed in chapter 3, the downside to both the intuitive-inductive approach to practice and the deductive, eclectic use of theory in practice is a lack of structure and guidelines for action. Without some dependable structure and guidelines, both the artistic and the theoretically eclectic approaches to practice can lack focus and direction and become haphazard—which is the common criticism from those who advocate following a single model of therapy. The problem-solving model provides such structure and guidelines for practice.

The problem-solving model's broad guidelines for each phase of practice provide sufficient structure for the eclectic use of various theories, but because they are not rigidly prescriptive, they also afford enough flexibility to allow for intuition and inductive reasoning. The general structure of the problem-solving model allows for an integration of, or at least an oscillation between, the scientific and artistic modes of practice. For instance, with regard to data collection and assessment, the general structure and guidelines of the problem-solving model remind practitioners to use a person-in-environment perspective and direct them to give consideration to a broad range of factors (micro and macro, stressors and strengths) in order to understand clients' life situations. The problem-solving guidelines in this phase of practice also direct practitioners to consider a broad range of theoretical perspectives to help make sense of clients' situations, including mid- and low-level practice theories, as well as high-level or metatheories. Furthermore, the general nature and the flexibility of these problem-solving guidelines allow for practitioners to use their intuition and inductive reasoning to develop together with their clients a complex understanding of unique problem situations. Thus, as with other phases of the problem-solving process, the general guidelines of the data collection and assessment phase allow for a synthesis of an eclectic use of theory and intuitive-inductive processes.

CHALLENGES FOR GENERALIST-ECLECTIC DIRECT SOCIAL WORK PRACTICE

Given the fact that we have tried to extol the virtues of and argue persuasively for generalist-eclectic direct social work practice, we would be remiss if we did not consider some of the challenges that exist for this approach to practice. Below, we discuss important challenges for research and for practice, as well as strategies for dealing with these challenges.

CHALLENGES FOR RESEARCH

Single-theory approaches have predominated in the helping professions, and thus most psychotherapy research to date has focused on the effectiveness of such approaches. Although cumulative research on psychotherapy has found no significant differences in the effectiveness of the various single-theory approaches (the "equal outcomes" phenomenon), the results indicate clearly that, overall, such psychotherapy is effective compared to nonintervention (Bergin & Garfield, 1994). What has not been established empirically is the superiority of eclectic approaches over single-theory approaches. Due to the newness of the movement toward eclecticism and integration in psychotherapy and to the preoccupation with theory development in this movement, research has been neglected. As Norcross (1997) has noted, "[T]he commitment to psychotherapy integration is largely philosophical rather than empirical in nature. The adequacy of various integrative and eclectic approaches remains to be proven" (p. 87). This is not to say that there is reason to doubt that eclectic approaches are effective. Lambert (1992) has argued that "to the extent that eclectic therapies provide treatment that includes substantial overlap with traditional methods that have been developed and tested, they rest on a firm empirical base, and they should prove to be at least as effective as traditional school-based therapies" (p. 71).

Research comparing the effectiveness of eclectic approaches to single-theory approaches, as well as research that compares the effectiveness of various types of eclectic approaches (including the generalist-eclectic social work approach), is needed. Comparative outcome research of both of these kinds needs to be undertaken with regard to specific problems and populations. Such research should focus on matching theories and techniques not only to specific client problems but also to other factors, such as client coping style and client stage of change (Norcross, 1997). Similarly, research on the therapeutic alliance should examine matching relationship styles to various client and process factors (Norcross, 1997).

CHALLENGES IN PRACTICE

A generalist-eclectic approach to practice does not provide the comfort and certainty for practitioners that following a single model of therapy can provide. Practitioners who adhere to one theoretical approach, particularly if it has a narrow focus and prescriptive guidelines, can gain comfort in "knowing" at the outset of counseling what the problem is and/or what they need to do to help ameliorate it. In generalist-eclectic practice, the emphasis on theoretical openness and broad-based assessment precludes this type of certainty. Furthermore, the emphasis on the intuitive-inductive/artistic elements of practice, as well as on collaboration and partnership with the client, involves giving up control and certainty in the generalist-eclectic approach to helping. Although the guidelines of the problem-solving model and understanding and/or techniques gleaned from a variety of theories provide helpful guidance for practice, a generalist-eclectic approach requires the practitioner to be creative and to find courage "in the face of the uncertain" (Papell & Skolnik, 1992, p. 22). This can be difficult, particularly for beginning practitioners who frequently yearn for " 'a secret handbook' of practical 'how-to-do-it' knowledge" (Mahoney, 1986, p. 169); however, it is our contention that clients respond better to this humble, open, and humane approach to practice than to theoretical certainty and prescriptive formulas.

Another obvious challenge in this approach to practice is that of becoming familiar with the wide variety of theoretical approaches that can be used eclectically. Although we have offered strategies for simplifying and demystifying the confusing array of clinical theories (i.e., conceptualizing levels and broad classes of theory, and identifying the central concepts and ideas for the latter), there is no denying that developing in-depth knowledge and skill in a variety of theoretical approaches is a formidable task. This is particularly difficult given the unfortunate but continuing use of "idiosyncratic jargon" by many theoretical orientations (Goldfried & Castonguay, 1992). This not only makes learning different theories more difficult and intimidating but also hinders the development of understanding about similarities across theories. With regard to the latter issue, we support the long-range goal of translating theories into ordinary English in order to further demystification and to facilitate cross-theory dialogue (Goldfried & Castonguay, 1992). With regard to the more general difficulty of becoming a "master of all trades" (i.e., of all theories and techniques), we think that practitioners should construe this as a career-long goal, in the context of understanding that theoretical knowledge and technical expertise can never be complete and that general interpersonal sensitivity and relationship skills are of prime importance to counseling effectiveness.

A third, general challenge to practicing from a generalist-eclectic orientation concerns the necessity of integrating a consideration of broader social issues, particularly issues of diversity and oppression, into both assessment and intervention. As noted earlier in this chapter, very few counseling theories pay much attention to these issues. Thus, from a generalist social work perspective, there is a need to use other sources of knowledge about working with issues of diversity and oppression. In addition to generalist social work literature, practitioners can draw upon other broad frameworks for social work practice, such as empowerment practice (Gutierrez, Parsons, & Cox, 1998) and the strengths perspective (Saleeby, 1997), that pay special attention to these issues.

Managed Care

The major transformation in counseling services that has been brought about over the last 10 years by the managed care industry deserves special attention as a potential challenge to a generalist-eclectic approach to practice. We surmise that the managed care industry, which frequently limits counseling to as few as 5 or 10 sessions, might be skeptical of an approach to practice that values holistic assessment, the development of in-depth understanding within the context of a good therapeutic relationship, and intervention that draws on a range of theories and techniques. In fact, in advising practitioners how to present themselves to case managers within the managed care industry, Nichols and Schwartz (1998) suggest that "calling yourself 'eclectic' is more likely to sound fuzzy than flexible" (p. 105). We do not doubt that this type of pejorative thinking about eclecticism continues to exist, particularly with regard to brief treatment, and we see this is as a challenge that needs to be addressed.

Although we do have concerns about the rigid enforcement of short-term counseling limits, particularly for clients who have multiple, severe, and/or longstanding stressors, we believe that a generalist-eclectic approach to practice can be used effectively in the context of brief treatment and managed care. As discussed in chapter 3, holistic assessment usually does not involve a long, drawn-out process of data collection. Practitioners can learn to focus a broad lens rather quickly, and some holistic assessments (which are always tentative and subject to change) can be completed in single sessions. Similarly, the development of a strong therapeutic relationship usually does not require long periods of time—research has shown that alliances predictive of outcome are usually formed within the first few sessions (Horvath & Greenberg, 1994). With regard to intervention, a generalist-eclectic approach to practice can be as focused and brief as necessary. Within a managed care context, practitioners and clients should plan and contract to focus on the most pressing problem that can be dealt with within the allotted time periods. From a generalist-eclectic perspective, however, practitioners working within the managed care industry would be obligated to attempt to secure longer-term help for those clients who want and require it. This could involve lobbying a case manager for extending the counseling limits, contracting with the client to continue work together after the managed care session limits have been reached (and working out payment issues), or referring the client to other services.

There seems to be an unfortunate myth that only therapeutic approaches that are labeled as "brief" are suitable for the managed care industry. In particular, brief solution-focused therapy's "seductive promise of quick and easy solutions has endeared it to the managed care industry. Indeed, . . . many applicants for provider status call themselves 'solution-focused' regardless of whether or not they have any training in this approach" (Nichols & Schwartz, 1998, p. 381). However, there are good reasons to believe that most models of therapy (whether single-theory or eclectic) are adaptable to the counseling parameters of managed care. First, a review of studies that have examined length of treatment across settings and theoretical orientations has established that the median number of sessions was between five and eight (Garfield, 1994). Thus, even traditional counseling approaches are often as brief as the so-called brief therapies. Second, even the psychodynamic school, which traditionally is the longest-term approach to counseling, has developed brief treatment models that can fit the constraints of managed care (Koss & Shiang, 1994). Thus, we see two specific challenges with regard to managed care. The first challenge is to educate the managed care industry to the fact that all theoretical orientations, including eclecticism, are adaptable for brief treatment. The second is to educate social workers that, although they need to be mindful of the inadequacies of brief treatment for some clients and to make appropriate adjustments (as discussed above), a generalist-eclectic orientation can be used effectively in the brief treatment context of managed care.

SUMMARY

In addition to providing a survey of contemporary theories for direct social work practice, this book represents an attempt to integrate a number of important and compatible ideas in the field of counseling into a broad framework for practice. To summarize, there are three major elements to what we have called the generalist-eclectic approach to practice. The first is represented by the movement toward eclecticism in the field of counseling/psychotherapy and includes the principles and guidelines for eclecticism that are being generated by this movement. The second is represented by the principles and values of a generalist social work orientation to direct practice. In addition to a general embracement of eclecticism, the generalist orientation includes commitment to a person-in-environment perspective, holistic assessment that includes attention to issues of diversity and oppression, the development of a good helping relationship that fosters empowerment, and the flexible use of a problem-solving model of practice. The third element of our framework for practice is the valuing of the artistic elements of practice, or what we have called intuitive-inductive practice. This includes the recognition that much of the time practice does not involve the conscious application of theory and technique and that intuition, inductive reasoning, and creativity play important roles in practice. A key idea in our framework is that the problem-solving model of generalist practice provides a flexible structure for guiding and combining the eclectic use of theory and the intuitive-inductive elements of practice.

In conclusion, we wish to stress that the generalist-eclectic approach is not meant to represent yet another competing approach to or framework for direct social work practice. It is a way of conceptualizing practice that encourages flexibility in the use of multiple theories, perspectives, and ideas, while placing the principles and values central to the profession of social work at the forefront.

REFERENCES

Bergin, A. E., & Garfield, S. L. (1994). Overview, trends, and future issues. In A. E. Bergin & S. L. Garfield (Eds.), *Handbook of psychotherapy and behavior change* (4th ed., pp. 821–830). New York: Wiley.

Garfield, S. L. (1994). Research on client variables in psychotherapy. In A. E. Bergin & S. L. Garfield (Eds.), *Handbook of psychotherapy and behavior change* (4th ed., pp. 190–228). New York: Wiley.

Garfield, S. L., & Bergin, A. E. (1994). Introduction and historical overview. In A. E. Bergin & S. L. Garfield (Eds.), *Handbook of psychotherapy and behavior change* (4th ed., pp. 3–18). New York: Wiley.

Goldfried, M. R., & Castonguay, L. G. (1992). The future of psychotherapy integration. *Psychotherapy, 29,* 4–10.

Gutierrez, L. M., Parsons, R. J., & Cox, E. O. (1998). *Empowerment in social work practice: A sourcebook.* Pacific Grove, CA: Brooks/Cole.

Horvath, A. O., & Greenberg, L. S. (1994). Introduction. In A. O. Horvath & L. S. Greenberg (Eds.), *The working alliance: Theory, research, and practice* (pp. 1–9). New York: Wiley.

Koss, M. P., & Shiang, J. (1994). Research on brief psychotherapy. In A. E. Bergin & S. L. Garfield (Eds.), *Handbook of psychotherapy and behavior change* (4th ed., pp. 664–700). New York: Wiley.

Lambert, M. J. (1992). Psychotherapy outcome research: Implications for integrative and eclectic therapists. In J. C. Norcross & M. R. Goldfried (Eds.), *Handbook of psychotherapy integration* (pp. 94–129). New York: Basic Books.

Mahoney, M. J. (1986). The tyranny of technique. *Counseling and Values, 30,* 169–174.

Nichols, M. P., & Schwartz, R. C. (1998). *Family therapy: Concepts and methods* (4th ed.). Boston: Allyn & Bacon.

Norcross, J. C. (1997). Emerging breakthroughs in psychotherapy integration: Three predictions and one fantasy. *Psychotherapy, 34,* 86–90.

Papell, C. P., & Skolnik, L. (1992). The reflective practitioner: A contemporary paradigm's relevance for social work education. *Journal of Social Work Education, 28,* 18–26.

Safran, J. D., & Segal, Z. D. (1990). *Interpersonal processes in cognitive therapy.* New York: Basic Books.

Saleeby, D. (1997). *The strengths perspective in social work practice* (2nd ed.). New York: Longman.

Stalker, C. A., Levene, J. E., & Coady, N. F. (1999). Solution-focused brief therapy— One model fits all? *Families in Society, 80,* 468–477.

Tolson, E. R., Reid, W. J., & Garvin, C. D. (1994). *Generalist practice: A task-centered approach.* New York: Columbia University Press.

Wachtel, P. L., & McKinney, M. K. (1992). Cyclical psychodynamics and integrative psychodynamic therapy. In J. C. Norcross & M. R. Goldfried (Eds.), *Handbook of psychotherapy integration* (pp. 335–372). New York: Basic Books.

Index